"This book is changing my mind on more themes that have long been important to me than any publication since Hans Frei's *The Eclipse of Biblical Narrative* (1974). It links recent developments in Pauline scholarship on justification, politics, Israel, culture, and the church in both constructive and critical but consistently surprising ways to the work of practitioners, especially Hauerwas and Yoder, of the theological approach Barth pioneered and Frei clarified well before the name 'postliberal' was launched in 1984. I do not always agree with the author, but I am invariably stimulated. His book belongs on the required reading list of those concerned from whatever theological or nontheological angle with the relation of Paul and the postliberal on any or all of these topics."

George Lindbeck, Yale University

"Seeking fresh insight, Doug Harink has linked up the new perspective on St. Paul with the work of certain postliberals and noted a very fruitful fit with some large implications for living faithfully as Jesus' disciples. The book to my mind represents the kind of generous orthodoxy toward which we should all be tending."

Clark Pinnock, author, *Most Moved Mover*

"Arguing that Paul was more concerned with cosmic apocalypse than with individual 'faith,' Harink shows us a deeply Jewish apostle, a faithful practitioner of the politics of Jesus. The author's readings of Karl Barth, John Howard Yoder, and Stanley Hauerwas as Pauline thinkers are wonderfully illuminating; the chapter on Galatians and Hauerwas is alone worth the price of admission. This is one fine book; read it."

Joseph Mangina, Wycliffe College, University of Toronto

"Can Paul the Apostle be placed in the company of such contemporary luminaries as John Howard Yoder and Stanley Hauerwas? Douglas Harink shows that such a conversation, in the form of an engagement between central Pauline themes and perspectives that lie at the heart of postliberal thought, is not only possible but also crucial. The result is an illuminating rendering of the significance of Pauline teaching for the church 'beyond Christendom and modernity.'"

Stanley Grenz, Baylor University

Paul among the Postliberals

*Pauline Theology beyond
Christendom and Modernity*

Douglas
Harink

Brazos Press

A Division of Baker Book House Co
Grand Rapids, Michigan 49516

3 -

Published by Brazos Press

a division of Baker Book House Company

P.O. Box 6287, Grand Rapids, MI 49516-6287

http://www.brazospress.com

Printed in the United States of America

Scripture is taken from the New Revised Standard Version of the Bible, copyright 1989 by the Division of
Christian Education of the National Council of the Churches of Christ in the USA. Used by permission.

Portions of this book were previously published in an article entitled "For or Against the Nations: Yoder
and Hauerwas, What's the Difference?" in the Toronto Journal of Theology 17/1 (2001): 167–85.

Library of Congress Cataloging-in-Publication Data is on file at the Library of Congress, Washington,
D.C.

For Debby, Elizabeth, and Allison

Contents

Preface

One thing Paul often did in his letters was to acknowledge and give thanks for his companions, co-workers, and friends. Obviously he knew, as I do, that no important work is accomplished alone. He depended, as I clearly do, in a thousand ways on the grace, generosity, patience, encouragement, admonishment, and concrete kindness of many people. So it is now both my responsibility and my joy to acknowledge and give thanks to some of the host of others who have had a share in making this book possible.

For the past twelve years I have had the privilege of working and teaching at The King's University College. King's is a small university college with a large vision—a vision of fostering the best of Christian scholarship across the whole range of university disciplines. Perhaps many such colleges have that vision, but King's has consistently stood behind it with time, money, and commitment. Consider: a teaching load that is the envy of many colleagues in similar institutions, a serious commitment to fund scholarly research and participation in conferences, a generous sabbatical policy, a genuine collegiality among faculty and administration. The writing of this book owes a huge debt to this wonderful institution. King's provided funding at both the earliest and latest stages of this project for student research assistants. I am grateful to Sheena Moodie for her very competent early assistance in seeking, gathering, and documenting a large number of the books and articles that inform this study. Late in the project Bronwyn Martin assisted in the preparation of the bibliography. King's granted me a sabbatical leave in 2000–2001, during which the bulk of the research and writing was completed. For all these things I am deeply grateful.

The support and encouragement of a number of colleagues and friends at King's have made it much more than simply a workplace for me. John Hiemstra, with whom I have had numerous valuable discussions about the nature of Christian political witness, has and is the best argument for the truth of the Reformed tradition, with which I nonetheless still have a few differences. Roy Berkenbosch is many things to me: on-site pastor, good preacher, colleague and conversation partner in many things theological (and nontheological), fellow lover of fine wine and good curry, and faithful friend. I am also blessed at King's by the friendships of Carol Everest, Arlette Zinck, Dawn Stiles-Oldring, and many others.

Other institutions must also be acknowledged. The Pew Foundation provided a Summer Research Grant in 1996, which was instrumental in getting this project under way. The Canadian Theological Society and the Canadian Evangelical Theological Association have over the last decade provided the forums in which just about every idea in this book was tested among my peers and friends—thanks to all of them. I am grateful to these societies and their members for patiently putting up with my many papers on Paul and the postliberals and more generally for the good work they do in fostering theological work in Canada. I am especially grateful in this regard to my dear and faithful friend John Franklin, with whom, through the years, I have regularly attended these and many other conferences. John, more than anyone else, has heard far too many of my papers, bearing them with great patience, not only listening to the ideas before they were presented, but then also debriefing with me afterward. It would be hard to imagine the theological life without John.

A number of people graciously read and commented on smaller or larger portions of the manuscript as it was produced. Thanks to JoAnn Badley, Roy Berkenbosch, Tim Fretheim, Larry Hurtado, Joe Mangina, Andy Reimer, David Reimer, and Jonathan Wilson. Richard Hays and Mark Thiessen Nation provided valuable comments and even more valuable encouragement in the earlier stages of writing. Michael Cartwright cast a careful eye over the bulk of the material and provided very discerning commentary. He also shared with me in manuscript form his and Peter Ochs's important work on Yoder and the Jews. I only wish I could have taken more account of it. Stanley Hauerwas took time to read and comment on everything he received from this unknown Canadian theologian; his enthusiastic support of the project sustained me through many a doubtful moment. Debby Harink's careful reading of the manuscript saved me from making some important theological and tactical errors. I am grateful to Rodney Clapp, editorial director of Brazos Press, for believing in this project from the beginning and for his encouragement throughout the process of writing. The editorial staff at Brazos has been a model of helpfulness, skill, and efficiency. If errors and problems remain, as I am sure they do, none of these fine people are responsible for them; I am.

I am profoundly thankful for and to First Baptist Church, Edmonton, which has nurtured me and my family for many years. It is a congregation that has often helped me to believe that what Paul imagined the church might be is not merely a dream. The Bible study group with which we have shared our lives for years has not only often listened patiently to a theologian in their midst but also, more importantly, continually sustained our family with love and prayer. Ed, Iris, Allana, and Emma Peters show us God's grace through their friendship and love.

My wife, Debby, in her ministry at First Baptist Church, surely knows Paul in ways that I do not—as pastor, advisor, spiritual director, pray-er, passionate lover of God. She practices what I often only preach. Despite all that, or because of it, she keeps on believing in me and encouraging me to press on. Her love, constancy, and friendship are the very specific shape of God's grace in my life. Our daughters, Elizabeth and Allison, are God's gifts and joy. I dedicate this book to these three, with a gratitude that words can never fully tell.

Introduction

Paul among the Postliberals

Getting Here

I'll be the first to say that this is an odd book. It claims to be a book on Paul. It draws heavily on recent biblical studies in Paul; yet it is not a work of biblical studies in the usual guild sense of that term. I am proposing no new paradigms for understanding the apostle, nor am I breaking new ground in reading his texts and contexts. Apart from continuing to read Paul's texts closely and carefully, I am largely dependent on the work of others who have done all those things.

This is a work of theology. It is an extended theological engagement with the letters of Paul in their contexts, done in the conviction that the Holy Spirit has much to teach the church in our time through this apostle and his writings. The reader will soon discover that Paul is a theologian of the people of God, and it is for the sake of this people, the church, that he writes his letters. In the same way I also write for the church, hoping that my work will in some measure be a faithful repetition in another time and place of some of the things Paul says.

The book before you is the product of the convergence of two primary streams in my studies over the past decade and a half. Both streams have their origins even further back than that, when in my graduate and doctoral studies in theology I made two discoveries which were to set the direction of my theological work thereafter. The first was Krister Stendahl's book *Paul among Jews and Gentiles*, which included his now (and even then) famous essay, "The Apostle Paul and the Introspective Conscience of the West."[1]

---

1. Krister Stendahl, *Paul among Jews and Gentiles* (Philadelphia: Fortress, 1976). The essay referred to (first published in English in 1963) is on pp. 78–96; equally important is the essay "Paul among Jews and Gentiles" (1–77). See also Stendahl's *Final Account: Paul's Letter to the Romans* (Minneapolis: Fortress, 1995).

Stendahl managed in one short essay to distinguish the apostle's concerns from centuries of individualizing, psychologizing, and spiritualizing interpretations, with the audacious claim that a great deal of Paul's theology was about Gentiles and Jews rather than about guilt-ridden individuals seeking to escape the punishment of an angry God. The essay and book not only revolutionized my understanding of Paul but also instilled in me a passion to understand the apostle as best I could, a passion that persists to this day and of which this book is a partial result.

The second discovery was Karl Barth. Already by the time I had reached graduate theological studies, I was convinced that the evangelical theology with which I was raised was constantly fighting a rearguard action against modernity, generally right in what it hoped to defend, but just as deeply indebted to the assumptions of modernity as its enemy, theological liberalism. Evangelicalism by and large rejected Karl Barth as a viable alternative, identifying him (tellingly—for evangelicalism) as an "existentialist" or "fideist" or "irrationalist" theologian who rejected biblical inerrancy and the rational defense of the faith. Somewhat prejudiced thus, I had not read any of his works before arriving at graduate school. When I did read him, however, I almost immediately discovered the missing voice: here was a theologian who boldly and confidently worked out his theology in the conviction that its foundation, its wisdom, its power, is the gospel itself, the world-constituting story of God's self-giving revelation in Jesus Christ. By comparison, the attempts by evangelicalism and liberalism alike to "establish" theology on other grounds, whether reason or experience, seemed hollow and self-defeating—and, often, boringly methodological. I discovered what is now known as Barth's "postliberal nonfoundationalism." At the time, it seemed to me that Barth was a theologian who believed and preached the gospel, as Paul had.

For me, the convergence of Paul and postliberal theology, as represented in this book, had begun. It was not something that I could explicitly pursue until I had finished the long detour through graduate and doctoral studies, though I continued to explore both streams—most directly Barth, by writing a dissertation on his critique of Schleiermacher. I also discovered Hans Frei and George Lindbeck, the two theologians best known as "postliberals," during my doctoral studies. But it was only after those studies that I returned with all seriousness to the apostle, reading his letters again and again and attempting to channel at least a trickle of the unending flood of Pauline studies into my theological scholarship.

At the same time another postliberal theologian, Stanley Hauerwas, became a determinative voice for me, convincing me not only of the truth of nonfoundationalism in theology but also of the coinherence of theology and ethics—and thus another natural ally of Pauline theology. Reading Hauerwas was an invigorating experience in itself, but it also led me to return to a book that I had read in my first year of graduate studies but had mostly forgotten about: John Howard Yoder's *Politics of Jesus.*[2] What I remembered was that it was a book about Jesus, a political Jesus based upon a reading of Luke's Gospel. What I rediscovered is that it is as much or more a book on *Paul's* theology; Yoder provided compelling political readings of several key Pauline texts. The rediscovery of Yoder is what led most directly to my beginning work on the present project, for I was already beginning to make many of the connections between theology, ecclesiology, social and political ethics, and Pauline studies that were being made in the second half of Yoder's book. Further, it seemed to me that even before the term *postliberal* became common theological currency, Yoder was already developing his unique theological-social-ethical-ecclesial vision in definitely postliberal and postconservative ways. Here were no rationalistic justifications of "belief"; no rationalizing evasions of the normative truth of Jesus. I was hearing the gospel all over again from him. I began a project of reading as much Yoder as I could lay my hands on, facilitated by new publications of his essays. At every turn in Yoder's work the influence of his reading of Paul is evident. I produced several conference papers exploring the convergence of Paul and Yoder, with Hauerwas and Barth often finding their way into the mix. The present book was underway.

Pauline Scholarship

Daunting to any attempt to say something responsibly about Paul is the simply overwhelming amount of scholarship on this apostle. I expect that only a very few have mastered most of it—for example, James D. G. Dunn, in his commentaries on Romans and Galatians and the huge (800 pages) *Theology of Paul the Apostle.*[3] Many have mastered some, and I, only a very little. What I have done is follow some of the strands in Pauline studies "since Stendahl" which seem most promising and helpful to me. I believe these strands can be combined in some fashion to produce a fuller picture of Paul and his theology without becoming merely eclectic or self-contradictory. Further, I am convinced that they will prove helpful for building up the church in its calling and mission in our time. Four such strands feature prominently in this study.

1 The "New Perspective."[4] Krister Stendahl's essay "The Apostle Paul and the Introspective Conscience of the West" marked the beginning of a major shift in Pauline scholarship, at least in North America. Stendahl's essay was effective in

2. John Howard Yoder, *The Politics of Jesus: Vicit Agnus Noster* (1st ed. 1972; 2d ed.; Grand Rapids: Eerdmans, 1994).

3. James D. G. Dunn, *Romans 1–8* and *Romans 9–16* (Word Biblical Commentary 38A–38B; Dallas: Word, 1988); idem, *The Epistle to the Galatians* (Peabody, Mass.: Hendrickson, 1993); idem, *The Theology of Paul's Letter to the Galatians* (Cambridge: Cambridge University Press, 1993); idem, *The Theology of Paul the Apostle* (Grand Rapids: Eerdmans, 1998).

4. The phrase *new perspective* comes from a now classic essay (first published in 1983) by James D. G. Dunn, "The New Perspective on Paul," in his *Jesus, Paul, and the Law: Studies in Mark and Galatians* (Louisville: Westminster John Knox, 1990), 183–214. This essay provides an account of the trajectory which Pauline scholarship has taken from Stendahl to Dunn himself. See also the helpful accounts by

shifting attention from the typically "Lutheran" or Protestant themes of individual justification, sin, guilt, grace, and faith to the more concrete, historical issues
of the relationships between Jews and Gentiles in Paul's mission and churches.
Justification, for example, is about how it is that Gentiles have come, through
Jesus Christ, to share in the life of God's people, Israel. It is these issues, Stendahl
argued, which Paul's letters, particularly Galatians and Romans, were written to
address, and it is against the background of his own Pharisaic Judaism, which in
many ways he never left behind, that Paul and his letters must be understood.

The latter task, assessing Paul within his Judaistic context, was taken up
with great learning and vigor by E. P. Sanders in another landmark book,
Paul and Palestinian Judaism.[5] At least four-fifths of this book is devoted to a
detailed description of the varieties of Palestinian Judaism in the time of Paul,
in an effort to show that the usual Protestant depictions of it as simply a system of "legalistic works-righteousness" are wrong and that Paul himself did
not respond to it as such. Sanders contributed as much or more to a "new
perspective on Judaism" as a living religion as he did to understanding Paul.
Since Sanders, discussions of Paul's letters and theology have paid much more
careful, detailed, and respectful attention to the Judaism(s) that form the context and also shape the content of Paul's message and mission. Paul is now
understood as a *Jew* who took a fundamentally *Jewish* message (christologically reordered) into a Gentile world. Sanders's work has been taken up,
worked with, modified, and argued against by many—James D. G. Dunn,
N. T. Wright, and Terence Donaldson, to name a few of the most notable—
but no one can now study Paul responsibly without engaging the issues he
raised. He has indeed inaugurated a "new perspective on Paul."

The Apocalyptic Perspective. The understanding of Paul as an "apocalyptic"
theologian goes back as far as the work on Paul by Albert Schweitzer.[6] It has
been given a vigorous revival by Ernst Käsemann, J. Christiaan Beker, and J.
Louis Martyn.[7] I explain Pauline apocalyptic in more detail in the chapters

Terence L. Donaldson, *Paul and the Gentiles: Remapping the Apostle's Convictional World* (Minneapolis:
Fortress, 1997), 3–27; and N. T. Wright, *What Saint Paul Really Said: Was Paul of Tarsus the Real Founder
of Christianity?* (Grand Rapids: Eerdmans, 1997), 11–23.

5. E. P. Sanders, *Paul and Palestinian Judaism: A Comparison of Patterns of Religion* (Philadelphia:
Fortress, 1977). See also Sanders's *Paul, the Law, and the Jewish People* (Philadelphia: Fortress, 1983); and
Paul (Past Masters; Oxford: Oxford University Press, 1991), the best introduction to Sanders's perspec-
tive on Paul and a fine introduction to Paul.

6. Albert Schweitzer, *The Mysticism of Paul the Apostle* (trans. William Montgomery; London: Black,
1931).

7. Ernst Käsemann, *Perspectives on Paul* (trans. Margaret Kohl; Philadelphia: Fortress, 1971); idem,
Commentary on Romans (trans. and ed. Geoffrey W. Bromiley; Grand Rapids: Eerdmans, 1980); J. Christiaan Beker, *Paul the Apostle: The Triumph of God in Life and Thought* (Philadelphia: Fortress, 1980);
idem, *Paul's Apocalyptic Gospel: The Coming Triumph of God* (Philadelphia: Fortress, 1982); idem, *The
Triumph of God: The Essence of Paul's Thought* (Minneapolis: Fortress, 1990); J. Louis Martyn, *Theological
Issues in the Letters of Paul* (Nashville: Abingdon, 1997); idem, *Galatians: A New Translation with Introduction and Commentary* (Anchor Bible 33A; New York: Doubleday, 1997).

that follow. For now it is important to note that the emphasis in the apocalyptic interpretation of Paul is on *God's action*. In the death and resurrection of Jesus Christ, the giving of the Holy Spirit, and the creation of the new community of God's people among the nations, God acted decisively to deliver humanity and the cosmos from the powers of "this present evil age" and inaugurated "the age to come" in which God's triumph over the powers is revealed or "apocalypsed" to Paul and among the nations.[8] The stress on God's action is an important corrective to the often decidedly sociohistorical focus of the "new perspective," with its concomitant emphasis on human agents and the workings of human communities. While this latter emphasis cannot be ignored, if we are to take the proper measure of Paul's theology we cannot ignore that for him every human action, whether personal or corporate, is always taking place within a context where other agents are also at work, whether the "principalities and powers" or God in Jesus Christ through the Holy Spirit. In my own readings of Paul presented here, the apocalyptic perspective thus consistently takes priority over sociohistorical perspectives.

3) The Faith of Jesus Christ. If the apocalyptic perspective marks one giant step away from anthropocentric readings of Paul, another major step was taken with the argument that the phrase *pistis Iēsou Christou*, traditionally translated "faith in Jesus Christ," is more appropriately translated "the faith of Jesus Christ." Richard Hays was not the first to make such an argument, but his 1981 doctoral dissertation, published in 1983 as *The Faith of Jesus Christ*, marks a turning point in the rendering of the phrase.[9] Hays's important claim is that *pistis Iēsou Christou* encapsulates a narrative about Jesus Christ rather than a narrative about the dynamics of faith in the believing subject. Combined with the apocalyptic perspective, that turn from "the doctrine of faith" to Christology has wide-ranging implications both for understanding Paul's theology, particularly his theology of justification, and for the shape of theology and ethics in our time.

4) The Political Perspective. Studies of Paul and his mission in the context of the politics, economics, and religions of the Roman Empire often combine the insights of the apocalyptic and new perspectives.[10] In particular, when the Roman imperial order is taken into account as an often dominating factor in the

8. The neologism *apocalypsed*, which will be used frequently in this book, is borrowed from J. Louis Martyn, who uses it in place of *revealed*, which is too weak to get at Paul's meaning. Two accessible and illuminating accounts of Pauline apocalyptic may be found in J. Louis Martyn, "The Apocalyptic Gospel in Galatians," *Interpretation* 54 (2000): 246–66; and Martinus C. de Boer, "Paul, Theologian of God's Apocalypse," *Interpretation* 56 (2002): 21–33. See also Beker, *Paul's Apocalyptic Gospel*.

9. Richard Hays, *The Faith of Jesus Christ: An Investigation of the Narrative Substructure of Galatians 3:1–4:11* (Chico, Calif.: Scholars Press, 1983). This volume was issued in a second edition (Grand Rapids: Eerdmans, 2002) with an new introduction and additional essays by Hays.

10. The best and most accessible introduction to political perspectives on Paul may be found in two volumes of essays edited by Richard A. Horsley: *Paul and Empire: Religion and Power in Roman Imperial Society* (Harrisburg, Pa.: Trinity, 1997); and *Paul and Politics: Ekklesia, Israel, Imperium, Interpretation: Essays in Honor of Krister Stendahl* (Harrisburg, Pa.: Trinity, 2000).

day-to-day life of the cities and citizens to which Paul brought his message, it becomes clear that Paul's gospel is an announcement of God's own "imperial order." God acts "apocalyptically" to reveal and establish his new political order in all clarity through Jesus' crucifixion (in which the powers of the "present evil age" attempted, through Roman imperial power, to destroy the purposes of God) and resurrection (in which God's power triumphed over the powers of the death-dealing Roman Empire). God's cruciform imperial power is now shaping a new people or "citizenship," called out from the old empire in the name of the Lord, Jesus Christ, into a sign of God's sociopolitical will for all humanity.

Each of these perspectives will feature from time to time and receive fuller explication in the discussions of the following chapters.

Postliberals

In a now famous entry in the "Lexicon" of his *Ethics after Babel* Jeffrey Stout defined "postliberal theology" (under the entry "Postmodern theology") thus: "The quest, initiated in recent years by the most interesting American followers of Karl Barth, to get beyond all forms of modernism in theology; either a *cul de sac* or the harbinger of a new theological age (too soon to tell)."[11] I am convinced it is the latter, as will become obvious in the following chapters, in large part because postliberal theology—in some of its forms—is a genuine recovery of the Pauline gospel. That recovery, of course, can be traced directly to Barth, whose theological revolution began with his powerful commentary on Romans. As I show below, I believe, despite many criticisms of that commentary as telling us more about Barth than Paul, that Barth was seized by the logic of Paul's gospel in a way that few have been since. Barth is the father of postliberal theology (he himself did not use the term) and still its most powerful proponent. His theology, whether earlier or later, bears the marks and shape of Paul's theology through and through.

Barth's theological revolution was slow in coming to North America. Categorized as "existentialist" or "neoorthodox" or "crisis" theology, it was often enough taken note of, but seldom seen for the total upheaval of modernist theology that it was. America's favorite theologians, Reinhold Niebuhr, H. Richard Niebuhr, and Paul Tillich, while marking important qualifications of liberal theology, were nonetheless still deeply entrenched in it.[12] Barth languished as "conservative" and passé. It was with the work of the so-called postliberals— Hans Frei and George Lindbeck and their students at Yale University—that

11. Jeffrey Stout, *Ethics after Babel: The Languages of Morals and Their Discontents* (Boston: Beacon, 1988), 301.

12. As argued persuasively, with reference to Reinhold Niebuhr, by Stanley Hauerwas in his Gifford Lectures, *With the Grain of the Universe: The Church's Witness and Natural Theology* (Grand Rapids: Brazos, 2001), 87–140.

Barth's theology began to be viewed in a different light.[13] Frei and Lindbeck argued that Barth represented a crucial and authentic alternative to liberal theology's persistent tendency to subject the gospel, Scripture, and Christian doctrine to criteria of credibility alien to them; in other words, to provide a "foundation" in those criteria for accepting the truth of the Christian message.[14] Barth worked from "no other foundation" than the gospel of Jesus Christ, because he was confident that it had the power to "destroy strongholds," not least the strongholds of post-Enlightenment rationalism and experientialism, which had for at least two centuries imprisoned theology within their constraints. For Frei, this meant that Barth recovered biblical narrative in its own world-constituting power; for Lindbeck it meant that Barth displayed an understanding of Christian faith as a language ruled by its own inherent grammar, Christian doctrine. The Barthian postliberal revolution was begun.[15]

It is not with Frei and Lindbeck, however, that I will have to do in the following chapters. Their valuable work is one step (the methodological step) removed from what I hope to accomplish with reference to two other postliberal theologians. The first is John Howard Yoder, a Mennonite theologian whose work has become increasingly recognized in the past two decades as a major contribution not only to the postliberal movement but also to North American theology as a whole. As I noted above, Yoder, like Barth (and significantly indebted to Barth, as his student), eschews the foundationalism of liberal and conservative theologies alike.[16] Confident that the Scriptures, as read by the Christian community, have the power not only to provide that community with direction but also to constitute the world for it, Yoder's theology carries on, like that of Barth, as a constant engagement with the Scriptures in an effort to describe how Jesus Christ is normative for

13. The important works to mention here are Hans W. Frei, *The Eclipse of Biblical Narrative: A Study of Eighteenth and Nineteenth Century Hermeneutics* (New Haven: Yale University Press, 1974); and the essays by Frei on Barth in *Types of Christian Theology* (ed. George Hunsinger and William C. Placher; New Haven: Yale University Press, 1992) and *Theology and Narrative: Selected Essays* (ed. George Hunsinger and William C. Placher; Oxford: Oxford University Press, 1993); George Lindbeck, *The Nature of Doctrine: Religion and Theology in a Postliberal Age* (Philadelphia: Westminster, 1984).

14. Cf. the definition of "liberal theology" in Stout's "Lexicon" (*Ethics after Babel*, 301): "Letting theoretical reason live in the optimistic modernist's machine while finding another home for reflective piety; post-Kantian epistemology (bad sense) or hermeneutics (bad sense) applied to theology."

15. For a helpful short description of postliberal theology, see William C. Placher, "Postliberal Theology," in *The Modern Theologians: An Introduction to Christian Theology in the Twentieth Century* (ed. David F. Ford; Oxford: Blackwell, 1989), 2:115–28. See also the essays in John Webster and George Schner (eds.), *Theology after Liberalism: A Reader* (Oxford: Blackwell, 2000).

16. Many of Yoder's works will be referred to in the chapters to follow, so I will not list any here. An excellent treatment of Yoder's thought as a whole is available in Craig A. Carter, *The Politics of the Cross: The Theology and Social Ethics of John Howard Yoder* (Grand Rapids: Brazos, 2001). Carter traces the influence of Karl Barth on Yoder's theology (61–90); the correspondences between Yoder and the work of Frei and Lindbeck are explored in a chapter entitled "Yoder's Narrative, Postliberal Christology" (93–111). Several essays on Yoder may be found in Stanley Hauerwas et al. (eds.), *The Wisdom of the Cross: Essays in Honor of John Howard Yoder* (Grand Rapids: Eerdmans, 1999).

understanding both God's action and human action, especially human social and political action. The gospel of Jesus Christ is sufficient to direct the life of the people of God, without that people seeking norms for its social and political existence in the wider world. Here too, as I demonstrate especially in chapter 3, we have a theological vision that resonates deeply with Paul's.

The other postliberal theologian (besides Barth and Yoder) featured in this book is Stanley Hauerwas. A student of Frei and Lindbeck at Yale, and also deeply indebted to Barth and Yoder, Hauerwas has just about all the credentials necessary to count as a postliberal theologian.[17] He has, moreover, almost single-handedly overturned the hegemony of the Niebuhr brothers in North American theology in the last two decades. Stout's ambiguity about postliberal theology being "either a *cul de sac* or the harbinger of a new theological age" seems to be finding some resolution in the influence that Hauerwas is having on the next two generations of theological students, of which one could draw up a long list who are now setting the agenda for theology in North America. I am particularly interested in the present work with Hauerwas's contributions along three lines: his rejection of the separation of theology and ethics; his decidedly "apocalyptic" stance; and his emphasis on the Christian community as the locus of God's coming reign. Each of these emphases, as I will show, is so thoroughly Pauline that Hauerwas must be reckoned as another means by which Paul's gospel to the nations is being heard on this continent (and beyond)—despite Hauerwas's infrequent display of readings of Pauline texts in his works.

Scripture and Theology

Since I am going to be reading together Paul and postliberal theology, a brief word is in order about the relationship between Scripture and theology at work here. The reader will soon discover that no overriding "method" is used consistently in each chapter. For example, the evangelical reader will search in vain for a single "exegetical method" which is employed to obtain "sure exegetical results," which are then used as the foundation upon which to "build" theology. While virtually every twentieth-century evangelical commentary on Scripture is written in that spirit, it is but another form of the modernist rationalism from which I hope Paul and the postliberals enable us to be delivered. For it assumes that the biblical scholar is "objectively" at work, without theological commitments, or at least holding them at bay, digging for scriptural "scratch," that is, the scripturally embedded propositions of divine revelation from which the church's life and theological

17. Hauerwas's debts to Barth and Yoder are on full display in his Gifford Lectures; *With the Grain of the Universe*, 141–241. An excellent introduction to Hauerwas's work is available as *The Hauerwas Reader* (ed. John Berkman and Michael Cartwright; Durham: Duke University Press, 2001). In addition to many essays by Hauerwas, the essays by Berkman, William Cavanaugh, and Cartwright help to place these essays in the context of Hauerwas's life and work.

reflection would start and to which it could always return for correction "on the basis of" further exegesis.

Other readers will search in vain for an analysis of a "human experience" or "religious experience," which in turn would constitute the common trans-historical and cross-cultural "basis" for thinking that the Paul of long ago might still continue to speak "out of his own religious experience" to like-minded religious people in our time. In this scenario, the Scriptures are searched as "expressions" of the religious experience that lies "behind" them, on the assumption that a common religious experience is the thing that binds us to the authors of Scripture and is the subject matter about which they primarily speak. This too is a form of modern foundationalism, the credibility of which is increasingly being called into question.

This is not the place to dispute those ways of approaching Scripture or to write a treatise on exegetical method and hermeneutics.[18] Instead, I will simply try to describe what I do here, with the suggestion that it might also work as a proposal about the relation of Scripture and theology. Each chapter that follows addresses in one way or another the question, What is a Pauline theology for our time? I try to answer that question on the one hand by making use of biblical scholarship that attempts to understand the apostle and his letters in their social, political, and religious contexts. A good deal of that biblical schol-arship (though certainly not all) is also attempting to hear, through Paul, what God is calling the church to be and do in our time. On the other hand, I try to answer the question by looking for what seem to me to be faithful repetitions (in this case, among the theologians) in our time of the Word that was spoken to Paul and through his letters in his time. In other words, it seems to me that the question cannot be answered except by this kind of reading together of witnesses: the witness of Paul in his context and under his conditions (with the discerning *help*—not control—of biblical scholarship) and the witness of con-temporary theology in its context and under its conditions. I cannot say where I started in this listening to witnesses, both Paul and the postliberals, and hear-ing a common voice. Did I begin with Paul and then start discovering corre-spondences to his voice and logic in the likes of Barth, Yoder, and Hauerwas? Or, did I begin with these theological voices and then find that I was hearing them all over again in Paul's letters? It is difficult for me to say, and the varying structures of the following chapters display that no univocal, "methodological" procedure clarifies the question. Nor need there be one. I ask the reader only to listen in on these conversations between Paul and the postliberals and to see whether they hear what I hear. Is God speaking again to the churches of North America through these postliberal theological voices in the way that he spoke to the churches in the Roman Empire to which Paul wrote his letters? Is the

---

18. For an excellent treatment, with which I am in fundamental agreement, of the issues of exegesis, hermeneutics, the doctrine of Scripture, and the work of Scripture in the life of the church, see Telford Work, *Living and Active: Scripture in the Economy of Salvation* (Grand Rapids: Eerdmans, 2002).

same Spirit speaking through each? The discernment that it is so will depend on whether we hear a shared language and logic, that of the gospel—something which I hope to show in this book. But it will also depend on whether the Pauline word which I hear these theologians speaking to the church today is aimed at producing the same faithful fruit in the church that Paul strove to produce in his day—and whether it is in fact producing it. That discernment will be made only over the long haul of the life of the churches. And that is the final test of theology, even theology which seeks to be faithful to Scripture. Every theological effort, this one included, must therefore put itself at the service of the triune God with the prayer that he might use it in his work of sustaining and shaping a people for his name and glory.

Getting There

Each of the chapters of this book can in some sense stand on its own, and the reader who wishes to read them according to his or her interests will not be at a great disadvantage in not reading them in order. At the same time, there is an overall logic and coherence that I think becomes most apparent by following the order I have set out. These final comments will, I hope, enable the reader to see the whole in the parts.

In chapter 1 I address the question of justification. The doctrine of justification is believed by most Protestant theologians to be at the very heart of Pauline theology, and there is a definite and strong tradition of construing this doctrine, going back to Martin Luther. Pauline scholarship has raised many critical questions about that construal, questions that I believe lead in turn to the possibility of shaping a powerful new understanding of Paul's doctrine necessary for the ongoing faithfulness of the church after modernity and Christendom. After addressing some of the problems with the traditional renderings of justification, both by taking account of scholarly criticisms of it and by reading 1 Thessalonians carefully, I go on to restate the theme in a way that I believe is more faithful to Paul's own rendering in the context of his mission and concerns. I follow this by showing how that restatement finds very clear correspondences in Barth's *Römerbrief* and *Church Dogmatics*, in Yoder's *Politics of Jesus*, and in Hauerwas's essay on the relationship of theology and ethics.

One of the arguments of chapter 1 is that justification is in fact an aspect of Paul's apocalyptic theology. In chapter 2 I take up the theme of Pauline apocalyptic, showing how it is the dominant orienting motif of his theology. That becomes especially evident in the letter to the Galatians, as demonstrated compellingly by J. Louis Martyn in his commentary on Galatians. At the same time, and alongside the letter to the Galatians, I introduce Hauerwas as an apocalyptic theologian, a witness together with Paul of God's invasion of an enslaved cosmos in the crucifixion and resurrection of Jesus Christ. For Hauerwas that invasion means that the people of God are rescued from enslaving worldly powers, in particular the powers of Americanism and liberal democracy that hold most North American Christians in bondage. Paul's urgent call to the Galatians not to submit again to the cosmic powers that enslaved them finds a faithful and powerful repetition in Hauerwas's voice.

By the end of chapter 2 it will be evident that Paul's proclamation of the gospel is intrinsically social and political good news. In chapter 3 I explore in detail Yoder's "politics of Paul." As I already indicated, not only in his *Politics of Jesus* but also in many of his other writings, Yoder is a thoroughly Pauline theologian who argues that Pauline theology is thoroughly political. To demonstrate this point, as well as to show how right Yoder was in many of his judgments already in 1972, I provide a close reading of his treatments of Pauline texts and themes in light of Pauline scholarship that supports those treatments. Yoder must be read as an important Pauline theologian as much as he is a theologian of "the politics of Jesus."

The strong emphasis on the apocalyptic character of Paul's gospel in the first three chapters raises the issue addressed in chapter 4. As those chapters show, in Paul's apocalyptic gospel God in Jesus Christ radically invades and interrupts the cosmic order, recreating all things, including the Sinaitic Torah, by the power demonstrated in the cross and resurrection. God in Christ destroys the *opposition* that that Torah creates between those who received it (Israel) and those who did not (the nations). Does this mean, then, that Paul's theology is inherently "supersessionist"? That is, does Paul teach the doctrine, prevalent in the history of Christian theology, that the *church* absorbs and replaces (supersedes) historic, fleshly Israel and therefore displaces Judaism, in God's purposes? My answer in chapter 4 is No! One of the most vigorous proponents of a supersessionist reading of Paul's theology is the widely influential New Testament scholar N. T. Wright. The first part of chapter 4 is a fairly extensive presentation and refutation of Wright's understanding of Paul on this matter, with a focus on reading Romans 9–11. Following this, I show how Wright's rendering of Paul as a supersessionist is itself rooted in what appears to be Wright's prior political commitment to a liberal democratic vision of personal, social, and political order, which will not allow him to accept a nontranscendable *difference* in the human community, a difference rooted in fact in God's own eternal decision to establish it—the difference between Israel and the nations, between Jew and Gentile. God is not a liberal democrat. Nor is the church, then, at one with the social and political agenda of the Western world. Supersessionism is itself an ecclesiology, and therefore also a politics—a politics at odds with the Pauline gospel. Following my critique of Wright, I look to Yoder's essays on Judaism as a possible alternative to Wright. These essays provide a description and strong appreciation of Diaspora Judaism as displaying a mode of being God's people in the world without having to be "in charge" of history. Yoder presents Diaspora Judaism to the church as a model of the shape of its own existence in the world. I find much that is compelling in Yoder's vision, but finally I find that he too comes up short in embracing the Pauline doctrine of Israel's nonsuperseded election. This raises the question of whether his ecclesiology, like Wright's, is itself still somewhat determined by an individualist voluntarism and liberalism that runs against the grain of his otherwise very Pauline vision of the church. Yoder's ecclesiology requires a more emphatic rooting in the Pauline theology in which Israel's election is not only not canceled or replaced, but in fact sustained and preserved in the apocalypse of Jesus Christ.

In chapter 5 I address questions of religious and cultural pluralism that face the church around the world, and in particular the church in the West after the decline of Christendom. I begin by providing a brief description of this context and asking whether Paul's own responses to pluralism in his time can help us. I then give a critique of the modern notion of religion, suggesting that it is not only inadequate for dealing with the topic of world religions but also for dealing with what Paul was about when he took his message to the Gentile world. Was he really asking the Gentiles to change religions? With the help of three postliberal (or postmodern) theologians, Paul Griffiths, John Milbank, and Kathryn Tanner, I replace the category "religion" with the category "form of life" or "culture." Only this, I argue, can deal with Paul's not calling his Gentile hearers to "accept a religion" but to "become a people"—a people called out from the nations and thus called to enact the difference in the totality of life which the apocalyptic gospel of Jesus Christ makes. I explore the relationship between peoplehood and culture in studies of Paul's letters to the Romans and Corinthians. I conclude this chapter with a set of "Pauline notes toward a theology of culture and religions," developing the themes of the difference of election, the scandal of universality, the politics of witness, and the face of the other.

In a brief conclusion to the book, I draw on the arguments of each of the chapters to set forth the orientation for preaching Paul "after Christendom and modernity." The purpose of the conclusion is to encourage the reader to get back to the apostle's texts, there to hear again the explosive and world-transforming Word of God, of which the apostle was nothing more, and nothing less, than a witness and servant.

At the end of the day, I remain painfully aware of how preliminary and incomplete the arguments in each of these chapters are. They are not tidy, finished "conclusions." Rather, I ask the reader to take them as hand-painted signs—rough, unsanded boards pointing along a road on which I believe there is great promise for drinking again from the apostolic springs of living water. Should theologians, preachers, and the churches follow these signs, there will, I pray, be "times of refreshing" for the people of God.

1

Justification

Beyond Protestantism

When Protestants think of Paul, they think of the doctrine of justification by faith in Jesus Christ. Justification means being made right before God through faith alone in Jesus' atoning sacrifice alone, apart from the law or any other human works or striving. That is the essence or core or peculiar contribution of Paul's theology. My aim in this chapter is to challenge that understanding of Paul in several ways. I argue, among other things, that it is based on a poor translation of an important Pauline phrase; that it misunderstands the notion of justification as an inner and individual matter; that it was not part of Paul's original message to the Gentiles; and that it gives the language of justification a more important place in Paul than it actually has. I show how Pauline scholarship is opening up many ways of getting a better understanding of Paul's teaching. Building on these arguments, I go on to show that, while not many theologians have taken account of or work with the new scholarship on justification in Paul, some (Karl Barth and John Howard Yoder) have in fact anticipated or even presupposed the "discoveries" of the new scholarship, and others (e.g., Stanley Hauerwas) are doing theology and theological ethics in a manner that receives a good deal of support from them. In this way I hope to show that a genuine Pauline theology of justification is in some significant respects quite different from that assumed by much of Protestant theology, and it may lead us, with the help of

25

a few theologians, beyond some of the misunderstandings and errors in theology and Christian life caused by the usual interpretations of Paul.

The Gospel to the Nations:
Without Justification by Faith in Jesus Christ

"Faith in Jesus Christ": History of a Bad Translation

Generations of readers of Paul since the time of Luther have understood that one must "have faith in" Jesus Christ in order to be "saved." Indeed, it is not enough to give "mental assent" to God's work in Jesus. God's work of justification is completed in the individual only through his or her *wholehearted trust in* Jesus Christ and his atoning sacrifice for sin on the cross and not in any effort, work, or merit of one's own. That is the meaning of being saved by faith, not works.

That reading of Paul is rooted deeply in Luther's consistent rendering of the Greek phrase *pistis Christou Iēsou* (Gal. 2:16 and its variants elsewhere) as *Glauben an Christus Jesus*—faith *in* or *toward* Christ Jesus. Jesus Christ is the *object* of the faith whereby the individual is saved, while faith is the way in which Jesus Christ and his "benefits" are subjectively received. Since Luther, "faith in Jesus Christ" has become the nearly universal Protestant translation of *pistis Christou Iēsou*. For example, while early editions of the Authorized Version (1611) did not follow Luther, but translated the phrase as a subjective genitive, "the faith *of* Christ," more recent editions of the Authorized Version, together with all the other English translations with which I am familiar, render it as an objective genitive, "faith in Christ." But it was not always so. In an important article entitled "Faith of Christ," George Howard notes that until the time of Luther virtually all translations, including the Vulgate (*fide Christi*), rendered the phrase as "the faith *of* Christ." While Howard's study of early translations is not exhaustive, he concludes: "It appears that Luther was the first in the history of NT translators to render *pistis Christou* as an objective genitive."[1]

Scholarship has, until recently, virtually matched the translations in its unanimity in taking *pistis Christou* as an objective genitive.[2] Only a few dissenting voices were raised in the late nineteenth and early twentieth centuries. Richard Hays notes that Rudolf Bultmann in his influential article entitled "πιστεύω, πίστις, πιστός, κτλ" in the *Theological Dictionary of the New Testament* "does not even consider the problem. A single footnote [in Bultmann's article] states, without supporting argumentation, that the genitives

---

1. George Howard, "Faith of Christ," in *Anchor Bible Dictionary* (ed. D. N. Freedman et al.; New York: Doubleday, 1992), 2:759. Howard's article is an excellent place to become familiar with the issues of translation and meaning surrounding the phrase; and it includes a substantial bibliography.

2. I use the phrase *pistis Christou* as inclusive shorthand for the variants of the phrase which appear in the Pauline letters.

following πίστις in Rom 3:22, 26; Gal 2:16, 3:22; Phil 1:27, 3:9; Col 2:12; Eph 3:12; and 2 Thess 2:13 are to be taken as objective genitives."[3] It is that almost unanimous, unargued assumption that Hays himself challenged in his 1981 dissertation (published in 1983), *The Faith of Jesus Christ*, and many publications since then. A growing number of Paul scholars have joined him.[4]

I propose below that reading *pistis Christou* as a subjective genitive, "the faith *of* Christ," is indeed the better way to understand Paul. First, however, I must show that the usual construals of the meaning of *pistis Christou* in Paul are subject to serious criticism. For while the issue of *pistis Christou* is in some measure a question of the translation of the Greek phrase, it is not only so. Issues in the wider context of Paul's theology both enter into and emerge from the rendering of the phrase. Hays writes:

> Little is to be gained by rehearsing the familiar arguments about syntax. . . . Such syntactical arguments are . . . finally inconclusive. . . . Our interpretative decision about the meaning of Paul's phrase, therefore, must be governed by larger judgments about the shape and logic of Paul's thought concerning faith, Christ, and salvation. Indeed, rather than defining the debate as a dispute between subjective ["faith of"] and objective ["faith in"] genitive readings, we would do better to speak—as some recent essays have suggested—of a distinction between the *christological* and *anthropological* interpretations of πίστις Χριστοῦ. The christological reading highlights the salvific efficacy of Jesus

3. Richard Hays, *The Faith of Jesus Christ: An Investigation of the Narrative Substructure of Galatians 3:1–4:11* (Chico, Calif.: Scholars Press, 1983), 160, referring to *Theological Dictionary of the New Testament* 6:204 n. 230. Hays provides a helpful discussion of the history of interpretation of the phrase (up to 1983) and the grammatical and theological issues involved (158–70), with bibliographical information (186–87 nn. 105–6).

4. A presentation of Hays's argument for *pistis Christou* as "the faith of Christ" may be found in his "Letter to the Galatians," in *The New Interpreter's Bible* (Nashville: Abingdon, 2000), 11:239–41. Hays's latest restatement of the argument in the light of Pauline scholarship since 1983 and in response to criticisms (in particular those by James D. G. Dunn) may be found in his "Πίστις and Pauline Christology: What Is at Stake?" in *Pauline Theology*, vol. 4: *Looking Back, Pressing On* (ed. Elizabeth Johnson and David M. Hay; Atlanta: Scholars Press, 1997): 35–60. Footnotes 2–4 (pp. 35–37) contain excellent bibliographies of the debate over *pistis Christou* from about 1980 to 1997. Hays's essay in *Pauline Theology* is followed by two valuable essays: James Dunn ("Once More, Πίστις Χριστοῦ," 61–81), in which Dunn responds to Hays and presents a vigorous argument for reading *pistis Christou* as an objective genitive—"faith in Christ"; and Paul J. Achtemeier ("Apropos the Faith of/in Christ: A Response to Hays and Dunn," 82–92). A valuable short essay by Hays addressing the question of *pistis Christou* in its significance for Christian social ethics is "Jesus' Faith and Ours: A Rereading of Galatians 3," in *Conflict and Context: Hermeneutics in the Americas* (ed. Mark Lau Branson and C. René Padilla; Grand Rapids: Eerdmans, 1986), 257–68. The following discussion is deeply indebted to Hays's work. The argument for "faith of Christ" is helpfully summarized by Michael J. Gorman in *Cruciformity: Paul's Narrative Spirituality of the Cross* (Grand Rapids: Eerdmans, 2001), 110–11. Gorman writes: "On the whole, at least in this country [America], a major shift has occurred in scholarship, and the acceptance of 'faith of Christ' is widespread and ever-increasing" (111).

Christ's faith(fulness) for God's people; the anthropological reading stresses
the salvific efficacy of the human act of faith directed toward Christ.[5]

In other words, each phrase in effect summarizes a different story. In the
rendering *faith in Jesus Christ* the story is predominantly *anthropocentric*—re-
volving around the creation-fall-redemption scheme that, it is thought, forms
the overarching narrative of scripture. Human beings (generically speaking),
originally created good, are now fallen, sinful, and rebellious against God at
the core and incapable of redeeming themselves by their own effort or
"works."[6] Instead, God alone can redeem human beings from their sinful state,
and he does so by atoning for their sins through the substitutionary and salvif-
ically efficacious sacrifice of Jesus Christ. Rather than relying on the merits of
our own (outward) effort or works to save us—which is always the greatest human temptation and source of pride before God—we must cast ourselves on
the undeserved mercy of God shown in Jesus Christ, through whom we are
saved strictly out of God's own gracious goodwill and through his work. Human beings must therefore have faith *in* Jesus Christ and his atoning sacrifice
in order to be rescued from bondage to sin and saved from the wrath of God.
Faith itself, in many tellings of this story, is not something that human beings
can muster or do or achieve, but is that purely passive (inner) *receiving* of
God's grace made possible by the Holy Spirit working in the human heart.
Thus the very core of the gospel which Paul preached is thought to be this: the
individual sinner is caught in an inescapable plight and thus in desperate need
of salvation, of being made right—justified—before God. This "righteousness"
is found in one's faith in Jesus Christ alone, rather than through one's own
striving; through faith, Christ's righteousness is "imputed" to the sinner, who
is thus enabled to stand before God without guilt or shame.

This outline of the classic Protestant reading of Paul is familiar to all who
have had some minimal induction into the mainstream Protestant or evangelical theological traditions. The roots of the story of "faith in Jesus Christ"

5. Hays, "Πίστις and Pauline Christology," 39–40.
6. The idea that Paul's basic narrative is about generic humankind's plight is often rooted in readings
of Rom. 1:18–32 as a commentary on the "fall" narrative of Gen. 3. Christ comes to save generically
fallen humankind. Stanley Stowers argues persuasively that Rom. 1:18–32 tells a different story: "What
Christian exegesis came to read as the consequences of the fall of humanity in the Garden of Eden, Paul
read as the corruption of the non-Jewish peoples. The first story explains how human nature got to be the
way it is; the second concerns the religious and ethnic other of Jews, how the gentiles became alienated
from God and from Israel. Human nature and ethnic other are quite differing subjects answering diver-
gent kinds of questions"; *A Rereading of Romans: Justice, Jews, and Gentiles* (New Haven: Yale University
Press, 1994), 83. If Stowers is right, we should pause before assuming that Paul presents anything like a
theory of human nature or of the religious subject, as is often thought on the basis of Rom. 1:18–32. A
strong argument against the assumption that Paul works with (or argues for) a notion of generic humanity, rather than a humanity constituted as Jew and Gentile or Israel and the nations, is made by Terence
L. Donaldson, *Paul and the Gentiles: Remapping the Apostle's Convictional World* (Minneapolis: Fortress,
1997), 107–64.

are founded deeply in a particular reading of Romans 1–3, guided decisively by Luther's grappling with that text and of course with Galatians, in the context of Luther's own crisis of conscience.[7] The story's deep entrenchment in Protestant theology, and in turn Protestant theology's deep investment in it, is evident in nearly every systematic theology, whether fundamentalist, evangelical, mediating, existentialist, or liberal, from the sixteenth century to the present day. That makes it difficult for Protestant theologians to hear another story from Paul. While the thought that Paul may be telling a different story is now common, perhaps even dominant, in Pauline scholarship, such a thought has barely touched the edges of consciousness in the guild of doctrinal and systematic theologians.[8]

One peculiarly modern way of telling the story of "faith in Jesus Christ" has been to ignore or bracket or postpone attention to the object or content of faith—"in Jesus Christ"—(which the Reformers, Luther in particular, never did) and to engage in extensive study of the "dynamics of faith." After Kant, and for those who take his philosophy of religion as critically normative, this has become the preferred way to address the "Pauline" language of faith. Here, a phenomenology of the believing subject, the "religious consciousness" or the "act" of faith becomes the central, sometimes exclusive, focus of attention.[9] Barth's comment is apropos:

> In the modern period there have been massive theological structures which have begun at the very point where we now end [i.e., Barth's exposition of the first part of the doctrine of reconciliation]. They started with the presupposition that, whatever may be the attitude to it, Christian faith as such is a fact and phenomenon which is generally known and which can, as such, be explained in the light of general anthropology. According to this type of structure the task of dogmatics is the description of Christian faith as such (the *fides qua creditur*) and the enumeration, exposition and explanation of its characteristic expressions (the *fides quae creditur*). And all on the further underlying presupposition that the really interesting and vital problem of the Christian is the one which is nearest to hand, that is to say, himself, his existence as a Christian, and therefore the fact and phenomenon of his faith. Dogmatics, therefore, is the "doctrine of faith."[10]

7. Of course, there is a particular understanding of Luther at work here as well, which tends to neglect the profoundly christocentric, ecclesial, and catholic shape of Luther's own theology. For a strong antidote to the usual ways of attributing individualizing, interiorizing, and spiritualizing understandings of faith to Luther, see an important essay by David S. Yeago, "'A Christian Holy People': Martin Luther on Salvation and the Church," *Modern Theology* 13 (1997): 101–20.

8. As I show below, Barth and Yoder are exceptions.

9. See, e.g., Paul Tillich's small classic, *Dynamics of Faith* (New York: Harper & Row, 1957), in which faith "in Jesus Christ" does not come up for discussion, except as one, perhaps "superior," "expression of ultimate concern," ultimate concern of course being the "true" meaning of "faith" (see, e.g., 54).

10. Karl Barth, *Church Dogmatics*, vol. 4.1: *The Doctrine of Reconciliation* (trans. Geoffrey W. Bromiley; Edinburgh: T & T Clark, 1956), 740.

The classic treatment along these lines, still unmatched in depth and brilliance, is Friedrich Schleiermacher's explorations in his *Speeches on Religion* and *The Christian Faith*. But the works of the great liberal theologians of the nineteenth and early twentieth centuries, as well as the works of such twentieth-century thinkers as Rudolf Bultmann, Paul Tillich, Hans Küng, Karl Rahner, Wolfhart Pannenberg, and Rosemary Ruether, all exhibit a common concern to explore the religious subject as the focal object of theological inquiry, to understand faith in terms of a universal religious a priori (cf. the concept of "other religions," also called other "faiths"), and to introduce Jesus Christ into the discussion as a modifying feature or directional motif within the basic structure of religion or faith.[11] In any case, the turn to the subject and the anthropocentrism of much of modern theology owes a great deal to the notion that salvation comes through "faith," but faith now understood not as, of necessity, always properly directed to its object, Jesus Christ, but as an intrinsic, essential dynamic of being human, which can be called upon to achieve a salvific relation to transcendent and worldly reality. Indeed, in these terms not only is faith understood to be "apart from works," but now also, in large measure, apart from Jesus Christ.

The Gospel without Justification by Faith: Paul's Call

The question is, Did *Paul* ever pay much attention to faith, either in the sense of being directed to its object, Jesus Christ, or in the sense of a basic dynamic or structure of human existence? It seems not.

First, Paul's "conversion" must be seen primarily in terms of the call narratives of the prophets of Israel, rather than in terms of moving from unbelief to "faith in Jesus Christ."[12] Paul does not emphasize his "faith in"

---

11. In my own academic context, a Reformed college with deep intellectual debts to Dutch philosopher Herman Dooyeweerd (1894–1977), similar attention is paid to "faith" as one of the "modal aspects" (albeit, the fundamental, integrating one—cf. Schleiermacher) of being human. Faith is a universal structure of human consciousness which is given specific "direction" by the "biblical worldview" of creation, fall, and redemption through Christ. The fundamental indebtedness to Kant and similarity to Schleiermacher in the conception of faith and religion seems to be neither recognized nor acknowledged by Dooyeweerd and his heirs.

12. The classic account of Paul's "conversion" as a specific, prophetic call to preach God's salvation to the Gentiles is Krister Stendahl, *Paul among Jews and Gentiles* (Philadelphia: Fortress, 1976), 7–23. Stendahl himself is largely indebted to Johannes Munck, *Paul and the Salvation of Mankind* (trans. Frank Clarke; London: SCM, 1959), 11–68. Studies of Paul's "conversion" abound, many of them supporting Stendahl's insight. See the excellent overview, discussion, and bibliography in J. M. Everts, "Conversion and Call of Paul," in *Dictionary of Paul and His Letters* (ed. Gerald F. Hawthorne, Ralph P. Martin, and Daniel G. Reid; Downers Grove, Ill.: InterVarsity, 1993), 156–63; also Larry W. Hurtado, "Convert, Apostate, or Apostle to the Nations: The 'Conversion' of Paul in Recent Scholarship," *Studies in Religion/ Sciences Religieuses* 22 (1993): 273–84. On Paul's sense of his unique mission Hurtado writes: "Paul seems to have thought that upon his work the larger salvation-historical plan of God depended" (284). Donaldson argues, contra Stendahl, that Paul's altered perception about Jesus precedes his sense of prophetic call: "The experience [conversion] in its initial impact and import . . . concerns Jesus and the belief that God had raised him, not Paul and the belief that God had called him" (*Paul and the Gentiles*, 251). Donaldson's volume is indispensable for understanding the sources, origins, and character of Paul's call and mission to the Gentiles and, thus, for understanding Pauline theology as a whole.

Jesus Christ in his accounts of his own conversion, even at points where it might have been advantageous to his argument to do so. In his (very brief) autobiographical reflections in Galatians, Paul does not depict his own moral and spiritual condition before his call/conversion as *anticipating*, whether positively or negatively, the world-shattering character of his encounter with the risen Jesus. He signals neither a sense of questing incompleteness requiring fulfillment nor of helplessness in the face of sin and guilt-consciousness through an inability to keep Torah, which would set the precondition of his "need" for "faith." Quite the contrary. He could say that, "as to righteousness under the law," he was "blameless" (Phil. 3:6). His "zeal" for God, for "Judaism," and for the "ancestral traditions" (Gal. 1:14; cf. Phil. 3:5–6) would have been regarded by himself and many of his contemporaries as exemplary faithfulness to God, rooted in and guided by the scriptures of Israel and modeled after some of the great heroes of the tradition of "zeal," such as Phinehas (Num. 25:6–18), Elijah (1 Kings 18:30–40; 19:10), and Mattathias (1 Macc. 2:15–28).[13] Paul would have considered his opposition against the Jesus movement to be appropriate and perhaps necessary disciplinary action in order to maintain the absoluteness of Torah against a deviant, troublesome, or perhaps politically dangerous group of Jews.[14] In other words—if Romans 10:2 may also be applied to Paul before his call—the "problem" with Paul was not that he was striving to please God rather than resting in faith in God's "acceptance" of him, but that he had a "zeal" which was not informed by knowledge (*ou kat' epignōsin*). The knowledge (the fact, so to speak) which he lacked was not that he must have faith rather than works, but that Jesus is indeed the messianic agent of the God of Israel, the Faithful One raised from the dead, in whom "the righteousness that comes from God" (10:3) is disclosed. Contrary to what he had thought as a zealous Pharisee, it was "the church *of God*" (Gal. 1:13) that he had been seeking to destroy, rather than an apostate sect of Jews; and Jesus was indeed the Christ

13. "As a Pharisee of the Diaspora (Phil 3:5), his [Paul's] ardent devotion to the traditions of the Law knew no limit, being the form of his worship of God. In this regard he was almost certainly conscious of standing in the noble tradition of several pious Israelites: Phinehas . . . , Elijah . . . , Mattathias"; J. Louis Martyn, *Galatians: A New Translation with Introduction and Commentary* (Anchor Bible 33A; New York: Doubleday, 1997), 155. See also Donaldson, *Paul and the Gentiles*, 284–92; James Dunn, *The Epistle to the Galatians* (Peabody, Mass.: Hendrickson, 1993), 60–62. On this evidence, it may be that Paul already had some sense of specific calling before his encounter with the risen Jesus; see Donaldson's discussion (275–84) of Paul's mention that he at one time "preached circumcision" (Gal. 5:11).

14. Donaldson, *Paul and the Gentiles*, 286–87. The precise nature of the perceived threat that the Jewish Jesus movement posed, and which evoked disciplinary action from the likes of Paul, is difficult to determine. Donaldson argues that the threat was primarily theological in nature—focused on the Christ-Torah antithesis. Paula Fredriksen ("Paul and Augustine: Conversion Narratives, Orthodox Traditions, and the Retrospective Self," *Journal of Theological Studies*, n.s. 37 [1986]: 3–34) suggests it was political—a group of apocalyptic, messianic Jews posed a threat to the fragile peace between Jerusalem and the Romans (13–14).

whose divine glory and power for salvation now transcended that of Moses and Torah (2 Cor. 3:7–11; 4:6).

Had Paul's central point in Galatians 2 (or indeed, in the whole letter) been, as many suppose, to stress that salvation comes by an inner disposition of faith (in Jesus Christ) rather than striving to please God, what better place to make that point than in this account of his own conversion—that is, that he was "working" vigorously to win God's approval, and then he learned that he must cease striving and "have faith" instead.[15] But in Paul's account *God interrupts! Christ comes!* When Jesus Christ enters into his frame of reference—or rather, shatters it, and himself becomes Paul's frame of reference—Paul can only speak of this in the language of God's electing and apocalyptic action. Borrowing the words of Jeremiah's call (Jer. 1:5; cf. Isa. 49:1–7), Paul writes of himself: God "set me apart" (*aphorizō*) from my mother's womb, "called" (*kaleō*) me, and "reveal[ed]" (*apokalyptō*) his Son to me, that I might "proclaim" (*euangelizō*) him among the nations (Gal. 1:15–16). The only thing that stands prior to God's apocalypse of his Son to Paul is God's own long-standing purpose to send Paul on a unique mission to the Gentiles. Paul goes then, not because he leaves behind his own prideful but vain efforts or "works," and learns to live by "faith"—which then becomes the content of his message. Rather, Paul goes because he believes that Jesus is risen in divine glory and because he does not resist the prophetic call from God to proclaim Jesus Christ among the nations. So, in Paul's own story of his prophetic/apostolic call, "faith" is not of focal concern—only God's revelation of the risen Jesus Christ, God's election, call, and commissioning of prophet/apostle Paul, and Paul's obedient response to all of this.[16]

The Gospel with Works: Paul's Early Preaching to the Gentiles

Second, Paul does not take a message of "faith, not works" to the nations. He takes a message about the one God of Israel and about his Son, Jesus Christ, crucified and risen, in whom the nations have been saved from God's wrath, freed from bondage to false gods and "powers," and called to serve the God of Israel in holiness through the gift of the Holy Spirit. The problem with the nations is their idolatry, their slavery to demonic powers, and the resulting dissolution of their way of life, all of which, apart from God's

15. To be sure, Paul's main point in telling of his conversion/call in Gal. 1:11–17 is to stress the divine rather than human origin of the gospel which he proclaimed to the Galatians. Still, if the point of the gospel—and the letter to the Galatians—was "faith in Jesus Christ" rather than in human effort, Paul missed the perfect opportunity to say that is exactly what he learned from his own experience as a Jew striving to please God rather than resting in faith.

16. See Martyn, *Galatians*, 157 and n. 191: "Paul does not speak . . . in a biographical fashion, as though it were his intention to say, 'Let me tell you about my life and experiences!' He speaks, rather, in a prophetic fashion, concentrating attention in the first instance on God. . . . Paul is thus conscious of standing in continuity with the prophetic traditions (cf. Rom 1:1–2; 11:1–6)." And: "Paul transforms the category of biography into a theological witness focused on God's activity in the gospel."

reconciliation of the nations through Jesus Christ, places them in the direct path of God's coming wrath.

One text which reflects in summary form the content of Paul's proclamation to the Gentiles is 1 Thessalonians 1:9–10.[17] The believers in Macedonia and Achaia, indeed, "in every place," writes Paul, speak about how the Thessalonians welcomed and responded to Paul and his message: "How you turned to God from idols, to serve a living and true God, and to wait for his Son from heaven, whom he raised from the dead—Jesus, who rescues us from the wrath that is coming" (cf. Phil. 3:20–21). The central characters in this story are the God of Israel ("the living and true God") who raises his Son from the dead, and Jesus who rescues from the coming wrath, but who is also coming again "from heaven." The response to his proclamation, which Paul calls for and receives from the Gentile Thessalonians, is in fact their "turning toward" (*epistrephō*) God from idols, their "serving" (*douleuō*) him, and "expectantly waiting for" (*anamenō*; see also 1 Thess. 5:6) Jesus. The first two verbs strongly suggest *active* responses to the gospel. The first requires a decisive rejection of idolatry and public confession of the one God of Israel, a confession which itself may have brought upon the Thessalonian church considerable social and political hardship.[18] If we ask what the verb *serving* means concretely in the lives of the Thessalonians, we discover an answer soon enough in the letter:

> Finally, brothers and sisters, we ask and urge you in the Lord Jesus that, *as you learned from us* how you ought to live and to please God (as, in fact, you are doing) [lit., how it is necessary for you to walk and to please God, as indeed you do walk], you should do so more and more. For you know *what instructions we gave you* through the Lord Jesus. For this is the will of God, your sanctification (*hagiasmos*): that you abstain from fornication, that each one of you know how to control your own body in holiness (*hagiasmos*) and honor,

17. "Much of the value of 1 and 2 Thessalonians as documents of Pauline theology is based on their apparent closeness to Pauline mission preaching. . . . Little of their content is prompted by special situational concerns, at least in comparison with other letters of Paul. . . . 1 Thessalonians 1:9–10 in particular allows us to see something of the general pattern of Paul's early preaching to Gentile audiences"; J. W. Simpson Jr., "Thessalonians, Letters to the," in *Dictionary of Paul and His Letters* (ed. Gerald F. Hawthorne, Ralph P. Martin, and Daniel G. Reid; Downers Grove, Ill.: InterVarsity Press, 1993), 938. Simpson goes on to note the typically Jewish character of Paul's preaching: emphasis on the one God, "the standard Jewish polemics against pagan idolatry," and the apocalyptic end of the age. See also Charles A. Wanamaker, *The Epistles to the Thessalonians: A Commentary on the Greek Text* (Grand Rapids: Eerdmans, 1990), 9–10, 84–89, who draws links from the themes of 1 Thess. 1:9–10 to other Pauline texts. The most important of these is, of course, Rom. 1:18–32.

18. See Karl P. Donfried, "The Imperial Cults of Thessalonica and Political Conflict in 1 Thessalonians," in *Paul and Empire: Religion and Power in Roman Imperial Society* (ed. Richard A. Horsley; Harrisburg, Pa.: Trinity, 1997), 215–23; and Donfried's contributions on 1 Thessalonians in Karl P. Donfried and I. Howard Marshall, *The Theology of the Shorter Pauline Epistles* (Cambridge: Cambridge University Press, 1993), 3–79. This latter work by Donfried provides, to my mind, the best theological analysis of 1 Thessalonians currently available. See also Wanamaker, *Epistles to the Thessalonians*, 112–14.

not with lustful passion, like the Gentiles who do not know God; that no one wrong or exploit a brother or sister in this matter, because the Lord is an avenger in all these things, *just as we have already told you beforehand and solemnly warned you.* For God did not call us to impurity but in holiness (*hagiasmos*). Therefore whoever rejects this rejects not human authority but God, who also gives his Holy Spirit to you. (1 Thess. 4:1–8)

As the italicized phrases in this text show, Paul's earliest preaching to the Thessalonian Gentiles included not only a criticism of their idolatry and a call to serve the one God of Israel, but also a call to holiness as they conduct themselves (i.e., "walk" [*peripateō*]; cf. 2:12: "lead a life worthy of God") in their bodily activities and relationships. From the very beginning Paul provided instructions "through the Lord Jesus" about the specific shape of their holiness, which is enabled by God, who "gives his Holy Spirit to you." Paul at first preached and now writes all of this, it should be noted, without reference to the faith/works contrast that becomes a focal theme primarily in Galatians and Romans. Paul assumes that the Thessalonians will become obedient in their actions, holy in specific ways, without worrying about whether they would be striving or working to please God. The Protestant notion of "works-righteousness" does not seem to bother Paul at all, nor does he anywhere warn the Thessalonians to be on guard against it. Quite the contrary: he urges them to "do so more and more" (*hina perisseuēte mallon*; 4:1, see also 4:10) in walking to please God.

It is not, of course, that by so walking the Thessalonians are saving themselves or making themselves worthy of God's grace. Their salvation and sanctification is all thoroughly the gracious work of the triune God. The third verb in 1:9–10, "expectant waiting," calls the believers to be confident in the promise of Jesus' parousia and *his* rescuing them from the coming wrath. But God's action is not only to be awaited from the future. The Thessalonian believers are already delivered from their enslavement to idols and already participate in a new theopolitical reality through the power of the Holy Spirit at work in Paul's message (1:5–6).[19] It is God "who calls you into his own kingdom and glory" (2:12).[20] God's word "works" in the believers (2:13). It is the Lord who makes the Thessalonians "increase and abound in love for one another," and "strengthen[s their] hearts in holiness" (3:12–13). God gives the enabling Holy Spirit together with the call to holiness (4:8). God will raise, through Jesus who died and rose again, all those who have died in him. (4:14–16). "God has destined us not for wrath but for obtaining salvation

19. For an excellent treatment of the Pauline apocalyptic tension between "not yet" and "already" at work in 1 Thessalonians, see Abraham Smith, "The First Letter to the Thessalonians: Introduction, Commentary, and Reflections," in *The New Interpreter's Bible* (Nashville: Abingdon, 2000), 11:678–80.

20. Donfried notes that "election by the living and true God" is a significant theological motif in 1 Thessalonians; see Donfried and Marshall, *Theology of the Shorter Pauline Letters,* 28–30. God's calling of the Thessalonians into his own "kingdom and glory" is what makes it possible for them for consider and enter into another political reality besides that of the Roman Empire.

through our Lord Jesus Christ, who died for us, so that whether we are awake or asleep we may live with him" (5:9–10). "May the God of peace himself sanctify you entirely; and may your spirit and soul and body be kept sound and blameless at the coming of our Lord Jesus Christ. The *one who calls you is faithful*, and *he will do this*" (5:23–24). From beginning to end in the letter, Paul thoroughly inscribes the walk of the Thessalonians within the faithful action of the Father, Son, and Holy Spirit, so that while their walk in holiness is always genuinely their own, it is always also wholly the work of God.[21] Paul is surely as clear here as anywhere that the Thessalonians are what they are in Christ solely through God's grace and Spirit.

The point to emphasize here is that for Paul the Thessalonian believer's participation in God's gracious work through Christ and the Spirit is not focused upon or localized in a single form of human response, that is, receptive faith (or "faith in Christ," a phrase which appears nowhere in the letter); rather, it is depicted as spread over the whole range of human life, active and passive, attitudinal and bodily, inner and outer, personal, social, and political. Indeed, in what is clearly the thematic statement for the whole letter, Paul writes that in his prayers he remembers "before our God and Father your *work of faith[fulness]* (*ergou tēs pisteōs*) and *labor of love* and *steadfastness of hope*" (1:3). These themes are struck throughout the letter.[22] The first, their "work of faithfulness," surely refers in the first place to the way in which the Thessalonians had stood fast in loyalty to the gospel in Paul's absence (3:7–8), not falling away from their confession of the one God of Israel (Paul writes of their "faith [or loyalty] in God" [*pistis . . . pros ton theon*] in 1:8) in the face of persecution, and in so doing imitating both Paul and Jesus (1:6; 2:13–16; 3:1–5).[23] When Paul writes in 3:5 that he "sent [Timothy] to find out about your faith[fulness] (*pistis*)," he was eager to know, not whether the Thessalonians were rightly disposed in their hearts toward Jesus, but whether they had withstood the temptation, under severe pressure from their own fellow citizens, to turn away from "the gospel of God" (*to euangelion tou theou*, 2:2, 9)

21. See Earl Richard, "Early Pauline Thought: An Analysis of 1 Thessalonians," in *Pauline Theology*, vol. 1: *Thessalonians, Philippians, Galatians, Philemon* (ed. Jouette M. Bassler; Minneapolis: Fortress, 1991), 43–44.

22. "These three themes form a prism through which Paul examines and then addresses a variety of concerns. Paul views the suffering of the Thessalonians and their separation from the apostles in the larger context of conflict between the God who calls and sustains and Satan who endeavors to destroy. He comforts the grieving with the promise that all believers will again be together when they are gathered to the returning and triumphant Jesus Christ. He offers ethical admonitions that build up the boundaries around this fledgling community, boundaries of love and respect that protect the community but also maintain its attractiveness to others"; Beverly Gaventa, *First and Second Thessalonians* (Louisville: John Knox, 1998), 2.

23. That *pistis* may properly be taken as "loyalty" (of a subject to a ruler) is argued persuasively by Dieter Georgi in *Theocracy in Paul's Praxis and Theology* (trans. David E. Green; Minneapolis: Fortress, 1991), 43, 83–84.

that Paul had preached to them.[24] Surely for Gentiles in the cities and towns
of the Roman Empire the crucial issue in Paul's preaching would be faith in
the one God of Israel—a faith made possible through God's triumph in Jesus
Christ over idols, demons, principalities, magical powers, and rulers in high
places—versus faith in the gods of the cities or the empire, and not the issue
of faith (in Jesus Christ) versus "law" or "works" as human striving. Paul's
gospel to the nations was, at core, a message about the truth of the one God
of Israel in a polytheistic, idolatrous context.[25] The Thessalonian church's
"work of faithfulness" is its loyalty to this gospel.[26]

The second theme, their "labor of love," encompasses all that Paul says
about the blamelessness and holiness in which the Thessalonians are walking
and in which he calls them to abound more and more. The active holiness in
which Paul encourages them has primarily to do, negatively, with not doing
wrong to one another (4:6) and, positively, with loving one another and "be-
hav[ing] properly toward outsiders" (4:9–12).

Finally, the third theme, their "steadfastness in hope," is the point of departure for Paul's encouragement of the Thessalonians to wait expectantly
and hopefully for the "coming of the Lord" (4:13–5:11) and not to lose
sight of this parousia as their sustaining hope in the midst of persecution.

In each and in all of these ways the Thessalonians participate in the grace
and work of God. There are inner and outer aspects, passive and active aspects, soulish and bodily aspects to all of these ways of participation, and no
aspect is prioritized above the others. The whole community and each person in the wholeness of life are drawn into the work of the Father, Son, and

24. Hays notes ("Πίστις and Pauline Christology," 39) that while "there are at least two passages
where Paul does use the verb πιστεύειν with Χριστὸν Ἰησοῦν (or the equivalent) as its object (Gal 2:16,
Phil 1:29; cf. also Rom 10:12 and Col 2:5)," "it is an interesting fact—not always fully appreciated by
defenders of the objective genitive interpretation—that such passages are relatively rare in Paul; more
characteristically, he speaks of God (Rom 4:3, 5, 17, 24; Gal 3:6; cf. 2 Tim 1:12, Tit 3:8 [Hays might
have added 1 Thess. 1:8]) or of the content of the proclaimed gospel (Rom 6:8; 10:9, 16, 1 Cor 15:11, 1
Thess 4:14) as the object of faith, or he uses the verb absolutely, with no expressed object."

25. Note how similar this account of Paul's gospel to the nations is to that recounted in Acts. There
Paul engages the realities of idols, demonic forces, and magical practices to which the Gentiles are enslaved, with the message of the one God of Israel who raised Jesus from the dead; he does not engage the
Gentiles' "works-righteousness" (what would that be?) with a gospel of "faith." So also in Rom. 4 faithful
Abraham must be read as the paradigmatic Gentile who, like the Thessalonians, left his idols behind and
placed his trust in the one God "who gives life to the dead" (4:17)—just what Paul called his Gentile hearers to do. On the content of the gospel as a christologically redefined Jewish monotheism in Acts, see the
illuminating article by C. C. Newman, "God," in *Dictionary of the Later New Testament and Its Developments* (ed. Ralph P. Martin and Peter H. Davids; Downers Grove, Ill.: InterVarsity Press, 1997), 414–17.

26. "Faith has as its object God (1 Thess. 1:8) and results in a turning away from idols so as 'to serve
a living and true God' (1 Thess. 1:9). The Old Testament theme of faithfulness is dominant. Since God
has called the Thessalonians they are no longer to be involved in idolatry and must avoid the continuous
temptation to apostasy"; Donfried, *Theology of the Shorter Pauline Letters*, 54. I would add only that it is
not that faith "results" in turning from idols, etc., but that faith is the turning from idols to serve the living God of Israel. A "faith in God" that is not precisely this act of turning and serving is empty.

Holy Spirit. There is no evidence that Paul called the Thessalonian Gentiles to "have faith in Jesus" as the first and all-important moment or stage in their salvation and then, as a second and perhaps secondary moment or stage, to "live out" or "express" that faith in loyalty and active service to God. Their participation in the work and grace of God (their faith, love, and hope) *is* their turning to God, their loyalty to God in the face of persecution, their abstaining from *porneia*, their active pursuit of holiness and love for one another, their eager anticipation of the coming of the Lord.

These brief studies of Paul's account of his conversion/call and of his letter to the Thessalonian church show that neither *faith in Jesus Christ* nor *faith* itself as a phenomenon of the human subject is central to the explication of Paul's own turn from persecutor to apostle or of his original apostolic preaching to the nations. That original proclamation is instead about the one-God-of-Israel's action for the nations in the crucifixion and resurrection of Jesus and in the outpouring of the Holy Spirit. The nations, ignorant or blind to the true God, suffer under the demonic influence of idols (1 Cor. 8:7–10; 10:14–22; 12:2; Gal. 4:8) and other antigod powers, from which they need a more powerful deliverance, a deliverance that God accomplishes among the nations through Paul's preaching of the crucified and risen Jesus Christ in the demonstrated power of the Holy Spirit (Rom. 15:17–19; 1 Cor. 2:1–5; Gal. 3:1–5; 4:9–11). Under the power of idolatry the Gentile peoples had slipped into a downward spiral of spiritual, moral, and social disorder and stand under God's wrath (Rom. 1:18–32; cf. Eph. 2:1–3). They need rescue and instruction in a new way of life pleasing to God. Paul preaches that in Jesus Christ they are not only delivered from the coming wrath of God and reconciled to God, but also that, through the Holy Spirit and baptism, they are made sharers in Jesus' death and resurrection life and members of a new people, the *ekklēsia*. In Jesus Christ they receive a new identity and the normative pattern of a new obedience (Rom. 6). Through the Holy Spirit they receive freedom from bondage to the powers of sin and death, power for a holy life, and confidence in the love of God (Rom. 8). They are recipients of and sharers in a "new creation" (Gal. 6:15; 2 Cor. 5:17–18).

All of that Paul preached among the Gentiles without reference to "the law," "works," or "justification by faith." We begin to see the point of the claim made by Pauline scholarship that these terms enter Paul's letters and discussion only under those circumstances where the relationship between Gentiles and Jews is in question; more specifically, where the identity of Gentile believers as full sharers in God's promise to Abraham and full members of God's people, apart from their doing the works of Torah, is being challenged. So, for example, when Paul speaks of "works" in Galatians and Romans it is clear that he specifically means "works of Torah" (*erga nomou*) and not striving to please God or doing good in general. Whether, with James Dunn, we should consider Paul's use of *erga nomou* more narrowly as "*particular observances of the law like circumcision and the food laws,*" that is, those observances of Torah which functioned in a Gentile context as "badges" or "identity markers" of Jewishness,[27] or whether we should take it in a more inclusive sense as the full observance of all of Torah which would be expected of proselytes to Judaism, the matter in question in Galatians and Romans, where *erga* and *erga nomou* occur most frequently, is whether the *Gentiles* are set right with God and made members of Abraham's family through Christ *alone* or through Christ *together with* (some or all of) Torah observance. Even a cursory tour through a concordance on the term *work* (*ergon*) will show that, except within these polemical contexts, Paul has nothing but good things to say about good works, and he nowhere discourages good works because they might become a source of pride before God. Rather, as we have seen, striving toward holiness and doing the works of obedience are ingredient in the Gentiles' hearing and believing the gospel of God, indeed, are precisely that which the power of the gospel frees and enables them to do (cf. Eph. 2:10).

The Gospel with the Law:
What Paul Does Not Say about Jews and Jewish Christians

Nor do we find anywhere in Paul an instruction that Jews who believe in Jesus the Messiah must cease their Torah observance. On the contrary, intrinsic to what God has done on behalf of Jew and Gentile in Jesus Christ is that the one, the Torah-observant Jew, may share life, worship, and table fellowship with the other, the non-Torah-observant Gentile (Gal. 2:11–13). The miracle of God's apocalyptic deed in Jesus Christ is that these two, who are *not the same* "deep down" or "in God's eyes," are yet made *one people* in Jesus Christ (Rom. 15:7–13; cf. Eph. 2–3). The Torah in its continuing role of *distinguishing*—not dividing—Jew (whether "Christian" or not) from Gentile remains a basic presupposition in Paul's thinking (Rom. 1:16 and Rom. 2–4, 7, 9–11, 14–15).[28] We search in vain in Paul's letters for a criticism of *Jews* (whether within or without the Jesus movement) who keep Torah. Indeed, in Galatians we find Paul positively affirming Peter's apostolic commission to Torah-keeping Jews:

> When they [the leaders in Jerusalem] saw that I had been entrusted with the gospel for the uncircumcised, just as Peter had been entrusted with the gospel for the circumcised (for he who worked through Peter making him an apostle to the circumcised also worked through me in sending me to the Gentiles), and when James and Cephas and John, who were acknowledged pillars, recognized the grace that had been given to me, they gave to Barnabas and me the right hand of fellowship, agreeing that we should go to the Gentiles and they to the circumcised. (2:7–10)

27. James D. G. Dunn, "The New Perspective on Paul," in *Jesus, Paul, and the Law: Studies in Mark and Galatians* (Louisville: Westminster John Knox, 1990), 191–92 (emphasis original).

28. This must be insisted upon, against the thesis of Daniel Boyarin in *A Radical Jew: Paul and the Politics of Identity* (Berkeley: University of California Press, 1994), that Paul spiritualizes particular Jewish identity by means of a Christian universalism in such a way that any continuing identity and role for fleshly Israel—in lineage, circumcision, and Torah obedience—is dissolved.

There is no suggestion here or elsewhere in Paul that Peter or anyone else should condemn or discourage Jewish Torah-keeping as either impossible, inherently full of pride and self-righteousness, or a sign of particularistic nationalism.[29] For in fact Paul attacks only "works of law" or "works" when Gentile believers themselves wished to take Torah obedience upon themselves (to come "under Torah") as a necessary completion of their justification or when anyone else, whether, Jew, Gentile, or "Christian" Jew wished to require Torah observance of Gentile believers as a necessary completion of their justification. Gentile justification is complete in Jesus Christ—period. Virtually all of Paul's comments with respect to "works" and "law" are directed to *that* issue, not to developing either a general theory of human action versus God's action or a specific theory about ongoing obedience or nonobedience to Torah by Jews, whether members of the Jesus movement or not.

Of course, for Paul, the Torah itself, understood now not as a set of nomistic practices but as a veritable ontic reality, does not have the power to deliver, set right, or vindicate either Jew or Gentile. Only God has that power, which is the power of resurrection. With respect to the attempt to place Gentiles "under Torah," the Torah speaks a curse (Gal. 3:10–12) and ministers condemnation (2 Cor. 3:9).[30] With the coming of Christ, the glory of Torah is a once and fading glory, not the permanent and unsurpassable and therefore transforming and saving glory of God visible in the face of Jesus Christ (2 Cor. 3:7–4:6). Only God has the power to deliver, set right,

29. Scholars such as James Dunn and N. T. Wright propose that "the Jewish problem" is the Jews' particularistic nationalism and exclusivism, fostered by "badges" or "identity markers" which set clear boundaries between Jews and Gentiles. As Paula Fredriksen shows, however ("What You See Is What You Get: Context and Content in Current Research on the Historical Jesus," *Theology Today* 52 [1995]: 75–97), this is but a variant on the theme of "Jewish" pride and self-righteousness based in Torah-keeping. For the various contemporary options on how scholars understand the phrase *works of law*, see Thomas Schreiner, "Works of the Law," in *Dictionary of Paul and His Letters* (ed. Gerald F. Hawthorne, Ralph P. Martin, and Daniel G. Reid; Downers Grove, Ill.: InterVarsity Press, 1993), 975–79. Schreiner himself makes an argument for a traditional understanding: "When Paul used the phrase 'works of Law' he referred to doing what the Law commanded. Paul maintained that no one can be justified . . . before God by doing what the Law commands, for no one can do everything which the Law demands and, should they experience some measure of success, they would sin in their pride of achievement" (975). The strangeness of this argument is palpable: the Jews, by virtue of being given the law and being called to obey it, were made to sin; indeed, to sin not only in their disobedience, but also and precisely in their obedience! This is a rather vicious "Lutheranism," in which God, by giving Torah, was intent only on setting a massive trap of condemnation for the Jews.

30. I am largely persuaded that Paul's letters have Gentiles as their implied or encoded audience (see Stowers, *Rereading Romans*, 21–33). That means that when Paul writes about Torah, he is writing about it to Gentiles in relation to Gentiles, not to and in relation to humanity in general or to Jews. It is important to keep the implied audience in mind especially when reading Galatians, or one easily slips into thinking that what Paul writes there is a letter to "humanity" or to "Jews and Gentiles" or a critique of "Judaism," when in fact it is a letter to Gentiles critical of an attempt (by Jews? "Christian" Jews? Christian Gentile proselytes to Judaism?) to require full Jewish practice from the Gentile believers in Galatia and their seeming willingness to accept this imposition. Making that distinction makes an important difference in how one reads Paul.

and vindicate both Jews and Gentiles, a power which, in keeping with the promise made to Abraham (Rom. 4), God demonstrated by raising Jesus from the dead, exalting him above all things—above the Torah as well as the idols, principalities, and powers—and sending the Holy Spirit. In fact, the Torah, while itself "holy and just and good" (Rom. 7:12), really lacks any power in itself and is therefore easily captured and used as an instrument by powers inimical to it, the "elemental principles of the cosmos (*stoicheia tou kosmou*; Gal. 4:3–10) or the powers of sin and death (Rom. 7). Thus for a Gentile to come "under Torah" is to be enslaved again to those powers through Torah, and for a Jew to "rely on Torah" is to rely on a reality without the power to give life. But, through God's power revealed in Jesus' crucifixion and resurrection, those who have and practice Torah (Jews) and those who do not (Gentiles) are delivered from hostile powers, reconciled to God, and made one people in the risen and exalted Lord, one people with one another. They are called to live together in this reconciliation and to live peaceably with a wider world that has not yet come to know the true state of affairs, namely, that "one has died for all; therefore all have died. And he died for all, so that those who live might live no longer to themselves, but to him who died and was raised for them" (2 Cor. 5:14–15).

I have attempted to address three questions in the foregoing discussion: (1) whether for Paul "justification by faith (in Jesus Christ)" is at the core of his conversion or of his original proclamation to the nations (i.e., a proclamation not contaminated by the controversies over Gentile Torah observance); (2) whether the faith/works dichotomy is about passive reception of grace versus active human striving to please God; and (3) whether ongoing Torah observance for Jews and a continuing distinction between Jews and Gentiles based on observance and nonobservance respectively are ruled out by the gospel which Paul preached. In each case I have answered the question in the negative. But that is all by way of establishing what *pistis Christou* is *not about*. I must now attempt to say what it *is about*.

The Gospel to the Nations: Justification through the Faithfulness of Jesus Christ

The Faith of Jesus Christ

I noted earlier that Richard Hays and others, in making a distinction between "faith in" and "the faith of" Jesus Christ, suggest that it is better to speak of *anthropological* and *christological*, rather than objective and subjective, interpretations of the phrase, each interpretation incorporating "larger judgments about the basic shape and logic of Paul's thought concerning faith."[31] In the rather extensive argument above I showed how the anthropological (or anthropocentric) interpretation is missing in Paul's preaching to the Gentiles. The

---

31. Hays, "Πίστις and Pauline Christology," 39.

christological interpretation, on the other hand, is central to that preaching. The positive case for the christological translation of *pistis Christou* has been thoroughly established and documented in Pauline scholarship. I will not myself make the exegetical case for it, but simply quote this summary by Michael Gorman of some of the most important arguments for it:

1. It expresses the most natural translation of the Greek phrase.
2. It makes God (rather than God and Christ) the consistent object of faith for Paul.
3. It is parallel in form and content to "the faith of Abraham" in Romans 4:12, 16.
4. It can be given coherent sense, as a reference to Christ's faith or faithfulness (the Greek word *pistis* can mean either) expressed in death, in the overall structure of Paul's experience and theology, making the most fundamental basis of salvation not anthropocentric (our faith) but theocentric and Christocentric (Christ's faith).
5. It grounds Paul's emphasis on the inseparability of faith and love in the one faithful and loving act of Christ on the cross.[32]

In what follows, I will set forth briefly "the basic shape and logic of Paul's thought" (Hays) surrounding this issue, following primarily the work of Hays and Martyn, in order to move on to the theological issues at stake in it.

Pistis Christou encapsulates a *story about God's faithfulness in relation to Jesus' faithfulness*. What is the story implied in the phrase "from/through the faith of Jesus Christ"? It is, in the first place, a story about Jesus' faithfulness or loyalty to God in doing what God sent him to do for humanity: "The phrase . . . points . . . to Jesus Christ's act of fidelity in undergoing death for our sake."[33] "The Lord Jesus Christ . . . gave himself for our sins to set us free from the present evil age, according to the will of our God and Father" (Gal. 1:3–4). Martyn helpfully notes the close parallel between Galatians 2:16 and 2:21, the beginning and ending sentences of a single argument: in 2:16 Paul contrasts "works of the law" with *pistis Iēsou Christou*; in 2:21 he contrasts "the law" with Christ's death:

> If beginning corresponds to end, then in 2:16, as in 2:21, Paul is referring to an opposition between rectification by Law observance and rectification by the deed of God in Christ. It follows that *pistis Christou* is an expression by which Paul speaks of Christ's atoning faithfulness, as, on the cross, he died faithfully for human beings while looking faithfully to God.[34]

32. Gorman, *Cruciformity*, 110–11.
33. Hays, "Letter to the Galatians," 239.
34. Martyn, *Galatians*, 271.

In the same way, in Romans 5:6–11 justification/rectification comes about because "Christ died for the ungodly/us," "we [are] justified by his blood," "we were reconciled to God through the death of his Son," "we [will] be saved by his life." The story of God's rectification and reconciliation of the ungodly and sinners is told without reference to the human disposition of faith, but consistently with reference to the history of Jesus Christ, his death and life.

In Romans 5:18–21 the "one righteous act" (*hena dikaiōma*) of Christ results in "justification and life" (*dikaiōsis zōēs*) for all; in contrast to the disobedience of "the one man" (Adam), the "obedience" (*hypakoē*) of "the one man" (Christ) makes the many righteous (*dikaios*). Romans 5:21 literally states that "grace may reign through righteousness (*dikaiosynē*) in eternal life through Jesus Christ our Lord." In these compact statements Paul again makes it clear that rectification and righteousness are rooted in and made effective solely through the obedience and righteousness of Jesus Christ, his death on the cross (cf. again 5:6–11), as the way in which the powerful rule of death and sin is broken. When Paul moves on in Romans 6 to address the question of how his Gentile readers may share in Christ's righteousness, he does not say, "put aside all human effort and have faith in Jesus." Rather, he speaks about their baptism into the death and resurrection of Jesus; about their deliverance through Christ from the powerful reign of death and sin; and about how, being dead to sin and raised to new life, they must present their "members" (*melē*; 6:13) as "instruments of righteousness"—what can this mean but the parts of their bodies in their physical moral agency?—indeed, themselves as "slaves . . . of obedience . . . to righteousness (*douloi . . . hypakoēs eis dikaiosynēn*)" (6:16). Hays writes:

> Romans 5 shows unmistakably that Paul regards Jesus' death as an act of obedience that carries the destiny of many; furthermore, Romans 6 goes on to contend that his death is not merely vicarious but that through baptism we have entered a union with Christ in such a way that his death and resurrection define a pattern for our obedience as well.[35]

Christ's obedient death leading to righteousness makes possible, calls forth, and expects a corresponding obedience leading to righteousness from those who now participate in Christ through baptism. Christ's faithfulness makes possible human faithfulness. Paul never prioritizes faith as one supposed kind of (inner, passive) human response, over obedience (bodily, active) as another kind; nor does he ever separate faith from obedience. Quite the contrary; he holds the two together as one: when he summarizes his mission to the nations he writes of calling forth from them their "obedience of faith[fulness]" (*hypakoēn pisteōs*; 1:5) or, quite straightforwardly, their "obedience" (*hypakoē*; 15:18). The way the Gentiles live, in their faithfulness to the one God of Is-

35. Hays, "Πίστις and Pauline Christology," 49.

rael, in their baptism into Christ's death and resurrection, and in their bodily acts of obedience, is the way in which they share in the righteousness of God revealed in the faithful death of Jesus.[36]

All of this sets the narrative context within which we must translate and interpret the phrase *pistis Christou* as it appears in the concentrated and controversial texts of Romans 1:17; 3:21–31; and Galatians 2:15–3:29. The many linguistic and semantic arguments which others have marshaled in favor of "the faith(fulness) of Christ" finally draw me to the larger theological question: Is it *our* faith that plays the decisive role in justification, the means by which the individual is put right before a righteous God? Or is it the faithful and obedient *Jesus* in his crucifixion and God's vindication of Jesus' faithfulness in raising him from the dead that are both decisive and powerful in setting the cosmos right and delivering it from the powers under which it is enslaved, in order that humans might obey God freely? If—as I have demonstrated in many ways—this latter story indeed pervades Paul's letters, excepting these few controversial texts, then this story is contradicted in a fundamental way by rendering *pistis Christou* in these texts as "faith in Jesus Christ." Martyn makes this point forcefully:

> The result of this interpretation of *pistis Christou* [as the faith *of* Christ] is crucial to an understanding not only of Galatians but also of the whole of Paul's theology. God has set things right without laying down a prior condition of any sort. God's rectifying act, that is to say, is no more God's response to human faith in Christ than it is God's response to human observance of the Law. God's rectification is not God's response at all. It is the *first* move; it is God's initiative, carried out by him in Christ's faithful death.[37]

God's right-making of the cosmos is not, and cannot be, achieved through our response of faith; it is rather what elicits faithfulness from us; faithfulness is at one and the same time God's deed and one of our own deeds.[38]

Justification

The meaning of justification has been more or less explicit throughout our discussion of the faith of Jesus Christ. It remains to draw out the main contours of Paul's meaning in the form of an expanded definition.[39] For Paul

---

36. Richard Hays's development of Paul's ethics in *The Moral Vision of the New Testament: Community, Cross, New Creation* (San Francisco: Harper San Francisco, 1996), 16–59, is a sustained attempt to show that Paul's moral instruction is theologically grounded in the faithfulness of Jesus Christ in his death and thus also in Jesus Christ's being put forward as the normative pattern of the moral life in the Christian community. The same themes pervade Hays's "Letter to the Galatians" and his discussion of the many moral issues raised in 1 Corinthians in *First Corinthians* (Louisville: John Knox, 1997).

37. Martyn, *Galatians*, 271.

38. On this point see ibid., 275–77.

39. This extended definition is indebted most deeply to Martyn, *Galatians*, 97–104, 246–80; idem, "Apocalyptic Rectification," in Martyn's *Theological Issues in the Letters of Paul* (Nashville: Abingdon,

justification or, preferably, rectification (Martyn's term) is the definitive, cosmic, apocalyptic act of the one God of Israel in Jesus Christ, whereby this God, through the death and resurrection of the Faithful One, conquers the powers which hold the nations in bondage and reconciles the world to himself, in order that he might create in Christ a new people, indeed, finally a whole new world, in which loyalty, obedience, and faithfulness to the one God of Israel is made possible among the nations in the power of the Holy Spirit. In this way God demonstrates his own justice, that is, his faithfulness to the promise which he made to Abraham to bless not only Israel but also the nations and so too the whole of creation. God's right-making faithfulness thus also calls forth and enables a corresponding right-making (justice) among the peoples of the earth; specifically it creates the theological-political space for a reconciliation between Israel and the nations, a reconciliation made concretely real and present in the baptism and table fellowship of Jews and Gentiles in the new community that hears and obeys the good news which Paul preaches.

If this is the meaning of justification/rectification in Paul, then we must say that while the *language* of justification by the faith of Jesus Christ appears only to arise in and be addressed to those contexts in which there is a controversy over whether Gentiles must take up Torah observance, nevertheless the *story* which is told there is consistent with what we read as central to Paul's missionary message in a letter like 1 Thessalonians, where such controversy is not on the horizon. This must be affirmed in response to those who claim that justification is not the central and determinative doctrine in Paul. The claim predates the "new perspective on Paul" by a half a century or more, but is reclaimed and further argued by much scholarship.[40] Albert Schweitzer (and, before him, Wilhelm Wrede) suggested that justification is of secondary importance (a "subsidiary crater") in Paul, that it is a concept which Paul uses only when he is engaged in controversy with Judaism. Krister Stendahl, E. P. Sanders, James D. G. Dunn, and N. T. Wright, among others, followed Schweitzer's lead. Dunn's comment is representative:

> The doctrine of justification by faith was formulated [by Paul] within and as a result of the early mission to the Gentiles. It was a polemical doctrine, hammered out in the face of Jewish Christian objections to that mission as law-free and not requiring circumcision. "Justification by faith" was Paul's answer

---

1997), 87–156; Hays, "Letter to the Galatians"; idem, "Justification," in *Anchor Bible Dictionary* (ed. D. N. Freedman et al.; New York: Doubleday, 1992), 3:1129–33. For somewhat different perspectives, see James D. G. Dunn, *The Theology of Paul the Apostle* (Grand Rapids: Eerdmans, 1998), 334–89 (which includes an excellent bibliography); and N. T. Wright, *What Saint Paul Really Said: Was Paul of Tarsus the Real Founder of Christianity?* (Grand Rapids, Eerdmans, 1997), 113–33.

40. See the helpful survey of various stances toward the centrality of justification in A. E. McGrath, "Justification," in *Dictionary of Paul and His Letters* (ed. Gerald F. Hawthorne, Ralph P. Martin, and Daniel G. Reid; Downers Grove, Ill.: InterVarsity Press, 1993), 522–23.

to the question: How is it that Gentiles can be equally acceptable to God as Jews?[41]

Such claims are largely correct. But, as we have seen, if we distinguish the contingent terminology from the underlying story (the "narrative substructure"— Hays), they are overdrawn. They are simply the mirror opposite of the traditional claim that in the few texts in which the language of justification (by faith in Jesus Christ) is prevalent we have the center and perhaps the sum total of Paul's gospel. In fact, rather, we have in these texts only one more way of stating that gospel in a contingent, conflictual context, in language appropriate to that context.[42] The story that the language of justification tells is the same story which Paul, in other language, originally preached to the nations.

Justification Reconfigured: Barth, Yoder, Hauerwas

As I noted earlier, the usual Protestant story of justification and faith is quite different from that outlined above. The anthropocentrism of the usual readings of *pistis Christou* in Paul has been fundamentally challenged and rendered suspect by the christological readings of Hays, Martyn, and others. Still, most modern theology, whether conservative or liberal Protestant, whether Lutheran or Roman Catholic, remains apparently either ignorant of, uninterested in, or perhaps hostile to this challenge to the usual readings. Justification through the believer's faith in Christ is still, as a rule, considered the central and determinative Pauline doctrine, to which all others are subordinate or of which they are secondary implications.[43] So also, when justification and faith come up for discussion in theological writings, the anthropological reading of *pistis Christou* almost invariably informs the treatment of these doctrines. But there are some notable exceptions.

Barth: Justification, Faith, Human Action

Karl Barth's theology, from his early commentaries on Romans to the later volumes of the *Church Dogmatics*, may be seen as an especially thorough outworking of the Pauline theme of "justification by the faithfulness of Jesus Christ" as I have laid it out above. That Barth's revolution in theology

41. Dunn, *Theology of Paul the Apostle*, 340.

42. On the relationship between the "coherence" of the gospel which Paul preached and the "contingency" which characterizes this gospel as it is present in the variety of Paul's letters, see J. Christiaan Beker, *Paul the Apostle: The Triumph of God in Life and Thought* (Philadelphia: Fortress, 1980, 1984), 11–36.

43. See, e.g., the discussions in Lutheran-Roman Catholic dialogues. In the groundbreaking *Joint Declaration on the Doctrine of Justification of the Lutheran World Federation and the Roman Catholic Church* (Grand Rapids: Eerdmans, 2000) we read that "in Paul's letters . . . , the gift of salvation is described in various ways," e.g., as freedom, reconciliation, peace with God, new creation, life, and sanctification. "*Chief among these* is the 'justification' of sinful human beings by God's grace through faith" (12, emphasis added). See also Dunn's comments in *Theology of Paul the Apostle*, 335–36.

began with five years (1916–21) of intensive study in and two commentaries on Romans (with a third in 1956) surely accounts in large measure for the fundamentally Pauline character and structure of his entire thought. And yet, within the whole of the *Church Dogmatics* the doctrine of justification receives, on its own, relatively few pages, and the doctrine of faith even less.[44] Barth's "Paulinism" is mostly found elsewhere. In what follows I want to draw attention to some features of the second edition of Barth's commentary on Romans and of the *Church Dogmatics* that warrant the judgment that his work stands in fundamental continuity with the Pauline theology of justification that I have presented above.

The second edition (1921) of Barth's *Römerbrief* (*The Epistle to the Romans*),[45] as is well known, marks a revolution not only in Barth's own theological development but also in the theological world of the early twentieth century. It remains *the* landmark of twentieth-century theology in the way that Schleiermacher's *Speeches on Religion* (1799) does for the nineteenth.[46] Among the many remarkable features of Barth's commentary, one which becomes immediately evident is its powerful *apocalyptic* tone and message. Commenting on Romans 1:16–17 as the theme of the epistle, Barth writes: "The Gospel is the victory by which the world is overcome. By the Gospel the whole concrete world is dissolved and established" (35). Even more powerful is the apocalyptic tone of his comments on the "but now" which begins Romans 3:21:

> We stand here before an irresistible and all-embracing dissolution of the world of time and things and men, before a penetrating and ultimate KRISIS, before the supremacy of a negation by which all existence is rolled up. The world is the world; and we now know what that means (i.18–iii.20). But whence comes this KRISIS? . . . Our origin evokes in us a memory of our habitation with the Lord of heaven and earth; and at this reminiscence the heavens are rent asunder, the graves are opened, the sun stands still upon Gibeon, and the moon stays in the valley of Ajalon. *But now* directs our attention to time which is beyond time, to space which *has* no locality, to impossible possibility, to the gospel of transformation, to the imminent Coming of the Kingdom of God, to affirmation in negation, to salvation in the world, to acquittal in con-

44. Barth's *Church Dogmatics* 4.1 contains about 130 pages entitled "The Justification of Man" (514–642), within which are about 40 pages entitled "Justification by Faith Alone" (608–42); and about 40 pages entitled "The Holy Spirit and Christian Faith" (740–79), within which are about 20 pages entitled "The Act of Faith" (757–79). In the whole scheme of *Church Dogmatics* 4.1 (entitled *The Doctrine of Reconciliation*), this is a small amount of coverage, perhaps roughly the same ratio of focal attention which these doctrines get within the total Pauline corpus.

45. Karl Barth, *The Epistle to the Romans* (trans. Edwyn C. Hoskyns; Oxford: Oxford University Press, 1933; repr. 1968).

46. The best available account in English of Barth's early theology is Bruce L. McCormack, *Karl Barth's Critically Realistic Dialectical Theology: Its Genesis and Development, 1909–1936* (Oxford: Oxford University Press, 1995); on the second edition of *Romans* (1921), see 241–90.

demnation, to eternity in time, to life in death—*I saw a new heaven and a new earth: for the first heaven and the first earth are passed away.* This is the Word of God. (*Epistle to the Romans*, 91–92, emphasis original)

For Barth this irruptive, disruptive, even destructive apocalypse of Jesus Christ, which is the overriding theme of Barth's entire commentary on Romans, means the eradication of all human pretensions of having God in hand and the world under control. That apocalypse has no other goal than exposing and destroying all idolatry: "The Gospel is not a truth among other truths. Rather, it sets a question-mark against all truths" (*Epistle to the Romans*, 35). Because of this, the person grasped by the gospel is immediately "engaged in a strife with the whole, even with existence itself," because the whole world and the whole human being is the ground of contention between God and the idols. The only hope in this battle is the gospel: "The Gospel of the Resurrection is the—**power of God** . . . the disclosing and apprehending of His meaning, His effective pre-eminence over all gods. The Gospel of the Resurrection is the action, the supreme miracle, by which God, the unknown God dwelling in light unapproachable, the Holy One, Creator, and Redeemer, makes Himself known" (35, emphasis original). Further, the power of the gospel is totally unlike the powers of the world: "The power of God is not the most exalted of observable forces, nor is it either their sum or their fount. Being completely different, it is the KRISIS of all power. . . . The power of God stands neither at the side of nor above—supernatural!—these limited and limiting powers. It is pure and pre-eminent and—beyond them all" (36). It is thus God's power of *salvation* for humanity in bondage to these other powers: "In this world men find themselves to be imprisoned. . . . Their sin is their guilt; their death is their destiny; their world is formless and tumultuous chaos, a chaos of the forces of nature and of the human soul; their life is illusion. This is the situation in which we find ourselves" (37).

In a rather surprising move, Barth's comments on Romans 1:16–17 and 3:21 are accompanied and informed by none other than Paul's speech on the Areopagus (Acts 17:16–34; see *Epistle to the Romans*, 35–37, 94–96), in which Paul engages the Athenians, their religion, and their gods with the message of the gospel. The "unknown god" for which the Athenians hold a place in their pantheon, Paul goes on to declare, is none other than the God of Israel, who cannot however be merely ranged among the gods, but is the Creator God, without form or place, the Lord who sets the nations in their places, gives life and breath to all, and who raised Jesus from the dead. By thus connecting the gospel of justification with the criticism of idolatry, Barth anticipates one of our key findings about Paul's message to the nations: justification, that is, the rectification of the nations, is in the first place about the first commandment, the exclusive priority of the one God of Israel, not only for Israel but for all the nations of the world. Barth emphasizes, with Paul, that God's revelation in Jesus Christ is *God's apocalyptic tri-*

umph over all the enslaving powers and gods of this world, a triumph that in turn delivers idolaters (for Barth, this means all of humankind) from their imprisonment to these other, finally immanent and impotent, powers and gods. Precisely so, it is also a demonstration of God's faithfulness:

> We proclaim that, because it is His nature to remain faithful [to humankind, to creation], the Godhead cannot be graven into any likeness by the skill and device of men. . . . By faith in the revelation of God we see men bounded, confined, and barred in, but even this is the operation of God. We see men under judgement, yet nevertheless thereby set aright. . . . We see salvation breaking through. We see the faithfulness of God remaining firm. (*Epistle to the Romans*, 94–95)

The revelation of God's righteousness is the revelation of God's faithfulness to the creation: "It is the redemption of all creation, and most particularly when the creature knows itself to be no more than a creature, and so points beyond itself" (*Epistle to the Romans*, 95).

"The faithfulness of God is established when we meet the Christ in Jesus" (*Epistle to the Romans*, 96). That statement comes out of Barth's rendering of *dia pistēs Iēsou Christou* in Romans 3:22 as "through his [God's] faithfulness in Jesus Christ."[47] While that translation may be finally unsustainable, it allows Barth to draw the closest possible connection between God's faithfulness and the revelation of Jesus Christ, who for Barth is the paradigmatic and normative human being, the only one in whom the truth of humanity is properly discerned:

> In Jesus we have discovered and recognized the truth that God is found everywhere and that, both before and after Jesus, men have been discovered by Him. In Him [Jesus] we have found the standard by which all discovery of God and all being discovered by Him is made known as such; in Him we recognize that this finding and being found is the truth of the order of eternity. Many live their lives in the light of redemption and forgiveness and resurrection; but that we have eyes to see their manner of life we owe to the One. In His light we see light. (*Epistle to the Romans*, 97)

That Jesus is this "One" is made known because in his life we see the faithful fulfillment of the will of God as testified by the law and prophets:

47. Barth's German translation of 3:22 reads: "**Die Gerechtigkeit Gottes durch** seine **Treue in Jesus Christus für alle, die glauben.**" The word *seine* (which Barth prints in nonbold) indicates that Barth is supplying his own word here. Barth must therefore use *Treue* (faithfulness) to translate *pisteōs*, rather than *Glaube* (faith); *Der Römerbrief* (Zurich: EVZ, 1940), 66; see also Barth's translations of Rom. 3:25–26, 27–28, 29–30 on pp. 79, 81–82, 87. In each case where *pistis* occurs, Barth renders it, unambiguously, as the "faithfulness" of God! Barth does not justify this rendering with linguistic and exegetical arguments, but it is crucial to the claims of his commentary on these passages, which emphasize the faithfulness of God.

That it is the Christ whom we have encountered in Jesus is guaranteed by our finding in Him the sharply defined, final interpretation of the Word of the faithfulness of God to which the Law and Prophets bore witness. His entering within the deepest darkness of human ambiguity and abiding within it is THE faithfulness. The life of Jesus is perfected obedience to the will of the faithful God. (*Epistle to the Romans*, 97, emphasis original)

God's faithfulness is revealed in the faithfulness of Jesus Christ; specifically, in the faithfulness of his standing "among sinners as a sinner," placing himself under God's judgment, and moving through slavery to the cross and to death, as Barth explicates with reference to Philippians 2:6–11.

Further, the faithfulness of God establishes human faith. But for Barth, faith, insofar as it is what humans are called to before the faithfulness of God, is a nonentity, a nothing rather than a something. In the power of the gospel, "only faith survives: faith which is not a work, not even a negative work; not an achievement, not even the achievement of humility; not a thing which exists before God and man in its own right" (*Epistle to the Romans*, 110). As such, human faith is neither "foundation" nor "atmosphere" nor "system" upon which or in which humans might take their own stand. Rather, "the *law of the faithfulness of God* [*nomos pistou*, Rom. 3:27], or, what is the same thing, the *law of faith*, is the place where we are established by God" (110, emphasis original). That human beings might be something again, and that they might do something again, resides wholly in being thus "established" in the faithfulness of God—and this exactly is faith, the being and doing established by God. "In the paradox of faith the faithfulness of God is sufficient, for through it we stand on firm ground and move forward with assurance" (113).

The goal of God's faithfulness is made clear in the way in which Barth construes the movement through Romans 5–6, a movement evident in the titles which Barth gives to the sections of those chapters. Once again drawing on the apocalyptic theme, he characterizes Romans 5 under the rubric "The Coming Day" (*Epistle to the Romans*, 149). By this Barth does not mean a day in a distant future, but the day which comes in the revelation of Jesus Christ. In his death and resurrection the old humanity and the old creation are canceled, and "The New Man" (5:1–11) and "The New World" (5:12–21) arrive in power. Romans 6 is presented under the rubric "Grace" (188). Grace is the power of God by which the new creation comes into being. Grace is revealed as God's power in two aspects: "The Power of the Resurrection" (6:1–11), by which humans are made sharers in the new man and the new world in Jesus Christ; and "The Power of Obedience" (6:12–23), by which participation in Christ's resurrection cancels the dominion of sin over humans and renders them "slaves of righteousness." Having said that, however, Barth does not say much about the concrete shape of that obedience which participation in the power of the resurrection renders possible, a point I shall return to below.

While there is a certain abstractness running throughout all of this, there is also a powerful grasp of the logic of Paul's gospel in Barth's commentary. Has any theologian been so decisively seized by the revelation of God in Jesus Christ as to write theology as "apocalyptic without reserve"—except perhaps Paul himself?[48] The recovery of the apocalyptic logic of Paul's theology by Ernst Käsemann, J. Christiaan Beker, J. Louis Martyn, and others certainly sustains and is perhaps also significantly sustained by Barth's reading of Romans—of course, not in all the details, but in the overall mood and tone and direction of that reading. For in Paul the apocalypse of Jesus Christ is indeed a world-dissolving and world-constituting event. As we shall see, Barth himself never loses sight of this throughout all of his later work. More important for the present discussion, in Barth as in Paul the language and meaning of justification and faith is consistently subsumed within this unreserved apocalyptic horizon. Barth sees that justification is simply another way of saying that in the cross and resurrection God puts to death the whole cosmos and raises it again from the dead. Justification is about God's deed of new creation, a deed that occurs in spite of and against and for the sake of an old creation held in bondage to powers from which it has not the power to escape.

Faith too is caught up into the apocalyptic horizon. As we have seen, Protestant theology has all too often rendered "faith" as a substantive noun, turned it into "something" that one must "have" to be saved, or that one perhaps always has as an essential human endowment that must be discovered, awakened, or redirected. For Barth faith is not a substantive, is not a something to be possessed, is not a "consciousness" or "standpoint" or "perspective" from which one might then move assuredly on in the business of self-realization ("freedom") and world ordering ("justice"). It is rather the event of being caught up into the action of God in order that human action might thereby be truly dissolved and constituted as service to God and to the neighbor. In an illuminating study of human action in Barth's theology, John Webster describes Barth's project in *The Epistle to the Romans* thus:

> Barth is at the beginning of a process of reconstituting human action on grounds quite other from those to which appeal was made in the dominant Protestant tradition of his day. . . . [That is, Barth is about] reattaching consideration of ethics to consideration of the being and action of God. . . . [He

48. The phrase is from Walter Lowe, "Prospects for a Postmodern Christian Thought: Apocalyptic without Reserve," *Modern Theology* 15 (1999): 23: "The suspension of all things human within an unqualified apocalyptic—a suspension which is unqualified because it is apocalyptic—is perhaps the possibility glimpsed by the Theology of Crisis." Lowe has in mind especially Barth's *Römerbrief.* See also Lowe, "Barth as Critic of Dualism: Re-reading the Römerbrief," Scottish Journal of Theology 41 (1988): 377–95.

is attempting] to ensure that properly theological affirmations about what human beings do can be grasped as what they are: *theological*.[49]

Barth himself writes: "There is no human action which is in itself fashioned according to the transformation of this world; but there are actions which seem so transparent that the light of the coming Day is almost visible in them" (*Epistle to the Romans*, 434–35). About this, Webster comments that for Barth there is "a real, if restricted, sense that human actions, transformed by their annihilation and reconstitution in the resurrection, are a pointer to divine action 'in their primal Origin.'"[50] That is the meaning of faith in Barth. And, as I showed above, it is the meaning of faith in 1 Thessalonians, where Paul calls the Thessalonians to stand fast in the face of persecution, live holy lives, love one another, and remain hopeful *because* they have been caught up into and transformed by the faithful action of the Father who raised Jesus from the dead, of the Son who is coming, and of the Holy Spirit whom the Father gives.

While, as we have seen, Barth lays heavy stress on the theme of God's faithfulness in *Epistle to the Romans*, he also addresses the matter of the faithfulness of Jesus Christ: "In Him [Jesus] we have found the standard by which all discovery of God and all being discovered by Him is made known as such. . . . His entering within the deepest darkness of human ambiguity and abiding within it is THE faithfulness. The life of Jesus is perfected obedience to the will of the faithful God" (*Epistle to the Romans*, 97, emphasis original). Further, in relation to Romans 5:18–19, Barth speaks of Christ as "the 'new' subject, the EGO of the coming world. This EGO receives and bears and reveals the divine *justification* and election—*This is my beloved Son, in whom I am well pleased*" (181, emphasis original). Noteworthy here is Barth's claim that Christ is the one toward whom God's justification is directed in the first place. In other words, God vindicates, justifies, the Faithful One, the Righteous One, "through the power of the Resurrection" and his appointment as the Son of God (181). Sinful humanity is justified only because God first justifies Jesus: "As a consequence of the righteousness of Christ there comes—**justification of life—unto all men**. . . . With this declaration of righteousness the new and eternal subject of all men has been directly created" (182, emphasis original).

For (v. 19)—**by the obedience of the one shall many be appointed righteous**. Here again, it is not merely that A personality, AN individual, has been illuminated by what is observable and appreciable in the obedience of the life and death of the one Jesus; rather, it is THE personality, THE individual, which has here been disclosed. In the One the *many* individuals are, here, for those

49. John Webster, *Barth's Moral Theology: Human Action in Barth's Thought* (Grand Rapids: Eerdmans, 1998), 27–28.
50. Ibid., 30.

who have eyes to see, appointed, illuminated, and disclosed: that is to say, Thou and I are appointed as righteous before God, as seen and known by God, as established in God, as taken unto Himself by God. In the light of this act of obedience there is no man who is not—in Christ. (*Epistle to the Romans,* 182, emphasis original)

Barth here attends to the faithfulness or obedience of Jesus almost exclusively in its salvific significance. He is concerned *not* to present Jesus' obedience, in the concrete historical detail of his life, as a norm and pattern of obedience in life for those who are "in Christ." In the background of that decision there certainly lies, for Barth, the specter of the many pietistic and liberal "lives of Jesus" which render him all too easily comprehensible and followable, one full of strictly human possibilities for the religious and ethical life. Where in those "lives," Barth would ask, is the strange, new apocalypse of God to which Paul and the rest of the New Testament attest? So when Barth goes on (in commenting on Rom. 6:8–11) to address the question of "the visible significance of the 'Life of Jesus'" (*Epistle to the Romans,* 202), he insists that the only *imitatio Christi* possible for sinful humans is in death and resurrection. The life of Jesus "is determined by the fact of the crucifixion, for we are clearly not intended to understand His life as an illustration of human possibility, nor indeed can we thus interpret Him." Thus, "the visible significance of Christian faith . . . consists in the perception that the line of death which runs through the life of Jesus is in fact the law and necessity of all human life" (202). But the crucifixion, suffering, and passivity of Jesus have this negative significance only in the light of its reversal, the revelation of "a standard of impossibility by which visible human possibilities are measured," that is, the active and triumphant Jesus of the resurrection: "Over against the crucified Jesus stands the risen Lord. The visible significance of His life cannot be understood apart from the disclosure and revelation of the invisible glorification of the Father" (203). Barth keeps his account of the Christian life strictly focused on God's action in revelation and glorification, against the easy moralizing of the liberal lives of Jesus; but we might ask again whether Paul would not have more to say than Barth does about how the shape of Jesus' faithful obedience might provide a visible, normative pattern for the concrete shape of the Christian life (Rom. 15:1–8; cf. Phil. 2). On that matter, Barth provides a more adequate account in the *Church Dogmatics,* to which I now turn.

The sections on justification and faith in the *Church Dogmatics* certainly warrant careful study.[51] Such study reveals, perhaps rather surprisingly, that in many respects the most important decisions about how to approach these topics are made already in the second edition of *The Epistle to the Romans.* Justification remains wholly God's work, directed first toward Jesus Christ, "who lives as the author and recipient and revealer of the justification of

51. Barth, *Church Dogmatics* 4.1:514–642, 740–79.

man" (*Church Dogmatics* 4.1:629); in and through Christ humanity itself is wholly justified. Therefore, justification cannot be "completed" or "made effective" through human faith. Now—and only in apparent contrast to what he says in *The Epistle to the Romans*—Barth understands faith itself as a "work," a human action (617), so how can it be thought to contribute to our justification? To think thus is to fail to recognize that as a sinful human being the believer "needs justification just as much in faith as anywhere else, as in the totality of his being" (616). Instead, faith is the first of the *works* that justification establishes: "Faith is the humility of obedience. . . . Faith differs from any mere thinking and believing and knowing, or indeed from any other trusting, in the fact that it is an obeying" (620). In each of these ways Barth reiterates—though not without certain corrections and many expansions—the positions he developed in *The Epistle to the Romans*.

We find the most significant movement *beyond* those positions in his presentation of a theology of the *imitatio Christi*. Faith, as "the obedience of humility,"

> imitates Jesus Christ in whom it believes, it corresponds to Him, it has a similarity with the One who "for your sakes became poor, that ye through his poverty might be rich" (2 Cor. 8:9). Similarity with Him in the high mystery of the condescension in which as the Lord He became a servant, in which as a child He lay in a crib in the stall at Bethlehem, in which in Jordan He entered the way of penitence, in which He was hungry and thirsty and had nowhere to lay His head, in which He washed the feet of His disciples, in which He prayed alone in Gethsemane, in which He was rejected by Israel and judged and condemned by the Gentiles, in which He hung in opprobrium on the cross of Golgotha. Faith is a weak and distant but definite echo or reflection of all this. It cannot be otherwise. For it is the mystery of the true Godhead of Jesus Christ that He was able and willing to do what He did do in obedience according to Phil. 2:7–8: that He emptied Himself, humbled Himself. And a man finds his justification as he believes in this One who became poor. Faith itself, therefore, becomes a poverty, a repetition of this divine downward movement. (*Church Dogmatics* 4.1:635)[52]

This is something that it was not impossible for Barth to say in *The Epistle to the Romans*, but it is something that he, perhaps rightly, refused to say and did not say in that context. But now, not only the death and resurrection but also the specific narrative of Jesus' earthly career, that is, his "condescension," becomes crucial for discerning the shape of Christian life. This is a significant move beyond *The Epistle to the Romans*. Barth is clearly and explicitly following the Pauline logic whereby the faithfulness of Jesus Christ becomes also the pattern of human faithfulness: "If we have become obedient to Him, it is in-

---

52. Note that Barth says that "a man finds his justification as he believes in the One." This is quite different from saying that one is justified because he or she believes in the One.

evitable that the divine humility in which Jesus Christ is the righteous man should be the pattern which we who believe in Him should follow" (*Church Dogmatics* 4.1:636).

There is much else in Barth's analysis of justification and faith that is worthy of note, and also some worthy of criticism, in relation to the Pauline logic that I have developed above.[53] There is, most obviously and notably, Barth's commitment to treat ethics as a discipline within dogmatics, that is, as an account of the priority of divine action over human action and at the same time the incorporation of human action into divine action in and through the Son and the Spirit. But perhaps the most remarkable imprint of Pauline logic on Barth's theology, an imprint which is already firmly in place in *The Epistle to the Romans*, is surely to be discerned in the very structure of the *Church Dogmatics*. The entire project begins with the "apocalypse," that is, with a doctrine of revelation which is determined from beginning to end by the world-dissolving and world-constituting event of God's advent in the cross and resurrection of Jesus Christ. This apocalypse epistemologically precedes and in turn determines everything that Barth will go on to say about the knowledge of God, the reality of God, the election of God, and the command of God.[54] For Barth as for Paul, Jesus Christ is constitutive for the Christian doctrine of God; for Barth as for Paul, the God of Israel is no longer to be identified apart from Jesus Christ.[55] Further, as already in *The Epistle to the Romans*, Barth in the *Church Dogmatics* will not treat the doctrines of creation and humanity apart from God's apocalypse in Jesus Christ, for we do not finally know their true shape and destiny apart from that revelation. In other words, Barth's entire project is governed by the same christological conviction, summed up powerfully and succinctly in texts such as 2 Corinthians 5:14–21 and Colossians 1:15–23, which controls Paul's entire theology.

Nowhere is this more evident than in the doctrine of reconciliation that makes up the entire fourth volume of the *Church Dogmatics*. There Barth structures the entire doctrine, following Philippians 2:6–11, around three

53. In *Church Dogmatics*, as in *Römerbrief*, Barth continues nonetheless to work with the faith/works dichotomy (typically abstracted from its contingent context in the Pauline writings) as a way of protecting the priority of God's action. And in truly Protestant fashion, Barth seems to have far more to say and speculate about the character of "faith" than Paul was ever interested in doing. This, to my mind, runs not only against the grain of Paul's logic, but also against Barth's own better insights into the character of faith itself as a "work" and as obedience.

54. On the epistemological centrality of God's apocalypse in the cross of Christ for Paul, see J. Louis Martyn's commentary on 2 Cor. 5:16–17 in "Epistemology at the Turn of the Ages," in *Theological Issues in the Letters of Paul*, 89–110.

55. This point, with respect to the New Testament, including Paul, is made vigorously and persuasively by Richard Bauckham in what is sure to become a definitive statement: *God Crucified: Monotheism and Christology in the New Testament* (Grand Rapids: Eerdmans, 1998). Bauckham rejects the polarized options of "functional" and "ontic" Christologies and argues that New Testament Christology is a Christology of divine identity.

themes: "the obedience of the Son of God," "the exaltation of the Son of Man," and "the glory of the Mediator." The first theme is developed as an extended reflection on "the way of the Son into the far country," the journey of the Son, as an act of obedience, from heavenly glory and communion with the Father into the midst of human sin and suffering, culminating in his death on the cross. Within the first theme he includes the doctrine of the fall as the sinful human contradiction of the Son's obedience. It is worth noting that the fall is not presented in a separate section following the doctrine of creation, nor is it treated prior to and separate from the doctrine of reconciliation (which for Barth is most fundamentally about Emmanuel, God with us) as the "plight" which makes the obedience of the Son of God necessary. Rather, the fall is revealed in its true character *only* in the bright light of God's eternal will always to be for and with humankind and creation in the person Jesus Christ. But also under "the obedience of the Son of God," Barth places the doctrine of justification. Nothing shows more clearly that Barth understands that the doctrine of justification is critically determined by the logic of "the faithfulness of Jesus Christ" and not by "faith in Jesus Christ"—although there is certainly also room for the latter ("the Holy Spirit and Christian faith"; §63) when it plays an important but *tertiary* role, subsumed beneath Christology ("the obedience of the Son of God"; §59) and ecclesiology ("the Holy Spirit and the gathering of the Christian community"; §62). While there is not space for it here, a detailed reading of *Church Dogmatics* 4.1 fully bears out this claim that Barth repeats the Pauline *logic* (if not precisely the translation) of *pistis Christou* as, in the first and determinative place, the faith of Jesus Christ. But also, retrieving crucial insights from *The Epistle to the Romans* in *Church Dogmatics* 4.2, Barth goes on to claim that Jesus Christ is not only the site of human faithfulness, the faithfulness of "the Lord as Servant," but also the site of God's faithfulness demonstrated in the resurrection of Jesus from the dead and his exaltation as Lord, "the Servant as Lord." Humanity is sanctified in this exaltation, the Christian community is built up through the Holy Spirit, and the same Spirit creates the space for Christian love.

In effect, Barth's entire doctrine of reconciliation is an exposition of the meaning of the Pauline phrases *in Christ* and *in the Holy Spirit*. Christian existence is described primarily as this participation, but a participation which in turn makes possible and generates human action which corresponds to the obedience and exaltation of Jesus Christ. Commenting on Barth's ethics of reconciliation, which he develops as an exposition of the Lord's Prayer, Webster writes:

> Underlying Barth's exposition of the Lord's Prayer is an affirmation that God's gracious divine action both constitutes human persons as agents, and furnishes a prototype to which human action corresponds and in which correspondence its goodness is found. Thereby, Barth seeks to exclude sole causality

on the part of either God or the human agent, proposing instead that the moral field is a diverse pattern of correspondences or analogies, of similarities and dissimilarities, between the actions of God and human actions.[56]

In the same way, in *The Epistle to the Romans* and *Church Dogmatics* Barth renders the faithfulness of God, the faithfulness of Jesus Christ, and the faithfulness of Christian obedience in a "diverse pattern of correspondences or analogies." But that is also as good a summary of the *Pauline* doctrine of justification by faith as one is likely to find. To the present day no one has matched Barth's power to elucidate this Pauline logic.

Yoder: Justification, Politics, Ekklēsia

As we have seen, standard Protestant accounts of the doctrine of justification tend to focus on the relationship between God and the individual believer—indeed, the *inner being* of the individual—effected by the atoning death of Jesus and by the believer's faith in him. The individual is justified through his or her faith in Jesus Christ. If the central Pauline doctrine is fundamentally about the individual in his or her inner spiritual condition before God, then exploring "the politics of Paul," as I will do in subsequent chapters, is at best a secondary and dispensable exegetical and theological enterprise—as virtually every summary of Pauline theology testifies, up to and including the magnum opus by James Dunn, *The Theology of Paul the Apostle*.[57]

For John Howard Yoder, however, a sociopolitical reading of Paul is not an add-on to the main event of explicating Paul's doctrine of justification. On the contrary, as I will show more fully in chapter 3, sociopolitical explication is intrinsic to Yoder's reading of Paul's theology, not least the Pauline doctrine of justification. In Yoder's understanding, Paul's doctrine of justification is only one more example—but a crucial one—of the way in which Paul's gospel is intrinsically and thoroughly sociopolitical in character. Yoder devotes an entire chapter in his *Politics of Jesus* to showing not only how that is the case, but also to how traditional Protestant readings of Paul on justification in fact distort the central issues of Paul's doctrine.[58]

56. Webster, *Barth's Moral Theology*, 177.

57. See, however, James D. G. Dunn and Alan M. Suggate, *The Justice of God: A Fresh Look at the Doctrine of Justification by Faith* (Grand Rapids: Eerdmans, 1993). Notable exceptions to the norm are Neil Elliott, *Liberating Paul: The Justice of God and the Politics of the Apostle* (Maryknoll, N.Y.: Orbis, 1994); Dieter Georgi, *Theocracy in Paul's Praxis and Theology;* Wright, *What Saint Paul Really Said,* 39–62. We can expect that Wright's forthcoming major work on Paul will include a significant treatment of the politics of Paul; in the meantime see also his "Paul's Gospel and Caesar's Empire," in *Paul and Politics: Ekklesia, Israel, Imperium, Interpretation: Essays in Honor of Krister Stendahl* (ed. Richard A. Horsley; Harrisburg, Pa.: Trinity, 2000), 160–83. This last named book and Richard Horsley's other edited work, *Paul and Empire: Religion and Power in Roman Imperial Society* (Harrisburg: Pa.: Trinity, 1997), are fundamental to the contemporary retrieval of the politics of Paul.

58. John Howard Yoder, *The Politics of Jesus: Vicit Agnus Noster* (2d ed.; Grand Rapids: Eerdmans, 1994), 212–27.

The classic Protestant position on justification that places it in an all-determining position at the center of Pauline doctrine has the effect of ruling out ethical and sociopolitical matters as integral to Paul's message and mission. The "legal fiction," whereby God graciously considers or declares the guilty individual sinner righteous before him (while the individual yet remains a sinner—*simil iustus et peccator*) through the sinner's faith in the work of Christ, and completely apart from human works, has the effect of creating a deep and wide gulf between faith and ethics. As Yoder puts it: "The act of justification or the status of being just or righteous before God is therefore radically disconnected from any objective or empirical achievement of goodness by the believer." And further: "Does not the insistence that justification is by faith alone through grace alone, apart from any correlation with works of any kind, undercut any radical ethical and social concern by implication, even if Paul himself might not have been rigorous enough to push that implication all the way?" (*Politics of Jesus*, 213). If that is the case, then Yoder's argument (which he makes in the four chapters previous to the one on justification), that Paul's theology is intrinsically sociopolitical in character, comes apart.

Yoder notes, however, that some proposals in biblical scholarship have put a question mark against the typical Protestant construal of Paul on justification. The problems of personal guilt, forgiveness, self-acceptance, and acceptance before a righteous God, which preoccupied such determinative interpreters of Paul as Augustine, Luther, John Wesley, and Kierkegaard, and which continue to bother modern Lutherans and conservative evangelicals, were perhaps not the problems which bothered Paul himself. Were Paul's preoccupations, Yoder asks, even "most fundamentally located on the individual level?" He proposes that we "posit as at least thinkable the alternate hypothesis that for Paul righteousness, either in God or in human beings, might more appropriately be conceived of as having cosmic or social dimensions" (*Politics of Jesus*, 215). Ground-breaking essays by Krister Stendahl, Markus Barth, Hans Werner Bartsch, and Paul Minear provided Yoder with the exegetical foundations he needed to make his alternate hypothesis not only thinkable, but highly plausible.[59]

Following Stendahl, Yoder notes that before his conversion Paul was not burdened (as Luther was) with guilt-consciousness over his inability to keep the law of God, but instead had a robust conscience before God and confidence in his achievement as a faithful Jew (cf. Phil. 3:4–6). For Paul the law's primary purpose was not to convince people of their failure to keep it per-

---

59. Yoder mines several essays: Krister Stendahl, "The Apostle Paul and the Introspective Conscience of the West," *Harvard Theological Review* 56 (1963): 199–215 (repr. in Stendahl's *Paul among Jews and Gentiles* [Philadelphia: Fortress, 1976], 78–96); Markus Barth, "Jews and Gentiles: The Social Character of Justification in Paul," *Journal of Ecumenical Studies* 5 (1968): 241–67; Hans Werner Bartsch, "Die historische Situation des Römerbriefes," *Communio Viatorum* 8 (1965): 199–208; Paul Minear, *The Obedience of Faith: The Purposes of Paul in the Epistle to the Romans* (London: SCM, 1971).

fectly; rather, the law was God's "gracious arrangement" for ordering Israel's life until Christ came. Thus faith for Paul is "not a particular spiritual exercise of moving from self-trust through despair to confidence in the paradoxical goodness of God; faith is at its core the affirmation that separated Jewish Christians from other Jews, that in Jesus of Nazareth the Messiah had come" (*Politics of Jesus*, 215–16). Sin, on the other hand, in particular Paul's own understanding of himself as a sinner, is his failure to recognize that Jesus is God's Messiah. God corrected that by his "inexplicable intervention" into Paul's life on the road to Damascus (217). Only later, when the Jewish context of Paul's mission and message was forgotten, did the meanings of sin and law become universalized, individualized, and existentialized. Indeed, even faith in Paul has been misunderstood. In an intriguing footnote, which otherwise goes unargued and unexplored, Yoder writes: "In general the New Testament word *pistis* would better not be translated 'faith,' with the concentration that word has for modern readers upon either a belief *content* or the *act* of believing; 'faithfulness' would generally be a more accurate rendering of its meaning" (221 n. 9). The "relationship of prelude and sequence" between faith and ethics does not reflect Paul's understanding (221).

Further, according to Yoder, Paul in his time continued to respect both the law and those Jewish Christians who continued to keep it. The "basic heresy" against which Paul strove was that of Jewish Christians not recognizing that, now that the Messiah had come, the Gentiles were welcomed through Christ into full covenant relationship with God without having to become Jews, that is, without keeping the whole law as Jews do. Yoder concludes: "In sum: the fundamental issue was that of *the social form of the church*. Was it going to be a new and inexplicable kind of community of both Jews and Gentiles, or was it going to be a confederation of a Jewish Christian sect and a Gentile one" (216, emphasis added)? That such *is* the issue at the heart of the Pauline message, according to Yoder, is made especially clear in the letter to the Ephesians (2:11–22), in which the writer (whether Paul or one of his earliest interpreters) speaks of God's eternal "mystery" as "precisely that Jew and Gentile are now reconciled in one community" (218). "The overcoming of this hostility [between Jews and Gentiles], the making of peace by eliminating the wall that had separated them, namely the Jewish law to which Jews were committed and which Gentiles ignored, is itself the creation of a new humanity" (219). Drawing now on the work of Markus Barth, Yoder shows how even in that central document of the Protestant Reformation, the letter to the Galatians, Paul's language of justification indicates primarily a social event, the necessary table fellowship of Jews and Gentiles established by their unity (not uniformity) in Jesus Christ. "To be 'justified' is to be set right in and for that relationship" (220). Likewise, the language of new creation in Galatians 6:15 (and 2 Cor. 5:17) names "not a renewed individual but a new social reality" (222). Paul's entire mission to the Gentiles is driven by his conviction that the end-time new creation has already begun in Jesus' death and resurrection and that he (Paul) is "a major actor in that drama" by calling the Gentiles to take their place in it.[60]

Finally, with the help of Hans Werner Bartsch, Yoder addresses the meaning of the letter to the Romans. Here again we find that "law" names neither a way of "soul salvation" (as in "legalistic works-righteousness") nor the obstacle in the way of it; it identifies rather "the historically concrete identity of the Jewish separateness which made the problem that justification resolves" (*Politics of Jesus*, 224). In fact, justification is a "verbal noun" specifying the action whereby God "sets things right" because "he is a right-setting kind of God" (224). What God sets right, according to the argument of Romans, is the relationships between humanity and God and between Jews and Gentiles, such that a new, healed community is created from former enemies, Jews and Gentiles. This is consistent with the radical nonviolent ethic of Jesus which, according to Yoder, is pervasive in the writings of Paul. In other words, not only is justification not something antecedent to or above or beside Paul's social ethics. Justification is necessarily and intrinsically already social, political, ethical through and through. "It is the Good News that my enemy and I are united, through no merit or work of our own, in a new humanity that forbids my ever taking his or her life in my hands" (226).

This often neglected chapter in *The Politics of Jesus* in fact receives more support in Pauline scholarship—particularly from the "new perspective"—than almost any other claims Yoder makes about the theology and politics of Paul. Without reiterating in detail what I have presented above, I note the following of Yoder's claims which have been vindicated by Pauline scholarship since he made them in 1972:

1. Paul's primary concerns, precisely in the language of justification, are cosmic and social more than inner and individual. The approach to justification through Paul's "cosmological apocalyptic eschatology" (Martyn) demonstrates this.
2. Justification is about God's right-making action in Jesus Christ and in the church and therefore about setting right what is wrong between persons and peoples (Martyn, Hays).
3. Matters of social/ethnic division and enmity between Jew and Gentile believers are central in the Pauline texts having to do with justification, as demonstrated extensively and persuasively by Dunn and others.

---

60. "Because the end-time is here, the Gentiles are now in the covenant. The ingathering of the Gentiles is not a means to an end or a precondition of the fullness of time; it is the beginning of the end. The fullness of time is the precondition of the Gentile mission" (*Politics of Jesus*, 219 n. 6). Yoder at this point cites Minear, *Obedience of Faith*, 91ff., making an argument against the view (of Oscar Cullmann and Johannes Munck) that "when the gospel has been proclaimed to all the nations, then the end will come" (219 n. 6, emphasis original).

4. Paul's "conversion" is not about relieving his guilt-consciousness or coming to realize that keeping Torah fosters self-righteous Jewish legalism. It is about Paul being overwhelmingly convinced that Jesus is the Messiah of Israel and risen Lord who sends Paul on a mission to the Gentiles (Stendahl, the entire "new perspective," and most recent Pauline scholars).

5. Paul criticizes the law (1) insofar as some (whether Jews, Christ-believing Jews, or Gentile proselytes) try to require observance of the law from Gentile believers rather than acknowledge them as full sharers, as Gentiles, in the promise to Abraham and in the people of God; and (2) insofar as it causes division between Jews and Gentiles in the Jesus movement (Stendahl, Sanders, Dunn, Donaldson, Wright). Paul continues to respect the law and Jewish Christian observance of it (Dunn, Donaldson, Stowers).

6. "Faith" is primarily an affirmation about Jesus the Messiah, rather than the movement from human striving to receptive trust. Faith is not opposed to human doing (Hays).

7. The *ekklēsia* is intrinsic to the meaning of justification, since justification is another word for the reconciliation of Jews and Gentiles in Christ and the creation of one new people out of the two. The new creation is a social rather than an individual reality—the gospel is the transformation of social and political existence (Markus Barth, Hays, Donaldson).[61]

Yoder's anticipation of the new post-Protestant Paul is impressive indeed, and it is remarkable that those aware of Yoder's chapter on justification have hardly recognized this.[62] This is not to say that there are not some gaps and weaknesses in this chapter. Given that Yoder's treatment of the issues surrounding justification by faith is executed in a fairly short chapter, we cannot expect that he said everything he wanted to say or should have said on the matter. There are certainly some ways in which his discussion could and should be deepened and improved.

In the first place, there is a certain theological "flatness" about the discussion insofar as Yoder remains focused primarily on the social reconciliation accomplished in God's justifying action. While he rightly stresses that justification is a doctrine of cosmic as well as social proportions and acknowledges that it is also about reconciliation with God, he misses the opportunity to draw close links between the content of this chapter and an earlier one entitled "Christ and Power." In that chapter Yoder concretely displays the apocalyptic character of Paul's thought in the way in which Christ's triumph over

61. Each of these points will reemerge and be explored further in the chapters that follow. Yoder's own thoroughly Pauline theology is examined in detail in chap. 3.

62. The notable exception is Hays, *Moral Vision of the New Testament*, 245.

the powers delivers human persons and groups from the many kinds of bondages (ethnic, cultural, social, national) to which they have become en-slaved and which thus separate them both from God and from one another. The conquest of those powers—idols, demons, authorities, cosmic "ele-ments"—is precisely the core meaning of God's action in Jesus Christ as Paul preached it to the Gentiles, while the language of justification is Paul's way of speaking about God's action in the contingent situation of the challenges to his law-free gospel to the Gentiles. In other words, God's apocalypse in Jesus Christ, God's triumph in the cross of Christ over the powers, God's vindication of Jesus Christ in the resurrection, and God's rectification of the Gentile peoples in Christ are all one and the same reality. Yoder's work in *The Politics of Jesus* leaves them somewhat disconnected, at least in relation to Paul's theology of justification.[63] As a result, a careful explication of the re-lation between God's action and human action that we find in Barth is left undeveloped.

Second, Yoder rightly, and against an overwhelming tradition of interpre-tation of Paul, preserves the Torah's integrity in Paul's thought and argues that Torah observance for Christ-believing Jews is not only legitimate, but to be expected. He does not, however, sufficiently recognize that the Torah among Jews of Jesus' time (and after) holds a highly exalted position not only as a set of instructions for the good ordering of Jewish life but also as an ontic reality which bears the coherence and meaning of the universe. Thus when Paul speaks of the exaltation of Christ over all things in texts such as Philippians 2:6–11 or Colossians 1:15–20, this can only mean that whatever else either Jew or Gentile might rightly go on to affirm about Torah, they cannot from a Pauline perspective affirm that it shares a status and glory equal to, or even in competition with, that of Christ. There is no indication that Yoder would dispute that, but again, because he focuses primarily on justification as social reconciliation in *The Politics of Jesus,* he neither makes this point clear nor explores its implications for an ongoing affirmation of Torah observance among those Jews who believe in Jesus Christ or those who remain within Judaism.[64] But Yoder cannot be blamed too much for this. One of the important unfinished tasks of Pauline scholarship is to sort out the differences between the Torah's ongoing proper function within Ju-daism as the Jews' faithful witness to the God of Israel and Torah's "end" in Christ as an exalted, universal structuring principle and primary locus of God's glory. That question will come up again for consideration in subse-quent chapters of this book.

63. Yoder leaves his most important discussion of apocalyptic for the Book of Revelation, rather than emphasizing that Paul is also, intrinsically, an apocalyptic theologian.

64. As I show in chap. 4, Yoder addresses these issues at some length in a variety of as yet unpub-lished writings.

Finally, however, as a lasting contribution Yoder crucially and forcefully
draws our attention to the fact that the primary, direct, and immediate result
of justification is not the "saved" individual, but the *ekklēsia*.[65] On that judgment he joins Karl Barth in testifying to the Pauline logic of the gospel, a
logic in which God's reconciliation and redemption of the cosmos through
Christ and the Spirit has as its first goal the creation of a new *people of God*,
made up of Jews and Gentiles, in which the calling of Israel and the nations'
unified witness to the one true God have their beginning. Justification creates the new sociopolitical reality called church.

Hauerwas: Justification, Doctrine, Ethics

The contributions of Barth and Yoder made a determinative impact on
the theology/theological ethics of Stanley Hauerwas. I treat Hauerwas's contribution to a post-Protestant understanding of Paul more extensively in the
next chapter. Here I simply want to draw attention briefly to the way in
which he addresses the division between doctrine and ethics, so typical in
the Protestant theological curriculum, as a reflection of certain ways of construing the doctrine of justification and the faith/works relationship.

In an important essay entitled "On Doctrine and Ethics,"[66] Hauerwas,
following Barth, argues that "something has already gone wrong if Christians have to ask what the relation might be between doctrine and ethics"
(20). Certainly in the Bible one looks in vain for any significant distinction,
let alone division, between the two; and the attempt to explicate them as
separate entities leads to anachronistic misunderstanding: "The New Testament and the early Christian theologians thought about little else than how
Christians were to live their lives" (23).

> That we now think, for example, that there is a "problem" for understanding
> the relation between Paul's discussion of justification in Romans 5:1–11 and
> the "moral" instruction he gives in Romans 12–14, says more about us than it
> does about Paul. Our assumption that Romans 5 is theology and that the later
> chapters of Romans constitute ethics is not a distinction Paul would recog-
> nize. There is nothing in Romans that indicates or suggests Romans 5 is more
> significant than or foundational to Romans 12. That we now think one of the
> tasks of Christian ethics is to provide some account of this "problem" in Paul
> is but an indication that the Pauline text is being read through the polemics of
> the Reformation. (*Sanctify Them in the Truth*, 21)

65. Markus Barth's *Ephesians* (2 vols.; Anchor Bible 34–34A; Garden City: Doubleday, 1974) is the
fruition of the research and essays which informed Yoder's work on justification and *ekklēsia*. This is a
rich and valuable resource alongside Yoder's chapter.

66. The essay appeared first in *The Cambridge Companion to Christian Doctrine* (ed. Colin Gunton;
Cambridge: Cambridge University Press, 1997), 21–40, and is reprinted in Hauerwas's *Sanctify Them in
the Truth: Holiness Exemplified* (Nashville: Abingdon, 1998), 19–36.

It is no accident that Hauerwas traces the problems with such readings of Paul to the Reformation. He does not suggest that Reformers such as Luther and Calvin themselves worked with a basic division between doctrine and ethics. In this way they were not different from the great figures of the early and medieval church, such as Augustine and Aquinas. Neither the early church nor Augustine and Aquinas distinguished between theology and pastoral direction; indeed a good deal of the work of medieval theologians was given to the writing of church law in relation to the rite of penance (hence the creation of the "penitentials," manuals that matched appropriate penance to sins committed and confessed) as a means of forming Christian life, while the sacraments as the core practices of the church were the focal and generative points of most theological/moral reflection on the character of the Christian life (*Sanctify Them in the Truth*, 23–27).

Something else, however, was introduced in the Reformation that set the stage for the division between doctrine and ethics: the faith/works dichotomy in which the relationship of "the sinner" (singular) to God is construed. "Works became associated with 'ethics,' particularly as ethics was alleged to be the way sinners attempt to secure their standing before God as a means of avoiding complete dependence on God's grace. So for Protestants the Christian life is now characterized in such a way that there always exists a tension between law and grace" (*Sanctify Them in the Truth*, 27). "Law" and "works of law" became associated with what is *outside* of God's grace; but keeping such law and doing such works were nonetheless necessary to the good order of society (but not to "faith"), where the Christian lived life in the body and acted in love toward the neighbor. Thus, in the Lutheran doctrine of the two kingdoms the Christian must live according to one rule within the church ("faith," which attends to the assurance of salvation) and another rule in the social order ("works," which attends to the question, How ought I to live?). "What was lost after the Reformation was exactly [the] understanding of the church as the indispensable context in which order might be given to the Christian life" (28). The gospel of justification thus also adds little or nothing to the understanding of what "good order" in society is supposed to mean. It is not a long step from there to the conviction that doctrine and ethics are distinct, perhaps even in some senses opposing, topics and tasks. Ethics on this understanding easily comes to be seen as the more publicly accessible reality (in contrast to the hiddenness of faith), that is, what can be spoken about and consensus reached on, even if there is no shared or widespread belief in the gospel of justification. In any case, under the powerful influence of Kant, ethics, now stripped of any connection to particular theological descriptions of moral order, comes to be seen as the site of hope for universal peace. And Christian "ethicists" debate issues of social order, which is seen to be their primary task, with as little reference to the gospel as possible (29–32).

It is precisely at this point that Hauerwas discerns the significance of Karl Barth. For Barth once again recovered Christian theology/ethics as a matter of developing a "moral ontology" (Webster's term) in which the gospel of Jesus Christ is the all-encompassing and determinative reality and the church is the necessary context for discerning the shape of the Christian life: "Barth does not seek to make the church a servant of a civilizing project and thus a supplement for what is a prior conception of ethics" (*Sanctify Them in the Truth*, 34). Hauerwas saw rightly, and certainly in accord with Pauline logic, that "the question of the relation between doctrine and ethics," if we are going to allow that distinction, "is not just a 'conceptual' matter but an institutional, or more accurately, an ecclesial issue" (20).

Hauerwas's essay helps to draw the threads of this chapter together. From a theological and historical perspective he lets us see that some of the crucial moves made at the time of the Reformation and after regarding justification by faith have historically led to truncated understandings of the gospel in relation to human action, the *ekklēsia,* and the *polis*—themes that are at the forefront of Barth's and Yoder's retrievals of Paul. But I argue, on the basis of fresh examinations of some Pauline texts and with the help of recent Pauline scholarship, that the Reformation moves that Hauerwas identifies are neither necessary nor warranted (at least for our time—I will leave the historical question aside) if we understand Paul's doctrine of justification within the wider perspective of his message and mission to the nations. That message and mission is precisely about God's deliverance of the Gentiles from their former religious-sociopolitical allegiances, in order that they might give their unreserved loyalty (*pistis*) to the one God of Israel who has invaded their world in Jesus Christ and the power of the Holy Spirit, in order that they might become a new people, under a new Lord and a new regime called the kingdom of God, the body of Christ, the *ekklēsia. That is justification.* The Gentiles share in this new people and new regime by being baptized into the body of Christ and, in their newfound freedom from other gods and other lords, by becoming obedient and faithful to their Lord, repeating the pattern of his obedience and faithfulness in their whole way of life, in body and in soul, social and personal, active and passive, economic and political, within the body of Christ and as the body of Christ. *That is faith.* Their justification, therefore, is or ought to be immediately marked by a specific and visible way of being and living in the world as a social body. Every letter of Paul is oriented to that end; one searches in vain for any section within those letters that is not oriented to it.[67]

67. The clearest and most powerful current argument in support of this statement is surely Hays's *First Corinthians.*

Conclusion

Beyond attempting to say what might be said, in light of recent Pauline studies and with the help of Barth, Yoder, and Hauerwas, about the doctrines of justification and faith, I hope I have also cleared the ground for the chapters to follow, such that these doctrines, whether in their Lutheran, evangelical, or liberal guises, would not be the means of subverting or skirting the challenge which Paul's theology addresses to the church at the end of modernity. The church is plagued with all-too-many individualized and spiritualized versions of its (or, rather, "the Christian's") purpose and mission, and these stand in the way of the church's calling to be the people of God as salt and light in the world. What we have discovered in this chapter is that, not only does Paul's language of justification and faith *not warrant* those versions of the church, but in fact *stands against* them and points to something very different indeed. Only by recovering, beyond Protestantism, something of the original theological, political, and ecclesial force of that language as Paul used it, will the church be enabled again to see its mission and message as the proclamation, in full power, of the justification of the nations through the faithfulness of Jesus Christ. The remaining chapters are devoted to that recovery.

2

Apocalypse

Galatians and Hauerwas

It takes a bold theologian in these postmodern days to write an essay, and even a whole book, with the title "The Truth about God." Stanley Hauerwas is a bold theologian.[1] Moderation is missing in most of his work, which is not to say that he does not engage in careful, even patient, reasoning about matters theological, in conversation with many others both within and without the theological guild. But Hauerwas understands that even patience, respectful listening, and a certain playfulness in theological reasoning can only serve his larger and primary aim, "to remind Christians that we are in a life-and-death struggle with the world."[2] Such a struggle, or warfare, is always engaged in the specific awareness that real enemies pose real threats, in relation to which the theologian may—playfully, but rightly—be labeled a "nonviolent terrorist."[3] In matters theological, talk of truth, of enemies and warfare, of life-and-death struggles with the "world," and of "terrorism," can only mean

---

1. Stanley Hauerwas, "The Truth about God: The Decalogue as Condition for Truthful Speech," in Hauerwas's *Sanctify Them in the Truth: Holiness Exemplified* (Nashville: Abingdon, 1998), 37–59. *The Truth about God: The Ten Commandments in Christian Life* (Nashville: Abingdon, 1999) is coauthored by Hauerwas and William Willimon.

2. Stanley Hauerwas, "The Christian Difference; or, Surviving Postmodernism," in Hauerwas's *Better Hope: Resources for a Church Confronting Capitalism, Democracy, and Postmodernism* (Grand Rapids: Brazos, 2000), 36.

3. Stanley Hauerwas, "The Non-Violent Terrorist: In Defense of Christian Fanaticism" and "No Enemy, No Christianity: Preaching between 'Worlds,'" in Hauerwas's *Sanctify Them in the Truth*, 177–200.

erwas theology is a thoroughly *apocalyptic* activity. Hauerwas is
with the apostle Paul, especially the Paul of Galatians.

ter is an attempt to read together Galatians and Hauerwas as a
way of coming to terms with Hauerwas's "struggle" with liberalism, or liberal
democracy, or "America." As we will see, on few other matters has he been so
roundly and vigorously criticized than in his criticisms of liberalism. And on
few other issues has he been so deeply misunderstood. I am convinced that
reading Hauerwas in the light of Paul's letter to the Galatians enables us to
understand Hauerwas better. Further, it enables us to gain a better understanding of Paul's letter. In the light of this mutual illumination, I hope to
show that Hauerwas's struggle with liberalism is a thoroughly and authentically Pauline affair.

Before going further, however, a statement is in order about what I mean
by the words *apocalypse* and *apocalyptic* so frequently used in the following
pages.[4] Most simply stated, "apocalypse" is shorthand for Jesus Christ. In the
New Testament, in particular for Paul, all apocalyptic reflection and hope
comes to this, that God has acted critically, decisively, and finally for Israel,
all the peoples of the earth, and the entire cosmos, in the life, death, resurrection, and coming again of Jesus, in such a way that God's purpose for Israel, all humanity, and all creation is critically, decisively, and finally disclosed and effected in the history of Jesus Christ. The language of apocalypse
/apocalyptic captures several elements in this claim in a way that, for example, the language of revelation and eschatology do not. First and foremost is
a strong emphasis on *God's* action in the history of Jesus Christ, rather than
on human action or response. God's action, further, is characterized (1) as
conflict with enslaving powers: the world and humanity, including both Israel and the nations, are held enslaved by cosmic powers (e.g., sin and death,
but also other powers) that oppose God's good purpose for all creation; (2)
as invasive/decisive: God's action in Jesus Christ is absolutely necessary because of the enslaved condition of the cosmos and absolutely clear and effective because its goal, the liberation and rectification of humanity and creation, cannot finally be mistaken or thwarted; (3) as judgment: Israel and
the nations are presented in Jesus Christ with the normative and critical
measure of their faithfulness or faithlessness to God and so stand exposed in
their deeds before the "throne of God," where they will be vindicated or
condemned; and (4) as final: what occurs in the history of Jesus Christ is un-

---

4. The following account of the character of apocalyptic theology, particularly as it occurs in Paul, is
largely informed by J. Christiaan Beker, *Paul's Apocalyptic Gospel: The Coming Triumph of God* (Philadelphia: Fortress, 1982), 29–53; and J. Louis Martyn, *Galatians: A New Translation with Introduction and
Commentary* (Anchor Bible 33A; New York: Doubleday, 1997), 97–105. Martyn persuasively establishes
the apocalyptic character of Galatians in particular, against the doubts of someone like Beker. Against
those who narrow the definition of *apocalyptic* to a specific genre of literature and its themes (e.g., the
Book of Revelation) and thus overlook Paul as an apocalyptic theologian, see especially Martinus C. De
Boer, "Paul, Theologian of God's Apocalypse," *Interpretation* 56 (2002): 21–33.

surpassed and unsurpassable; there is no reality, no historical or mythical figure, no system, framework, idea, or anything else that transcends the reality of Jesus Christ, for, in the strongest possible sense, God's action and the history of Jesus Christ are both one and singular. The language of apocalypse/apocalyptic is therefore always also (5) cosmic/universal in scope: it is not language merely about human matters or "spiritual" realities or faith-perspectives or states of mind or consciousness, but language about mutually different worlds or ages: on the one hand, the world that was and is ("this age") and, on the other hand, the world that has begun and will come to fulfillment through God's action in Jesus Christ ("the age to come"). It is language about the action of God in Jesus Christ as both determining and revealing "the grain of the universe" (John Howard Yoder). Finally, apocalyptic is indeed language about "disclosure" or "revelation" (the most straightforward translation of the Greek word *apokalypsis*), but again this must be taken in the sense of the timely and effective disclosure of God's critical, decisive, and final action and purpose for the cosmos, and not as the unveiling of a previously hidden state of affairs immanent within human nature or the cosmos—God's *apokalypsis* is not only a showing, but also a doing which effects what is shown.

All of that means that apocalyptic theology is theology "without reserve," that is, theology which leaves no reserve of space or time or concept or aspect of creation outside of or beyond or undetermined by the critical, decisive, and final action of God in Jesus Christ. Discriminating judgments, definitions and differentiations, even "totalizing" claims, are intrinsic to the grammar of apocalyptic theology—not, of course, as the proud and "authoritarian" prerogative of the theologian or the church, but as the manner in which Christian theology participates in the apocalypse of Jesus Christ. I have not yet spoken of *how* apocalyptic theology engages this grammar, but *that* it must do so is central to the claim of this chapter. Indeed I propose that that is the only adequate appropriation of the logic and content of Paul's message. To do otherwise, for example to "contextualize" Paul's apocalyptic as the "conditioned" product of his time, is to escape the grip of his message, to depart from the road on which Paul travels and on which he invites, indeed implores, his hearers/readers to travel. In an essay whose importance stands in inverse proportion to its brevity, Walter Lowe writes:

> The rationalist response to apocalyptic is to treat it, or belief in it, as a historical phenomenon. In doing so, the historian asserts a priori the very continuity of history which apocalyptic would question—into the dustbin of history goes the notion that history is headed for the dustbin. But a similar distortion occurs when believers inscribe apocalyptic within a cosmic timeline, be it ever so celestial. . . .
>
> Reason spontaneously seeks to contextualize that with which it deals. But Christian theology proceeds upon the quite different premise that we our-

selves have been contextualized; and not just conceptually, but actually. It is
we who have been inscribed.[5]

Lowe goes on to note that "the suspension of all things human within an unqualified apocalyptic—a suspension which is unqualified *because* it is apocalyptic—is perhaps the possibility glimpsed by the Theology of Crisis."[6] Now,
however, the theology of crisis, along with Jesus and Paul, "has been returned to the relativizing embrace of history, its apocalyptic circumscribed
within the events of a distant day. But it was that apocalypticism which gen-
erated Christianity's distinctive postmodernism. And it is that apocalypticism which needs to be reclaimed and rethought today."[7] By reading Galatians, Paul's most apocalyptic of letters, together with Hauerwas's critique of
liberalism in the name of a contemporary apocalyptic theology, I hope to
contribute to that reclaiming and rethinking and therefore also to the shaping of the "distinctive postmodern" theology of which Lowe speaks.

Servants of the Apocalypse

Virtually every reader of Paul's letter to the Galatians, if he or she has also
read Paul's other letters, is soon struck by its unusually sharp and angry
tone—Paul displays here a palpable sense of dismay over the Galatians' confusion about the gospel and of anger toward those who are causing it (5:7–
12). He wishes he could change his tone (4:20), but since he is not present
with the Galatians, the letter will have to bear to them not only a powerful
message but also the full weight of Paul's emotions of dismay and perplexity.
Paul is to the Galatians as a mother groaning in the pain of childbirth
(4:19)—which certainly goes a long way toward explaining his extreme
curses upon those who are hindering the delivery of the child (1:8–9; 5:12).
Paul's birth pains are deep, the birth itself of cosmic significance. A whole
new world is at stake in this labor. Paul's is a life-and-death struggle for the
birth of the new world among the Galatian churches.

It is important not to come up short in describing what is at stake in
Paul's letter. It happens all too often. For example, Paul is often thought to
be concerned to defend a religion of "faith" against a religion of "works," or
a religion of grace against a religion of law, or Christian freedom against

---

5. Walter Lowe, "Prospects for a Postmodern Christian Theology: Apocalyptic without Reserve,"
Modern Theology 15 (1999): 23.

6. Ibid., 23. This possibility is being glimpsed again, in another way, by radical orthodoxy. See, e.g.,
John Milbank, Catherine Pickstock, and Graham Ward (eds.), *Radical Orthodoxy: A New Theology* (London: Routledge, 1999), 1–4. Whether the apocalyptic vision of radical orthodoxy is faithful to or compatible with that of Paul, as I believe the apocalyptic visions of Barth, Yoder, and Hauerwas are, remains a
question for further exploration. David Toole's critique of Milbank is a good place to begin that exploration; see *Waiting for Godot in Sarajevo: Theological Reflections on Nihilism, Tragedy, and Apocalypse* (Boulder, Colo.: Westview, 1998), 53–87.

7. Lowe, "Prospects for a Postmodern Christian Theology," 23.

(Jewish) legalism, or Christian universalism against Jewish ethnic particular-
ism, or social unity in Christ against the divisions of race, class, and gender,
and so on. These and so many other ways of construing the life-and-death
struggle in Galatians are often focused on anthropocentric concerns, the
conflicting patterns of religion or social relationships that confronted the
Galatians. There is a certain reductionism in such construals. They all more
or less ignore the apocalyptic reality that lives at the heart of the letter—that
God, in the death and resurrection of Jesus Christ, by the power of the Holy
Spirit, has inaugurated among the nations nothing less than a new cosmos,
the new creation, in which the Galatian churches are being called to share
and thus to be its first and most visible evidence. Will God's new creation be
made manifest in these churches, or will it be only another version of the old
creation? To construe the issue in terms of anything less than the arrival, the
revelation, the apocalypse of God's new creation in Christ is not only to
come up short of the theme of the letter but also to render that theme a servant to another.

   Such, I believe, is one of the persistent shortcomings of some of the work
from the "new perspective on Paul." E. P. Sanders, J. D. G. Dunn, N. T.
Wright, and others often borrow from the repertoire of historical, sociological, and religious studies to name the terms of Paul's theological concerns. It
is supposed that he is wrestling with questions about the conditions for "getting in and staying in" a certain religious group (i.e., the covenant people of
God); or with group "boundary markers" which distinguish and separate
groups from one another, but which in Christ are eradicated, making all
groups into one; or with "inclusion" and "exclusion," that is, the difference
between "Jewish ethnic nationalism" which is by definition "exclusive" and
the new message of God's gracious "acceptance" of all in Jesus Christ and
which is therefore "inclusive."[8] Without denying the element of truth in
these and similar construals, they are insufficiently apocalyptic/theological.
They miss the crucial point that in Galatians Paul is concerned to affirm
"the singularity of the gospel"—that God's relationship to and purpose for
the nations and all creation is exclusively determined by and through God's
cosmic-eschatological-healing in the cross and resurrection of Jesus Christ
and the outpouring of the Holy Spirit.[9] For this reason, and this alone, any
other cosmic principle (*stoicheion tou kosmou*) such as Torah—the contin-

   8. See, e.g., James Dunn: "Paul's chief target is a covenantal nomism understood in restrictively nationalistic terms—'works of the law' as maintaining Jewish identity, 'the curse of the law' as falling on the
lawless so as to exclude Gentiles as such from the covenant promise"; "The Theology of Galatians: The
Issue of Covenantal Nomism," in *Pauline Theology*, vol. 1: *Thessalonians, Philippians, Galatians, Philemon*
(ed. Jouette M. Bassler; Minneapolis: Fortress, 1991), 137.
   9. The phrase *the singularity of the gospel* is from an important essay by Beverly Roberts Gaventa,
"The Singularity of the Gospel: A Reading of Galatians," in *Pauline Theology*, vol. 1: *Thessalonians, Philippians, Galatians, Philemon* (ed. Jouette M. Bassler; Minneapolis: Fortress, 1991), 147–59. Gaventa's essay and the one following it by J. Louis Martyn (see the next note) have contributed substantially to my

gently relevant issue in Galatians—is ruled out as constituting and determining God's relationship with the cosmos and humanity. Will the Galatian Gentile churches continue to receive their place in Abraham's family and their share in God's life only through participation in Christ and the Spirit, or will they seek these things also through another participation, in this case also through the way of Torah?

Paul himself is the servant of only one apocalypse, one theme, one gospel, one God, the Father, and one Lord, Jesus Christ (1:1–5). It is this Jesus Christ and God the Father "who raised him from the dead" who commissioned Paul as messenger of the singular gospel, the gospel of deliverance from "the present evil age" (1:4). God's deed in raising Jesus from the dead is precisely that which determines the present time of Paul's speech and sets it off from that other time which is also still "present" but no longer determinative, the evil age of the old creation. The matter which Paul addresses throughout Galatians is already defined here: it is the struggle of the present evil age against the new creation, which has already been inaugurated in Jesus' crucifixion, in Paul's proclamation to the nations, and in the Galatian churches' reception of the Holy Spirit in power. This present evil age has found an all-too-effective voice and instrument in those who attempt to persuade the Galatian churches with a "different gospel," leading them (as Paul sees it) to desert the God who had already called them into the new creation in Christ. What is at stake is the life or death of the Galatian churches, their participation in the new creation or their reversion back to the present evil age of the old creation. For this reason, Paul's letter is more than a "paper presence" or an "argument"; it intervenes in the Galatian situation as one of the instruments of battle in the struggle over the allegiance of the Galatian churches. "Paul wrote Galatians in the confidence that *God* intended to cause a certain event *to occur* in the Galatian congregations when Paul's messenger read the letter aloud to them. . . . The author we see in the course of reading Galatians is a man who *does* theology by writing in such a way as *to anticipate* a theological *event*."[10]

The letter both is and calls for an act of critical, indeed apocalyptic, discernment. The "different gospel" (*heteros euangelios*; 1:6) that has been announced among the Galatians is in fact emphatically *not* a gospel, not the good news of new creation, even though it has been presented as such, as au-

understanding of the central issue in Galatians; indeed these essays and Martyn's commentary on Galatians persuaded me decisively against Dunn's understanding of the central issue in Galatians, which for many years I had taken as basically correct. Dunn's detailed and extensive work on Galatians is in many respects still very useful; see especially *The Epistle to the Galatians* (London: Black, 1993) and *The Theology of Paul's Letter to the Galatians* (Cambridge: Cambridge University Press, 1993).

10. J. Loius Martyn, "Events in Galatia: Modified Covenantal Nomism versus God's Invasion of the Cosmos in the Singular Gospel: A Response to J. D. G. Dunn and B. R. Gaventa," in *Pauline Theology,* vol. 1: *Thessalonians, Philippians, Galatians, Philemon* (ed. Jouette M. Bassler; Minneapolis: Fortress, 1991), 161 (emphasis original). See also Martyn, *Galatians,* 105–6.

thentic gospel alongside of (*par*; 1:8–9) the gospel which Paul preached. The whole point of Paul's letter is to expose in the light of God's apocalypse of Jesus Christ that this other gospel is false and as such stands under God's judgment. Thus Paul's anathemas in 1:8–9 must be read not only as expressions of his own dismayed response to *his* opponents, but also and far more important, as his apostolic discernment of *God's* judgment upon their activity as enemies of the one gospel. Their error is exposed, as was Peter's in Antioch (2:11–14), by "the truth of the gospel" (2:14). That truth of the gospel, when told directly and boldly, creates enemies (4:16) of those who do not receive and obey it to the exclusion of all other "truths," which in any case do not come from God, "who calls you" (5:7). At stake in the matter of the gospel in the Galatian churches is nothing less than truth or falsehood, life or death, the new creation or the present evil age.[11] Such is Paul's discernment of the situation.

Whatever might have seemed acceptable in Paul's time, however, does not seem so in post-Christian, postmodern, third-millennium North America. We are in the habit of believing something is profoundly wrong about staking religious claims in terms of conflicting worlds, life and death, truth and falsehood. In this context, those terms are reserved for such matters as national survival (whether political or economic), the institutions of democracy and free markets, and inalienable individual rights and freedom of choice. Nonetheless, a contemporary theology which aims to stand in faithful continuity with Paul's cannot, I contend, bypass or "contextualize" the thoroughly apocalyptic character of Paul's message in order to render it ei-

---

11. According to Martyn ("Events in Galatia," 161), "Paul wrote this extraordinarily angry letter because his Galatian churches had been invaded by traveling evangelists teaching a theology he considered to be untrue and thus lethal." Many students of Galatians accept Martyn's version, or some variation of it, that those causing trouble for the Galatian churches were intruders from outside, likely Jewish Christ-believers. Mark Nanos proposes, however, that the ones pressuring the Galatian Gentiles were members of the Jewish communities in the cities of Galatia; *The Irony of Galatians: Paul's Letter in First-Century Context* (Minneapolis: Fortress, 2002). According to Nanos, "Those influencing the addressees [i.e., the Galatian Gentile believers], the influencers, are not opponents of Paul or of the Christ-gospel per se. Nor are they outsiders who have only arrived in the several Galatian communities addressed after Paul's departure. They are Galatians too. They are members of the larger Jewish communities in Galatia entrusted with the responsibility of conducting Gentiles wishing more than guest status within the communities through the ritual process of proselyte conversion by which this is accomplished" (6). The Galatian Gentile believers are receptive to the efforts of these Jews because, as Gentiles who have left behind their pagan beliefs and practices, they have become marginalized and vulnerable to criticism, perhaps even persecution, in their Gentile communities. The "good news" which members of the Jewish communities tell these Gentile believers is that they can become full proselytes to Judaism, thus finding identity and perhaps even social and political protection as converts, members of Abraham's family under the umbrella of the Torah. Paul himself considers his Gentile converts as already full members of Abraham's family (i.e., full proselytes) through Christ and the Spirit, without having to take up full Torah observance. While I find Nanos's proposal both plausible and intriguing, it is as yet quite untested. The present apocalyptic interpretation of Galatians (dependent on Martyn) would, I believe, stand, even if Nanos's proposal about the historical context is correct.

ther irrelevant or acceptable within the terms and conditions of modernity and postmodernity. In this respect Stanley Hauerwas has proven to be a formidable *Pauline* theologian.

Hauerwas rarely declares his own apocalypticism explicitly or overtly, even though it pervades his thought. His clearest declarations in fact come as affirmations of the apocalyptic character of others' thoughts, notably Yoder and lawyer-theologian William Stringfellow.[12] In an essay (written with Jeff Powell) on Stringfellow, Hauerwas notes the usual discomfort in academic theological circles with Stringfellow's "apparently unembarrassed use of mythical [apocalyptic] language" as a means of critically analyzing American society.[13] The way to deal with such language, as we have already seen with Lowe's help, is to conceptualize it as "a primitive or poetic use of myth" as "a way of getting control of what he [Stringfellow] was saying, of fitting it into our intellectual categories" (*Dispatches from the Front*, 107–8). It is "of course" impossible to take the biblical imagery of, for example, angelic powers and principalities and demonic powers seriously: it has nothing to do with the "social reality" that we have to engage in the modern world. So, we "translate" ancient apocalyptic language into categories more readily available and comprehensible to the modern mind. But in so doing, Hauerwas insists, we *evade* rather than engage the disturbing things that both Stringfellow and the biblical apocalypticists were saying.

First, apocalyptic was for Stringfellow "always a way of reminding us of the intrinsically political character of salvation. . . . Apocalyptic is Stringfellow's—and we believe the authentic Christian—mode of taking seriously Christ's Lordship over the public, the social, the political" (*Dispatches from the Front*, 109). Apocalyptic theology treats issues of concrete enslavement and power within a political-cosmic horizon and in terms of final judgment. It disavows all privatization of Christian faith. Second, it rejects the notions ("presupposed by liberal politics and social science"; 110) of the cosmos as "a seamless web of causal relations" and of "the social world [as] a sealed network of causally determined functions" in which there is merely the endless repetition of the same (109). That is, in fact, the way of death in which the "principalities and powers" are regnant. "Stringfellow's apocalypticism enabled him—and demands of us—that we reject the 'causal point of view' for a construal of 'how things are' as the creation of a God who cannot be excluded from creating new possibilities for our lives through our lives"

12. See also Hauerwas's attempt (written with Mark Scherwindt) to recover a more apocalyptic understanding, over against purely "ethical" versions, of the "kingdom of God" in "The Reality of the Kingdom: An Ecclesial Space for Peace," in *Against the Nations: War and Survival in a Liberal Society* (Notre Dame: University of Notre Dame Press, 1992).

13. Hauerwas and Jeff Powell, "Creation as Apocalyptic: A Tribute to William Stringfellow," in *Dispatches from the Front: Theological Engagements with the Secular* (Durham: Duke University Press, 1994), 107.

(109).[14] Third, for Stringfellow, "God's creation [is] caught in a dramatic and final battle" (112) in which *God* accomplishes the decisive victory in the death and resurrection Jesus, leaving us free to participate in this victory rather than to try to accomplish it ourselves through optimistic social engineering or cynical violence. Such participation is the very meaning of the Christian community: "The church becomes the necessary correlative of an apocalyptic narration of existence. It is the eucharistic community that is the epistemological prerequisite for understanding 'how things are'" (112). The eucharistic community is thus also enabled to tell the very truth about the world and to offer resistance to the lies the world tells us, namely that we must "accept, with despair and relief, the inevitability and thus the goodness of things as they are" (114). Against those lies, "truth is the way of apocalyptic resistance" (114).

While Hauerwas and Powell are here describing Stringfellow's apocalyptic theology, those at all familiar with Hauerwas's writings can easily detect here many of the main themes to be found in his own work: the intrinsically political character of the gospel and church; the rejection of privatized understandings of Christian faith; the challenge to the hegemony of secular social-scientific rationality and its solutions to the basic issues of human life; the Christian life as a struggle with the powers; the centrality of the church in the gospel; witness as telling the truth in preaching and ecclesial action. In other words, if Stringfellow's approach is apocalyptic, so also, very clearly, is Hauerwas's. In fact, he has a decided predilection toward theologians writing in an apocalyptic mode. Yoder comes most immediately to mind and surely is the most important influence on Hauerwas's work—one testimony to which is the fact that Hauerwas prefaces his Gifford Lectures with a quotation from Yoder.[15] The quotation comes from "Armaments and Eschatology," an important essay in which Yoder explores the significance of the "apocalyptic stance" in relation to the arms race:

> The point that apocalyptic makes is not only that people who wear crowns and who claim to foster justice by the sword are not as strong as they think—true as that is: we still sing, "O where are the Kings and Empires now of old that went and came?" It is that people who bear crosses are working with the grain of the universe. One does not come to that belief by reducing social processes to mechanical and statistical models, nor by winning some of one's bat-

14. Hauerwas is quoting some comments by Wittgenstein on apocalyptic. In a letter (Feb. 9, 2001) to me, Hauerwas wrote, "I always love Wittgenstein's account of apocalyptic—it means 'it did not have to happen that way.'" In *Ethics as Grammar: Changing the Postmodern Subject* (Notre Dame: University of Notre Dame Press, 2001), Brad Kallenberg shows how Hauerwas engages the work of Christian ethics in a Wittgensteinian mode. What has apocalyptic to do with Wittgenstein? That is a question worthy of further consideration.

15. Stanley Hauerwas, *With the Grain of the Universe: The Church's Witness and Natural Theology* (Grand Rapids: Brazos, 2001), 6.

tles for the control of one's corner of the fallen world. One comes to it by sharing the life of those who sing about the Resurrection of the slain Lamb.[16]

Hauerwas delivered his Gifford Lectures under the title *With the Grain of the Universe*. With that title he declares that the apocalyptic stance that Yoder describes is fundamental to his own attempt in the Gifford Lectures (a lecture series dedicated to the promotion of "natural theology") to claim that the truth about "the way things are" with the universe can finally be told only through concentrated attention on God's action in the life, death, and resurrection of Jesus Christ, by those caught up in the life and practices of the new-creation people called church.[17] The life-and-death struggle into which such a conviction places the Christian theologian is therefore nothing less than a struggle rightly to identify the God of the gospel and rightly to tell the story of humanity and the cosmos. That Hauerwas finds himself caught up in this struggle should then not surprise us. Any theologian faithful to the witness of the New Testament, and faithful in particular to the witness of Paul in Galatians, can do nothing other than engage the theological task in the conviction that gods, worlds, and lives are at stake.[18]

If that is so, what should theology in an apocalyptic mode look like? We already know what it looks like in Galatians: dismayed, angry, vigorous, seeking conversion to the truth, demanding agreement or separation, even

16. John Howard Yoder, "Armaments and Eschatology," *Studies in Christian Ethics* 1 (1998): 58. See also Yoder, *The Politics of Jesus: Vicit Agnus Noster* (2d ed.; Grand Rapids: Eerdmans, 1994): "When read carefully, none of the biblical apocalypses, from Ezekiel through Daniel to Mark 13 and John of Patmos [author of the Book of Revelation], is about either pie in the sky or the Russians in Mesopotamia. They are about how the crucified Jesus is a more adequate key to understanding what God is about in the real world of empires and armies and markets than is the ruler in Rome [or Washington] with all his supporting military, commercial, and sacerdotal networks. Then to follow Jesus does not mean renouncing effectiveness. It does not mean sacrificing concern for liberation within the social process in favor of delayed gratification in heaven, or abandoning efficacy in favor of purity. It means that in Jesus we have a clue to which kinds of causation, which kinds of community-building, which kinds of conflict management, go with the grain of the cosmos, of which we know, as Caesar does not, that Jesus is both the Word (the inner logic of things) and the Lord ('sitting at the right hand'). It is not that we begin with a mechanistic universe and then look for the cracks and chinks where a little creative freedom might sneak in (for which we would then give God credit): it is that we confess the deterministic world to be enclosed within, smaller than, the sovereignty of the God of the Resurrection and Ascension" (246). "'Cross and resurrection' designates not only a few days' events in first-century Jerusalem, but also the shape of the cosmos" (160).

17. The theological "hero" of Hauerwas's Gifford Lectures, which treat the "natural theologies" of former Gifford lecturers William James, Reinhold Niebuhr, and Karl Barth at length, is clearly Barth. Hauerwas argues (*With the Grain of the Universe*, 10) the startling thesis "that Karl Barth is the great 'natural theologian' of the Gifford Lectures because he rightly understood that natural theology is impossible abstracted from a full doctrine of God." In this conviction, Hauerwas also puts his finger on Paul's "natural theology," which is nothing other than Paul's reading history and the cosmos in the bright light of God's revelation in Jesus Christ (even in Rom. 1:18–32).

18. Further indications of Hauerwas's enthusiasm for apocalyptically oriented theology may be found in his responses to Toole's *Waiting for Godot in Sarajevo* (see Hauerwas, *Better Hope*, 36) and Dale Aukerman's *Reckoning with Apocalypse: Terminal Politics and Christian Hope* (New York: Crossroad,

possibly creating enemies. The opposition is powerful, the stakes are high, the time is short. But the point of the apocalyptic mode is not for the theologian to win followers or personal allegiance. Richard Hays notes that in Paul's caustic comments in Galatians 1:8–9 he pronounces a curse not only on others who might proclaim a "different gospel" but also upon himself, should he do so:

> Paul certainly does not anticipate proclaiming a different gospel, but by including himself hypothetically under the threat of a curse, he makes an important point. He is not asking for the Galatians' personal allegiance to him; rather, what matters is their allegiance to the gospel message. Even if Paul should ever stray and begin preaching something different, the Galatians should reject him and cling to the gospel.[19]

Hauerwas, too, writes consistently in an apocalyptic mode that, in the current privatized, individualized, and consumerized climate in which religious claims are made, strikes many as objectionable, even wrong. Consider, for example, his account of what he is doing when he is teaching:

> As a way to challenge such a view of freedom [i.e., the view that freedom is always to do what we want to do], I start my classes by telling my students that I do not teach in a manner that is meant to help them make up their own minds. Instead, I tell them I do not believe they have minds worth making up until they have been trained by me. I realize such a statement is deeply offensive to students since it exhibits a complete lack of pedagogical sensitivities. Yet I cannot imagine any teacher who is serious who would allow students to make up their own minds.[20]

In so approaching his teaching, Hauerwas seems to be possessed of a sense of "apostolic" authority—albeit a derivative authority, one that requires and is dependent upon the prior authority of the New Testament witnesses. He is self-consciously engaging the task of theological teaching not simply as a talking-about the gospel, but as a participation in the work of the gospel. He aims to *effect* what he teaches and not simply to make available the current

---

1993). On Aukerman, Hauerwas writes in his preface to Aukerman's book: "Aukerman helps us see how our current politics is intelligible only as judged by God's lordship. [He reminds] us that apocalypse is the disclosure of God's truth in Jesus Christ for the consummation of history. . . . Aukerman reclaims apocalyptic as not just one other aspect of the gospel, but as at the very heart of the good news of God's call to Israel and the Cross and Resurrection of Christ. Accordingly he helps us see that our lives are embedded in forces and powers that can be understood and resisted only to the extent that we understand that as Christians we have been made citizens of a Kingdom of the end times" (*Reckoning with Apocalypse*, ix).

19. Richard Hays, "Letter to the Galatians," in *The New Interpreter's Bible* (Nashville: Abingdon, 2000), 11:206.

20. Hauerwas, "Christian Schooling *or* Making Students Dysfunctional," in Hauerwas's *Sanctify Them in the Truth*, 220.

intellectual options as mere consumer goods awaiting the students' choices. Indeed, as he makes clear in the same essay, that latter notion of the teaching task is precisely the bondage in which students and teachers find themselves in the modern and postmodern age: "We think our task is to be free to be what we want even if we think what we want is to be Christian. As a result, we fail to see that nothing is more destructive, nothing makes us less free, than to have to do what we want to do. Indeed, I can think of no better description of hell than the condition of always having to do what I want to do."[21] The appropriate way to speak about such notions of "freedom" is, for Hauerwas, to name them as Paul does in Colossians 2:8–15: "Put simply, the kind of education as professors we represent and as students you receive is exactly what Paul would identify as an 'elemental spirit,' a 'power!'"[22] There is no way for professors and students to be delivered from such powers except that someone name them as such and announce the gospel which is the only hope of freedom from them. That is what Hauerwas aims to do in his teaching, and in doing so he is doing nothing other than what Paul with his demanding rhetoric in Galatians was aiming to do—to see the Galatians freed from bondage to the "elemental spirits of the cosmos" which formerly held them in bondage, and to which they were ready to enslave themselves (albeit in different terms) again.

Not surprisingly, we are already not only close to the apocalyptic *mode* of Paul's letter to the Galatians, but also to the apocalyptic *content* of the letter. The gospel as a message of deliverance from bondage is at the heart of the letter. We must now attend to that content in greater specificity and detail, for there too we will discover remarkable convergences between Paul's letter and Hauerwas's writings.

The Apocalypse of Jesus Christ

For Paul the apocalyptic mode is not adopted in order to justify or serve apocalyptic. That is, it is not apocalyptic itself which interests Paul, but rather the very specific fact that God apocalypsed Jesus Christ to Paul. As I noted above, Jesus Christ *is* the apocalypse for Paul. While Galatians 1–2 are usually treated, rightly, as Paul's defense of his own apostolic credentials and authority, especially vis-à-vis the claims of those "disturbers" who troubled and influenced the Galatian churches, these chapters do more than warrant Paul's apostolic "rights." Their aim is also to enclose the Galatian hearers/readers (and not only them, but also the disturbers, as we will see) within the very same apocalyptic event by which Paul himself became an apostle and in which he now speaks to them with apostolic authority. Insofar as Paul has

---

21. Ibid., 220.

22. Ibid. "Ironically no institution is more supportive of the powers today than universities, including those supported by the churches, and the knowledge the universities legitimate and in turn by which they are legitimized" (221).

been laid hold of by the *apokalypsis* of Jesus Christ and thereby made apostle to the nations (*ethnē*), so too the Galatian Gentiles (*ethnē*) have already, through Paul's apostolic preaching, been laid hold of by that same *apokalypsis*, caught up into it: "It was before your eyes that Jesus Christ was publicly exhibited as crucified" (Gal. 3:1). The apocalypse of Jesus Christ is this public exhibition of his crucifixion. When this crucified Messiah was proclaimed to the Galatians (Paul speaks of the "hearing of faith," *akoēs pisteōs*; 3:2, 5) they were laid hold of by the Holy Spirit, the sign of full apocalyptic blessing (3:2–5). That both Paul and the Galatians were seized (*exaireō*—to pluck out, rescue; 1:4) by God through the same revelation/apocalypse is Paul's point ("become as I am, for I also have become as you are"; 4:12). The burden of the letter to the Galatians is that the Galatian Gentile believers do not "supplement" the Christ apocalypse with some supposed other (Torah), for to do so is in fact not to add to what is already theirs in Christ, but to lose it.

Briefly stated, Galatians 1–2 incorporates both Paul and the Galatians into God's decisive action in the cross of Christ. Hays and Martyn make the crucial point that *ex akoēs pisteōs* in Galatians 3:2 must not be taken in the way that, for example, the New Revised Standard Version and New International Version render it: "by believing what you heard."[23] Just as in 2:15–16, where Paul contrasts "works of the law" not with the human possibility of "having faith" but with "the faith of Jesus Christ," so here also he contrasts works of law not with the human action of believing but with the message about Jesus Christ which he proclaimed, a message which both announces God's action and effects God's action of "supplying the Spirit and working miracles" (3:5). Martyn notes: "From the epistle's beginning to its end, Paul draws contrasts not between two human alternatives, such as works and faith, but rather between acts done by human beings and acts done by God (1:1; 6:15)."[24] The apocalypse of Jesus Christ and the outpouring of the Spirit are the acts by which God invaded the world and laid claim to the Galatians' lives, rendering both them and their world a new creation. It is precisely God's "invasive action" (Martyn's term) which has made the Galatians sharers in God's new world order established in Jesus Christ.

God's apocalyptic act of new creation reveals that the Galatians could not have contributed by their own actions to their rescue and rectification. Before the apocalypse ("before faith came"; 3:23) they were, as Gentiles, "confined" (*sunkleiō*) under sin (*hypo hamartian*), under law (*hypo nomon*), under a guardian (*hypo paidagōgon*), and enslaved "under the elemental

23. See Hays, "Letter to the Galatians," 251–52; Martyn, *Galatians*, 281–89.

24. Martyn, "The Apocalyptic Gospel in Galatians," *Interpretation* 54 (2000): 246–66. By contrast, Dunn's construal ("Theology of Galatians," 143) of the focal issue in Galatians is: "*either* covenantal nomism *or* faith." Martyn's argument ("Events in Galatia," 165) against Dunn is that such a construal is in fact the way the disturbers (Martyn calls them "the Teachers") have put the issue, but Paul *reconstrues* it: "The Teachers' fundamental issue is covenantal nomism, if you like; Paul's is evangelical, cosmic, history-creating christology."

spirits of the world" (*hypo ta stoicheia tou kosmou*) (3:22–4:3). This constant
repetition of *hypo* in the central section of the letter is the strongest argument against any notion that, for Paul, the Galatians were or are being presented with two human possibilities or ways—that is, either works or faith,
doing or believing—and being asked to choose one. Rather, what is at issue
is what kind of world the Galatians were and are living in. So confined and
enslaved were they "under" a world of many powers (or levels of power)
that their only hope for deliverance rested with God the Father alone, who,
at the appointed time (4:2), "when the fullness of time had come, . . . sent
his Son, born of a woman, born under the law, in order to redeem those
who were under the law, so that we might receive adoption as children"
(4:4–5). Here Paul claims that it is precisely through God's act of placing
his Son under the condition of enslavement ("born under the law") that he
redeems those who are enslaved and makes them his children, thereby creating both a new world and a new sociopolitical reality in which the powers
are no longer in control.

The pattern of Christ's humiliation and exaltation, so clearly laid out in
the Christ hymn of Philippians 2:6–11, is, while less explicit, not less constitutive of the core of Paul's gospel in Galatians.[25] While in the Philippians
hymn the Son is himself the agent of his own humiliation, here Paul
stresses that the *Father* sends the Son, inserts the Son into slavery, invades
the territory of the enslaving powers, and defeats them by subjecting his
Son to them. All of this is done so that the Galatian Gentiles might be free
of the enslaving powers and find themselves alive by the Spirit (Gal. 5:16),
slaves of one another (5:13), bearing one another's burdens (6:2), testing
their own work (6:4), doing what is right (6:9), "work[ing] for the good
(*ergazōmetha to agathon*) of all" (6:10). In other words, the Father's decisive
and invasive action through the Son opens up a space in the world—new-
creation space—in which the Galatians' own faithful action is called forth
and becomes concretely possible. That space is indicated by the phrase *in
Christ.* The new creation is in the first place Jesus Christ himself; in the second place it is the cosmos delivered of enslaving powers through the crucifixion; in the third place it is the Galatian Gentiles participating in Christ's
death and resurrection through baptism into his community and living life
in the Spirit through loyalty to Christ and service to one another in the
congregation.

Absent from all of Paul's discussion of the nature and effect of God's
apocalypse and from his discussion of the tempting alternative being pushed
by the disturbers is any notion that the Galatians are free agents in a theologically neutral space who might "choose" one way or another. They either

25. This is, of course, the main thesis, compellingly argued, of Richard Hays, *The Faith of Jesus Christ: An Investigation of the Narrative Substructure of Galatians 3:1–4:11* (Chico, Calif.: Scholars Press, 1983).

receive "sonship" and are made heirs through God (*dia theou*; 4:7) or they are slaves of the powers: "Formerly, when you did not know God, you were enslaved to beings that by nature are not gods" (4:8). Not to be missed is Paul's rhetorically effective "self-correction" in the next verse: "Now, however, that you have come to know God, or rather to be known by God, how can you turn back again to the weak and beggarly elemental spirits" (4:9)? "To be known by God" is their one hope of deliverance. Conversely, to turn away from being so known amounts to immediate exit from the space of the new creation—the space in which they are known by God and therefore free—into the space of enslavement and to their own "not knowing" God. It is to fall out of blessing and back under curse, to be "cut off" from Christ and to fall away from grace (5:3–4). It is also important to notice that Paul does not see the disturbers as free agents either: "You [Galatians] were running well; who prevented you from obeying the truth? Such persuasion does not come from the one [i.e., God] who calls you. A little yeast leavens the whole batch of dough" (5:7–9). Where does such prevention, persuasion, "yeast," come from? Surely the implication is that it comes from the very powers that would see the Galatians enslaved again. The truth about the disturbers' agenda is exposed clearly only in the light of the apocalypse of Jesus Christ. Apart from that apocalypse, which is itself the truth of the cosmos and which as such exposes the truth or falsehood of all things, perhaps the message of the disturbers might be seen as a relatively harmless addendum or alternative to the message that Paul himself preached. But Paul does not see in Christ one religious option among others. He sees in Christ nothing less than the whole of creation and all of humanity under God's final judgment and grace.

There is something profoundly illiberal and intolerant about Galatians in this reading. Paul is uncompromisingly focused on a single, incomparable, final, and exclusive theological reality which constitutes, includes, and determines all other reality: Jesus Christ. The habit of focusing our sights immediately on the new social reality adumbrated in a text such as Galatians 3:28 or on Paul's arguments about Abraham, the promise, and the law misses that point. Such a habit is often the result of believing that large-scale theological claims ("metanarratives") are latecomers to an argument already under way which is about more "fundamental" social agendas, causes, and facts such as class, race, and gender or about a mainstream tradition and a sectarian group or about various relationships of power and weakness.[26] Does Paul's apocalyptic gospel address social reality, tradition, and power relationships? There is no doubt about it. But it addresses these things precisely because God is remaking the cosmos and humanity in Christ and the Holy Spirit, and hu-

26. No more vigorous and persuasive critique of this understanding of the relationship between theological claims and social reality can be found than that of John Milbank in *Theology and Social Theory: Beyond Secular Reason* (Oxford: Blackwell, 1990).

man beings are being invited to participate in that triune remaking through the *ekklēsia*.

If understanding the theologic of Paul's social vision is crucial, it is as much so for Hauerwas. Many misunderstandings of Hauerwas's work fail to recognize that he works from a position which can be characterized in the same terms that Martyn uses of Paul in Galatians: "Paul's [fundamental issue] is evangelical, cosmic, history-creating christology."[27] Hauerwas's theology assumes the singular primacy of the christological apocalypse of the one God of Israel, the nations, and the cosmos and aims to be consistently oriented to and by that apocalypse. Such a stance has far-reaching consequences not only for the mode of theologizing, which, as we have seen, Hauerwas exhibits in most of his writing; it also shapes the subject matter of his theology in basic ways.

For Hauerwas, Jesus Christ or the gospel or the Christian story (Hauerwas employs many ways to speak about the "evangelical, cosmic, history-creating" reality of God's revelation in Christ) is an all-encompassing event that not only reveals the truth about God but also constitutes the truth about all of humanity and creation. The truth of humanity and creation is not finally and rationally grasped apart from the gospel. Commenting on the character of Christian witness in the modern period, Hauerwas writes:

> Our preaching and theology has been one ceaseless effort to conform to the canons of intelligibility produced by the economic and intellectual formations characteristic of modern and, in particular, liberal societies.
>
> Christians in modernity thought their task was to make the Gospel intelligible to the world rather than to help the world understand why it could not be intelligible without the Gospel. Desiring to become part of the modernist project, preachers and theologians accepted the presumption that Christianity is a set of beliefs, a worldview, designed to give meaning to our lives. As a result, the politics of Christian discourse was relegated to the private in the name of being politically responsible in, to, and for liberal social orders. We accepted the politics of translation believing that neither we nor our non-Christian or half-Christian neighbors could be expected to submit to the discipline of Christian speech.[28]

Several elements in this excerpt are worthy of notice. First, "intelligibility," far from being an independent criterion by which the gospel is "warranted," in fact *requires* the gospel in order for intelligibility to be what it is. Since there is no larger and more determinative truth or norm than that revealed in Jesus Christ, intelligibility depends on critical judgment formed in the light of the gospel. So the first task of the theologian is to narrate, inscribe,

---

27. Martyn, "Events in Galatia," 165.
28. Hauerwas, "No Enemy, No Christianity," in Hauerwas's *Sanctify Them in the Truth*, 193.

encode, and otherwise enclose the world within the apocalypse of Jesus Christ. This move is necessary because of the very character of the gospel. Jesus Christ is not one very significant moment among others on the cosmic or historical time line, nor one very great feature among others in the make-up of the cosmos, nor one very powerful agent among others in the movements of the universe. Christ is in no sense one among other "principles" or "symbols" through which the inherent intelligibility of things manifests itself. To say with Paul that there is no other gospel than the one he preached is to say that there is no other way, except by publicly exhibiting Jesus Christ as crucified, to rightly name the truth of history and the cosmos. In Hauerwas's words, to "conform [the Christian message] to the canons of intelligibility" produced by modern, liberal societies is to consider another account of the truth of things as a "gospel" of equal or higher authority than the gospel of Jesus Christ. But that is to say that Jesus Christ is in fact not himself the good news, but only "embodies" or "illustrates" or "symbolizes" a truth and a rationality—a gospel—learned from some other revelatory source or event. Or it is to suggest that Jesus Christ serves only to enable a "perspective" or "view" of a world that exists independent of the new creation which he himself in the first place constitutes. Neither Paul nor Hauerwas will allow these moves as anything other than a defection from "the one who called you in the grace of Christ" (Gal. 1:6).

I expect that Hauerwas learned these convictions about Christian intelligibility more from Barth and Yoder than from Paul. Nevertheless, he is at one with Paul in declaring that the singular apocalypse of Jesus Christ excludes any other decisive and critical theological norm, whether that be the Torah in Paul's situation or modernist, liberal canons of rationality in Hauerwas's situation. But for Hauerwas (as also for Paul—see Colossians and Philippians) there is more than one way in which modern theology subordinates Jesus Christ to other norms, visions, and purposes. The issue of "intelligibility" is not the one that figures most prominently in Hauerwas's work. Rather, he engages most directly, vigorously, and critically with the fact that in much of modern American theology and ethics the reality of liberalism/Americanism is the supposed larger and more determinative truth which the Christian gospel is meant to serve. The affinities between Hauerwas and Paul's letter to the Galatians emerge most clearly in a close examination of Hauerwas's engagement with liberalism in America. Before listening to him in this engagement, however, consider the claims of one of his harshest critics, American Christian ethicist Max Stackhouse:

> Stanley Hauerwas hates liberalism. He hates liberal theology, liberal ethics, liberal churches, liberal politics, liberal economics, and liberal democracy. He uses military terms . . . to signal that he is part of a great battle against liberalism, waged on behalf of virtue, character and pacifism.

But, claims Stackhouse, "Christianity has a liberal element at its core."[29]

Stackhouse's charge may at first glance seem right to those who have read a modest amount of Hauerwas. But a more careful look at his work suggests that Hauerwas's criticism of liberalism is both motivated by and has a purpose very different from that which Stackhouse attributes to it. Hauerwas is indeed engaged in a "great battle against liberalism," but the clue to the reason for this battle comes in Stackhouse's claim that "Christianity has a liberal element at its core." For precisely this conviction, according to Hauerwas, is what has resulted in and goes on perpetuating the crisis of faithfulness in the church in America.

It is important to state that for Hauerwas the crisis does not in the first place have to do with "virtue, character and pacifism." Rather, it has first to do with the first commandment, the exclusive loyalty which the God of Israel and Jesus Christ requires from his people.[30] The churches of America, whether conservative or liberal, are divided in their loyalty; divided between allegiance to American liberal democracy and society on the one hand and to the triune God revealed in Jesus Christ on the other.[31] When it comes to

29. Max L. Stackhouse, "Liberalism Dispatched vs. Liberalism Engaged," *Christian Century* (Oct. 18, 1995), 962. This review of Hauerwas's *Dispatches from the Front* is a rather sad, or perhaps comical, exercise in incomprehension. While Stackhouse certainly provides a fine statement of how liberalism works, he does not even come close to representing fairly how Hauerwas works, which means his critique of Hauerwas is simply beside the point and amounts to nothing more than a restatement of Stackhouse's own liberal assumptions. In any case, he presents a prime example of the habit of engaging other norms besides the gospel in the theological task. For example: "It is impossible to understand the Renaissance, Enlightenment, or the liberalism that has brought us, among other things, modern science and technology, constitutional democracy, and the struggle for human rights without understanding that they rest on assumptions worked out by theology. At each point, the 'liberal' impulse of Christianity has selectively used resources from beyond itself and was willing to modulate contextual aspects of the faith's own roots. Christianity, in other words, does not simply trust religion as a given. It demands critically interpreted and socially engaged theology in which philosophy and ethics and social analysis play decisive roles" (962). Three things to note in this excerpt: (1) the main task of theology seems to be to function as midwife to (the seemingly unquestionable great goods of) science and technology, democracy, and human rights; (2) "faith" or "religion"—Stackhouse's words, I take it, for "the Christian thing" (Jesus Christ?)—cannot be "trusted" to fulfill its maieutic function in the modern context without being "modulated" by critical interpretation and social engagement; and (3) other criteria besides faith/religion play "decisive roles" in rendering Christianity usable in its modern context. At the very least it is absurd for Stackhouse to claim to be "guided by Paul" (962) in this understanding of the task and method of theology.

30. See Hauerwas and Willimon, *Truth about God*, 13–39; Hauerwas, "Truth about God." I believe there has been a shift in Hauerwas away from his earlier primary attention to the themes of virtue, character, and narrative toward a more recent emphasis on the first commandment as the necessary condition under which the earlier themes might rightly be established in their importance. But I think the earlier themes were always ways in which Hauerwas wished to speak about the faithfulness of the church as the people of the one true God of Israel who was apocalypsed in Jesus Christ. This judgment about the trajectory of Hauerwas's work is borne out, I believe, by Samuel Wells, *Transforming Fate into Destiny: The Theological Ethics of Stanley Hauerwas* (Carlisle, Cumbria: Paternoster, 1998).

31. This is the theme of many of Hauerwas's writings. See especially "On Keeping Theological Ethics Theological," in *Against the Nations: War and Survival in a Liberal Society* (Notre Dame: University of Notre Dame Press, 1992), 23–50; *After Christendom? How the Church Is to Behave If Freedom, Justice, and a Christian Nation Are Bad Ideas* (Nashville: Abingdon, 1991).

the decisive moments—the apocalyptic, revelatory moments, when America goes to war in the name of "freedom," "justice," and "democracy"—the latter loyalty almost always takes second place to the former. What Hauerwas "hates" is idolatry. American liberal democracy is the One Great Thing for which most American Christians are prepared to make the costliest sacrifice: the lives of their own and others' children. Such human sacrifices declare final—apocalyptic—allegiances. How has American liberal democracy so thoroughly confused the American churches about their loyalty to the gospel? It is as if Hauerwas were saying, with genuinely Pauline passion (cf. Gal. 3:1; 5:7–9), "You foolish Americans! Who has bewitched you? Who prevented you from obeying the truth? Such persuasion does not come from the one who calls you. A little yeast leavens the whole batch of dough." [32]

The confusion runs deep into the tradition of American theological ethics. In that tradition, according to Hauerwas, "the subject of Christian ethics in America *is* America," [33] that is, "the first subject of Christian ethics is how to sustain the moral resources of American society" (*Against the Nations*, 36). Such is the case with Protestant theologians from Walter Rauschenbusch and the Niebuhrs to Paul Ramsey and James Gustafson and (now Catholic) Richard John Neuhaus. Hauerwas argues that America has "no other imaginable public philosophy" than liberalism (18). Unless a public theologian is going to work on other grounds and thus risk not being heard or understood in America (a risk Hauerwas is prepared to take), then the public philosophy of liberalism must also be accepted as providing the terms within which Christian social ethics must work.

Hauerwas is less inclined to define a priori what he means by a liberal society than he is to depict its workings in relation to a variety of issues and events. He does, however, provide something of a definition in his introduction to *Against the Nations:*

> In the most general terms I understand liberalism to be that impulse deriving from the Enlightenment project to free all people from the chains of their historical particularity in the name of freedom. As an epistemological position lib-

32. The perceptive reader will notice that I left out the Pauline phrase *you were running well* (Gal. 5:7). Hauerwas would not be inclined to think the American church has been "running well" for much, if any, of its history. The confused loyalty of the American churches has been a problem for many generations—and not only in America, for the problem is that of Constantinianism, which goes back many centuries.

33. Hauerwas, *Against the Nations*, 10. I will primarily follow the arguments against liberalism found in *Against the Nations*, since I think this collection is representative of Hauerwas's thinking on the theme. Other essays might have been drawn into the discussion; e.g., the first five chapters of *Better Hope* (9–107) or "The Democratic Policing of Christianity," in *Dispatches from the Front: Theological Engagements with the Secular* (Durham: Duke University Press, 1994), 91–106. See Arne Rasmusson, *The Church as Polis: From Political Theology to Theological Politics as Exemplified by Jürgen Moltmann and Stanley Hauerwas* (Notre Dame: University of Notre Dame Press, 1995), for an excellent account of Hauerwas's "theological politics" in general (174–351) and his critique of liberalism in particular (248–302).

eralism is the attempt to defend a foundationalism in order to free reason from
being determined by any particularistic tradition. Politically liberalism makes
the individual the supreme unit of society, thus making the political task the securing of cooperation between arbitrary units of desire. (*Against the Nations*, 18)

Liberalism on these terms is a comprehensive ordering of thought and life
that "is not simply a theory of government but a theory of society that is imperial in its demands" (*Against the Nations*, 18–19). In this sense liberalism
may properly be labeled (borrowing Paul's terms) another apocalypse, another revelation, another definitive gospel, which seeks not only to provide a
comprehensive vision of the cosmos and human nature, but to shape the entire social order according to that vision. In describing it as "imperial in its
demands," Hauerwas reveals the totalizing way in which liberalism persistently attacks and dissolves the political significance of all particular social
groups and historical traditions that might stand between the individual and
the state, by recognizing the individual alone as the only important political
unit of liberal society. Particular groups and traditions "are now understood
only as those arbitrary institutions sustained by the private desires of individuals" (124). There is in America, argues Hauerwas, as much a "monism"
of political existence as in the Soviet system. "Though it is less immediately
coercive than that of the Soviet Union, it is the monism of the freedom of
the individual" (125). The freedom of religion in America is guarded only
insofar as particular religious traditions, including the Christian churches,
do not promote themselves as particular political alternatives, but rather provide religious support for and promotion of the wider liberal political regime. We should not be led to believe, then,

> that democratic societies and states by being democratic are any less omnivo-
> rous in their appetites for our loyalties than non-democratic states. Indeed ex-
> actly because we assume that democracies protect our freedoms as Christians
> we may well miss the ways the democratic state remains a state that continues
> to wear the head of the beast. For example, democratic societies and states, no
> less than totalitarian ones, reserve the right to command our conscience to
> take up arms and kill not only other human beings but other Christians in the
> name of relative moral goods. (*Against the Nations*, 127)

"Omnivorous in its appetite." "Imperial in its demands." Hauerwas makes
these claims concrete when he shows liberalism in action in relation to Jews,
the Jonestown suicides, and the black civil rights movement led by Martin
Luther King Jr.

In "Remembering as a Moral Task: The Challenge of the Holocaust,"
Hauerwas engages a book by Jewish author Eliezer Berkovits, *Faith after
the Holocaust*.[34] In it Berkovits states his conviction that liberalism is the

---

34. Eliezer Berkovits, *Faith after the Holocaust* (New York: Ktav, 1973).

only means by which to avoid a repetition of the Holocaust. He cites as universal moral bedrock the liberal principles of "the dignity of every human being" irrespective of religion, of "interhuman understanding . . . based on our common humanity and wholly independent of any need for common religious beliefs and theological principles" (quoted in *Against the Nations*, 69). Hauerwas notes that this may be one strategy for Jewish survival, but it comes with a high cost to any meaningful Jewish identity. On these terms the call to remember the Holocaust certainly cannot be based on a *theological* conviction about the Jews as God's chosen people. It can be made only on broadly humanitarian grounds, and on those grounds the emphasis on the destruction and survival of the *Jewish* people in particular can appear only arbitrary and perhaps even ethnocentric in a peculiarly illiberal way. "For Berkovits fails to understand that societies putatively founded on values of 'universal validity' cannot help but interpret the particularistic commitments of the Jewish people at best as a moral curiosity, and more likely as morally retrogressive" (70). In other words, in American liberal society it is all right to be Jewish, so long as one does not take one's Jewishness very seriously as making comprehensive claims not only on the souls but also on the bodies of Jews. In this regard it is important to be American first, Jewish second. This may be a relatively less coercive form of anti-Judaism, but it appears to be one form nonetheless. Jewishness disappears behind the larger realities of human rights, democracy, and Americanism.

In a rather striking juxtaposition, Hauerwas places next to his discussion of the Holocaust an essay on the Jonestown cult led by Jim Jones, which ended in mass suicide. Hauerwas argues that what happened at Jonestown is incomprehensible in a liberal society where "the lowest possible priority for anyone should be the willingness to die in a religious cause" (*Against the Nations*, 91). Insofar as the Jonestown people understood their convictions to lay claim not only to their "individual consciences" but also to their bodies and sociopolitical hopes, what happened there must be viewed as "an act of revolutionary suicide" (92). "Jones offered people something more profound than just meaning and status" (97), which is what liberal society considers a legitimate function of religion. Rather, "he offered a mission" (97) and engaged his followers in "a task [that] was fundamentally political" (99).

Hauerwas's point is not to justify Jonestown; he believes and argues that the beliefs of Jones were false and his actions wrong. But he does not argue, in liberal fashion, that the Jonestown people took their convictions too seriously or illegitimately transferred them from the "purely religious" sphere to the political. His point is that the Jonestown convictions and community, false and falsely based though they were, were coinherently religious, social, political, and revolutionary through and through, and this is the only means of rendering the suicides comprehensible, even meaningful. For liberal

America, the event can be understood only as a meaningless tragedy. For the Christian church, the Jonestown mass suicide presents an opportunity for the church to give witness to its own alternative politics, in which the church shows "first, why it is so important that Christians prohibit suicide and, second, what kind of community we must be to maintain such a prohibition" (*Against the Nations*, 13).

A final example of liberal America's "omnivorous appetite" for the loyalties of its people is the way in which American interpreters of Martin Luther King Jr. have coopted King's movement as simply one more achievement in liberal democracy, rather than a movement by a particular people rooted in a particular memory in the cause of freedom for *that* people:

> Liberal memory makes King the great hero of the liberal ideals of "freedom of the individual" and "equality," but King did not represent "individuals." He did not seek individual freedom for African Americans. King sought freedom for African-Americans as a people to remember slavery and the triumph over slavery by the black church. But "America" does not want to remember that slavery (and, even less, genocide) is a part of our history.[35]

Precisely because the historical memory of the slavery of a particular people is dangerous to liberal America, the memory itself must be dissolved into the abstract, ahistorical, universalist categories of "individuals," "rights," and "freedoms."

These three examples of American liberalism in action, while important in themselves, also serve for Hauerwas as tales of warning: there also go the gospel and the church. If American liberalism can get gospel and church to serve its cause, then it will have triumphed in its "imperial demands"; it will have consumed gospel and church with its "omnivorous appetite." And all of this happens precisely in the place where the church in America believes it will be saved: separation of church and state and freedom of religion. Implicit in each of these phrases is the prior conviction that religion is in the first place a "matter of the heart," an inner, private event of the experience of the sublime, which may serve the emotional or spiritual well-being of the individual but has no intrinsic social or political character. Indeed, even the church is understood not primarily, appropriately, and necessarily as a sociopolitical body, but only secondarily, intrusively, and accidentally so, since its primary purpose is thought to be encouraging and nurturing the "interior dimension" of human life. On this understanding, while the church may be given the freedom to "touch the soul" of the "believer" (if one chooses to believe), America as a society, economy, polity, and nation nevertheless makes

---

35. Hauerwas, "Remembering Martin Luther King Jr. Remembering," in Hauerwas's *Wilderness Wanderings: Probing Twentieth-Century Theology and Philosophy* (Boulder, Colo.: Westview, 1997), 230.

an absolute claim on—*seizes*—the bodies and therefore the public actions of its subjects.[36]

But this way of "saving" *religion* by securing a safe but innocuous place for it is at the very same time the way of killing the *church*. For, as we have seen in Galatians, the apocalypse of Jesus Christ is not a religious event, but a world-making event. It is an event in which the lordship of the crucified Christ is both revealed and announced, bringing about the new creation, the cosmos delivered from enslaving powers, in which a new social body called the *ekklēsia* has been called out, laid hold of, *seized* by the God of Israel to bear testimony to this good news. In other words, the apocalypse of Jesus Christ is itself imperial in its demands, omnivorous in its appetite. The gospel creates and names a world, a "kingdom," a people, a social and political body and practice in which the reign of Christ dissolves the loyalty claims of all other kings, lords, powers, empires, social orders, economies, and nations. But, as Hauerwas shows, that kind of dissolving of resistance is precisely what American liberalism also aims to do and claims as its "lordly" right to enforce by creating and maintaining religion as a purely private thing. Seen in the light of the gospel, American liberalism is thus exposed as nothing other than "another gospel," the work in fact of "the elemental spirits of the cosmos," of "beings which by nature are not gods," to which, when we did not know God, we were enslaved until Christ came. Hauerwas's most fundamental criticism is that, by allowing American liberalism to be the larger cause which it is ready to serve, the American church has "turned back again to the weak and beggarly spirits" and become enslaved again to them (Gal. 4:1–9). There can no more be a "liberal element at the core" of Christianity (Stackhouse), than there can be a Torah element at the core of the Galatian Gentiles' loyalty to Jesus Christ. American Christians (and Christians of any other nation) can no more give their bodies to the flag and nation than the Galatian Gentiles can let themselves be circumcised. With Paul, the only marks which Christians may bear in their bodies will be "the marks of Jesus" (6:17). The national flag in the church sanctuary is the mark of the beast on the Christian body. Hauerwas's thoroughly Pauline claim is this: America and American liberal democracy is wrong because it directly and powerfully makes an imperial claim on its subjects which is precisely counter in scope and substance to the claim which the risen Jesus Christ makes on humanity through the proclamation of his crucifixion and the creation of the church in the power of the Holy Spirit.[37]

36. For an illuminating account of how the invention and promotion of religion as a private affair functions to serve the modern nation-state, see William Cavanaugh: "A Fire Strong Enough to Consume the House: The Wars of Religion and the Rise of the State," *Modern Theology* 11 (1995): 397–420; idem, "The City: Beyond Secular Parodies," in *Radical Orthodoxy: A New Theology* (ed. John Milbank, Catherine Pickstock, and Graham Ward; London: Routledge, 1999), 182–200.

37. Since I write as a Canadian, I should make two things clear. First, I do not exempt Canadian liberalism or the Canadian church from precisely the same criticisms. Indeed, Canadian churches have accepted the privatization of religion far more thoroughly than have American churches. Second, Canadi-

"Sectarian Temptations"?

By focusing attention on the apocalyptic character of Paul's message in the letter to the Galatians, I have placed much of his discussion of justification, faith, works of law, Abraham, the promise, and Torah somewhat in the background of the discussion. There are good reasons for this. As I have already hinted, that Paul must engage in a criticism of the role of Torah in this letter is a result of a contingent situation: some other teachers, whose identity remains uncertain, had approached the Galatian Gentile believers after Paul left, insisting that the Galatians must be circumcised and in other ways become observers of Torah in order to complete what is necessary toward becoming full sharers in the family of Abraham. The Galatian Gentiles' being in Christ is not enough: they must also be in the way of Torah. As I argued in the previous chapter, Paul's original message to the Gentiles was a message about the one God of Israel who, through his messianic agent Jesus Christ, delivered the nations from their bondage to idolatry and the corresponding dissolute way of life, in order that they might become full sharers in a new people of God in the power of the Holy Spirit. That original message did not come with lengthy diatribes on justification by faith versus works of Torah or Abraham versus Moses. These themes in all likelihood moved into the center of discussion in Galatians only because they were part of the message that the disturbers were teaching to the Galatian churches. While Paul had to engage his more basic apocalyptic convictions in this struggle with these other claims, the specific content of those claims itself becomes the battleground over which Paul had to defend the singular and exclusive sufficiency of the *apokalypsis* of Jesus Christ. Because of the apparent strength and persuasiveness of the alternative message, perhaps precisely as a scriptural argument, and the great vigor with which Paul had thus to counter it, also with much scriptural argument, many readers of Galatians have been confused into thinking that the very core of Paul's message centers on issues of law, works, promise, faith, and justification. But it doesn't. In letters like Colossians (which I take to be Pauline) or 1 Corinthians very different challenges are brought against Paul's message of "Christ crucified and risen." In those letters Paul again announces his apocalyptic gospel and engages it against the challenges, but with very little reference to the so-called classic Pauline themes of law, works, faith, justification, etc.

Still, that the Galatians were apparently almost or already persuaded about the necessity of walking in the way of Torah in addition to believing the message about Jesus points to one of the most significant differences between the situation Paul was dealing with and the one with which Hauerwas is confronted. It has to do with the matter of separation from the wider social and cultural milieu. Paul assumes that his Galatian congregations are already to some extent on a tra-

---

ans have no escape from the "imperial demands" that American culture, society, and politics make upon us daily in every aspect of our lives. American problems are our problems.

jectory of separation from their pagan surroundings. "Formerly, when you did not know God, you were enslaved to beings that by nature are not gods. . . . How can you want to be enslaved to them again" (Gal. 4:8–9)? In other words, the Galatians had left their typical Gentile habits and practices behind in at least this very important respect—they had turned from their idols to serve the one God of Israel (cf. 1 Thess. 1:9–10). Paul suggests that with respect to this primary act of separation, this "obeying the truth," the Galatians were "running well" (Gal. 5:7). Further, he had already taught them about "the works of the flesh" which they were to avoid (5:19–21). "I am warning you, as I warned you before: those who do such things will not inherit the kingdom of God" (5:21). In some measure the Galatians are already a distinct community of believers in the God of Israel in the midst of a predominantly idolatrous pagan culture.

In fact, it may be the desire to give concrete shape to their difference from the wider culture, or the desire to join the already different Jewish community by taking up full Torah observance, that disposed the Galatians toward the Torah as a way of life that would make them stand out from their surroundings. What if, as the disturbers were teaching, Torah *is* the very principle of cosmic order and life, the means by which God makes the cosmos right; and what if participation in Torah through full obedience to it *is* the means by which God brings the Gentiles close to himself and joins them with his people, the Jews. Jesus' atoning death is the Gentiles' way into the Torah; the Torah is their way of sharing in God's life and purpose for them and the cosmos. Certainly this would confirm the Galatians in what appears to be their genuine desire to distinguish themselves from their surroundings as very specifically and concretely the people of the one God of Israel. They really wanted to be a separate people, and Torah obedience gave them a way to do so. Further, it promised a new, relatively unambiguous focus of identity, Judaism, which already had a reputation and raison d'être for marking off a separate people.

It might be concluded, in view of these considerations, that Paul's rejection of the idea that the Galatian Gentiles should take up the way of Torah is also his firm rejection of any Gentile desire to become "sectarian" as the Jews were sectarian. Gentile believers must not separate themselves from their unbelieving Gentile neighbors by the practice of Torah; for that matter, even Jewish believers should cease Torah practice so as to enter into full table fellowship with Gentiles. In other words, in this view Paul's thrust in Galatians is nonsectarian, nonparticularist; it is inclusivist and universalist. In Christ all humanity is "the same"; differences have ceased to count for anything "in God's eyes"—Paul is the first liberal. "What drove Paul was a passionate desire for human unification, for the erasure of differences and hierarchies between human beings, and . . . he saw the Christian event, as he had experienced it, as the vehicle for this transformation of humanity."[38] Perhaps, after

---

38. Daniel Boyarin, *A Radical Jew: Paul and the Politics of Identity* (Berkeley: University of California Press, 1994), 106.

all, there is "a liberal element at the core" of the gospel Paul preached, a strategy of getting beyond all sectarian temptations to separate the people of God from the rest of humanity by specific identifying narratives, traditions, habits, practices.

> Christians have been willing to challenge tradition when it becomes legalistic, ethnic, or impervious to prophetic insight. Guided by Paul and John . . . it has engaged philosophies and cultures from beyond its own roots. . . . Some of us . . . remain convinced that some forms of liberal thought are not foreign to the faith but intrinsic to it. For instance, many of us believe that we are not bound to the cultural-linguistic traditions of the socio-historical contexts from which we come. Not only can we critically reflect on the faith and morals handed down to us, but we can convert or transform what we inherit—and offer a reasonable account of why we do so.[39]

While such a vision of Protestant liberalism as "guided by Paul" is attractive and self-affirming for those who find themselves in that tradition, there is little warrant for it in Galatians.

First, Paul's quarrel is not with legalism in general or Judaism in particular, but with the way in which the disturbers are presenting Torah as the final cosmic principle (the "basic element") through which God's relationship with creation and humanity (and so also the Gentiles) is established. But Paul, who saw the apocalyptic resurrection glory of the crucified Christ, learned that nothing in all creation is higher or more basic or more "elemental" than Jesus Christ. New creation means just this for Paul: what was formerly thought to exist in and through and for Torah, God's "firstborn" of all creation, he now knows to exist in and through and for Jesus Christ who is the "firstborn" (cf. Col. 1:15–20). In other words, Paul is not arguing for a "more inclusive," less particularist view of humanity and creation; he is arguing that God's relationship to all creation is established through Jesus Christ alone and not through Torah. The claim some were making about Torah is as all-inclusive as Paul's; only the particular terms of inclusiveness are different and therefore (because it is *all*-inclusiveness) opposite. So particular is Paul's specific claim about all-inclusiveness that it *excludes* any other particular claim, and radically so. The Galatian Gentiles cannot be both *hypo nomos* and *en Christō* at the same time: "You who want to be justified by the law have cut yourselves off from Christ; you have fallen away from grace" (Gal. 5:4).[40] Paul's claims about how God creates and rectifies the cosmos and humanity are as "sectarian" as one could imagine.

Second, while the possibility of making those claims—in Marcionite fashion—apart from the Scriptures and traditions of Israel may have pre-

39. Stackhouse, "Liberalism Dispatched vs. Liberalism Engaged," 962–63.
40. In chap. 4 I ask in what sense, if any, this is also true of Jews. It is important to recognize that Paul does not have Jews in view when he writes Galatians.

sented itself to Paul, it was a path he did not take. Paul's claim was not that something about an already generally available *theos* had in some sense been glimpsed or discerned through Jesus; it was that the very particular God of the very particular people Israel had apocalypsed himself in Jesus Christ. Paul makes that claim by showing how Jesus Christ himself, the promised Holy Spirit, and the church called into being by God, are already inscribed and anticipated in Israel's Scriptures—indeed, in Torah. Torah bears witness not to itself, but to the Christ and the church: "Tell me, you who desire to be subject to the law, will you not listen to the law? For it is written that Abraham had two sons" (Gal. 4:21–22). Paul in no sense allows himself to float free of the traditions and scriptures of Israel, nor does he establish a "critical" relationship to them; on the contrary, he takes up the task of reading them again and again (albeit, differently from the way the disturbers were reading them) in order that the Galatians might know themselves also to be written into those Scriptures from the beginning. Hays puts this point well with reference to Paul's reading of the Abraham stories in Galatians 3:1–14 and 4:21–31:

> Scripture speaks not only to the church but also about it. If the ends of the ages have come upon Paul and his readers, then all God's dealings with Israel in the past—as recounted in Scripture—must have pointed toward the present apocalyptic moment. If God was authoring the sacred story, then all the story's narrative patterns must foreshadow the experience of the community that has now encountered the apocalypse of God's grace.

> Paul reads the Bible in light of a central conviction that he and his readers are those upon whom the ends of the ages have come. They are God's eschatological people who, in receiving the grace of God through Jesus Christ, become a living sign, a privileged clue to the meaning of God's word in Scripture. This hermeneutic conviction demands a fresh reading of Scripture.[41]

Note that Paul's claims demand a "fresh reading of Scripture." Paul looks nowhere else to establish his position vis-à-vis those with another message. He does not draw on available theological or philosophical convictions from the Galatians' Gentile world, convictions which might have worked well to free him from the very particular sectarian perspective of the Scriptures of Israel. Rather, the whole history of the Galatian Gentiles, both before and after "faith was revealed," is subsumed within that perspective, read into it, made comprehensible by it. Even the Gentiles' prior enslavement is so inscribed in Israel's Scripture that the word of Scripture itself in some sense *effects* that condition: "But the scripture has imprisoned all things under the power of sin" (Gal. 3:22). The true condition of the Gentiles under sin, the law, and

41. Richard Hays, *Echoes of Scripture in the Letters of Paul* (New Haven: Yale University Press, 1989), 105, 121.

the promise is unavailable to them apart from the stories of Scripture, since sin, the law, and the promise are realities rendered only in and by those stories. Thus, while Paul wants to tell a very different story about the Torah, Christ, and the Gentiles than the disturbers are telling, he considers himself bound to the same "cultural-linguistic traditions" as they and refuses to advance his claims on any other ground, for there is no other God and no other world than that which those traditions faithfully attest. Paul's sources and patterns of theological reasoning are thoroughly particular and sectarian not because his "sociohistorical context" is inescapable, but because there is no other way in which God has chosen to reveal and enact his cosmic and historical purpose for all creation than through Israel, Jesus Christ, and the church.

Third, the shape of ecclesial life to which Paul calls his Galatian congregations is itself patterned very specifically after the shape of Jesus' own life, death, and resurrection. The Galatian churches live their life in the world not as a participation in the Torah principle, but as a participation in the crucifixion and resurrection of Jesus Christ and the work of the Holy Spirit. The Galatians received the Spirit when they heard the message of Christ's faithfulness: "Before your eyes . . . Jesus was publicly exhibited as crucified! . . . Did you receive the Spirit by doing the works of the law or by hearing of [Christ's] faith" (3:1–2)? Having been incorporated into Jesus Christ through baptism, they share a unity in Christ and the Spirit which is the very reality of what was promised to Abraham (3:14, 25–29). The Galatians overcome the "passions of the flesh" by sharing in Christ's crucifixion (5:24) or, which is the same thing, by living by the Spirit. In other words, the habits of the Gentiles (5:19–21) are replaced by the fruit of the Spirit (5:22–23) in order that "the law of Christ" (6:2) might be fulfilled in the Galatian churches. "The law of Christ" is the pattern of his self-offering for the sake of the Gentiles (1:4), his "becoming a curse for them" (3:13–14), in order that in their new freedom from the enslaving powers they might reflect that pattern in their life together, in a fellowship marked on the one hand by the absence of conceit, competition, and envy (5:26) and on the other hand by the actions of restoring transgressors "in a spirit of gentleness," bearing one another's burdens, testing one's own work rather than that of others, sharing generously with teachers of the word, doing what is right, and working for the good of all (6:1–10). "To fulfill the Law of Christ . . . is to play out over and over again in the life of the community the pattern of self-sacrificial love that he revealed in his death. . . . Fulfilling the law of Christ will follow as a consequence of the church's simple daily acts of assuming responsibility for one another."[42]

In brief, the shape of the corporate life of the Galatian churches is itself given in and with the *apokalypsis* of Jesus Christ, the proclamation of his

---

42. Hays, "Letter to the Galatians," 333. Hays's detailed argument for his understanding of the "law of Christ" may be found in his "Christology and Ethics in Galatians: The Law of Christ," *Catholic Biblical Quarterly* 49 (1987): 268–90.

crucifixion as a way of life. While Paul radically rejects drawing the Galatians into a Torah way of life, as some others hoped to do, he does not go on to draw on a general ethical ideal or on the common wisdom of the Gentiles in instructing the churches in their way of life. Rather, on this matter from beginning to end in the letter he inscribes the Galatian churches' life into the story of the self-offering of the crucified Christ on their behalf. This cruciformity is no less particular, no less "sectarian" and exclusive than living by Torah; and certainly Paul has every expectation that a cruciform way of life will distinguish, even separate, the Galatian churches from their idolatrous surroundings in radical ways—as radical as the difference between living "by the flesh" or "by the Spirit," living according to "passions and lusts" or according to "the fruit of the Spirit." There is nothing to suggest that Paul wishes to encourage the Galatian churches toward a greater "inclusiveness" or openness to their religious, cultural, and social surroundings by having them refuse the works of Torah. He only wants them to live fully and exclusively in the new creation constituted in Jesus Christ and the Holy Spirit. But that makes all the difference in the world. Or rather, it *is* a different world, and at the same time it is the only world there is.

In view of these reflections on Galatians, what does it mean to accuse Hauerwas of being "sectarian"?[43] The charge has been leveled by many of his critics, among them Stackhouse, whom we have already encountered, and James Gustafson, a former teacher of Hauerwas. Gustafson's argument may be taken as representative of those who think of Hauerwas as sectarian.[44] Scott Holland summarizes four of the main "temptations" that Gustafson detects in Hauerwas's work. First, Hauerwas is susceptible to the temptation to "withdraw from the world," that is, "to isolate the language of the church from the discourse of public life . . . not to take seriously the wider world of science and culture, thus limiting the participation of Christians in the ambiguities of the moral and social life."[45] Second, Hauerwas is

43. The following discussion is informed by the important work of clarification on the idea of sectarianism by Philip D. Kenneson, *Beyond Sectarianism: Re-imagining Church and World* (Harrisburg, Pa.: Trinity, 1999); see also Rasmusson, "The Genealogy of the Charge of Sectarianism," in *Church as Polis*, 231–47.

44. Gustafson's critique appears in "The Sectarian Temptation: Reflections on Theology, the Church and the University," *Proceedings of the Catholic Theological Society* 40 (1985): 83–94. I am following the helpful summary provided by Scott Holland, "The Problems and Prospects of a 'Sectarian Ethic': A Critique of the Hauerwas Reading of the Jesus Story," *The Conrad Grebel Review* 10 (1992): 157–68. Holland's own response to Hauerwas in this essay is of a piece with the critiques of Gustafson and Stackhouse. Hauerwas's response to Gustafson appears in his introduction to *Christian Existence Today: Essays on Church, World and Living in Between* (Grand Rapids: Brazos, 2001), 1–21. For a qualified defense of Hauerwas against the charge of sectarianism, see Nigel Biggar, "Is Stanley Hauerwas Sectarian?" in *Faithfulness and Fortitude: In Conversation with the Theological Ethics of Stanley Hauerwas* (ed. Mark Thiessen Nation and Samuel Wells; Edinburgh: T & T Clark, 2000), 141–60. Rasmusson's discussion in *Church as Polis*, 248–302, is an extended defense of Hauerwas against the charge of sectarianism.

45. Holland, "Problems and Prospects," 162.

tempted by "Wittgensteinian fideism." The languages of theology and science are thought to be incommensurable, leaving theology as a "privileged and often fideistic discourse" that cannot be corrected and revised from the perspective of other discourses such as the social and physical sciences.[46] Third, Hauerwas is tempted by a "communitarian hermeneutic" that rejects all universalisms, leaving the church to think of itself as a "a special tribe, indeed resident aliens living in a cultural-linguistic ghetto" worshiping "a tribal God," protecting itself from the messy, dirty, and ambiguous wider world.[47] Finally, Hauerwas succumbs to the temptation to "resist a theology of creation." "The exclusive arena of God's activity appears to be the church. God appears to be absent in the world of nature and culture beyond the sanctuary doors."[48]

Hauerwas himself responded to these charges at length in his writings. I will not take the time to summarize his specific counterarguments. One thing is certain, however: the difference between Hauerwas and defenders of liberalism such as Stackhouse, Gustafson, and others can only be described as a clash of paradigms. The dogmatic certainties about universal rationality, morality, and experience preached by Enlightenment modernity have been rejected by Hauerwas in such a radical and decisive way that Gustafson's charges simply bypass Hauerwas's theology, since it is precisely those certainties that fund Gustafson's liberal paradigm. Hauerwas's theology is not recognizable in the accusations. He himself has noted in response to another critic, Gloria Albrecht: "I am not accusing Albrecht of wilful misunderstanding. If anything, I think she has tried very hard to be a sympathetic reporter and critic, but she continues to misunderstand me precisely because she insists on reading me as saying what only someone who thinks like she thinks can and must think I must think."[49] I think these comments are equally appropriate about Gustafson and Stackhouse. Each shares in a failure of understanding because he cannot think or grasp Hauerwas's position in any terms other than those supplied by a culturally dominant liberalism, thus confirming Hauerwas's consistent charge that liberalism itself is "imperial in its demands." Hauerwas sees his own work as trying "to help Christians, particularly in North America, discover in what ways liberal speech (and practices) subverts the way we must speak as Christians. I have done so not because liberalism is peculiarly perverse, but simply because liberalism has been and is the speech that dominates our lives."[50] The guardians of that speech can only imagine that if someone is not using it, he or she must be irrational, "fi-

---

46. Ibid., 162–63.

47. Ibid., 163.

48. Ibid.

49. Hauerwas, "Failure of Communication *or* A Case of Uncomprehending Feminism," *Scottish Journal of Theology* 50 (1997): 230. Hauerwas is responding to Albrecht's article in the same journal: "Article Review: *In Good Company: The Church as Polis*," 219–27.

50. Hauerwas, "Failure of Communication," 231.

deist," "against culture," and simply enamored of his or her own particularity and location.

Still, it is worthwhile to consider Gustafson's description of the four "sectarian temptations" to which he thinks Hauerwas is susceptible. I will respond to Gustafson's charges, not primarily by drawing on Hauerwas's writings, but by bringing to bear on the issues what we have learned from Paul's letter to the Galatians. I begin with the last temptation: Hauerwas "resists a theology of creation." It depends on what one has in mind as a theology of creation. Usually that means a theological account of what can and must be said about the world and humanity "before" the fall into sin and redemption through Christ and "in general" apart from the appearance of Jesus Christ. Typically, it involves paying a great deal of attention to Genesis 1–2 and on that basis developing statements about the status, structures, relationships, and order of creation and creatures in relation to God and to one another. Christology is a later theme in the order of theological loci, having primarily to do with how the world is rescued from the fall.

While such a procedure is typical in much Christian theology, it receives no warrant from Paul. For Paul a doctrine of creation is impossible apart from the *apokalypsis* of Jesus Christ. In fact, the apocalypse of Jesus Christ *is* Paul's doctrine of creation, since for him the *kosmos* that preceded the crucifixion of Jesus Christ is itself in some sense destroyed in the crucifixion: "May I never boast of anything except the cross of our Lord Jesus Christ, by which the *kosmos* has been crucified to me, and I to the *kosmos*. For neither circumcision nor uncircumcision is anything, but a new creation is everything!" (Gal. 6:14–15). Commenting on this verse, Martyn writes:

> What do things look like when, having entered the present evil age in Christ, God has begun to set things right? To give the climactic answer to this question, our radical apocalyptic theologian does not refer to an improvement in the human situation. In an unbridled way, Paul speaks rather of nothing less than the dawn of the new creation. . . . Paul speaks about what does and does not exist, not about what should and should not exist. There *are* two different worlds, the (old) cosmos and the new creation. . . . The liberating dawn of the new creation is death? God's idea of good news includes the crucifixion of God's Son, of the world, and of human beings? . . . [Paul] says in effect that the foundation of the cosmos has been subjected to a volcanic explosion that has scattered the pieces into new and confusing patterns.[51]

What could it mean then, to develop a theology of creation in which the Christ apocalypse, the coming of the Holy Spirit, and the creation of the *ekklēsia* are not the *first* things to be treated, as Paul does not only in Galatians, but also in Romans 8, Colossians 1, and Ephesians 1? It could only mean that one is attempting to shape a normative understanding of creation

---

51. Martyn, "Apocalyptic Gospel in Galatians," 255–56.

out of the religious resources provided by the "elemental spirits of the cosmos" (*stoicheia tou kosmou*). While that is a bold claim, consider that Paul would not allow the Galatians to think of the God/world relationship even in terms of the very best resource that the tradition of Judaism had to offer, the Torah. For even the Torah, if it is thought of as a cosmic mediating principle higher than or alongside of Jesus Christ, must as such be judged to be one of the enslaving *stoicheia tou kosmou* under the power of sin in "the present evil age."

In view of this, consider the following criticism of Hauerwas by Holland:

> [Hauerwas's] Wittgensteinian, pure narrative approach to theological discourse, which demands a clean self-referential consistency if theologians are to play by the rules of this proposed language game, fails to address the fact that the entire vocabulary of the Christian community, including central signifiers like God, revelation, faith, love, and justice are ordinary terms grounded in the language and culture of general experience. Because no community is an island in the contemporary world, there is no language of revelation or peoplehood that does not have its beginning in broader human experience.[52]

There is in neither Paul nor Hauerwas any such quest for a "pure" and "self-referential" theological discourse. Each engages the ordinary linguistic idiom of his culture to speak truthfully about Jesus Christ. But the language must be disciplined by that aim, and that means that it must be uprooted from its "ground" and "beginning" in "general" or "broader" human experience. For any claimed ground or origin which is not Jesus Christ must be viewed, in light of the *apokalypsis* of Jesus Christ, as one of those "beings that by nature are not gods" (Gal. 1:8), that is, as opposed to the gospel insofar as it is claimed they are more fundamental or more original than the Son of God revealed in the gospel. Nor is there a general world that is broader than the one in which the crucified Jesus Christ is Lord or that can be discerned in its truth apart from the public exhibition of Christ crucified (3:1). In a theology determined by the apocalypse of Jesus Christ, as all Christian theology must be, any other way of telling the world's story as God's creation must itself only be viewed as a parochial, provincial, "sectarian" perspective enabled by devotion to one or another of the many *stoicheia tou kosmou*. If Paul is to be taken seriously, precisely insofar as Hauerwas's theology of creation is rigorously oriented to and disciplined by the Christ apocalypse as also the apocalypse of the new creation and the end of the old, that theology, or something like it, also offers the possibility of the only truly nonsectarian account of creation available.[53]

---

52. Holland, "Problems and Prospects," 166.

53. Hauerwas's indebtedness to Barth on the theology of creation is evident. Kathryn Tanner, commenting in an illuminating essay on Barth's theology of creation and providence, writes: "Christian accounts of creation that hope to be biblical . . . cannot give isolated attention, as they usually do, to the first

Apocalypse   99

2 /· 95-6
/

Hauerwas is also accused of succumbing to the sectarian temptation of Wittgensteinian fideism.[54] The charge of fideism is a standard one leveled by those who are quite convinced that reason is on their side and that reason supplies universally available criteria—derived apart from any narrative, tradition, community, habits, or practices—by which anything not meeting those criteria may be judged irrational, or at best available only to faith. Alternatively, in company with Schleiermacher, faith or religion is more positively construed as a fundamental prerational mode of consciousness without an intrinsic rationality, which then seeks expression in the modes of rationality available within a given intellectual cultural context. Fideism on this account would be the refusal to hand faith over to the rationality of its wider context, seeking instead to isolate it within its own particular primary language, tradition, and community.

I have already noted above that Paul speaks in no other language and idiom than that with which the Galatians are already familiar—the language of *stoicheia tou kosmou* is surely part of the Galatian theological vocabulary. But his theologic both presupposes and offers something very different from that with which the Galatians are familiar. Critical to the message of Galatians is that truthful speech about Jesus Christ cannot be rendered *within* the concept of the *stoicheia* but only *against* it. To render Jesus Christ as one of or even the highest of the *stoicheia* is to fail to recognize that the *stoicheia* are themselves considered by pagan Galatia to be in some sense "revelatory" of the way things are and as such in competition with the *apokalypsis Iēsou Christou* that excludes all rivals, including Torah. So while Paul borrows some of the theological vocabulary of the Galatians, the theological grammar is fundamentally different, indeed "wholly other." Further, since it is precisely the God of Israel who is apocalypsed in Jesus Christ, truthful speech about God cannot be rendered without making it clear that *this* God is the one who calls the Galatian Gentiles into community with himself and commands them to turn from all other "beings that by nature are not gods." While it is important for Paul in this letter to "relativize" Torah (as "law" or "cosmic principle") with respect to the Christ apocalypse, it is equally important for Paul to establish the continuity of the logic of the Christ apocalypse with the story of God's dealings with Israel inscribed in Torah (as Scrip-

---

two chapters of Genesis, *filling out their theological meaning from who knows where.* Instead, the meaning of those chapters must be developed in the light of the Bible's treatment of the whole covenant history of God and Israel that culminates in Jesus, in such a way that what the New Testament proclaims about Jesus is the key to understanding all that comes before it in the Bible. . . . God's decision to be for us in Jesus is not a reaction to previous events in the history of God's relations with us, but has a reality in its own right preceding the whole of that history"; "Creation and Providence," in *The Cambridge Companion to Karl Barth* (ed. John Webster; Cambridge: Cambridge University Press, 2000), 114 (emphasis added).

54. The argument for Hauerwas's genuinely Wittgensteinian mode of rationality is made by Kallenberg, *Ethics as Grammar.* I am arguing that Hauerwas's mode of rationality is also genuinely apocalyptic.

ture).[55] This is not simply due to the contingent fact that those who are con-
fusing the Galatians are no doubt exploiting the stories of Abraham and
Moses. It is also due to the abiding fact that those stories are crucial to identifying the God of whom Paul speaks when he proclaims the gospel to the
nations. It would have been inconceivable for Paul to draw on the pagan
theological traditions of the Gentiles to speak truthfully of God. Paul's theological task is to offer a new reading of *Israel's* Scriptures and traditions in order to display the rationality of God's apocalypse in Jesus Christ. While it is
certainly true that for Paul, Jesus Christ himself establishes the logic of the
cosmos, it is also true that the logic of Jesus Christ is not discernible apart
from the work of God toward his people, the Jews, for that work is also, precisely, the logic of the Son, the "one seed" of Abraham, who for the sake of
the nations God sends in "the fullness of time." Thus the rationality of Jesus
Christ is rendered in and through the stories of Abraham, Sarah, Hagar, Ishmael, and Isaac, because Christ himself in a prior way constitutes the rationality of those stories. That claim is central to Paul's use of Israel's Scriptures.
The biblical stories are thus indispensable and unsubstitutable for rendering
the identity of the God of Israel, of Jesus Christ, and of the Holy Spirit and
also for providing a truthful characterization of the cosmos and human history. The possibility of the Galatians' sharing in that theological rationality
requires that they hear the stories of Israel's Scriptures along with Paul,
rather than that Paul "translate" the stories into the rationality of the wider
Galatian world. Induction into the biblical stories and traditions enables the
Galatians to realize that they have to do with the one true God of Israel who
promised both Jesus Christ and the Holy Spirit, whom they have received as
the very truth of the way things are.

In responding to the charge of fideism or confessionalism Hauerwas
writes: "Of course, I think it is true that God has saved all creation in the
cross and resurrection of Jesus Christ, but such a 'confession' is not required
by an assumed necessity of human beings to have a 'faith.' . . . If I am anything I am a 'rationalist,' just to the extent I have tried to show that Christian convictions do in fact provide the skills necessary to help us see the
world as it is."[56] In doing so Hauerwas has in no sense rejected rationality,
but he has rejected the notion of a universally available rationality by which
Christian convictions are to be judged, as well as the notion that faith is an
ineffable, prerational experience of the divine awaiting expression in the
forms of rationality provided by a given cultural context. To be rational after
the manner of Paul in a letter like Galatians, Hauerwas has found it necessary to engage the linguistic and narrative philosophies of Wittgenstein,
George Lindbeck, Alasdair MacIntyre, and others. He does this not in order
to establish the claims of the gospel in terms of these philosophies, but, with

55. See Martyn, *Galatians*, 364–70.
56. Hauerwas, "Failure of Communication," 232.

the aid of these philosophies, to show that for rationality to be properly Christian—that is, determined by the Christ apocalypse—it is necessary to read the stories of Israel and Jesus Christ within the community, tradition, and practices formed by those stories as creating the very possibility of rationality. And since those stories do not so much speak of the world as constitute its very intelligibility in Christian terms, they also set the conditions for judging all other claims to rationality. 3/-96

Two other temptations attributed to Hauerwas are that of embracing tribalism with a tribal God and of withdrawing from the world. How this could hold true for Hauerwas is as difficult to imagine as how it could be a temptation for the apostle to the nations. Would Paul agree that any other God—one perhaps more generally accessible to the Gentile peoples through their religious or cultural experience—than the one God of Israel apocalypsed himself in the crucifixion of Jesus for the sake of the nations? And it was precisely for the sake of the nations that Jesus was crucified, that he was apocalypsed to Paul, and that Paul was commissioned as apostle to the nations. While Israel and the church are certainly the "tribes" chosen by God as witnesses to God's action for the world in Jesus Christ, these tribes nevertheless exist as fully public signs of God's work among the peoples and nations of the world. Indeed, as I showed above, for Paul and theologians such as Hauerwas the gospel of Jesus Christ is "imperial in its demands" and "omnivorous in its appetite." A kind of "totalizing" universalism is as intrinsic to the apocalypse of Jesus Christ as it is to liberalism or Americanism, even as the provenance of those universalisms is, despite their disclaimers, just as particular as the universalism of the gospel. But as Hauerwas notes, Christians are (or should be) more capable and ready to name the particular provenance of their universal mission: "Our universalism is not based on assumed commonalities about humankind; rather it is based on the belief that the God who has made us his own through Jesus Christ is the God of all people. Christian universality is too often based on a high view of the human, rather than a high view of Jesus."[57] Ultimate allegiances must, therefore, be declared, enemies identified, battles engaged, territory taken, in the task of declaring the name *Jesus Christ* to every tribe and nation, calling them to confess Jesus as Lord and to become obedient to him through the church in the power of the Holy Spirit. In this sense, Hauerwas has never disavowed a certain kind of Constantinianism.[58] In a description of Hauerwas's theological agenda, which Hauerwas himself fully endorses, Gerald Schlabach writes:

57. Hauerwas, "Remembering as a Moral Task: The Challenge of the Holocaust," in *Against the Nations: War and Survival in a Liberal Society* (Notre Dame: University of Notre Dame Press, 1992), 77.
58. The implicit reference here is to John Howard Yoder's important essay defining "Constantinianism": "The Constantinian Sources of Western Social Ethics," in *The Priestly Kingdom: Social Ethics as Gospel* (Notre Dame: University of Notre Dame Press, 1984), 135–47.

Hauerwas has discovered a dirty little secret—Anabaptists who reject historic Christendom may not actually be rejecting the vision of Christendom as a society in which all of life is integrated under the Lordship of Christ. On this reading, Christendom may in fact be a vision of shalom, and our argument with Constantinians is not over the vision so much as the sinful effort to grasp at its fulness through violence, before its eschatological time. Hauerwas is quite consistent once you see that he does want to create a Christian society (polis, societas)—a community and way of life shaped fully by Christian convictions. He rejects Constantinianism because "the world" cannot be this society, and we only distract ourselves from building a truly Christian society by trying to make our nation into that society, rather than be content with living as a community-in-exile.[59]

As Schlabach recognizes, there is a dual key to the kind of Constantinianism that Hauerwas affirms. It is nonviolent, and it is ecclesiocentric. Here again Hauerwas may be understood to be sustaining two central Pauline convictions. I showed, with the help of Hays, that for Paul in Galatians the pattern of Jesus' self-offering for the sake of the Gentiles is the pattern that must be repeated in the life of the Galatian churches as they have been chosen by God and set apart from their pagan surroundings. The dissolute, violent, and destructive habits of idolaters give way to the peaceable building up of the community through the fruit of the Spirit, in which violence is inconceivable; conceit, competition, and envy give way to fulfilling "the law of Christ" and working for the good of all. While Paul does not make an explicit call to nonviolence in Galatians, as he does elsewhere (Rom. 12:14–21), nonviolent witness to the universal lordship of Jesus Christ is everywhere implicit in Galatians.[60] Most important, the new creation is inaugurated in the crucifixion and resurrection of Jesus Christ and is solely the work of God in the church through Jesus Christ and the Holy Spirit. The church participates *in* the new creation; it does not bring it about by its own actions. It can only bear the marks of the crucifixion in its body. Its conquest of the world is never its own; it is only ever a participation in the "the cross

59. Quoted in "Christian Difference," 44. In a footnote to this quotation Hauerwas speaks of "what might be described as my lingering longing for Christendom" (227 n. 39). At the 1999 meeting of the Society of Christian Ethics, Hauerwas, in positioning himself vis-à-vis John Howard Yoder, declared, "I am much more Catholic, more Constantinian, than John."

60. If the fruit of the Spirit (Gal. 5:22–23) defines the habits and virtues of the *ekklēsia*, violence is simply ruled out by definition, as Philip Kenneson makes abundantly clear in *Life on the Vine: Cultivating the Fruit of the Spirit in Christian Community* (Downers Grove, Ill.: InterVarsity Press, 1999). In a note to me (Aug. 28, 2001) about this chapter, Mark Thiessen Nation made the following perceptive observation on this point: "It is intriguing to read Paul's autobiographical statement at Gal. 1:13: 'I was violently persecuting the church of God and was trying to destroy it. . . .' It never occurs to him to make the same zealot approach a mission strategy for the church after he is a follower of Jesus. That is rather remarkable, given that he is still quite zealous for the faith (as Galatians makes clear). Also, is it accidental that, in light of this autobiographical comment, so much of the reflection in his comments on the works of the flesh and fruit of the spirit deals with conflict?"

of our Lord Jesus Christ, by which the world has been crucified to me, and I to the world" (Gal. 6:14); and a participation in the resurrection, by which God vindicates the cruciform way of the Righteous One and those who share in his life. But it is nonetheless the *world* that is the sphere of conquest of the crucified Christ. For the church to participate in that conquest can have no other consequence than that the church make known among the nations, to the nations, that they too have already died in Christ's crucifixion (which means that there is never any need for Christians to kill idolaters— God has already done that in the death of Christ—2 Cor. 5:14) and that they can now only live "by the faith of the Son of God." The church's universal mission is therefore to bear testimony to the faithful Jesus Christ through its own cruciform, nonviolent life among the nations—a nonviolent, ecclesial Constantinianism that has no other goal than the conversion of all nations, by publicly exhibiting before them the crucified Jesus Christ. To that mission Hauerwas has committed himself as a "nonviolent terrorist." "The issue is not whether Christian claims are imperial, but what institutional form that takes. If one believes as I do that the church rules nonviolently, I think the questions of 'imperialism' are put in quite a different context."[61] The *ekklēsia* is the institutional form of an appropriate Christian imperialism that seeks to conquer the world through the nonviolent politics of the cross rather than the sword. Not only does that sum up Hauerwas's response to sectarian tribalism; it sums up the message and driving motivation of Paul's apostolic mission to the nations.

An indissoluble coinherence of theology, cosmology, hermeneutics, politics, and ethics in Paul's letter to the Galatians resists all attempts to separate out a "level" or "dimension" in which one is free of the others. In an effort to avoid sectarianism every liberal theology in some sense or another seeks a level or dimension in which the theologian has to do with something supposedly more common, more universal, less particular than the apocalypse of Jesus Christ; or if not less particular, at least less all-inclusive in the claims made about that particular apocalypse—surely that claim can be "contextualized." Paul excludes both options and thus proves himself, in Lowe's terms, as a theologian of "apocalyptic without reserve." Hauerwas's consistent refusal to do theology as anything other than thinking all of human existence and creation only through the *apokalypsis Iēsou Christou*, joins him with the company of Barth, Yoder, and others as a faithful imitator of the apocalyptic apostle to the nations. Whether that makes Paul or Hauerwas sectarian should not be a matter of much concern. For neither sectarian nor nonsectarian is anything; but the new creation in Christ is everything.

---

61. Hauerwas, *After Christendom?* 169 n. 23.

3

Politics

Yoder's Pauline Theology

In the previous chapter I showed how one postliberal theologian, Stanley Hauerwas, demonstrates a mode of theology that corresponds well with Paul's apocalyptic mode in the letter to the Galatians. Since Hauerwas engages in very little Pauline exegesis in his work, the task was to discern formal and substantial correspondences between the theologies of Hauerwas and Paul. In this chapter, by contrast, I examine the work of another postliberal theologian, John Howard Yoder, who engaged Pauline texts extensively in his work. Here it is a matter not of searching for correspondences, but of displaying, testing, and promoting Yoder's many readings of Paul.

In the Protestant imagination the appellation *Pauline theologian* almost certainly suggests one who emphasizes "justification by faith"; that is, one who stresses the radical inability of humans to find acceptance with God through their own will or effort and the necessity of believing in Jesus Christ alone and attributing the whole of human salvation to God's grace alone. The names Augustine, Luther, Calvin, and Barth spring immediately to mind. The name John Howard Yoder is not the first, or even last, to come to mind. To be sure, he wrote very little on the "great Reformation theme" of justification by faith, supposed by many to be the very center of Pauline theology. Yet it may come as a surprise to many who know Yoder's most famous book, *The Politics of Jesus*,[1] but who have not read it, that it devotes more

1. John Howard Yoder, *The Politics of Jesus: Vicit Agnus Noster* (2d ed.; Grand Rapids: Eerdmans, 1994).

space to the letters and theology of Paul (93 pages) than it does to Jesus and the Gospels (75 pages). In addition Yoder devoted a full volume to a study of the theme of ministry and another to the church, with Paul as the anchor.[2] In many other essays he addressed other Pauline themes. In his later years Yoder was especially interested in reading the letters of Paul as a way of engaging the conversation between Christians and Jews.[3]

In this chapter I show how the writings and theology of the apostle to the Gentiles are as crucial in Yoder's theological project as is the story of Jesus' mission to Israel. Indeed, the Pauline writings form for Yoder the most important link in the theological chain that leads from the politics of Jesus to the church's political witness in history and the present day. If there were no "politics of Paul," Yoder's entire argument in the first half of *The Politics of Jesus*, that the politics of Jesus are of direct relevance to the question of Christian political existence today, could by Yoder's own admission be easily dismissed. So the Pauline element in Yoder's theology is indispensable. Further, I show that the angle from which Yoder approached the Pauline letters in *The Politics of Jesus*, namely as an extension into the Gentile world of Jesus' political mission to Israel, enabled Yoder (already in 1972) to render a version of Pauline theology that incorporated and anticipated some of the most important developments in recent Pauline scholarship. In order to display the Pauline character of Yoder's theology in what follows, I offer a close reading of the latter half of *The Politics of Jesus*, showing first how an understanding of Paul's theology and mission are intrinsic to Yoder's entire argument in that book; second, how Yoder's insights and arguments receive support from some of the best Pauline studies from the past two decades and in fact point toward a new construal of Pauline theology as a whole;[4] and, third, how Yoder's political reading of Paul is critical for the life and mission of the church in our time.

From the Politics of Jesus to the Politics of Paul

Yoder's aim in *The Politics of Jesus* is to persuade readers that the writings of the New Testament present Jesus as "a model of radical political action"

2. On ministry: John Howard Yoder, *The Fullness of Christ: Paul's Revolutionary Vision of Universal Ministry* (Elgin, Ill.: Brethren, 1987); on the church: idem, *Body Politics: Five Practices of the Christian Community before the Watching World* (Nashville: Discipleship Resources, 1992).

3. Yoder's reading of the story of the Jews is examined in chap. 4.

4. The point here is not to "prove" that Yoder's reading of Paul is right by surveying the entire range of Pauline studies in search of "support" for his reading. (As anyone even slightly familiar with Pauline scholarship knows, that is a feat far beyond the capabilities of all but a few—certainly beyond my own.) The point is rather that Yoder asks some particular kinds of questions of Paul that (1) seem to receive some important answers from the Pauline writings and (2) seem to shed some new light on the character and themes of Paul's thought. My question then will not be whether there is unanimous or even widespread agreement with Yoder's readings, but whether others have asked the same or similar kinds of questions of Paul and whether they have come to conclusions similar to or supportive of Yoder's.

(2), that is, as the normative bodily enactment of God's political will for God's people. As Richard Hays summarizes, Yoder

> argues for three fundamental theses: (1) that the New Testament consistently bears witness to Jesus' renunciation of violence and coercive power; (2) that the example of Jesus is directly relevant and normatively binding for the Christian community; (3) that faithfulness to the example of Jesus is a political choice, not a withdrawal from the realm of politics.[5]

In the early chapters of *The Politics of Jesus* Yoder offers a reading of Jesus in his social and political context as a way of substantiating these three theses. He discovers a Jesus whose entire mission was pervaded with political significance and an explicit political self-consciousness in the context of first-century Palestine, evident in Jesus' own deeds, teachings, and crucifixion and retained in the gospel witnesses (Yoder focuses particularly on the Gospel of Luke). Already in 1972 this was not an entirely novel or controversial thesis. Yoder's references to works by S. G. F. Brandon, Oscar Cullmann, Martin Hengel, and others testify to an emerging scholarly awareness of Jesus as in some sense a sociopolitical figure with a sociopolitical mission who was crucified as a threat to the ruling powers in Jerusalem. Since 1972 a considerable consensus has grown among scholars that this description, when worked out in careful historical detail, is accurate with respect both to Jesus and to the Gospel witnesses.[6] While the detailed shape of Yoder's arguments and proposals is disputable, his understanding that the Jesus of history and gospel was a political figure has been vindicated. Hays, reflecting on Yoder's exegetical work in the first edition, concludes: "At numerous points, his readings reflect an astute—indeed, almost prescient—grasp of important developments in the field of New Testament studies."[7]

5. Richard Hays, *The Moral Vision of the New Testament: Community, Cross, New Creation* (San Francisco: Harper San Francisco, 1996), 239–40.

6. Yoder discusses recent literature on Jesus in the 1994 epilogues to chaps. 1 (13–15) and 2 (53–59) in *Politics of Jesus*. He finds that "there continues to be deep diversity among scholars as to detail [regarding Jesus as a political figure] but less than ever does any of them make Jesus apolitical" (13). See also the essays in E. Bammel and C. F. D. Moule (eds.), *Jesus and the Politics of His Day* (Cambridge: Cambridge University Press, 1984), and the massive work by N. T. Wright, *Jesus and the Victory of God*, vol. 2 of *Christian Origins and the Question of God* (Minneapolis: Fortress, 1997). For a survey and significant bibliography on the political character of Jesus' mission, see W. R. Herzog II, "Sociological Approaches to the Gospels," in *Dictionary of Jesus and the Gospels* (ed. Joel B. Green et al.; Downers Grove, Ill.: InterVarsity Press, 1992), 760–66.

7. Hays, *Moral Vision*, 245. Hays goes on to cite some areas in which Yoder's judgments have proven sound: "For instance, his attention to the social context and meaning of the texts, his placement of Jesus within the political matrix of first-century Palestine, his emphasis on the apocalyptic horizon of the 'powers' language in the Pauline traditions, his interpretation of Galatians as an argument about the social form of the church (rather than about the problem of individual guilt), his sympathetic understanding of the Torah as a vehicle of grace within Jewish tradition" (245).

Chapter 6 in *The Politics of Jesus* forms a crucial bridge from Yoder's explication of the politics of Jesus (as presented in the Gospel of Luke) to the rest
of the New Testament. Is the message of the "ethical-social Jesus" of the Gospels sufficiently persuasive to reach into the present day? "Did it even reach
into the other parts of the New Testament? Did it even survive the translation into the cultural idiom of the early non-Jewish churches?" (*Politics of
Jesus*, 93). It is these questions that motivate Yoder's examination of other
New Testament texts and the Pauline texts in particular. The history of interpretation of the New Testament often seriously hampers attempts to read the
texts in pursuit of the kinds of questions which Yoder wants to address to
them. The Pauline texts especially have been subject to individualizing, interiorizing, and spiritualizing interpretations which make a sociopolitical reading almost impossible. So Yoder makes it his task to pay "special attention to
those points where it has often been assumed that we are farthest from his
[Jesus' sociopolitical] influence, or that his influence is of the least concrete
kind" (93).

Yoder's argument is straightforward, but its point is critical and pervades
all of the subsequent chapters. The "transposition" of the politics of Jesus
into "the cultural idiom of the non-Jewish churches" takes place around one
specific theme: "Only at one point, only on one subject—but then consistently, universally—is Jesus our example: *in his cross*" (*Politics of Jesus*, 95,
emphasis added). It is at this point that a theology of the imitation of Christ
can be developed. What is the concrete meaning of Jesus' disciples "bearing
the cross?"

As a first step in answering that question, Yoder provides in chapter 7,
"The Disciples of Christ and the Way of Jesus," a series of quotations from
the New Testament; indeed, the greater part of the chapter is little more than
these quotations, interspersed with only a small amount of commentary. Yoder's aim is to clarify the character of the imitation of Christ. The epistles of
the New Testament call Jesus' disciples to imitate, participate in, correspond
to, the character of God or Jesus Christ. But what does that look like? To answer that question Yoder sets out a series of categories under which he col-
lects his lists of quotations (*Politics of Jesus*, 115–27):

    I. The disciple/participant and the love of God
       A. Sharing the divine nature as the definition of Christian existence
           (Col. 3:9; cf. Eph. 4:24)
       B. Forgiving as God has forgiven you (Eph. 4:32; Col. 3:13)
       C. Loving indiscriminately as God does
   II. The disciple/participant and the life of Christ
       A. Being in Christ as the definition of Christian existence
       B. Having died with Christ and sharing his risen life (Rom. 6:6–11;
           8:11; Gal. 2:20; cf. 5:24; Eph. 4:20–24; Col. 2:12–3:1)
       C. Loving as Christ loved, giving himself

    D. Serving others as he served (Rom. 15:1–7; 2 Cor. 5:14–21; 8:7–9; Eph. 5:25–28)

    E. Subordinating (here Yoder refers the reader to chap. 9, an extended study of the New Testament *Haustafeln*, including Col. 3:18–4:1 and Eph. 5:21–6:9)

III. The disciple/participant and the death of Christ

    A. Suffering with Christ as the definition of apostolic existence (Phil. 3:10–11; 2 Cor. 4:10; 1:5; Col. 1:24; 1 Cor. 10:33–11:1; 1 Thess. 1:6)

    B. Sharing in divine condescension (Phil. 2:3–14)

    C. Giving your life as he did (Eph. 5:1–2)

    D. Suffering servanthood in place of dominion

    E. Accepting innocent suffering without complaint as he did

    F. Suffering with or like Christ the hostility of the world, as bearers of the kingdom cause (Phil. 1:29)

    G. Death is liberation from the power of sin (Gal. 5:24)

    H. Death is the fate of the prophets; Jesus, whom we follow, was already following them (1 Thess. 2:15)

    I. Death is victory (Col. 2:15; 1 Cor. 1:22–24)

I included in this list only references to the passages that Yoder quotes from the Pauline literature.[8] He draws in many more from other New Testament texts. Of the total passages quoted, the Pauline texts represent the majority. What does Yoder make of his catena of texts?

> As long as readers could stay unaware of the political/social dimension of Jesus' ministry (which most of Christendom seems to have done quite successfully [and which Yoder seeks to reverse]), then it was possible to perceive the "in Christ" language of the epistles as mystical or the "dying with Christ" as psychologically morbid. But if we may posit . . . that the apostles had and taught at least a core memory of their Lord's earthly ministry in its blunt historicity, then this centering of the apostolic ethic upon the disciple's cross evidences a substantial, binding, and sometimes costly social stance. (*Politics of Jesus*, 127)

Stated otherwise (which Yoder does frequently to stress the point), "the believer's cross must be like his Lord's, the price of his social nonconformity" (*Politics of Jesus*, 96). In contrast to the use of the cross in "Prot-

---

8. Yoder does not commit himself to any particular view of the authorship, Pauline or otherwise, of letters such as Colossians and Ephesians. He simply includes them within the "Pauline" orbit. He is not concerned in these lists to set apart authentic Pauline texts from other New Testament texts. Together with the Pauline texts identified above he includes in his lists quotations from the whole range of New Testament writings, since he is intent on making a point about the entire New Testament witness here, not only a point about Paul.

estant pastoral care" to deal with suffering from illness and natural disaster or inner experiences of the self or to encourage humility, brokenness of spirit, or confession of sin—all of which, according to Yoder, entail "the abuse of language and misuse of Scripture" (129)—Yoder writes: "The cross of Christ was not an inexplicable or chance event, which happened to strike him, like illness or accident. . . . The cross of Calvary was not a difficult family situation, not a frustration of visions of personal fulfillment, a crushing debt, or a nagging in-law; it was the political, legally-to-be-expected result of a moral clash with the powers ruling his society" (129). Paul in particular never uses the concept of the imitation of Jesus to warrant his (Paul's) own or his disciples' practices of celibacy or his "tent ministry," even though Paul might have pointed to Jesus' own practices on these matters. The concept of imitation in Paul and the rest of the New Testament is exclusively focused on "the concrete social meaning of the cross in its relation to enmity and power. Servanthood replaces dominion, forgiveness absorbs hostility. Thus—and only thus—are we bound by the New Testament to 'be like Jesus'" (131). The cross of Christ together with the community that takes up that cross as the shape of its own mandate are thus found in the sociopolitical space where the new creation is in conflict with the old.[9] "Representing as he [Jesus] did the divine order now at hand, accessible; renouncing as he did the legitimate use of violence and the accrediting of the existing authorities; renouncing as well the purity of non-involvement, his people will encounter in ways analogous to his own the hostility of the old order" (96). The cross, whether borne by Jesus or by his community, "is the social reality of representing in an unwilling world the Order to come" (96).

As these excerpts demonstrate, the theme of the imitation of Jesus or participation in Christ is for Yoder not about mystical, existential, or pietistic communion with Christ; it is, rather, a thoroughly *apocalyptic* theme. It is about participating with Christ in a conflict with the structures and powers of "the present evil age" in the manner pioneered by Jesus in his life, trial, and crucifixion.

That the cross of Christ is of central significance in Paul's theology, indeed that it is the very heart of his thinking, is recognized in much of Pauline scholarship. As only one example, James D. G. Dunn writes, "[Paul's] gospel, and so also his theology, focused on the cross." The cross and resurrection are the "centre of gravity of Paul's theology."[10] But the significance of the cross is often rendered solely in terms of atonement theology. Dunn (in historically typical Protestant fashion) directs his entire dis-

9. The three themes which this sentence draws out of Yoder's chapter—cross, community, and new creation—form the infrastructure of Hays's presentation of New Testament ethics in *Moral Vision*. Hays presents this infrastructure as the theological framework of Paul's theology/ethics (19–36), and the same three themes, now "focal images," are extended into New Testament ethics as a whole (196–200). As I show below, Hays's interpretation of Pauline theology offers considerable substantiation of Yoder's reading.

10. James D. G. Dunn, *The Theology of Paul the Apostle* (Grand Rapids: Eerdmans, 1998), 208–9.

cussion to various dimensions of atonement theology; he does not address the theme of the cross in Paul as, among other things, the focal point for Paul's social ethics. Nor does Yoder's contention, that the imitation of Christ in his cross is central to Paul's social ethics, receive widespread attention in Pauline scholarship. Dunn, again for example, gives the theme of the *imitatio Christi* only a few pages of consideration, and he is not inclined to link the theme to that of the cross or to social ethics.[11]

Yoder's *mode* of argument in chapter 7, or rather, his *lack* of argument— he expects the texts to speak for themselves—does less than it might to strengthen his proposal that the language of the imitation of Christ is focused on the sociopolitical significance of the cross. The Pauline texts especially (noted under the categories outlined above) would have benefited from some commentary, since they do not obviously make the point that Yoder wants to clinch by merely quoting them. Of the Paul texts, only Philippians 2:3–14 receives a short comment and a few footnotes (*Politics of Jesus*, 121–22).[12] That text indeed may have been a good place for Yoder to spend more time in careful exegesis, as he does with so many other texts in previous and subsequent chapters. Yoder observes in a footnote that Protestant interpreters have often sought "to undermine any possibility of moralism"—no doubt in strict obedience to the rule of "justification by grace"—and so have tried even in relation to Philippians 2:5–11 to steer clear of any notion of direct imitation of Christ when the apostle exhorts the Philippians to have "the same mind . . . that was in Christ Jesus" (122 n. 26). Several features of this section of Philippians in the context of the whole letter are worth dwelling on in support of Yoder's overall argument in chapter 7, particularly in light of studies of the political context of the letter to the Philippians.

First, Paul himself is suffering imprisonment under the Praetorian Guard (Phil. 1:13), quite possibly in Rome,[13] for his apparently subversive preaching of the gospel (cf. Acts 16:11–40). While he hopes not to "be put to shame," he continues even in his imprisonment to speak boldly, hoping that "Christ will be exalted (*megalynthēsetai*) now as always in my body, whether by life or by death. For to me, living is Christ and dying is gain" (1:20–21). The language of participation is clear, and the motifs (though not the specific terms) of Christ's humiliation and exaltation depicted in 2:8–9 are an-

11. See the discussion in ibid., 194–95, 654–58.

12. Yoder includes a reflection on this passage in the final chapter of *Politics of Jesus* (234–36): "The War of the Lamb."

13. The traditional position is that Paul wrote Philippians while imprisoned in Rome, a position which Markus Bockmuehl defends in *The Epistle to the Philippians* (Peabody, Mass.: Hendrikson, 1998), 30–32. A review of arguments for other provenances may be found in ibid., 25–30, and in G. F. Hawthorne, "Philippians, Letter to the," in *Dictionary of Paul and His Letters* (ed. Gerald F. Hawthorne, Ralph P. Martin, and Daniel G. Reid; Downers Grove, Ill.: InterVarsity Press, 1993), 709–11. Richard Cassidy, *Paul in Chains: Roman Imprisonment and the Letters of St. Paul* (New York: Herder & Herder/Crossroad, 2001), 124–42, makes an extended and careful argument for Rome as the place of writing.

ticipated in Paul's account of his own suffering. His preaching in imprisonment, in this condition of shame and bondage, is in fact one way in which
Christ is exalted, since for Paul his living "is Christ."[14]

Second, the Philippians themselves are confronting opposition, quite possibly as a result of their refusal to participate in the imperial cult in Philippi,
a Roman colony loyally devoted to the emperor.[15] The very character of
Paul's message would have created this opposition, since, as Richard Horsley
shows, the terms in which Paul preached Christ to the Philippians set that
message directly against the imperial cult:

> During the 50's the apostle Paul moved systematically through eastern Medi-
> terranean cities such as Philippi, Thessalonica, and Corinth proclaiming "the
> gospel of Christ." . . . Yet by then "the gospel of Caesar" had already become
> widespread and well established in those very cities. Paul reassured the Philip-
> pians that they could expect a "Savior from heaven." But the imperial savior
> had long since established "peace and security" throughout the Mediterranean
> world, and the cities of Greece and Asia Minor had long since established
> shrines, temples, citywide festivals, and intercity games in which to honor
> their savior. Paul taught that God had "highly exalted [Jesus Christ] . . . so
> that every knee should bend . . . and every tongue confess that Jesus Christ is
> Lord" (Phil. 2:9–11). However, the divine lord, to whom all did obeisance
> and to whom all declared loyalty ("faith"), was already enthroned in Rome.[16]

Paul encourages the Philippian community not to fear their persecution,
but to receive it as "graciously granted" (*echaristhē*) by God as sharing both
in the suffering of Christ and in the same struggle in which Paul himself is
engaged (1:27–30). In face of this opposition, Paul affirms the Philippians
for "standing firm in one spirit, striving side by side with one mind" for the
faith of the gospel. Paul's concern for unity in the Philippian church, so
strongly expressed in 2:1–4, is then not merely in the interests of the believ-

14. An account of how Paul reads his life in Christ is provided by Stephen Fowl, "Learning to Narrate Our Lives in Christ," in *Theological Exegesis: Essays in Honor of Brevard S. Childs* (ed. Christopher
Seitz and Kathryn Greene-McCreight; Grand Rapids: Eerdmans, 1999), 339–54.

15. On Philippi as a Roman colony in which the cult of the emperor played a significant role, see
Bockmuehl, *Philippians*, 2–8.

16. Richard A. Horsley, "General Introduction, " in *Paul and Empire: Religion and Power in Roman
Imperial Society* (ed. Richard A. Horsley; Harrisburg, Pa.: Trinity, 1997), 3–4; see also Neil Elliott, "The
Anti-Imperial Message of the Cross," in the same volume (167–83); and Bockmuehl, *Philippians*, 19,
100–101. It is not certain that devotion and loyalty to the emperor always or even usually meant that the
emperor was considered divine; see Clinton D. Morrison, *The Powers That Be: Earthly Rulers and Demonic Powers in Romans 13:1–7* (London: SCM, 1960), 131–6. Nor should persecution possibly motivated by loyalists of the imperial cult in Philippi be generalized as the reason for persecutions in other cities of the empire (a tendency in Horsley's volume); see Leonard Victor Rutgers, "Roman Policy toward
the Jews: Expulsions from the City of Rome during the First Century c.e.," in *Judaism and Christianity in
First-Century Rome* (ed. Karl P. Donfried and Peter Richardson; Grand Rapids: Eerdmans, 1998), 93–
116, esp. 111–16.

ers "getting along" with one another (there is no obvious indication of a crisis of unity in the church in Philippi)[17] but also, and likely more important, for the sake of strengthening the community's resolve not to falter in the face of opposition. They are to "live as citizens" (*politeuesthe*) in a manner worthy of the gospel (1:27) as those whose citizenship (*politeuma*) is in heaven, that is, in that place from which the exalted Lord (*kyrios*) Jesus Christ reigns and will soon come as Savior (*sōtēr*) (3:20). Their unity is that of citizens of a *polis* under threat. So the purpose of the "Christ hymn" (2:6–11) in this context is to present to the Philippians the picture of Christ, who, of his own free will, was enslaved, humiliated, and suffered death, "even death on a cross," at the hands of his political opponents, but who then also was vindicated and exalted and given rule over all things.[18] In the pattern of Christ's costly and humiliating self-emptying, the Philippian community certainly receives a model of how it must bind itself together as a *polis* of citizens who seek the common good rather than engage in individual self-promotion. But it also receives a model of how it is to respond to its political enemies. As Yoder points out, for imperial Rome and its subjects there was no dichotomy between the religious and sociopolitical aspects of life.[19] Neither is there for Jesus and his imitators. "The 'cross' of Jesus was a political punishment; and when the early Jesus-movement is made to suffer by government it is usually because of the practical import of their faith, and the doubt they cast upon the rulers' claim to be 'Benefactor'" (*Politics of Jesus*, 125). In thus following the example of Christ, the Philippian believers show themselves to be "blameless and innocent, children of God without blemish in the midst of a crooked and perverse generation" (2:15). They do so concretely both in their life together and in their response to opposition. By "holding fast to the word of life" they prove that Paul has not worked in vain, even if he himself, also on the model of Christ, is—in chains in Rome—"being poured out as a libation over the sacrifice and the offering of [their] faith" (2:16–17).

Third, Paul enjoins the Philippians to imitate him as he imitated Christ. Paul himself "want[s] to know Christ and the power of his resurrection and the sharing of his sufferings by becoming like him in his death" and then to "attain the resurrection from the dead" (3:10). Paul's account of his privileged heritage as faithful Jew in 3:4–6—his "reason to be confident in the flesh" (3:4)—and his regarding of all of this as "loss" and "rubbish" because of the surpassing value of knowing Christ as Lord, is not presented in this letter as a response to an imminent threat from Judaizers. It is presented,

17. See Bockmuehl, *Philippians*, 33, 108.

18. It is widely agreed that the phrase "even death on a cross" is Paul's own addition to the Christ hymn in Phil. 2:6–11 (if the hymn in fact is borrowed by Paul). The phrase is certainly the focal point of the hymn as it appears in Philippians. On the political significance of the phrase in context of the practice of crucifixion in the Roman Empire, see Elliott, "Anti-Imperial Message."

19. This point is also emphasized by Horsley, "General Introduction," 7–8. Horsley also points out that it is an "essentialist anachronism" to think of Paul as the founder of a religion or of Judaism as a religion.

rather, as the way in which Paul imitated Christ, who himself did not retain his privilege but freely gave it up, humbled himself, became a slave, and suffered the horror of crucifixion.[20] Paul's close identification with the Crucified One is the basis on which he in turn calls the Philippians to

> join in imitating me, and observe those who live according to the example you have in us. For many live as enemies of the cross of Christ. . . . Their minds are set on earthly things. But our citizenship is in heaven, and it is from there that we are expecting a Savior, the Lord Jesus Christ. He will transform the body of our humiliation that it may be conformed to the body of his glory, by the power that also enables him to make all things subject to himself. (3:17–21)

Here all the themes of Christ's suffering, cross and humiliation, exaltation and rule are held up for imitation and participation by Paul himself, as example, and by the Philippian community, all within the context of pressure from imperial opposition. Yoder's thesis that the political stance of Paul's Gentile churches recapitulates the politics of Jesus thus finds strong confirmation in Paul's letter to the Philippians. "This centering of the apostolic ethic upon the disciple's cross [as imitation of or participation in the cross of Christ] evidences a substantial, binding, and sometimes costly social stance," as the Pauline community comes into conflict with the powers of the wider world (*Politics of Jesus*, 127).[21]

From "Principalities and Powers" to Structures and Institutions

At critical junctures in his letters Paul refers to "authorities," "rulers," "principalities and powers" (among other terms)—hereafter referred to in shorthand as "powers"—as those creatures or features of the cosmos which are opposed to God's purpose and which Christ has in some sense conquered in his crucifixion.[22] For Yoder it is crucial to show that Paul's lan-

20. Cf. Hays, *Moral Vision*, 30–31. Note that on this reading Paul considers his impeccable Jewishness as an asset (*kerdē*)—analogous to Christ's privileged status of "equality with God"—which Paul freely relinquishes, "accounts" (*hēgēmai*) as loss (*zēmia*), as a way of sharing in Christ's *kenosis*. "For his [Christ's] sake I have suffered the loss of all things . . . in order that I may gain Christ and be found in him" (3:7–9). The persuasive power of Paul's example depends upon the privilege of Jewishness not being diminished in itself, but only in relation to Paul's reckoning that gaining Christ is a surpassing privilege (3:8).

21. This same story, with local variations, could be told about the church in Thessalonica. See Karl P. Donfried, "The Imperial Cults of Thessalonica and Political Conflict in 1 Thessalonians," in *Paul and Empire: Religion and Power in Roman Imperial Society* (ed. Richard A. Horsley; Harrisburg, Pa.: Trinity, 1997), 215–23. The same logic of imitation and participation in Christ's death, through persecution, for both Paul and the believers in his churches, is strongly scripted in 2 Cor. 4:15.

22. For lists of Paul's terms on this theme and their occurrence in the Pauline literature, see Dunn, *Theology of Paul*, 105; Clinton Arnold, *Powers of Darkness: Principalities and Powers in Paul's Letters* (Downers Grove, Ill.: InterVarsity Press, 1992), 218; D. G. Reid, "Principalities and Powers," in *Dictionary of Paul and His Letters* (ed. Gerald F. Hawthorne, Ralph P. Martin, and Daniel G. Reid; Downers Grove, Ill.: InterVarsity Press, 1993), 747–49, which includes a helpful discussion of each term.

guage of the powers names, among other things, sociopolitical realities, both in Paul's contexts and our own. If in fact Christ engaged the principalities and powers in a conflict and triumphed over them, and if what is named with these terms are social and political realities, then the meaning of the cross is directly relevant to Christian social ethics. In chapter 8 of *The Politics of Jesus*, "Christ and Power," Yoder argues that "this set of passages [about the powers] from the Pauline corpus demonstrates an astoundingly sweeping and coherent 'translation' of the political meaning of Jesus into the world-view of the audience of Paul's missionary witness" (160).[23]

Yoder begins by noting that in most Lutheran, Pietist, existentialist, and personalist (and I would add "spiritual" and evangelical) readings of Paul, the believer's response to Jesus "has nothing to do with the structures of society" (*Politics of Jesus*, 134). Since it was usually assumed that Jesus had little or nothing to contribute to the Christian understanding of sociopolitical structures and institutions, when Christians found themselves participating in these, "they had to go for their ethical insights to other sources than Jesus" (135). But that was based on a misunderstanding of Paul, in whose language of the powers we do indeed find him paying attention to what we in our time would call structures. Yoder points out that the term *structure* functions in modern social science "to point to the patterns or regularities that transcend or precede or condition the individual phenomena we can immediately perceive" (138). Drawing extensively on Hendrik Berkhof's *Christ and the Powers*,[24] which Yoder himself translated from the 1953 Dutch version, Yoder suggests that the Pauline "principalities and powers" are analogous to what we identify as "religious structures (especially the religious undergirdings of stable ancient and primitive societies), intellectual structures (-ologies and -isms), moral structures (codes and customs), political structures (the tyrant, the market, the school, the courts, race and nation)" (143). Referring to a variety of Pauline texts which use the language of the powers,[25] Yoder (again following Berkhof) argues that the powers are characterized in three ways. First, they are created by God, and therefore originally good: "Society and history, even nature, would be impossible without regularity, system, order—and God has provided for this need. . . . The creative power worked in a mediated form, by means of the Powers that regularized all visible reality" (141). Second, however, the powers are now "fallen," that is, in rebellion against God's purposes. Rather than serving only to share in and mediate creation's goodness, they now also enslave humanity and history. Every form

23. This statement is from the 1994 epilogue to chap. 8; that is, it was not part of the original 1972 text of *Politics of Jesus*.

24. Hendrik Berkhof, *Christ and the Powers* (Scottdale, Pa.: Herald, 1962; 2d ed. 1977).

25. It is important to note that here again Yoder does not distinguish between generally agreed-upon authentically Pauline letters and those usually assumed to be pseudo-Pauline (e.g., Colossians and Ephesians). Making such a distinction may in fact strengthen Yoder's case for the political nature of the powers in Paul's thinking; see Elliott, "Anti-Imperial Message," 176–81.

of religious, cultural, social, and political structure is encountered as both an ordering and an oppressive reality. Nonetheless, third, the powers have not fallen beyond God's providential care of his creation. Though the powers are rebellious, God's superior power can still co-opt them to serve God's purposes in the world; the powers "continue to exercise an ordering function" (141), even though they do so in distorted ways. Yoder concludes about the powers that as elements within God's good creation "*we cannot live without them*," but as fallen "*we cannot live with them*" (143, emphasis original):

> We are lost in the world, in its structures, and in the current of its development. But nonetheless it is in this world that we have been preserved, that we have been able to be who we are and thereby await the redeeming work of God. Our lostness and our survival are inseparable, both dependent upon the Powers. (*Politics of Jesus*, 143)

Yoder goes on to argue that in the Pauline writings (particularly Col. 1:15–20) the structures of human life also come within the universal scope of God's reconciling work in Christ. This is crucial if humanity itself is to be saved. "If . . . God is going to save his creatures *in their humanity*, the Powers cannot simply be destroyed or set aside or ignored. Their sovereignty must be broken. That is what Jesus did, concretely and historically, by living a genuinely free and human existence" (*Politics of Jesus*, 144–45, emphasis original). Jesus' obedience to God even in the face of death is at the same time his freedom vis-à-vis the religious, social, and political structures which crucify him. His obedience is "in itself not only the sign but also the first-fruits of an authentic restored humanity" (145). Yoder draws at length from Berkhof's exegesis of Colossians 2:15: Christ "disarmed" the powers, "made a public example of them, triumphing over them." The claims to ultimacy and the demands for ultimate allegiance that social and political structures make for themselves are unmasked as the deceptions of false gods. When the true God is revealed in Christ's crucifixion and resurrection, the powers are exposed and defeated, and their ability to deceive is stripped from them.

Christ, having thus triumphed over the powers, now redeems them by putting them into service for doing good in that new sociopolitical order that God is creating in Christ Jesus, the *ekklēsia*. Central to Yoder's argument here is Ephesians 3:8–11: Paul's mission to the nations is a revelation of the "wisdom of God in its rich variety" which "through the church . . . [should] now be made known to the rulers and authorities in the heavenly places." The obedient church is that place, in the midst of creation and the nations, in which God's redemption of social and political structures begins. Again drawing from Berkhof's study, Yoder writes:

> For Paul, as interpreted by Berkhof, the very existence of the church is its primary task. It is in itself a proclamation of the lordship of Christ to the powers

from whose dominion the church has begun to be liberated. . . . The church must be a sample of the kind of humanity within which, for example, economic and racial differences are surmounted. (*Politics of Jesus*, 150)

Yoder's point is made even clearer by a quotation that he includes from Amos Wilder: "The believers [in the early church] were shaping a new pattern of the human community and realizing very concrete social values in a widening movement which collided increasingly with existing institutions and vested interests economic, social and political."[26] It is in the church that those various structures or powers—religious, cultural, social, economic, political—that make human community possible at all are reordered to their proper function under the rule of Christ. In turn the church, as redeemed and reordered humanity, presents to the wider world and its structures a picture of the world's own redemptive promise, should it submit to the lordship of Christ. Yoder sums up the argument of chapter 8 thus: "The Powers have been defeated . . . by the concreteness of the cross; the impact of the cross on them is . . . the sovereign presence, within the structures of creaturely orderliness, of Jesus the kingly claimant and of the church who herself is a structure and a power in society" (*Politics of Jesus*, 158).

As Yoder notes, interest by biblical scholars and theologians in the Pauline doctrine of the principalities and powers as a means of addressing concrete social and political issues began after World War II and has continued to the present day.[27] In his 1994 epilogue to this chapter Yoder writes that "exegetical scholarship has continued to confirm that in the Pauline witness Jesus is confessed as foundationally relevant to the political realm . . . in the cosmological sense that 'cross and resurrection' designates not only a few days' events in first-century Jerusalem but also the shape of the cosmos" (*Politics of Jesus*, 160).

While it is true that Yoder's interpretation of the principalities and powers found significant support in his own time and later,[28] not all exegetes come to his conclusions, as Yoder himself was aware. He draws attention to evangelical exegetes (e.g., John Stott) who continue to insist that the principalities and powers are "personal, demonic intelligences" beyond, though perhaps having an influence on, structures and institutions. He notes Walter Wink's extensive study of the powers in which Wink argues that the powers are present and effective as "the inner and outer aspects of any given manifestation of power." Every structure, institution, organization, or system has

26. From Amos Wilder, *Otherworldliness and the New Testament* (New York: Harper, 1954), 116; quoted in Yoder, *Politics of Jesus*, 150 n. 11.

27. See the bibliographies in Arnold, *Powers of Darkness*, 236–38; and Reid, "Principalities and Powers," 752.

28. Besides the work of Berkhof, see the works listed in Yoder, *Politics of Jesus*, 140 n. 5, and in the 1994 epilogue (159 and footnotes). N. T. Wright, *What Saint Paul Really Said* (Grand Rapids: Eerdmans, 1997), 153–56, 160–61, also reads the powers in this way. See also Marva J. Dawn, *Powers, Weakness, and the Tabernacling of God* (Grand Rapids: Eerdmans, 2001), 1–34.

both a "spirituality" and a "tangible manifestation" that together constitute its power.[29] Other exegetes focus little or no attention on Paul's language of the principalities and powers, choosing rather to give primary attention to the "demythologized" powers of death, sin, law, and flesh.[30]

While the exegetical debates about the specific meaning of the powers for Paul remain unsettled, at least two of Yoder's central claims have been widely supported even in the midst of other disagreements. First, whatever the character of the powers "in themselves," most exegetes agree that the powers have some relationship to and influence on the structured character of the cosmos and human society, even where the identification of the powers with those structures is denied. In other words, the language of the principalities and powers is understood as one way of speaking, even if indirectly according to some exegetes, about how human life is ordered by and subject to social and political realities not wholly under human control.[31]

Second, and more important, the context of Paul's language of the powers is consistently *apocalyptic*, in the sense that it always points to the cosmic— which must certainly include the sociopolitical—scope of the conquest of Christ on the cross. The cross is an event of cosmic reordering, the *apokalypsis* of God's rectification of all things, the intrusion of the new creation into the midst of the old. As such, it is an event which triggers a battle over the entire direction of cosmic and human destiny: "The challenge to which the proclamation of Christ's rule over the rebellious world speaks a word of grace is not a problem within the self but *a split within the cosmos*" (*Politics of Jesus*, 161, emphasis added). J. Louis Martyn states this same claim in bold images:

> It is this apocalyptic vision . . . that has given Paul his perception of the nature of the human plight. God has invaded the world in order to bring it under his liberating control. From that deed of God a conclusion is to be drawn, and the conclusion is decidedly apocalyptic: God would not have to carry out an

---

29. Walter Wink, *Naming the Powers: The Language of Power in the New Testament* (Philadelphia: Fortress, 1984), 5. This is the first volume in a trilogy that includes *Unmasking the Powers: The Invisible Forces That Determine Human Existence* (Philadelphia: Fortress, 1986) and *Engaging the Powers: Discernment and Resistance in a World of Domination* (Minneapolis: Fortress, 1992). In a review of *Unmasking the Powers* (*TSF Bulletin* 10 [May–June 1987]: 34–35) Yoder expresses serious misgivings about Wink's project. A critique of Wink from a perspective fully in line with Yoder's is provided by Dawn, *Powers, Weakness, and the Tabernacling of God*, 12–19. Arnold in *Powers of Darkness* presents a strong defense of the understanding of the powers as personal beings which intervene in human affairs, though primarily in relation to individuals. See also Dunn, *Theology of Paul*, who concludes: "Paul himself did not have a very strong, or at least very clear, belief regarding these heavenly powers. That there were real powers, supraindividual, suprasocial forces, spiritual realities which influenced events and conduct, he had no doubt. But he never thought it of relevance to describe or define these powers in any detail" (108–9).

30. See J. Christiaan Beker, *Paul the Apostle: The Triumph of God in Life and Thought* (Philadelphia: Fortress, 1980), 189–92. Dunn, *Theology of Paul*, 110, also leans in this direction.

31. See Arnold, *Powers of Darkness*, 194–209; and Dunn, *Theology of Paul*, 110. Nevertheless, Yoder (*Politics of Jesus*, 156–57) is critical of positions like those of Stott and Arnold which focus attention on the individual believer as the primary locus of the powers' influence and of Christ's conquest of the powers.

invasion in order merely to forgive erring human beings. The root trouble lies deeper than human guilt, and it is more sinister. The whole of humanity—indeed, the whole of creation ([Gal.] 3:22)—is, in fact, trapped, enslaved under the power of the present evil age. That is the background of God's invasive action in his sending of Christ, in his declaration of war, and in his striking the decisive and liberating blow against the power of the present evil age.[32]

As apocalyptic language, Paul's talk of principalities and powers cannot be less than talk about the social and political shape of human existence, although it may well be about more than that. So too, God's conquest of the powers in the cross of Christ, as the *apocalypse*, must be at least about the reshaping of the sociopolitical character of the community of the cross, though it will also be about more than that. Exegetes who insist on understanding the principalities and powers as "personal, demonic intelligences" that primarily attack individual human hearts have failed to read seriously enough the apocalyptic context of Paul's language. Yoder on the other hand provides a consistently apocalyptic interpretation of Paul, a fact that is more critical to his case for the politics of Paul than the specific interpretation he presents about the character of the principalities and powers.[33]

More subtle in his chapter entitled "Christ and the Powers" but not less important for Yoder's overall argument is the way in which the discussion of the principalities and powers provides him with an approach to the doctrine of creation, which Yoder uses to get beyond some of the problems of other approaches. In particular he believes the Pauline doctrine of the powers yields "a far more refined" analysis of "the problems of history and society" than "some traditional theologies [which] have sought to treat this theme under the heading of 'orders of creation'":

> Rarely, if ever, has it been possible under this heading ["orders of creation"] to combine with such clarity and precision the simultaneous recognition of humankind's fallen condition and the continuing providential control. Nor has it generally been the case within traditional thought regarding the orders of

32. J. Louis Martyn, *Galatians: A New Translation with Introduction and Commentary* (Anchor Bible 33A; New York: Doubleday, 1997), 105. See also Martyn's *Theological Issues in the Letters of Paul* (Nashville: Abingdon, 1997), 87–156. Martyn follows Ernst Käsemann and joins J. Christiaan Beker in emphasizing the cosmic and apocalyptic character of Paul's thought. For an excellent description of Jewish "cosmological apocalyptic eschatology" and Paul's christological modification of it, see Martinus C. de Boer, "Paul and Jewish Apocalyptic Eschatology," in *Apocalyptic and the New Testament: Essays in Honor of J. Louis Martyn* (ed. Joel Marcus and Marion Soards; Sheffield: JSOT Press, 1989), 169–90; and idem, "Paul, Theologian of God's Apocalypse," *Interpretation* 56 (2002): 21–33.

33. Given Stanley Hauerwas's deep indebtedness to Yoder, it is likely that the correspondences discovered in the previous chapter between Paul and Hauerwas are in some measure attributable to Yoder's reading of Paul as an apocalyptic theologian. At the same time, Hauerwas makes less use of the language and concept of the principalities and powers than Yoder does; see my analysis of this point in Douglas Harink, "For or against the Nations: Yoder and Hauerwas, What's the Difference?" *Toronto Journal of Theology* 17 (2001): 167–85.

creation that religion or ideology has been included. Nor has it generally been affirmed that it is in Christ that these values all find their meaning and coherence. As a matter of fact, the theology of the orders of creation has generally affirmed that Jesus Christ has little directly to do with them, but that rather these several orders (the state, family, economy, etc.) have an autonomous value *unrelated to redemption and the church*, by virtue of their having been created by the Father. (*Politics of Jesus*, 144, emphasis added)[34]

The point is also made in Yoder's preface to Berkhof's *Christ and the Powers*. Without a study like Berkhof's, Yoder writes, theologians "resolutely ignored" the theme of the principalities and powers, and thus were "free to develop a philosophy of history, a view of the state, and a theology of culture according to [their] own tastes and leanings." What Berkhof's book provided was the possibility of developing, through Paul's thought, "an up-to-date, yet Christian worldview, capable of understanding the state and the structuredness of culture, yet without overvaluing them."[35] In the 1994 epilogue to chapter 8 in *The Politics of Jesus* Yoder also writes, suggestively, "It would not be too much to claim that the Pauline cosmology of the powers represents an alternative to the dominant ('Thomist') vision of 'natural law' as a more biblical way systematically to relate Christ and creation" (159).

In fact, Yoder does go on to develop these three themes in many of his other writings: (1) a philosophy of history in which the weakness and foolishness of the cross of Christ and his community, rather than the shifting power and conquests of empires, is the normative clue for discerning God's work in history; (2) a view of the state in which the civil authorities are not beyond God's providential ordering for his service, but also not the normative bearers of the meaning of "the political"—which belongs to Christ and his church; and (3) a theology of culture which allows for the recognition of the complexity and variety of human cultural production as well as a nuanced and differentiated Christian critique of culture in its complexity and variety.[36] I explore these themes further below. For now, I will demonstrate the Pauline

---

34. In a footnote Yoder refers to H. Richard Niebuhr's "distribution of different kinds of ethical thought" to each of the persons of the Trinity. In the essay by Niebuhr to which Yoder refers, Niebuhr attempts to assign creational ethics to the Father as a way of unloading some of the emphasis on the normativity of Jesus for all of ethics; "The Doctrine of the Trinity and the Unity of the Church," in *Theology Today* 3 (1946): 371–78; repr. in *Theology Today* 60 (1983): 150–57.

35. In Berkhof, *Christ and the Powers*, 5–6.

36. The best sampling of Yoder's essays on these themes is found in his *For the Nations: Essays Evangelical and Public* (Grand Rapids: Eerdmans, 1997). His theology of culture is worked out most carefully in dialogue with Niebuhr in "How H. Richard Niebuhr Reasoned: A Critique of *Christ and Culture*," in Glen H. Stassen, D. M. Yeager, and John Howard Yoder's *Authentic Transformation: A New Vision of Christ and Culture* (Nashville: Abingdon, 1996), 31–89. Yoder's philosophy of history is powerfully presented in the final chapter of *Politics of Jesus*: "The War of the Lamb" (228–47). See also his "War as a Moral Problem in the Early Church: The Historian's Hermeneutical Assumptions," in *The Pacifist Impulse in Historical Perspective* (ed. Harvey L. Dyck; Toronto: University of Toronto Press, 1996), 89–110. An excellent discussion of Yoder's "apocalyptic historiography" in conversation with Nietzsche, Foucault,

character of Yoder's doctrine of creation through reading some texts from Paul's letter to the Romans.

Yoder develops what may be characterized as a christocentric, ecclesiocentric, apocalyptic theology of creation and history. God's avenue to the retrieval of an enslaved creation runs through the suffering-servant people of Israel and through the people gathered in Jesus Christ and the Holy Spirit. "From Genesis to Apocalypse, the meaning of history [has] been carried by the people of God as people, as community."[37] In this Yoder is thoroughly Pauline. Romans 8:12–39 is widely agreed to be one of the most overtly apocalyptic of Pauline texts.[38] There the apostle declares that the community of God's *apokalypsis* (1:16–17) already knows and lives in Christ and in the freedom of the Spirit; it has already been delivered from a spirit of slavery (*pneuma douleias*); it has already received the spirit of adoption (*pneuma huiothesias*) as God's children and heirs; and in its worship already calls upon God as "Abba! Father!" (8:14–17). But the community lives in this way in the midst of a wider creation that has yet to be redeemed. The community's deliverance is not yet complete—it cannot be insofar as it continues to dwell in a fallen creation. For what is promised in Christ and the Spirit is not the community's escape from its enmeshment in the created order, but rather the redemption of the whole created order *with* the children of God. As Yoder notes, the structures/powers of creation, though fallen and therefore often oppressive, are nonetheless necessary for human life to be fully human. For the time being the people of God must continue to share in Christ's suffering (8:17) and in creation's groaning (*stenazō* in 8:22–23). While they have already received the spirit of adoption in their obedience and worship, God's people still wait for adoption as the redemption of the body. The community remains deeply embedded in the created order, which continues in its subjection to futility (*mataiotēs*, 8:20) and its "bondage to decay" (*tē douleia tēs phthoras*, 8:21). In this condition the creation eagerly waits for the *apocalypse* of the children of God (8:19), in which creation itself will come into the same glory promised to the children of God (8:18, 21). In the interim, the suffering-servant community, as it lives in the power and prayer of the Holy Spirit, does indeed bear the meaning of creation. The Spirit himself takes up the groanings (*stenagmoi*, 8:26) of both the community and the creation and prays them in such a way that they accord with the will of God (8:27), since the community itself does not often know how God's purposes are being

---

and others may be found in David Toole, *Waiting for Godot in Sarajevo: Theological Reflections on Nihilism, Tragedy and Apocalypse* (Boulder, Colo.: Westview, 1998), 205–25.

37. Yoder, "The Constantinian Sources of Western Social Ethics," in *The Priestly Kingdom: Social Ethics as Gospel* (Notre Dame: University of Notre Dame Press, 1984), 138. This entire essay is relevant to Yoder's philosophy of history.

38. I have found most helpful the reading of Rom. 8:12–39 by Luke Timothy Johnson, *Reading Romans: A Literary and Theological Commentary* (New York: Crossroad, 1997), 122–38.

worked out in a given moment or place in history or creation—no doubt because of its continuing to suffer under powers that often still *seem* to be in charge and that still do in fact wreak considerable havoc (8:35–39).

In this remarkable text Paul both differentiates the community of Christ from the rest of creation by virtue of its already sharing in the Spirit's freedom and at the same time places that community in solidarity with creation by virtue of its continuing to share in some way in creation's futility and enslavement. To understand this enslavement, we must go back to Romans 1:18–32. There Paul writes of how the Gentile peoples suppressed the truth of God which it was the purpose of creation to make known to them. When the Gentiles failed to honor God the Creator or give thanks to him, they "became futile" (*emataiōthēsan*; 8:21) in their reasoning and "exchanged the glory of the immortal God for images resembling a mortal human being or birds or four-footed animals or reptiles" (1:23). The futility of the Gentiles in their thinking about God led them to exalt creatures into the place of divinity, which introduced a profound disorder into creation itself. Idolatry was born. What is more, God "handed over" (*paredōken*; 1:24, 26, 28) the Gentiles to their idolatry and to its disordering and destructive effects in their bodies (1:24–25), their sexuality (1:26–27), and their society (1:28–32). In this condition of being handed over as prisoners (cf. 11:30, 32), now in subjection to futility and in slavery to dissolute idolatry, the Gentiles remained, until the gospel of God's power and justice was apocalypsed in Jesus Christ (1:16–17; 3:21–22).[39] Romans 8 speaks of how the Gentile believers already experience something of their release from subjection and slavery, but also something of their continuing to be conditioned by it. They wait in hope, with the whole creation.

But while the community of Christ and the Spirit waits in hope for its full deliverance it is assured that no creaturely power, whether in earth or in heaven, whether visible or invisible, whether political or "spiritual," will be able to separate it from the love of God in Jesus Christ the Lord (8:31–39). Paul's list (8:35, 38–39) of the powers which present potential threats to the safety of the community is comprehensive in scope, ranging from "hardship" and "distress" (perhaps inflicted by human opponents?), to natural disasters such as "famine," to human hostility from seemingly authorized power ("persecution," "nakedness," "sword"), to suprahuman "angels," "rulers" (*archai*), and "powers" (*dynameis*), to the cosmic realities of life and death, time and space. At the mention of the "sword" (*makaira*—perhaps government-authorized execution? 13:4; cf. Acts 12:2) Paul breaks his list to speak of those who, like Christ, are not spared, who do have a charge brought against them, who are condemned (cf. 8:32–34) and killed by worldly power "for your

---

39. I owe the verb *apocalypsed* to J. Louis Martyn, who uses it to convey the fact that the arrival of Jesus Christ into human society and creation is not simply an "unveiling" of something hidden but always present; rather it is God's *invasion* into a world order enslaved by powers opposed to God's purpose. See Martyn's *Galatians*, 97–105.

[God's] sake" (8:36). And yet even these are not separated from the love of Christ. On the contrary, precisely in this way, these are the ones who are "more than conquerors" of the power of the sword through Christ (8:37).[40] All of the idolatry, disorder, and dissolution of earthly and heavenly reality, to which we were introduced in Romans 1:18–32, can no longer be any *final* threat to the community's destiny of becoming "conformed to the image of [God's] Son" (8:29). The powers, though often disordered, threatening, and destructive, are already subject to God's purposes in Christ. They serve God's purposes even in their power to kill God's servants, for in this the conquest of the Lamb/lambs (Ps. 44:22 is quoted in Rom. 8:36) is most directly revealed, and the conformity to Christ in his death and resurrection is made evident— in fact, made possible![41] Yet the powers too, with all creation, or rather as intrinsic to the very reality of creation (they are all identified as "creatures"—*oute tis ktisis hetera*; 8:39), await their final redemption. In the meantime, the community in Christ and the Spirit lives as the embodiment of at least a part of creation—the new creation—which knows (in part) the reality of its redemption. Martyn's comments with reference to Galatians are appropriate here:

> Paul speaks of the church's incorporation in this new-creation Christ. It is by being Christ's—by being baptized into him, by putting him on as though he were their clothes ([Gal.] 3:27), by having his Spirit in their hearts (4:6), by having him determine the form of their communal life (4:19), by belonging utterly to him, the cosmocrator of the new creation (5:24)—that the Galatians (with all other members of God's church; 1:13) are Abraham's corporate seed and God's new creation in Christ (3:29).[42]

The "form of their communal life" is the sign that the "cosmocrator" has begun not only to heal persons, but also and precisely—because a "person" is nothing without them—the social structures that make communal life possible. The powers are being redeemed in and with the community of Christ and the Spirit.

Yoder himself pays most careful attention to Colossians 1:15–20 and Ephesians 3:8–11 in developing his apocalyptic theology of creation, and rightly so since the key themes of Christ's creation, reconciliation (also of the powers), and new creation in the church are most explicit in those texts. Whether Colossians and Ephesians are "authentic" letters of Paul remains a matter of dispute. But as our reading of (indisputably Pauline) Romans makes clear (with Martyn's reading of Galatians), the apocalyptic logic of Paul's theology of creation is at the very heart of his gospel to the nations. The powers (false gods, authorities and institutions of human societies, structures of creation) that have not freely acknowledged and submitted to Christ's lordship still do

40. The similarity in Paul's logic here to that in his letter to the Philippians (see above) is unmistakable.
41. See Johnson, *Reading Romans*, 136–38.
42. Martyn, *Theological Issues*, 122.

what they can to assail the new creation that is now invading their old-creation territory. The powers beyond the community of Christ often show no signs of redemption—otherwise why would they attack the church, as it is presumed they do in Romans 8:35–39?—and so in themselves, that is, in their self-presumed autonomy, they provide no reliable point of departure for a theology of "the orders of creation" or of "natural law." God continues providentially to use these powers in their own spheres, but this is not a matter of the powers doing freely what they were originally intended to do as the good creatures of God.[43] Like the Gentiles without Christ, the rebellious powers remain subjected to futility and enslaved to dissolution. That the creation remains relatively habitable, cosmos and not chaos, indeed, a good place to live, is not attributable to a great benevolence inherent in the powers—as the powers themselves would like their subjects to think (cf. Luke 22:25)—but to *God's* providential kindness and patience, the faithfulness and justice by which he holds the creation together, through the instrumentality of the powers, until his righteousness is revealed—until the apocalypse of Jesus Christ (see Rom. 2:4; 3:4–5, 21–26). Then, under the lordship of Christ, through the power of the Spirit, within the community of the new creation, the powers may be restored to their proper purpose.

A theology of "the orders of creation" must therefore begin with Christ, the Spirit, and the *ekklēsia* in its concrete worship and obedience in time and place. Does the *ekklēsia* show forth a model of ordered, structured existence that is conformed to the image of Christ in his cross—that is, does the church present a model of the powers redeemed? Where it does, something of creation in its divinely intended wholeness may be glimpsed. The truth about creation is a christocentric, ecclesiocentric, apocalyptic truth. In this context the "orders of creation" are taken account of not as an unchanging set of relationships (an ontology), but as "the powers"—plural in number, rebellious and therefore threatening to the *ekklēsia*, nonautonomous in relation to Christ's lordship, and therefore within the scope of reconciliation and redemption, a redemption which has a beginning in the *ekklēsia*.[44] This

---

43. "The notion of an order of creation is not necessarily all wrong, but since sin came into the world we cannot discern which traits of 'the way things are' are the way God wants them and which are fallen, disobedient, and oppressive"; Yoder, *Body Politics*, 26–27.

44. I believe something like this is being claimed also by Bernd Wannenwetsch in "The Political Worship of the Church: A Critical and Empowering Practice," *Modern Theology* 12 (1996): 269–99. He writes, "The church, living faithfully to her worship as the particular event bearing the church over and over again, must not trace her practice back to an ontological level. She must refrain from the wish to have something 'more solid' in the background which exceeds her vulnerable practice." God "institutes" a practice, the ministry of reconciliation. "*Insofar* as the church lives up to this ministry, from which her own life is derived, she is enabled to live peacefully. Thus her very being is determined not by ontology but by practice, so that worship is at the same time the critical and forming power of the church." Such faithful worship amounts to the "eschatological removal of ontologies" (or orders of creation), and itself constitutes the church's witness, which "is to become involved in the non-violent struggle against the rule of violence, which [its] Lord already has fought and won" (276–77).

much, I believe, can be said on the basis of a reading of Romans 8. We must now see how this Pauline theology of creation is worked out concretely in Yoder's social ethics.

The Church among the Powers:
New Creation, Creative Transformation, Victorious Patience

It is now clear Yoder takes the church to be the primary sphere in which Christ's triumph, reconciliation, and redemption with respect to the powers becomes visible as a way of life. We can expect that Christ's work vis-à-vis the powers will have its most radical effect on the sociopolitical structures of that other *polis* within which those who confess the lordship of Christ live, that is, on the social body called "church." In other words, we would expect Yoder now to turn his attention to ecclesiology in *The Politics of Jesus*. He does not, however, do so. Rather, he first (chap. 9) examines New Testament texts (the so-called *Haustafeln,* or household codes in Colossians, Ephesians, and 1 Peter) that describe the impact the gospel must have on some social structures that members of the early Christian communities share in common with the wider world, namely the extended household relationships of husband and wife, parent and child, master and slave. Following that (chap. 10) he directs attention to Romans 13 and its instructions regarding the relationship of the Christian community to the "governing authorities." In fact, Yoder does not make any explicit attempt at ecclesiology in *The Politics of Jesus*, and for this reason, I suggest, he leaves himself open to a serious challenge with respect to his discussion of the *Haustafeln*—a challenge that might have been avoided had Yoder followed more carefully Paul's (or "Paul's") own approach to the issues in the household codes.

Yoder elsewhere wrote extensively on ecclesiology, perhaps more extensively than on any other subject.[45] His vision of the church as the primary locus of God's new creation through the reordering of social structures must be placed *before* what he has to say about the *Haustafeln* and the "governing authorities." Only thus can a proper account of "the politics of Paul" according to Yoder be outlined. So I must turn for a moment to sources other than *The Politics of Jesus;* in fact, primarily to a book which must be regarded as the essential ecclesiological companion to *The Politics of Jesus;* its title should already make this clear: *Body Politics.*

45. Yoder's *Body Politics* is the fullest single treatment of ecclesial practice. For the best representative sampling of Yoder's essays on ecclesiology, see *The Royal Priesthood: Essays Ecclesiological and Ecumenical* (ed. Michael G. Cartwright; Grand Rapids: Eerdmans, 1994). The introductory essay, "Radical Reform, Radical Catholicity: John Howard Yoder's Vision of the Faithful Church," by the editor is an excellent study of Yoder's ecclesiology. Yoder's *Fullness of Christ* focuses primarily on the theme of "universal ministry," that is, the ministry of all believers in contrast to the notion of a separate, ordained ministry.

New Creation: The Ekklēsia as Body Politics

I have already noted above that Yoder makes the claim in *The Politics of Jesus* that "the church must be a sample of the kind of humanity" within which the destructive and disordering effects of the powers (e.g., poverty and racism) are undone or reversed (*Politics of Jesus*, 151). The concrete sociopolitical reality of the gathered community in Christ must come to reflect the actual lordship of Christ over the powers. The church must be a living example of the new creation in Christ, a paradigm of humanity's sociopolitical healing:

> The Christian community, like any community held together by commitment to important values, *is* a political reality. That is, the church has the character of a *polis* . . . , namely a structured social body. It has its ways of making decisions, defining membership, and carrying out common tasks. That makes the Christian community a political entity in the simplest meaning of the term. . . .
>
> The will of God for human socialness as a whole is prefigured by the shape to which the Body of Christ is called. Church and world are not two compartments under separate legislation or two institutions with contradictory assignments, but two levels of the pertinence of the same Lordship. The people of God is called to be today what the world is called to be ultimately.[46]

In spelling out specifically what that means, Yoder draws heavily on Pauline texts to identify the structures and practices which constitute the *ekklēsia* and to show how these reflect the new social order which God is bringing into being through Christ and the Spirit in the church, as the church freely submits to his lordship in a way that the world does not. I will briefly outline those which are most directly rooted in Pauline texts.

What does the *ekklēsia* look like when it gathers? Yoder notes that the term *ekklēsia* has its original home in the ancient Greek *polis*; it is the town meeting, the assembly of full citizens in a given city to enact the city's business.[47] What was the "business" which the early Christian assemblies were to conduct? In a variety of essays and most expansively in *Body Politics*, Yoder

---

46. *Body Politics*, viii–ix.

47. "The popular assembly of the competent full citizens of the *polis*, city"; Lothar Coenen, "Church, Synagogue," in *The New International Dictionary of New Testament Theology* (ed. Colin Brown; Grand Rapids: Zondervan, 1975), 1:291. This article spells out in illuminating detail how the *ekklēsia* functioned in the ancient *polis* and also how the term in the Septuagint incorporates the idea of the people of God and the synagogue. Coenen goes on to note that for Paul the term "represents for this place [i.e., in a particular city] God's new creation, the eschatological order of salvation and thus the people of God. . . . Coming together . . . must be reckoned an essential element in *ekklēsia* (cf. 1 Cor. 11:18). Hence the *ekklēsia* can be thought of in purely concrete terms, and any spiritualizing in the dogmatic sense of an invisible church . . . is unthinkable for Paul" (299). Dunn denies any significance in the original political setting of the term (*Theology of Paul the Apostle*, 537). By contrast, Yoder's political understanding of the Pauline *ekklēsia* which I explicate here is supported by, among others, Richard A. Horsley, "1 Corinthians: A Case Study of Paul's Assembly as an Alternative Society," in *Paul and Empire: Religion*

lists five practices that characterized the early church's gathered life: "fraternal admonition," "the universality of charisma," "the Spirit's freedom in the meeting," "breaking bread," and "induction into the new humanity."[48] According to Yoder, each of these is a specific, noncultic, nonesoteric practice by which the community lives the new way of life in Christ in the power of the Holy Spirit—and "before the watching world." The one practice of these five that is less specifically rooted in Pauline texts is that of "fraternal admonition" or "binding and loosing." This practice is prescribed in Matthew 18:15–20, where Jesus sets out a process whereby a community member who sins may be admonished by another member, with a view to confession, forgiveness, and the restoration of the offending member to the community. Yoder finds testimony to this practice also in Paul, particularly in Galatians 6:1–2, but he does not develop his discussion in relation to that text. Thus, while the practice of fraternal admonition plays an important role in Yoder's ecclesiology, I will not give it further attention here.[49] Each of the other four practices is deeply rooted in Pauline texts that Yoder explicates in the development of his ecclesiology.

"Breaking bread" or the Lord's Supper or Eucharist is the practice of table fellowship in the Christian community. It is very concretely the practice of sharing food at a common meal. Yoder interprets Jesus' instruction, "Do this," as meaning, "Whenever you gather for the common meal" (*Body Politics*, 14–16). As a "simple social fact" in the early Jesus movement, "men and women left their jobs, homes, and families to constitute with Jesus a new 'family,' a community of consumption, in which he exercised the role of head-of-the-household" (17). As the head of the household, Jesus gave thanks (Eucharist) and distributed food to all at his table. That was to become the pattern for all times and places when people gather in his name around a common meal. Central to this pattern "is that people were actually sharing with one another their ordinary day-to-day material sustenance" (20). As such, the first and primary purpose of the meal is not as a ritual to "stand for" or "signify" something else; rather, "bread *is* daily sustenance. Bread eaten together *is* economic sharing" (20, emphasis original). The primary purpose of the meal is to ensure that none of the members of the family of Jesus are in need of the basic materials to sustain life, indeed, to ensure precisely that the poor are fed. Economic sharing in the name *Jesus* is at the

---

and Power in Roman Imperial Society (ed. Richard A. Horsley; Harrisburg, Pa.: Trinity, 1997), 242–52; and Michael J. Gorman, *Cruciformity: Paul's Narrative Spirituality of the Cross* (Grand Rapids: Eerdmans, 2001), 349–67.

48. This list of the practices is taken from Yoder's essay "Sacrament as Social Process: Christ the Transformer of Culture," in *Royal Priesthood*, 360–73. The same five practices are presented in a different order and with different names in *Body Politics*: "binding and loosing," "the fullness of Christ," "the rule of Paul," "breaking bread," and "baptism."

49. In addition to chap. 1 in *Body Politics*, see "Binding and Loosing," in *Royal Priesthood*, 323–58.

heart of eucharistic practice. Referring in particular to 1 Corinthians 11:17–34, Yoder argues that the meal is also the place at which social stratification is rendered null and void. To continue to observe social rank and economic standing at the meal, as happened in the Corinthian church in a division between rich and poor, is to contradict the basic character of the Eucharist as the table at which Christ alone is host, and everyone is welcomed by him on the same terms—as servants of one another (18, 22). On the basis of this text in 1 Corinthians, Yoder presents the Eucharist as a practice which challenges worldly economic and social structures and within the community of believers fundamentally alters those structures to conform to the way of the cross.[50]

In similar fashion, Yoder stresses the social and political character of baptism. "Baptism introduces or initiates persons into a new people. The distinguishing mark of this people is that all prior given or chosen identity-definitions are transcended" (*Body Politics*, 28). On the basis of texts such as 2 Corinthians 5:17, Galatians 3:27–28, and Ephesians 2:14–15, Yoder argues that the new creation or new humanity created in Christ, marked by baptism, is not to be understood individualistically as a person receiving a new "nature" or a new "self" in Christ. On the contrary, in Christ a whole new social reality is brought into being in which dividing walls are broken down, former enemies are reconciled, and God creates a new people. The church's mission is to make this fact known and celebrate it as a reality in its life together, in the concrete actions of meeting together, sharing meals, and worshiping the one God of Israel. Commenting on 2 Corinthians 5:17, Yoder writes: "The messianic age has begun; Paul simply proclaims that fact. He does not seek to bring it about, as it were for him or his readers to attain. What they are to do is only to announce and celebrate it. Because it has begun, status differences—whether sexual, ritual, ethnic, or economic—are overarched in a new reality" (37).[51] Baptism into Christ is a

---

50. Traditional interpretation focuses on 1 Cor. 11:28–29 and understands the Corinthian eucharistic problem to be "a disagreement about the interpretation of the elements of the Lord's Supper or a simple deficiency in piety in its observance"; Dale B. Martin, *The Corinthian Body* (New Haven: Yale University Press, 1995), 74; cf. 194. Martin, with many others, understands the "divisions" among the Corinthians to be primarily socioeconomic in character. Martin's discussions of this passage (74–75, 194–96) are illuminating in many ways. See also the excellent treatments by Markus Barth, *Rediscovering the Lord's Supper: Communion with Israel, with Christ, and among the Guests* (Atlanta: John Knox, 1988), 42–76; and Richard Hays, *First Corinthians* (Louisville: John Knox, 1997), 192–206.

51. Second Cor. 5:11–20 plays a significant role in Yoder's ecclesiology and theology of mission. He addresses the translation and interpretation of this text at length in "The Apostle's Apology Revisited," in *The New Way of Jesus: Essays Presented to Howard Charles* (ed. William Klassen; Newton, Kans.: Faith & Life, 1980), 115–34. Cf. the comment by Ralph P. Martin on 2 Cor. 5:17: "Paul is not describing *in this context* the personal dimension of a new birth; rather he is announcing as a kerygmatic statement *the advent of a new creation 'in Christ,'* the dramatic recovery of the world, formerly alienated and dislocated, by God who has acted eschatologically in Christ, i.e., the world is placed now under his rule"; *2 Corinthians* (Word Biblical Commentary 40; Waco: Word, 1986), 146 (emphasis original).

person's entry into and participation in that new social reality, the reality of reconciliation and friendship among those who were formerly strangers and enemies.

Of all the ecclesial practices that Yoder addresses, he devotes more attention to that of ministry than to any other. Note that Yoder does not write about "*the* ministry," except to criticize the very concept of "the religious specialist" and "professionalism" in ministry.[52] While the two previously discussed practices call for a redefinition of their meaning to include or reemphasize their social relevance, the practices nonetheless remain and are nameable by familiar terms: Eucharist, baptism. With respect to ministry, however, Yoder proposes a significant revolution of the shape of the *ekklēsia* in which, extending the meaning of Galatians 3:28, "there is no longer ordained or lay"; where "the ministry" of a few ordained persons is replaced by the "universal ministry" of everyone in the congregation on the basis of the gifts which Christ gives to the *ekklēsia* out of his fullness (cf. Eph. 4:7–16). "According to the standard account, a very few persons—one or, at the most, two or three in a congregation or parish—has the special role of 'minister.' Only this especially qualified person can do the special thing that makes the church what it is supposed to be" (*Body Politics*, 48). In stark contrast to that standard account (which is prevalent in virtually all denominations), Paul, in 1 Corinthians 12, Romans 12, and Ephesians 4 (cf. also 1 Pet. 4:8–11), "describe[s] a new mode of group relationships, in which every member of a body has a distinctly identifiable, divinely validated and empowered role"; in which "*every* member is the bearer of . . . a 'manifestation of the Spirit for the common good' (1 Cor. 12:7)"; where "the dignity of every part of the organism should lead his [Paul's] readers to ascribe the greater value to the less honored members"; in which "Paul tells his readers to see all of this diversity of enablements as a specific working of God the Spirit, present in, with, and under a particular pattern of social process" (47–48, emphasis original). In Ephesians 4:7–10 (which incorporates Ps. 68:18) the universal ministry of all believers is in fact one of the sure signs of Christ's triumph over the powers and the introduction of a new social order as a result: "It had to be achieved by Christ; it is a part of the triumphal procession of YHWH/Adonai leading captives in his train and sharing with his people the booty of his victory" (49). The new social order based on sharing gifts is thus "not mere human potential"; it is, rather, "a miracle" (48).

According to Yoder, for Paul "this pattern for the definition of roles in the group differed profoundly from the patterns that already were present in his world, just as it differs profoundly from our own. Sharing roles was

---

52. See chap. 1: "The Universality of the Religious Specialist," and chap. 6: "Professionalism," in *Fullness of Christ*, 1–8, 71–83; see also *Body Politics*, 55–58. While the present account follows the discussion in *Body Politics*, Yoder's treatment of the theme of ministry in *Fullness of Christ* is much more complete.

not a culturally available social model" (*Body Politics*, 48). There was and is always the tendency to overvalue some gifts or roles and depreciate others. In the Corinthian community in Paul's time some of the gifts were exalted above the others as being more "spiritual"; in later times, right up to the present day, some functions of ministry are exalted above others and "ordained." These recurring habits—Yoder calls them "the powerful alternative" (55)—run against the grain of Paul's vision of ministry. Hence, to work to pry open the "ordained" ministry or priesthood to a greater inclusiveness (e.g., to women or other "underrepresented" groups) is simply to perpetuate the mistake. The problem is the notion of "the" ministry itself.[53] Nor should the Pauline vision be mistaken for modern egalitarianism, individualism, antiauthoritarianism, or antistructuralism. Rather, Paul "confesses, even proclaims, that in the midst of a fallen world the grace of God has apportioned to everyone, without merit, a renewed potential for dignity in complementarity" for the purpose of building up the one social organism, the body of Christ (55). Here the Pauline teaching about the powers has as its goal a christologically and pneumatologically defined vision of the new-creation community, in which the ancient and present worldly structures of domination are uprooted and replaced by Jesus' pattern of service and gift-giving for the common good. That is the basis for the kind of sociality and the kind of politics in the *ekklēsia* that would present to the wider world a concrete image of the new order in Christ and the Spirit that is replacing the old.[54]

Finally, Yoder presents the practice which he calls "the rule of Paul." This phrase (originating among Zwingli and the early Anabaptists) refers to Paul's instructions in 1 Corinthians 14 about how the church is to conduct its meeting. "Paul tells his readers that everyone who has something to say, something given by the Holy Spirit to him or her to say, can have the floor. The others who were speaking before are instructed to yield the floor to him or her" (*Body Politics*, 61). The purpose of the assembly of believers is to engage in a process of discernment about the ongoing shape of the com-

53. "There are as many ministerial roles as there are members of the body of Christ, and that means that more than half of them belong to women. . . . To let a few women into an office that men have for generations wrongly restricted and that did not even exist in the apostolic churches may be a good kind of 'affirmative action,' but it is hardly the most profound vision of renewal. To debate about feminine access to the patriarchally defined ministry is like trying to say that Golda Meir, Margaret Thatcher, or Indira Gandhi transformed the nature of power politics" (*Body Politics*, 60). The analogy in that last sentence should not be taken lightly. Yoder wants to see the "power politics" of the churches transformed. Will the churches' politics reflect the politics of Jesus? That is the question that the Pauline notion of the universal ministry addresses.

54. Dunn's treatment of the church as a "charismatic community" and of ministry in the church in Paul's theology is illuminating and largely supportive of Yoder's reading of ministry in the Pauline churches; see *Theology of Paul the Apostle*, 552–64, 580–86. By making a distinction between ministry and authority, Dunn provides a more nuanced description of the ministry of women in the Pauline churches (586–93).

munity's faithfulness. A model of such discernment is provided in the account in Acts 15, the so-called Council of Jerusalem, where a decision about the acceptance of Paul's mission and of uncircumcised Gentiles was made based on open discussion and consensus about what "seemed good to the Holy Spirit and to us" (Acts 15:28). The practice of the open meeting is rooted in the conviction that the Holy Spirit does indeed guide the church and in "the trust that truth will be found in open conversation" (69) where different, sometimes opposing or minority, points of view are heard. The promise of this manner of discernment is that it "will enable wholesome and realistic flexibility in adapting to local occasions and needs" and, "because Jesus Christ is always and everywhere the same, any procedure that yields sovereignty to the direction of his spirit will have ultimately to create unity" (70).

In another important essay on this practice Yoder speaks of it as the basic form of the church's "practical moral reasoning," the "communal hermeneutic" by which the church asks and answers the questions of the character of its ongoing obedience in particular times and places.[55] Here Yoder explicates in more detail the kinds of contributions that go into congregational discernment by speaking specifically of various "agents" necessary to the process. The process requires "agents of direction," the "prophets" of whom Paul speaks in 1 Corinthians 14:3, and those who "weigh" the words of the prophets in 14:29. It requires "agents of memory," those who bring the light of Scripture (the "collective scribal memory") to bear on the questions at hand. It requires "agents of linguistic self-consciousness," the *didaskaloi* or teachers who are able to analyze and clarify the terms and context of the discussion, though of these there will be only a few in the community, and they must be aware of the dangers of their particular function (James 3:18). There will be "agents of order and due process," those who are "accountable for assuring that everyone else is heard, and that the conclusions reached are genuinely consensual."[56]

"The rule of Paul" at work is the community's authority to discern what the Holy Spirit is telling the church in the present.[57] For Yoder, that everyone within the community (dissenters included) is involved in the process of discernment is evidence that the ancient and present structures of interpretive oligarchy are to be decisively routed and replaced by a structure in which everyone is regarded as a potential instrument of the Spirit's speaking

---

55. "The Hermeneutics of Peoplehood," in *Priestly Kingdom*, 15–45. For what follows see 28–34.

56. Ibid., 33.

57. Dunn's accounts of "the authority of the congregation" and "discerning the spirits" in *Theology of Paul the Apostle*, 593–98, lend support to Yoder's reading of 1 Cor. 14. A full theological account of what Yoder calls "the hermeneutics of peoplehood," in many respects similar to Yoder's, is provided by Stephen E. Fowl, *Engaging Scripture: A Model for Theological Interpretation* (Oxford: Blackwell, 1998); see also Stephen E. Fowl and L. Gregory Jones, *Reading in Communion: Scripture and Ethics in Christian Life* (Grand Rapids: Eerdmans, 1991), in which the authors declare indebtedness to Yoder (24–25 n. 20).

and guiding and in which final judgments about communal direction are a matter of consensus following open discussion.[58]

My primary point in describing briefly each of these ecclesial practices which Yoder finds in Pauline texts is to show that in just these ways he depicts the church as a "body politic" in which the "principalities and powers," those created-yet-fallen social and political structures necessary for human life, undergo a fundamental transformation. The church is the sociopolitical sphere where the lordship of Christ is willingly and openly declared and practiced by its citizens; as such it is the *polis* in which Christ's conquest, reconciliation, and redemption of the powers/structures is (or ought to be) actualized in the world. These practices are "sacraments," because when they are engaged, God is working. "Each is a way God acts" (*Body Politics*, 71). "They are actions of God, in and with, through and under what men and women do. Where they are happening, the people of God is real in the world" (72–73). But being sacraments does not render the practices religious. Quite the contrary. Precisely as one *polis* among many, or rather as *the polis* among others, the people of God engage in practices which are in some sense recognizable by the other cities and nations of the world—recognizable as ways of social and political life. The strangeness or otherness of the ecclesial *polis* is not that it engages in practices of another order or kind (say, religious or spiritual) but that it engages in sociopolitical practices in the new way of Jesus Christ. Yoder writes of "the new humanity as pulpit and paradigm." The church's practices proclaim good sociopolitical news to the world.

> In each case [of the several practices] the shape of grace is described and prescribed *and practiced* in the early church as a social process pattern, *enabled* and *mandated* as a part of the good news of redemption. Yet in each case that way of interacting in the faith community is so concrete, so accessible, so "lay," that it is also a model for how any society, not excluding the surrounding "public" society, can also form its common life more humanely. The church is called to live, and is beginning to live (to the extent we get the point), in the way to which the whole world is called.[59]

Or, as Yoder (interpreting Barth) states in another way, in an essay entitled "The Paradigmatic Public Role of God's People":

---

58. The issue which Yoder does not address is the fact that Paul himself speaks with apostolic authority, an authority with which he interprets Scripture and provides binding instruction for his churches. The question is whether in the postapostolic era this authority dissolves into the Scriptures which the church receives from the apostles and the congregations as interpretive communities or whether God also provides the church with an ongoing teaching authority, an "apostolic succession," through which the congregations are instructed.

59. "The New Humanity as Pulpit and Paradigm," in *For the Nations*, 46 (emphasis original).

> *The order of the faith community constitutes a public offer to the entire society* ... It is not that first we set about being a proper church and then in a later move go about deciding to care prophetically for the rest of the world. To participate in the transforming process of becoming the faith community *is itself* to speak the prophetic word, *is itself* the beginning of the transformation of the cosmos.[60]

This is an important point to make before we move to an examination of Yoder's understanding of the *Haustafeln* in *The Politics of Jesus*. While Christ is already Lord of all families and peoples, cities and nations, not all make the good confession that it is so. The visibility of Christ's lordship will or ought to be most radically evident among those who make that confession, not only in word but also in deed. This is the primary form of the church's sociopolitical witness. But there are many forms of human life beyond and sometimes overlapping with the form of life of the Christian community. Some of these forms, the social and political structures and institutions of life in the world (the powers), will be directly impacted by the fact that followers of Jesus live in and among them, perhaps even, under some circumstances, as the "majority." Where possible, and in a manner consistent with their own confession of the triumph of the Crucified One, Christians will not only be there among the rebellious powers, but also seek their transformation according to the way of Jesus.[61] According to Yoder, this is what Paul aims for in the instructions to first-century households.

Creative Transformation: The Household Codes

Chapter 9 of *The Politics of Jesus*, "Revolutionary Subordination," is a treatment of the so-called *Haustafeln,* or household/domestic codes in Colossians 3:8–4:1; Ephesians 5:21–6:9; and 1 Peter 2:13–3:7.[62] Yoder chooses these texts for many reasons. First, in them we encounter concretely the social structures (in terms of Yoder's discussion in the previous chapter, "the Powers") that would most directly shape the life-in-the-world of the early believers: husband and wife, parent and child, master and slave. These relationships were the givens of the social context in which the gospel of Jesus Christ was announced and lived. Second, it is worth asking whether there is any sense in which these structures, now under the lordship of Christ in the *ekklēsia*, undergo a process of redemption in which the cross of Christ is the primary shaping power.

60. *For the Nations*, 28–29 (emphasis original).

61. Important treatments of the role of the church among the powers—significantly indebted to Yoder's work but also developing beyond it—are Rodney Clapp, *A Peculiar People: The Church as Culture in a Post-Christian Society* (Downers Grove, Ill.: InterVarsity Press, 1996); Barry Harvey, *Another City: An Ecclesiological Primer for a Post-Christian World* (Harrisburg, Pa.: Trinity, 1999); Philip D. Kenneson, *Beyond Sectarianism: Re-imagining Church and World* (Harrisburg, Pa.: Trinity, 1999); and Duane K. Friesen, *Artists, Citizens, Philosophers: Seeking the Peace of the City: an Anabaptist Theology of Culture* (Scottdale, Pa.: Herald, 2000).

62. I accept, with many scholars, the Pauline authorship of Colossians. I take Ephesians to be a development of the Pauline tradition.

Third, critical exegesis tends to view these texts as borrowed from the wider culture and dropped into the New Testament letters more or less unchanged.

This last point, says Yoder, has three implications. First, "if the early church could borrow from nonbiblical sources of moral insight" (*Politics of Jesus*, 165), if "borrowing ethical guidance from nonbiblical, non-Christian sources is necessary, possible, and legitimate" (165–66), instead of the church developing them out of its own peculiar resources, then there is no reason why Christian social ethics in other times and places should not also borrow from other sources or even be required to do so. Second, in relation to the specific social structures in question (the extended household), social ethics would then amount merely to accepting one's duties vis-à-vis one's role or status in the given order. Third, in this light the social ethics of the early church vis-à-vis the wider world (at the time of the writing of Colossians, Ephesians, and 1 Peter) appears "essentially conservative," a move away from "the radicality of the ethic of Jesus," either to a position of "realistic" compromise with the wider society or to a position of accepting the "orders of creation" as God-given (166–67). Depending on whether one's own social ethics is conservative or progressive, the New Testament authors of these passages will be praised or blamed for this move. Or, perhaps, they will be seen to be engaging in a kind of "natural theology"—and again this can be thought to be for good or ill, depending on one's stance vis-à-vis natural theology.

The question of the sources of the *Haustafeln* thus becomes for Yoder a matter of some significance. In the background of his discussion is the work of Martin Dibelius, who pioneered the form-critical analysis of these texts in his commentary on Colossians, Ephesians, and Philemon.[63] Dibelius argues that the (apocalyptic, enthusiastic) gospel of Jesus was inadequate for Christian communities of the second and third generations, who no longer expected an immediate *parousia* and had to get on with daily life in the societies and cultures of which they were a part. So they adopted moral instructions for the household from the popular Greek philosophy and Jewish *halakah* that were available in their context and so "came to grips with the World."[64]

Over against that understanding of the source of the New Testament household codes, Yoder presents an extended case for finding in them "an ethic that is derived in its shape and in its meaning and even in its language, from the novelty of the teaching and the work and the triumph of Jesus" (*Politics of Jesus*, 179). His argument consists primarily in exposing the points of difference between Stoic codes and those in the New Testament.[65]

63. Martin Dibelius, *An die Kolosser, Epheser und Philemon* (3d ed.; Handbuch zum Neuen Testament 12; Tübingen: Mohr, 1953); cited in Yoder, *Body Politics*, 165 n. 5.

64. Dibelius, *An die Kolosser*, 49; cited by Yoder, *Body Politics*, 165.

65. Yoder follows closely the argument of the 1959 Hamburg dissertation by David Schroeder, *Die Haustafeln des Neuen Testaments: Ihre Herkunft und ihr theologische Sinn*. A statement of Schroeder's thesis may be found in his "Lists, Ethical," in *The Interpreter's Dictionary of the Bible: Supplementary Volume* (ed. Keith Crim; Nashville: Abingdon, 1976), 546–47.

In contrast to the Stoics, who construed morality as living up to one's own nature, the *Haustafeln* call persons to live up to their relationships—the emphasis is on reciprocity between the pairs wife/husband, child/parent, slave/master. Where the Stoic pattern inculcates moral insight into the nature of things, the *Haustafeln* draw their pattern of moral exhortation from the apodictic (direct command) law of the Old Testament—they are imperative in style. The vocabulary is different: for example, the New Testament uses *doulos* (slave) and *kyrios* (master); the Stoics use *oiketai* (slaves) and *despotai* (masters).[66] The Stoic codes address the "dominant man in society" while in the *Haustafeln* the instruction "is addressed *first to the subject.*" "The *subordinate* person in the social order is *addressed as a moral agent*" (171, emphasis original). This, for Yoder, is a "revolutionary innovation" in the early church for which there is no parallel in Stoicism.

The "second revolutionary axiom" in the New Testament codes is that the persons at the bottom of the social order are called to be subordinate ("*hypotassein* . . . in the middle voice . . . means 'to accept one's lower place'"; *Politics of Jesus*, 172 n. 23), that is, freely to choose to remain where they are in the social order. In receiving and responding to this command the subordinates are treated as and become moral agents. Further, such "a call to willing subordination is not explainable unless there has been a temptation to insubordination," a temptation "which assumes that they have heard a message which calls into question the subjection they have hitherto not been able to challenge" (175). That is the message about how the gospel and baptism into Jesus Christ placed the early believers into a community where "there is no longer Jew or Greek, there is no longer slave or free, there is no longer male and female; for all of you are one in Christ Jesus" (Gal. 3:28). "Where had they heard such a message if not from Paul?" (175). In another crucial point of difference, while the Stoic ethic is about doing "what is fitting," the New Testament message is consistently about doing what is fitting "in the Lord" or according to the pattern of Jesus.

Finally, another revolutionary trait of the *Haustafeln* is the way in which, unlike in any other codes, "the *dominant* partner in the relationship [is called] to a kind of subordination in return" (177, emphasis original). This call, of course, makes far more practical, behavioral difference for the dominant partner than the call to the subordinate freely to remain as he or she is. Yoder goes on to show how the revolutionary dynamic of the *Haustafeln* is present elsewhere in the New Testament, notably in the difficult Pauline texts on slavery and women in 1 Corinthians 7 and 11.

In light of the fundamental differences which Yoder finds between the Stoic domestic codes and the various New Testament household codes, he

66. Yoder does not make the point that the New Testament rather than the Stoic terms in this pair are consistently those which Paul uses to speak of his own standing vis-à-vis Jesus Christ the Lord. Perhaps he thought this point was simply self-evident.

concludes that there is no evidence that the latter were borrowed from the former. On the contrary, "this kind of teaching was present in the very earliest years of the church. It must have grown directly out of the meaning for the young church of confessing Christ as Lord and the impact that proclamation had upon its listeners. The only remaining source we very logically suspect is that somehow this tradition comes from Jesus" (*Politics of Jesus*, 178–79). It comes from the message of the inbreaking power of the gospel which liberates believers from bondage to "the enslaving or alienating powers of this world" (185), to live in the freedom of obedience to Christ and service to the neighbor. That freedom is not a freedom simply to overthrow the existing social structures: "The new world or the new regime under which we live is not a simple alternative to present experience but rather a renewed way of living within the present" (185). Mutual subordination as shown in the *Haustafeln* and elsewhere in Paul's letters is intrinsic to the missionary task of the church. It is a pattern of "creative transformation":

> Since in the resurrection and in Pentecost the kingdom which was imminent has now in part come into our history, the church can now live out, within the structures of society, the newness of life of that kingdom. The early church did not need to borrow from Stoicism the concept of living one's own role. The apostles rather transformed the concept of living within a role by finding *how in each role the servanthood of Christ, the voluntary subordination of one who knows that another regime is normative, could be made concrete.* (*Politics of Jesus*, 187, emphasis added)

In other words, the given social structures in the world into which the gospel is announced and lived are neither accepted in their sheer facticity as "the way things are" nor are they simply rejected as the instruments of oppression. Rather, they are invaded by the gospel and become something that, apart from the gospel, they could never become—the means by which the cross of Jesus Christ is made concretely visible as the way of life. Perhaps the structures themselves will change, not only in the new community but also in the wider society through the living testimony of the followers of Jesus to another way of living socially. Whether wider social structures change or whether the gospel is proclaimed in a context where the structures are very different from those of first-century Greco-Roman society, the way of the cross remains normative in every time and place.

In his 1994 epilogue to "Revolutionary Subordination" Yoder writes: "No other single chapter provoked as much angry objection as this one when *The Politics of Jesus* first appeared." This was because, Yoder suggests, it failed to announce a form of "liberation as the preferred agenda of our age," and it failed to uphold "the autonomy of the independent individual [which] is the center of the modern liberal vision" (*Politics of Jesus*, 188). In the footnotes of the 1972 edition Yoder frequently warned against anachronism (167 n.

10, 173–75 nn. 25–28, 30), noting in particular how the "doctrinaire egalitarianism of our culture" distorts our ability to read these texts in their own social contexts and see in them something revolutionary in view of the fact that "Jesus' suffering is the law of his disciples' life" (174 n. 25, 175 n. 30). Still, contrary to his own intentions, Yoder's argument was taken to support the entrenchment of oppressive patriarchal patterns present in the *Haustafeln*, rather than to destabilize those patterns under the implications of the cross and Christology. Even Hays, a reader clearly sympathetic toward and deeply indebted to Yoder's contribution to Christian social ethics, finds the argument unpersuasive, suggesting that in this chapter Yoder "leans toward apologetic wishful thinking."[67] That is a rather surprising judgment from Hays, since his own treatment of Ephesians 5:21–6:9 repeats the central claims of Yoder's discussion: the call to mutual submission in Ephesians 5:21 subverts "conventional authority structures of the ancient household . . . even while they are left in place"; the subordinate persons in the relationships are addressed "as moral agents who must *choose* to be subject" (emphasis original);[68] there is reciprocity in that the dominant person in the relationship is also called to self-sacrificial care of the subordinate; the "commandments laid down" in the code "are warranted by the gospel." "In all these respects, then, the household code of Ephesians articulates a vision for community whose social relations are impacted by the gospel of Jesus Christ." Further, while "the vision is not egalitarian, if measured anachronistically by twentieth-century ideals of social equality," nonetheless "the conventional patterns" of the relationships are "unsettled" and "deconstructed" with a view to greater maturity in the relationships over time.[69]

In other words, Hays's reading, while perhaps more qualified than Yoder's, nonetheless seems to corroborate the main thrust of Yoder's most important points. Yoder's argument is further corroborated in the household code in 1 Peter 2:13–3:7 by Miroslav Volf. Volf argues that to regard that code as an example of the early churches' cultural accommodation for the sake of wider societal acceptance is mistaken. The instructions in 1 Peter are issued primarily in response to opposition and injustice coming from the wider social world; under those conditions the exhortations in the letter "are in fact an example of differentiated acceptance and rejection of the surrounding culture."[70] The church's identity in 1 Peter is christologically and eschatologically established; it is not established in mere opposition to the world. In fact, as Volf shows, the church continues to live in the midst of the old cre-

67. Hays, *Moral Vision*, 246. Reading Hays against a background of study in Yoder's theology will reveal how (perhaps often subliminally) indebted Hays is to Yoder.

68. At this point Hays refers in a footnote to Yoder's chapter.

69. Hays, *Moral Vision*, 64–65.

70. Miroslav Volf, "Soft Difference: Theological Reflections on the Relation between Church and Culture in 1 Peter," *Ex Auditu* 10 (1994): 8, an on-line article accessed October 26, 2000, at http://www.northpark.edu/sem/exauditu/papers/volf.html.

ation and to draw selectively from the old, even as the apparent stability of
the old creation is called into question by the presence in the church of a
new way of being in the world shaped by the life, death, and resurrection of
Christ. It is precisely by being consistent with the nonviolent way of Jesus
Christ that the church is present in the world as "witness and invitation," as
"soft difference" lived without guile, as "ontic gentleness," rather than as violent opposition to worldly order.[71] "A gentleness that refuses to help itself
with guile is no strategy of the weak. It is the open life-stance of the strong,
who feel no need to support their own uncertainty by aggression toward
others. Gentleness is the flip-side of respect for the other."[72] This, according
to Volf, is what we see reflected in 1 Peter and in particular in the instructions of the household code—not cultural accommodation nor a survival
strategy nor even simply a "missionary method" whereby those still outside
the church might be converted or the social orders changed. "Rather, the
soft difference is the missionary side of following in the footsteps of the crucified Messiah."[73] It is the church being true to its specific identity. Yoder
could not have said it better.

While Hays does not make it quite clear why he thinks Yoder's argument
is "apologetic wishful thinking," a good deal of scholarship on the *Haustafeln*
may support Hays's judgment, though possibly for a different reason—a reason that exposes what to my mind is a significant weakness in this chapter of
The Politics of Jesus. Yoder spends a great deal of effort addressing the question of the *sources* of the New Testament household codes. Since the time of
Dibelius this question has been addressed over and over again, and a variety
of proposals have been made for finding sources in Hellenism (Stoics, Aris-
totle), Hellenistic Judaism, or early Christianity.[74] There is still very little
consensus about possible sources, perhaps less so now than in 1972. If Yoder's argument depends upon establishing scholarly agreement about the
sources of the *Haustafeln*, it is in trouble. Scholarly consensus, however, is
not the issue in the 1972 edition; rather, Yoder appears to want to establish
that no source in the literary domain is available to the authors of the New
Testament *Haustafeln* from which they might have drawn any of the substance of these texts. In other words, Yoder argues that these texts are original, unique, completely different from anything found in the wider culture;
and therefore (which is Yoder's concern here) no appeal can be made to these

71. Ibid., 10–11.

72. Ibid., 10. Cf. Toole, *Waiting for Godot in Sarajevo*, 232–35, 252–57. The intriguing account of
"revolutionary subordination" as "tactical resistance" which Toole offers seems to miss the point that Volf
makes about gentleness being *without guile.*

73. Volf, "Soft Difference," 10.

74. See the bibliography, summary, and discussion in Peter T. O'Brien, *Colossians, Philemon* (Word
Biblical Commentary 44; Waco: Word, 1982), 214–18; and the bibliographies and discussions by John
T. Fitzgerald, "Haustafeln," and David L. Balch, "Household Codes," in *Anchor Bible Dictionary* (ed. D.
N. Freedman et al.; New York: Doubleday, 1992), 3:80–81, 318–20.

texts that would suggest that they warrant Christian cultural accommodation—a "coming to grips with the world," a social conservatism, a theology
of "created orders," or a natural law.

But why would borrowing a given cultural *form* of moral instruction (a
household code) necessarily make way for those kinds of appeal? The crucial
fact about the character of the New Testament household codes is not that
they are original (i.e., not borrowed as a form), but rather that as a fairly
widely used form of moral instruction they have been reshaped by the New
Testament authors in a such way that they are *transformed* by the gospel,
made to conform to the way of the cross as the shape of Christian moral order. In fact, this is what Yoder also shows in and with his argument for the
originality of the New Testament *Haustafeln* within the Jesus tradition. In
the 1994 epilogue Yoder himself seems to agree (without saying so) that the
argument in the first edition for the originality and independence of the
Christian household codes was not very useful. Commenting on a review of
scholarly opinions "on the derivation of the *Haustafeln* substance from the
several environing cultures," Yoder remarks: "For our purposes this does not
matter much; why should there not have been borrowings from all kinds of
sources? Can we really disentangle three quite separate streams? What matters is how those borrowed materials were transformed as they were taken
into the witness of the apostles" (*Politics of Jesus*, 189 n. 55). This comment
stands in rather stark contrast to the oft-repeated claim in the first edition of
this chapter that all of the comparative evidence fails to substantiate any borrowing at all, at least from Stoic sources.

As a matter of fact, what Yoder signals in the 1994 comment, without
dismissing his earlier effort, is a shift in his approach to understanding the
nature of the presence of the Christian community in the wider world and
how that presence establishes the difference of the Christian community
from the wider world—an approach which now looks much more like Volf's
notion of "soft difference." In essays published in 1983 and 1992, Yoder
pays careful attention to the way in which various New Testament writers
both borrow from a given current cultural idiom *and* bend and shape that idiom in such a way that it becomes a fit instrument for the communication of
the gospel.[75] "The evangelical strategy does not accept being walled into a
ghetto by the outside world. Not only does it accept the language of the environs: it seizes it, expropriates it, and uses it to say things that could not
previously have been said in its prior language; nor could they have been
said by anyone else using the world's wider language."[76] While Yoder uses as
examples texts which have more to do with the borrowing and bending of

75. Yoder, "'But We Do See Jesus': The Particularity of Incarnation and the Universality of Truth,"
in *The Priestly Kingdom*, 46–62; and idem, "On Not Being Ashamed of the Gospel: Particularity, Pluralism, and Validation," *Faith and Philosophy* 9 (1992): 285–300.

76. "On Not Being Ashamed of the Gospel," 296.

language and concepts with which to communicate the truth about Jesus (in John 1; Heb. 1; Col. 1; Rev. 4; Phil. 2), the move which Yoder identifies in those texts applies equally to the cultural idiom embedded in social structures. The primary question to ask about Christian existence in the midst of a wider social world is not whether a Christian has borrowed from the world's social structures, nor even whether the social shape of Christian existence is original, distinctive, or unique vis-à-vis its environs:

> To make "distinctiveness" a value criterion is to measure the truth value of meaning system A in terms of the other systems (whether B or C or N or X) that happen to be around, from which [A] is supposed to differ. That is a method mistake. Some of the neighboring systems may be very much like it. Some of them may be historically derived from it, which is true of most of the post-Christian value systems in the West. To ask that Christian thought be *unique* is nonsense. What we should ask of Christian statements is that they be *specifically* or *specifiably* Christian, i.e., true to kind, authentically representing their species. Whether a specifiably Christian statement [or social structure] is "distinctive" depends on the other guy.[77]

Yoder proposes that instead of asking questions about distinctiveness, we employ questions that probe whether what takes shape in a given context (whether linguistic/conceptual or social) is a "valid communication" of the gospel. Those questions (here in relation to concepts, which is Yoder's focus in this essay) are:

- Is the content of what is "said" in the new setting faithful to its origin? This is like a fuller form of asking whether a proposition is "true."
- Is the transition into the "flesh" of the receptor culture accurate? This is like checking the accuracy of a translation from one language to another. No two sentences in two languages can be absolutely identical, but a translation can be adequate.
- Is the "enfleshment" in the host setting authentic, nonimperial, uncoerced?[78]

If we return now to Yoder's discussion of the *Haustafeln*, we find that he does indeed spend too much time asking about their distinctiveness, but these other questions are not ignored. Central to his description of the *Haustafeln* is the claim that the existing social structure of the extended household is precisely the cultural idiom into which the gospel is spoken, and in which it must be-

---

77. Ibid., 294. See also Yoder's "On Not Being in Charge," in *War and Its Discontents: Pacifism and Quietism in the Abrahamic Traditions* (ed. J. Patout Burns; Washington, D.C.: Georgetown University Press, 1996), 87 n. 13.

78. "On Not Being Ashamed of the Gospel," 292.

come enfleshed. It is precisely these actual structures that must become specifiably Christian, "true to type," conformed to the way of the cross. The New Testament writers do not present an ideal type of household structure (whatever that would look like—would it be the egalitarian household of the modern Western world?), a utopia that must then become the distant social goal of the early Christians. Rather, the early recipients of the *Haustafeln* were consistently, in each text, shown the way in which even in those worldly social structures (far from perfect though they be) they were freed to enact their own "translation" of the way of the crucified Christ and thus to transform life within those structures into a visible sign of the gospel's reordering power in the social order, while the more radical enfleshment of gospel social order occurred, as we have already seen, in the actual assembly and practices that constituted the early *ekklēsia* as the people of God in the world.

This reading of the *Haustafeln* by Yoder is nicely corroborated by Bernd Wannenwetsch, which I quote here at some length:

> Whereas the *oikos* [household or realm of the private] hitherto had been structured by the arbitrary power of the *pater familias*—now the patron himself was subject to the apostolic *paranesis* [instruction], which told him to *act at home in exactly the same way as in the public of the church*. "Submit to one another out of reverence for Christ." This phrase in Eph 5:21 represents not so much the beginning of the *Haustafeln* (starting at verse 22 by explicitly addressing women first) as rather a hinge between the *Haustafeln* and the prescriptions given above for the public worship of the church (verses 18–20)—applying to both spheres. More significant still is that the *Haustafeln* also feature exhortations for women and slaves as well as for children. Those who were once restricted to a "pre-political" world (as Aristotle puts it for the household), restricted to mere "behaviour," are now found worthy of the apostolic exhortation concerning how they are to *act* in Christ. Thus in a way the political form is implanted into the *oikos*. On the other hand, we see the public realm in the church not being anxiously enclosed against all moments of the *oikos*, but itself described by terms of emotional and bodily commitment: to love one another as brothers and sisters, share one bread, give one another the kiss of peace, and so on.[79]

Wannenwetsch thus shows, as I have also tried to do, the intimate connection between *ekklēsia* and household in Paul and the deconstruction thereby of the tight boundary between public and private, as the normative sociopolitical existence achieved in the cross of Jesus Christ makes its way not only into the *ekklēsia*, but also into the social structures of daily life.[80]

79. Wannenwetsch, "Political Worship of the Church," 280–81.

80. It would be instructive to compare (as I cannot here) Yoder's treatment of the *Haustafeln* with the reflections by feminist theologian Sarah Coakley on the idea of *kenosis* as it appears in Phil. 2:6–11, the theological tradition, and feminist criticism; see "*Kenosis* and Subversion: On the Repression of 'Vulnerability' in Christian Feminist Writing," in her *Powers and Submissions: Spirituality, Philosophy, and Gender*

Victorious Patience: The Church and the Governing Authorities

The people of God always lives among other peoples. The social and political order of God's new *polis* in Jesus Christ is always being enacted in the
midst of other societies and polities. The lordship of Jesus Christ and the
power of the Holy Spirit are always being exercised in the face of claims to
superiority by other powers, other gods, and other lords. That the church
has often forgotten this, particularly in that long stretch from the time of its
"Constantinian" establishment in the West in the fourth century to its mar-
ginalization in the twentieth century, may be the fundamental reason why
Romans 13:1–7 presents such a massive interpretive stumbling block for
students of Paul.[81] Yoder's aim is not to forget. His own approach to this passage is an extension of the logic of the gospel that he develops throughout
The Politics of Jesus, a logic that leads from the politics of Jesus in Israel to the
politics of Paul and the Pauline churches. Yoder explicates the way in which
Romans 13 is also the good news of Jesus' nonviolent victory over the powers and structures which hold humankind in bondage.

The traditional Protestant approach to Romans 13:1–7 "as the foundation of a Christian doctrine of the state"—an approach which became fundamentally suspect after the rise of Nazism—has, Yoder notes, long since
been abandoned by New Testament scholarship, even as "it persists in the
systematic-theological and ethical thought of Protestants, especially of theologically conservative Protestants" (*Politics of Jesus*, 193). Yoder states that
tradition thus:

> It is that by virtue of the divine institution of government as a part of God's
> good creation, its mandate to wield the sword and the Christian's duty to obey
> the state combine to place upon the Christian a moral obligation to support
> and participate in the state's legal killing (death penalty, war), despite contrary
> duties which otherwise would seem to follow from Jesus' teaching or example.

As a means to unsettle the persistence of that understanding of Romans 13,
Yoder engages in an argument which both challenges many of the wider assumptions which the traditional approach brings to the reading of this text
and offers a close reading of the text itself. First, Yoder observes that Romans
13 is written with respect to a "pagan government" that would certainly have
been seen by Paul as a "power" (*exousia*) in some sense fundamentally
compromised by its paganism, that is, in rebellion against the one God of

---

(Oxford: Blackwell, 2002), 3–39. Coakley's reading of the concept of *kenosis* as crucial to feminist theology is, I believe, very compatible with Yoder's understanding of the transformative power of the cross on
the structures of everyday life.

81. As an indication of the extent of interpretive effort and diversity on Rom. 13:1–7, see the bibliography in Joseph A. Fitzmyer, *Romans* (Anchor Bible 33; New York: Doubleday, 1993), 670–76. This is
the largest bibliography on a single Romans passage in Fitzmyer's entire commentary.

creation. Whatever God may be doing with this *exousia*, it is not a willing participant in God's purpose; quite the contrary, it is willingly and self-consciously serving other gods, other lords. It is idolatrous. Romans 13 can hardly be read as "a kind of charter or constitution for the political realm" (*Politics of Jesus*, 195–96).

Second, Romans 12–13 must be read as a seamless unit that "begins with a call to nonconformity" in Romans 12 and continues with a discussion of "transformed life" within the Christian community and a readiness to suffer at the hands of enemies rather than repay with vengeance (*Politics of Jesus*, 196). Romans 13:8–10 is a call to love the neighbor. "Therefore any interpretation of 13:1–7 which is not also an expression of suffering and serving love must be a misunderstanding of the text in its context" (196). Further, the overarching theme of the entire epistle is about the dynamic movement of "the mercies of God" (12:1) among Gentiles and Jews, "God's triumphant movement from the merciful past into a triumphant future" (197), a future which is even now, in its nearness, pressing in upon the present (13:11–12). Romans 13:1–7 cannot, then, be read as "a static or conservative undergirding of the present social system," since it is precisely that system which is passing away under the pressure of God's saving purpose (197). Finally, the language of vengeance and wrath in 12:9 and 13:4 requires that we read these texts in light of one another. While Christians are never to exercise "wrath," repaying evil for evil, but must rather leave wrath to God, the existing powers *may* be the means by which God exercises his wrath on evildoers. But Paul does not allow us to conclude that, because God may use "idolatrous Assyria (Isa. 10) or Rome" to enact his purpose, these "pagan powers" are morally good or that God's people are obligated to participate in their actions. Paul argues the opposite.

Third, "the subordination [to governing authorities] that is called for recognizes whatever power exists, accepts whatever structure of sovereignty happens to prevail" (*Politics of Jesus*, 198). Paul makes no moral judgment about the existing powers; he neither affirms their actual way of ruling nor presents an ideal of "just" rule. The believers in Rome are neither called to approve of the authorities nor to subordinate themselves only insofar as the authorities live up to the ideal. They are simply called to be subordinate to them. The *exousiai* are there because God "put[s] them in order, sovereignly . . . tell[s] them where they belong, what is their place" (200). In so doing, God may make use of them as a means of ordering human life, but again, that does not mean that God approves of their actions: "God did not approve morally of the brutality whereby Assyria chastised Israel (Isa. 10)" (202).

Fourth, it is very unlikely that the early Roman believers—whether Jews or Gentile members of the Jesus movement—could have (under the existing political situation) participated in the military or police actions of the governing authorities, since such services "were considered either as hereditary professions or as citizens' privileges" (*Politics of Jesus*, 203). When Paul says, "let every person be subject" he can hardly mean that *every* person (women and children too?) must be ready to contribute to the war efforts of the empire, since most would not be allowed to do so.

Fifth, the "sword" which the governing authority wields is for Paul not a symbol of the empire's military dominance over other nations, but of its authority to punish wrongdoing within the empire. The sword represents the internal policing function of the state, which believers are not to resist.

Finally, the call to be subordinate to the governing authorities does not rule out the possibility of discriminating among the actions of those authorities. Romans 13:6 is notoriously difficult to translate, and it is possible that Paul here calls believers to consider "public servants" (*leitourgoi*) as God's servants only insofar as they "continue to attend to" (*proskarterountes*) the right administration of justice to the wrongdoer. Further, the list of "things due" in 13:7 calls for discrimination. "Taxes and revenue, perhaps honor, are due to Caesar, but fear is due to God" (*Politics of Jesus*, 208). Finally, while the call to "be subject" is unqualified (13:1), Paul does not use the verb *obey*. "Subordination is significantly different from obedience. . . . The Christian who refuses to worship Caesar but still permits Caesar to put him or her to death, is being subordinate even though not obeying" (209). This last point again calls to mind the pattern of Jesus Christ who willingly accepted subordination and suffering, while never agreeing to the justice or legitimacy of the verdict that the worldly powers pronounced upon him:

> The willingness to suffer is then not merely a test of our patience or a dead space of waiting; it is itself a *participation in the character of God's victorious patience* with the rebellious powers of his creation. We subject ourselves to government because it was in so doing that Jesus revealed and achieved God's victory. (*Politics of Jesus*, 209, emphasis added)

Christians are thus "not to perceive in the wielding of the sword their own reconciling ministry" (*Politics of Jesus*, 210). Rather, the church's victorious patience and reconciling ministry are the modes of its participation in God's apocalyptic healing of the world through the cross.

Here we see that neither Paul nor Yoder is interested in providing a "theory of the state" through what is said in Romans 13:1–7. Besides being anachronistic eisegesis of Paul's concerns, the attempt to construct such a theory on this text misses three points that *are* central to Paul. First, the "governing authorities" are simply another level of worldly power with which both Jews and the Jesus communities have to do, and those authorities stand in no more positive or negative relation to God's purposes than any other power. The church exists in a tactical relationship to the governing authorities as it does to other authorities, a relationship in which it is the church's task to witness to Christ's defeat of the authorities and powers through the cross by living the way of the cross. Second, the church is empowered for this witness by its knowledge that the "governing authorities" are in fact subordinate to the exalted Jesus Christ (cf. Phil. 2:9–11) and must finally serve God's purposes, whether knowingly and willingly or not. These authorities cannot separate the church from the love of God that is in Christ Jesus. Vis-à-vis the governing authorities and their use of the sword, the subordinate church in Christ is more than conqueror (cf. Rom. 8:35–37), even when it is persecuted.[82] The church is in no sense indebted to nor does it receive any order or mandate from the ruling authorities for its existence, its meaning, its message, or its mission. The church is simply subordinate to the powers that are. Third, the church is free to be thus subordinate because it knows that the destiny of history and the cosmos is not finally in the hands of the ruling authorities, but in the hands of God and his crucified and risen Christ, a destiny that is embodied concretely in the new-creation communities of Christ in the power of the Holy Spirit.

That is about as much as can be said about the state from within a Pauline perspective. For Yoder, following Paul, the true shape and direction of world history is discerned in the apocalypse of God's "imperial rule" in the cross of Christ, not in the power plays of worldly emperors and the rise and fall of worldly empires. In other words, Yoder reads Romans 13 as a section of Pauline writing within the context and perspective of Paul's apocalyptic theology as a whole. In fact, the main contours of that theology with respect to the church's existence vis-à-vis the reality of imperial Rome can be discerned in letters other than Romans. I showed above how the letter to the Philippians has a strong message about the church's relationship to the Roman imperial cult. A similar story can be told about 1 Thessalonians. Once we begin reading Paul politically, we see that Romans 13 is far from being the only Pauline text that addresses the issues of the churches' existence among the powers; and we also begin to see that what Paul writes in Romans

82. Neil Elliott notes the correspondences in language and content between Rom. 8 and Rom. 13 and explores the implications for understanding Rom. 13 in "Romans 13:1–7 in the Context of Imperial Propaganda," in *Paul and Politics: Ekklesia, Israel, Imperium, Interpretation: Essays in Honor of Krister Stendahl* (ed. Richard A. Horsley; Harrisburg, Pa.: Trinity, 2000), 184–204, esp. 194–95. Elliott's reading, while somewhat different from Yoder's, provides substantiation of Yoder's interpretation on many key points. For example, the variations on the verb *tassō* in 13:1–2 are not about Christian obedience to a divinely ordained political institution; rather Paul simply calls the Roman Christians to rank themselves under the political authorities which God "has set in rank" (195). The authorities are part of "the way things are" (cf. Yoder's analysis of "the powers") and as such must be reckoned with. For another intriguing and illuminating but also problematic reading of this text, see Mark Nanos, "Romans 13:1–7: Christian Obedience to Synagogue Authority," in his *Mystery of Romans: The Jewish Context of Paul's Letter* (Minneapolis: Fortress, 1996), 289–336. The "expanded contextual translation" which Nanos provides (334–36) gives a quick overview of his interpretation of 13:1–8. Nanos's perspective is especially valuable in stressing that any misbehavior (e.g., not paying taxes) of believing Gentiles in Rome would have a direct impact on the Jews in Rome, with whom the Gentile believers would be in close contact, and that this would be a matter of concern for Paul. This insight that Elliott exploits is missing in Yoder.

13 is both illuminated by and consistent with what he says elsewhere. Paul sometimes displays little more than holy indifference to worldly rulers and at other times little less than holy opposition, but nowhere does he display an embrace of the "ruling authorities."[83] God's apocalypse in Jesus Christ radically relativizes the significance of the Roman imperium within a wider and finally more decisive political reality—the victory of Jesus Christ over the powers:

> The crucified Jesus is a more adequate key to understanding what God is about in the real world of empires and armies and markets than is the ruler in Rome, with all his supporting military, commercial, and sacerdotal networks.
>
> In Jesus we have a clue to which kinds of causation, which kinds of community-building, which kinds of conflict management, go with the grain of the cosmos, of which we know, as Caesar does not, that Jesus is both Word (the inner logic of things) and the Lord ("sitting at the right hand"). It is not that we begin with a mechanistic [or otherwise fated] universe and then look for cracks and chinks where a little creative freedom might sneak in (for which we would then give God credit): it is that we confess the deterministic world to be enclosed within, smaller than, the sovereignty of the God of the Resurrection and Ascension. (*Politics of Jesus*, 246)

In dependence upon that sovereignty the church waits, prays, and acts in anticipation of the coming great revolution, in which the great rulers, powers, and authorities of the world are led in triumphal procession as the captives of Jesus Christ the Lord.

A Future for Yoder's Paul?

Does Paul have a politics, and if so what is its shape? By asking that question, a question rarely before asked so pointedly and persistently as Yoder did in 1972, indeed, a question which would have been thought to lead down irrelevant paths, Yoder was able to discover a Paul that had rarely before been seen. Previous Pauline theologies were often structured around Paul's Christology, anthropology, an *ordo salutis* focused on individual salvation and, to be sure, discussions of the church and sacraments and the Christian's "duty to the state." But the rubric *the politics of Paul* as a means of presenting a coherent sketch of the whole of Paul's theology was unheard of. Yoder's achievement is surely impressive in this historical light.

83. This assessment differs from that of Cassidy, *Paul in Chains*, who argues that in Rom. 13 Paul is "extremely accommodative" to imperial Rome, while in Philippians, when Paul is himself suffering in Rome at the hands of the governing authorities, he has changed from an accommodative to a resistant approach to the Roman imperium. I believe Cassidy is right about Philippians (as I show above), but fails to account for the apocalyptic context within which Paul's discussion of the ruling authorities is set in Rom. 13.

Of course, as he himself insisted, Yoder was building on a substantial body of Pauline scholarship available to him in 1972. For one thing, the emphasis on Pauline apocalyptic, crucial to Yoder's understanding, had been around for some time, going back as far as Albert Schweitzer. While that emphasis was not at first seen for its social, historical, and political significance, it at least set the stage for asking the question whether and how Pauline apocalyptic might be of such significance, if its claims to say something about history and the cosmos are taken seriously.

In another line of development, not unrelated to the recovery of Paul's apocalyptic mode but distinct from it, the basic character of Paul's conversion and mission was being reexamined. Krister Stendahl's groundbreaking essay "The Apostle Paul and the Introspective Conscience of the West"[84] dealt a severe blow to the ubiquitous individualistic, introspective, psychologizing, and spiritualizing grids through which Paul's conversion and message were interpreted. Stendahl (and before him Johannes Munck) was able to demonstrate that Paul's "plight" was not his guilty conscience occasioned by the "legalism" and "burden" of Torah and Judaism, but the fact that he had been chosen, seized, and commissioned by the risen Christ to announce the good news of God's reconciliation of the non-Jewish peoples. Following up on this insight, Pauline scholars such as Markus Barth were able to show that at the heart of Paul's message is the social and political reconciliation of Jews and Gentiles into one new people of God whose calling it is to bear witness to that reconciliation as God's message, even in contexts and social relationships far beyond the conflicts of Jews and Gentiles.

Finally, as I noted above, the renewed interest in the "principalities and powers" as a way to address some of the deep theological-political issues raised by two world wars was also a development which predated Yoder's first edition of *The Politics of Jesus*. Nonetheless, Yoder's Paul arrives in 1972 as something quite unique and unprecedented. Yoder combined the key elements of each of these strands of current Pauline scholarship into a compelling rendition of the coherent center of Paul's theology as a political theology focused on the cross of Jesus Christ.

What has happened in Pauline scholarship since 1972 has only served to lend broader and deeper credibility to Yoder's reading. Since Käsemann the apocalyptic perspective has been advanced and refined (in North America) most notably by the work of J. Christiaan Beker and J. Louis Martyn. Beker points suggestively toward some of the social and political implications of Pauline apocalyptic.[85] Martyn, in his commentary on Galatians (and its

---

84. First published in English in *Harvard Theological Review* 56 (1963): 199–215; repr. in *Paul among Jews and Gentiles* (Philadelphia: Fortress, 1976), 78–96.

85. See J. Christiaan Beker, *Paul's Apocalyptic Gospel: The Coming Triumph of God* (Philadelphia: Fortress, 1982), 105–21.

companion volume of essays),[86] pursues an apocalyptic interpretation of Paul with remarkable vigor and consistency, insisting that for Paul the crucifixion is the cosmic-apocalyptic axis upon which all history and the universe itself turns. Central to the significance of Paul's theology of the cross is that in it God engages in warfare with the anti-God powers that hold the cosmos and humans in bondage, in order to make possible the new creation in which those who believe are set free from their enslavement to these powers.

The apocalyptic perspective has been combined with programs of research into the social, economic, and political contexts into which Paul preached his gospel and established communities of believers in Jesus.[87] More than any other, this approach has proven the legitimacy and heuristic fruitfulness of the question which Yoder addressed to the Pauline letters in 1972—Does Paul have a politics, and if so what is its shape?—and shown that Yoder's answer to that question as I presented it above is at the very least a plausible and, surely much more than that, a compelling and revolutionary reading of the apostle. It remains to summarize briefly its main contours.

Christ. Jesus Christ crucified and risen is, for Paul, the Lord, the beginning and end, center and coherence of all things, all creation, all powers, and so too of the new creation and new humanity inaugurated by God in his apocalyptic arrival in Jesus Christ. Because he is this, Jesus Christ is also the single normative criterion of anything that claims to come from God and the single normative criterion of all human action, personal and political, that claims to be directed by and to God.

Cross. For Paul the cross is the focal point of history and cosmos, precisely in the sense that it is the site of Jesus' costly, nonviolent stance vis-à-vis worldly power as God's triumph over rebellion, power, and violence and therefore the site of the normative pattern of social and political existence that must characterize the Christian community in its internal and external relations.

Powers. For Paul the human plight is more characteristically rendered as enslavement to rebellious, larger-than-human powers which also constitute the context for and shape the way in which humans wield power. Paul's language of the powers blurs distinctions between the heavenly and earthly spheres and modes of operation of anti-God principalities and powers— imperial thrones manifest the reality of spiritual authorities. Flesh-and-blood manifestations of the powers are, however, to be confronted by believers in the same manner as Jesus confronted the powers of Jerusalem and Rome—in truthfulness and readiness to suffer, rather than in arms and

---

86. Hays describes Martyn's *Galatians* as "the most profound and powerful biblical commentary since Karl Barth's *Römerbrief*" (review of *Galatians* by J. Louis Martyn in *Journal of Biblical Literature* 119 [2000]: 378).

87. See the representative essays in Horsley (ed.), *Paul and Empire*, referred to often above; and Horsley (ed.), *Paul and Politics*.

readiness to do harm. Therein lies the corresponding triumph of believers over the powers.

Ekklēsia. For Paul the spiritual and moral space created by God through Christ's triumph over the powers in the cross is also the space in which a new human community is created, a community that is called to embody the reality of the powers conquered, redeemed, and reordered. In this community the new creation is announced, enacted, and celebrated through Spirit-enabled practices that reveal in concrete ways that the rule of the rebellious powers has been broken in Christ—practices of identification and incorporation, of forgiveness and reconciliation, of sharing earthly goods, of building up the corporate body of Christ through gifts of service, of giving everyone a voice in the discernment of corporate direction. Through these practices the church becomes God's people, a body, a *polis,* that reflects the way of Jesus Christ amid other peoples, bodies, and cities.

Witness. The *ekklēsia,* the people of God, continues to live in the world, not only as a paradigmatic sign of the world's destiny under the lordship of Christ, but also as a witness within and to the world's structures and powers. The *ekklēsia* and its members continue to dwell (as resident aliens) in social and political spaces other than the church. It is their calling in those places to be there in the way of Jesus Christ. Even oppressive social and political structures may become precisely the sites of Christian witness—witness as proclaiming and transforming presence and action, or as *martyria*—when Christians adopt the stance of Jesus' costly "revolutionary subordination" to the powers.

That is the heart of Pauline theology according to Yoder.

4

Israel

"Who Will Bring Any Charge against God's Elect?"

Many Christian theologians and Paul scholars since the 1940s agree on at least one fact: their work cannot go on as if Jews do not exist. That should always have been the case, but we must attribute this realization most directly to the reality of the Holocaust and the apocalyptic shock waves that emanated from it during the past half century. While most theology and biblical scholarship prior to the Second World War did not directly intend to be anti-Judaistic, it is also true that the doctrinal and theological systems of that period rarely assigned any constitutive role either to the Israel of the Old Testament or to present-day Jews and the synagogue. The Jews were simply not visible in systematic theology. In Pauline scholarship they were more often visible, but frequently only as the dark backdrop against which more clearly to outline the bright contours of the Pauline gospel.

Much has changed. Christian theologians are now frequently producing important theological accounts of Israel and Judaism. And it would not be wrong to view the "new perspective on Paul" as largely a thoroughgoing attempt to reverse the deep and long-standing conviction that Paul was the first anti-Judaistic theologian. But it would hardly be true to say that these changes have taken deep or far-reaching root in Christian theology. Both liberal and evangelical theologies continue to occlude Israel and the Jews in important ways, either by relativizing Judaism (and Christianity) as one reli-

151

gious path among many (the liberal option) or by continuing to view Christians and the church as replacing the Jews and the synagogue in God's purpose (the traditional and evangelical "supersessionist" option). Each of these modes of occlusion seeks and usually claims to find support in the Pauline letters. Paul scholars themselves also often move in these familiar tracks, depending on whether their angle of approach to Paul is primarily oriented by the sociology of religion or by traditional Lutheran, Reformed, or evangelical theological convictions. But I am convinced that any such occlusion of Israel, the Jews, and the synagogue, any relativizing of their constitutive role in Christian theology, whether of the liberal or the evangelical kind, is not only a kind of anti-Judaism, but also and more important for the present work, fundamentally un-Pauline. My task in this chapter is to support that claim.

First, I show how one very prominent Pauline scholar, N. T. Wright, while deeply indebted to the new perspective, nonetheless provides a vigorous supersessionist reading of Paul on Israel's election.[1] Wright's work is gaining widespread influence in evangelical biblical studies and theology, but also well beyond. A nonsupersessionist theology will have to engage Wright's reading critically. Hence, in the second and central part of this chapter I provide a sustained counterreading of Israel's election, challenging Wright's construal of key Old Testament texts and, most important, of Romans 9–11. It becomes clear here (as it may not have before) that the apocalyptic reading of Paul I developed in the preceding chapters not only does not warrant a supersessionist reading of Paul, but in fact stands against it: God's apocalyptic action in Jesus Christ both encloses and sustains God's irrevocable election of the Jews as his people. Third, I turn to the important and promising work on a Christian theology of Judaism that John Howard Yoder was doing in the later years of his life. Yoder comes to conclusions about the nature and promise of Judaism that are virtually the opposite of those of Wright and provides important resources for developing a contemporary theology of Judaism. Finally, in a critical comparison of Wright and Yoder in light of the

---

1. By "supersessionism" I mean the doctrine about Israel which George Lindbeck describes (and rejects): "On this view, the church, and the church alone, is Israel. Old Testament promises and prophecies are fulfilled not only in Jesus (an assertion essential to mainstream Christian identity), but also in the church—and in such a way that it replaces Israel. The church is the 'New' Israel (an expression not found in the New Testament) and has become the sole heir to the entirety of Israel's heritage." In this view, according to Lindbeck, the church "expropriates" Israel. Lindbeck himself proposes the church's "appropriation" of Israel; that is, the church shares in Israel's nonsuperseded covenant by being "Israellike" as the people of God among the nations; "What of the Future? A Christian Response," in *Christianity in Jewish Terms* (ed. Tikva Frymer-Kensky et al.; Boulder, Colo.: Westview, 2000), 359. As Lindbeck indicates, there are ways in which essential Christian affirmations about Jesus Christ in some sense claim that Christ fulfills Old Testament promises and prophecies and, as I indicated particularly in chaps. 1–2, that Christ transcends the Torah as the final mediation of God's will and salvation to both Jews and Gentiles. But, as I argue in this chapter, God's election of historic, fleshly Israel, far from being abrogated, is in fact caught up into and sustained by God's apocalyptic act of reconciliation in Jesus Christ.

Pauline doctrine of God's election of Israel, I draw attention to some differences as well as common points of departure—and weakness—in their theologies of Judaism. I conclude by drawing attention to promising proposals for a Christian theology of Israel and Judaism made by Kendall Soulen, Scott Bader-Saye, and Bruce Marshall, which give a central place to the Pauline doctrine of God's election of Israel.

Israel's Fall into Paganism:
Wright's Supersessionist Reading of Paul

Few New Testament scholars working today can match the prolific production of N. Thomas Wright, now Canon Theologian at Westminster Abbey in London. His most ambitious project is a five-volume work entitled *Christian Origins and the Question of God*, of which the first two large volumes have now appeared.[2] The next projected volume is on Paul. But while this awaited work, which promises to be a massive and comprehensive treatment of the apostle's life and theology, is not yet finished, Wright published significant studies in Paul's theology that are, no doubt, the groundwork for the promised volume. Among these studies is a volume of essays on significant Pauline texts,[3] major essays on the theology of Romans and Galatians,[4] an essay on Paul's political theology,[5] and a summary of Pauline theology.[6] There is much to be admired and much of value in Wright's vigorous and confident presentations of "what Saint Paul really said." I especially appreciate his (critical) joining cause with the political interpretations of Paul being offered by Neil Elliott and Richard Horsley, among others. But there is a problem at the heart of Wright's understanding of Paul, rendering Paul a supersessionist of the most rigorous kind, which has serious and damaging repercussions for a Pauline theology of Israel. If Wright is correct in this understanding, then Paul is indeed the most significant enemy of Judaism in the history of Christianity, since he would warrant a supersessionist doctrine at the very foundations of Christian theology.

2. N. T. Wright, *The New Testament and the People of God* (Minneapolis: Fortress, 1992); idem, *Jesus and the Victory of God* (Minneapolis: Fortress, 1996).

3. N. T. Wright, *The Climax of the Covenant: Christ and the Law in Pauline Theology* (Minneapolis: Fortress, 1991).

4. N. T. Wright, "Romans and the Theology of Paul," in *Pauline Theology*, vol. 3: *Romans* (ed. David M. Hay and E. Elizabeth Johnson; Minneapolis: Fortress, 1995), 30–67; idem, "The Letter to the Galatians: Exegesis and Theology," in *Between Two Horizons: Spanning New Testament Studies and Systematic Theology* (ed. Joel B. Green and Max Turner; Grand Rapids: Eerdmans, 2000), 205–36.

5. N. T. Wright, "Paul's Gospel and Caesar's Empire," in *Paul and Politics: Ekklesia, Israel, Imperium, Interpretation: Essays in Honor of Krister Stendahl* (ed. Richard A. Horsley; Harrisburg, Pa.: Trinity, 2000), 160–83.

6. N. T. Wright, *What Saint Paul Really Said: Was Paul of Tarsus the Real Founder of Christianity?* (Grand Rapids: Eerdmans, 1997).

Central to Wright's entire project on the New Testament, and of great importance to his understanding of Paul, is his conviction that in Jesus Christ *"the promises of Israel's restoration had in fact been fulfilled."*[7] That is, according to Wright, for many Jews in the time of Jesus and for Saul the Pharisee in particular, Israel was still suffering in exile despite the fact that many Jews had returned to the land and were living there in Jesus' and Paul's time. Saul before his conversion was a Shammaite or "hard-line" Pharisee, a revolutionary who believed that "Israel [should] be free from the Gentile yoke" (*What Saint Paul Really Said,* 27). A Pharisee like Saul would look back to characters such as Phinehas and Elijah and to the Maccabeans as models of revolutionary "zeal"; "zealous for God, zealous for Torah, ready to go anywhere and do anything, up to and including violence, that would achieve the longed-for liberty, the long-awaited kingdom of God" (28). The vision that moved Saul was "the great prophetic promises [which] had not yet been fulfilled," a vision rooted in apocalyptic texts such as Daniel 2, 7, and 9, in which the end of Babylon was predicted (30). Babylon was seen as a figure for Rome. The "Babylonian" captivity of Israel under Roman rule meant that Israel remained in exile. Saul the Pharisee and many other Jews of his time "were still waiting for the great events to happen 'according to the scriptures.' They were still in exile." They were living in "a story in search of an ending" (30).

> The story ran like this. Israel had been called to be the covenant people of the creator God, to be the light that would lighten the dark world, the people through whom God would undo the sin of Adam and its effects. But Israel had become sinful, and as a result had gone into exile, away from her own land. Although she had returned geographically from her exile, the real exilic condition was not yet finished. The promises had not yet been fulfilled. The Temple had not yet been rebuilt. The Messiah had not yet come. The pagans had not yet been reduced to submission, nor had they begun to make pilgrimages to Zion to learn Torah. Israel was still deeply compromised and sinful. (*What Saint Paul Really Said,* 30–31)

But there was a promised conclusion to this story. "One day soon YHWH would be king of all the earth; evil would be decisively defeated; Israel, or at least the true Jews within Israel, would be vindicated as the true people of the one true God" (*What Saint Paul Really Said,* 31). Saul the Pharisee perceived his own zealous, revolutionary activity as hastening the day of YHWH, as helping to move this story to its climactic conclusion.[8] Such, according to Wright,

---

7. Ibid., 82 (emphasis original).

8. This story, or "worldview" as Wright is also inclined to name it, is worked out in detail in Wright's *New Testament and the People of God,* part 3. In another essay, Wright produces a statement of this "worldview . . . which was assumed by a majority of Jews in the period" ("Romans and the Theology of Paul," 33). I quote it here for comparison and for confirmation of the way in which it sets the background for and determines much of Wright's interpretation of Paul. For, while Wright on the one hand draws Paul's worldview by inference from Paul's writings (and others by Second Temple Jews), on the

was Saul's conviction and practice before his encounter with the risen Jesus Christ.

The climax of the story, however, turned out to be radically different from what Saul the Pharisee had expected:

> The significance of Jesus' resurrection, for Saul of Tarsus . . . was this. The one true God had done for Jesus of Nazareth, in the middle of time, what Saul had thought he was going to do for Israel at the end of time. Saul had imagined that YHWH would vindicate Israel after her suffering at the hand of the pagans. Instead, he had vindicated Jesus after his suffering at the hand of the pagans. (*What Saint Paul Really Said*, 36, emphasis original)

Commenting on Romans 1:4, Wright concludes that for Paul the Christian, "the resurrection demarcated Jesus as the true Messiah, the true bearer of Israel's God-sent destiny" (*What Saint Paul Really Said*, 37). "Israel's destiny had been *summed up* and *achieved* in Jesus the Messiah" (37, emphasis added). All of Israel's eschatological hopes find their end here in the death and resurrection of Jesus, which "were themselves the great eschatological event, revealing God's covenant faithfulness" (37). For Wright this has far-reaching and revolutionary implications for the previous vision which moved Saul as a Pharisee, for in fact that vision, that story, found its completion, its ending, in Jesus. In Jesus Christ, God has indeed led Israel in a new exodus, he has indeed ended Israel's exile, and he has indeed restored the kingdom to Israel, all in Jesus' very own person, as the one in whom all of Israel was represented, embodied, summed up, and redefined.[9] The implication for all Jews and their hopes is

---

other hand it becomes the key by which to unlock the meaning of those writings. There may be a problematic circularity here. According to Wright, a worldview has four elements: a symbolic world, a nonreflective praxis, an assumed narrative framework, and fundamental answers to key questions of life: Who are we? Where are we? What's wrong? What's the solution? (31–32). "The symbolic world of Judaism focused on temple, Torah, land, and racial identity. The assumed praxis brought these symbols to life in festivals and fasts, cult and sacrifice, domestic taboos and customs. The narrative framework which sustained symbol and praxis, and which can be seen in virtually all the writings we possess from the Second Temple period, had to do with the history of Israel; more specifically with its state of continuing 'exile' (though it had returned from Babylon, it remained under Gentile lordship, and the great promises of Isaiah and others remained unfulfilled) and the way(s) in which its god would intervene to deliver it as had happened in one of its foundation stories, that of the exodus. Its fundamental answers to the worldview questions might have been: We are Israel, the true people of the creator god; we are in our land (and/or dispersed away from our land); our god has not yet fully restored us as one day he will; we therefore look for restoration, which will include the justice of our god being exercised over the pagan nations" (32–33).

9. Wright's conclusions are again nicely summed up in a paragraph: "Paul's Christian theological reflection begins . . . with the realization that *what the creator/ covenant god was supposed to do for Israel at the end of history, this god had done for Jesus in the middle of history.* Jesus as an individual, instead of Israel as a whole, had been vindicated, raised from the dead, after suffering at the hands of the pagans. . . . Jesus had somehow borne Israel's destiny by himself, was somehow its representative. . . . Paul made exactly this connection [between Jesus and Israel's destiny], and indeed made it central to his whole theology. The creator/covenant god has brought his covenant purpose for Israel to fruition *in Israel's representative, the*

equally as revolutionary, or perhaps we might say devastating: "God has *rede-fined Israel* through certain climactic and revelatory—in other words, apocalyp-tic—events [i.e., the coming of Jesus Christ and the Holy Spirit] and all forms of Judaism that do not recognize this and conform are at best out of date and at worst dangerous compromises and parodies."[10] In other words, according to Wright, in Paul's understanding anything that remains of "Judaism," after Christ's death and resurrection, which does not acknowledge that Israel's prom-ised destiny is fully fulfilled in Jesus Christ cannot but be an anachronism, the obstinate persistence of a now obsolete and compromised people and practice, a mere parody of the truth of Jesus Christ.

Indeed, according to Wright, Paul after his conversion and throughout his letters engages in an ongoing and rigorous criticism of Judaism and of Israel's "failure" to fulfill its calling. Wright does not deny the truth of the *election* of Israel. But it is important to note that he construes that election in purely functional terms: "The God of Israel had called Israel into being in order to save the world; that was the purpose of election in the first place" (*What Saint Paul Really Said*, 82). Paul's "critique of Israel should not be read as a denial of the doctrine of election, a rejection of the belief that the Jewish people were chosen by the one true God to be his means of saving the world" (83–84). But Israel "failed" in that role, failed its true purpose, failed as God's means to save the world: "The Jews, despite being given the covenant through which God intended to redeem the world, have failed in their task" (106).

> Paul argues that ethnic Israel has failed in the purpose for which she was called into being. . . . Israel, the chosen people, has failed to accomplish the mission to which she was called. That is, Israel as a whole has failed; Israel's representa-tive, the Messiah, Jesus, has succeeded. . . . He was the true, representative Is-raelite. . . . Israel's true fulfillment is now to be found in Jesus Christ and the Spirit. Israel rejected the call of Jesus, and now rejects the apostolic message about Jesus, because it challenges that which has become her all-consuming interest: her relentless pursuit of national, ethnic and territorial identity. (*What Saint Paul Really Said*, 84)

While Wright, following the arguments of the new perspective on Paul, cer-tainly rejects the typical Protestant accusations that the Jews were "legalists" trying to "earn" their way "into heaven" through meritorious "works," he re-places that image of the Jew with one much more hideous, even dangerous:

> In seeking to establish a status of righteousness, of covenant membership, which will be for Jews and Jews only, she has not submitted to God's righ-

---

Messiah, Jesus" ("Romans and the Theology of Paul," 34, emphasis original). The use of the phrase "Jesus . . . instead of Israel" (here and elsewhere) and Israel's purpose brought "to fruition" in Jesus is worth not-ing. Here is a fully realized eschatology of Israel's purpose.

10. Wright, "Paul's Gospel and Caesar's Empire," 178 (emphasis added).

teousness. The covenant always envisioned a worldwide family; Israel, clinging to her own special status as covenant bearer, has betrayed the purpose for which that covenant was made. It is as though the postman were to imagine that all the letters in the bag were for him. (*What Saint Paul Really Said*, 108)

Here Israel, the Jew, is now selfishly consumed with hoarding covenant membership, as if it were "inalienably hers and hers alone" (*What Saint Paul Really Said*, 108), and with matters of nationality, ethnicity, and territory, dismissing Gentiles with "a sense of effortless racial superiority" (75). "She is, Paul reckons, in danger of making herself simply a nation 'like all the others.' Blood and soil were the marks of pagan nations; Israel was using Torah and circumcision to emphasize exactly those things" (84). For Wright's Paul, the "non-Christian" Jew has become a pagan, indeed, a type of Nazi.[11]

The only hope for Jews and Judaism under these conditions is to convert to Christianity. "Paul holds firmly to the hope that the renewal of the covenant which has taken place in Jesus the Messiah will be effective not only for the Gentile but also for Jews who will come, as he himself has done, to faith in Jesus as the Jewish Messiah" (*What Saint Paul Really Said*, 109). Paul "still saw the great mass of Judaism as being disloyal to the true God, and needing to be brought into line. But the line in question was now the Christian, the fulfilled Israel, line" (85).[12] Indeed, the church now fully replaces Israel, according to Wright's Paul: "The Christian community actually is . . . the fulfilment of the community of Israel, with its symbols picking up the Jewish symbols, particularly those which evoked the exodus from Egypt (1 Corinthians 10). The Eucharist is, for Paul, the feast which shows that the church is the true exodus community" (87).

Nonetheless, Wright insists that Paul "did not (as it were) abandon Judaism for something else" (*What Saint Paul Really Said*, 39). What might this mean in light of Wright's understanding of Paul displayed thus far? It means, first, that the only true Judaism is in fact the "Christian" one. With reference to Philippians 3:7–11, Wright says: "Paul is by no means saying . . . that Ju-

11. With reference to Col. 2 Wright argues (ibid., 176): "Paul warns the young church . . . against Judaism described in terms of paganism. This is a familiar trick [i.e., for a group of Jews in the Second Temple period to define themselves as the true Jews over against other groups as false Jews]. From Paul's Christian point of view, those Jews who do not embrace Jesus as their Messiah are thereby embracing instead an identity marked out by blood and soil, by ancestry and territory, in other words, by the 'flesh.' They are, therefore, subject to the same critique as paganism." For the complete argument for Wright's rigorous supersessionism, see his discussion of Phil. 3 in "Paul's Gospel and Caesar's Empire," 173–81.

12. "There can therefore be no covenant future for those Israelites who refuse to abandon their 'own,' that is, their ethnic, status of covenant membership ([Rom.] 10:3). Christ is the end of that road, the final goal of the covenant purpose which always intended to deal with sin and its effects (10:4, with all its deliberate ambiguities in play). But those who see, in Christ, the clue to what the creator/covenant god has righteously been doing in Israel's history, and who grasp this in faith—these Israelites can always regain their full covenant status, and when this happens it is to be a cause of great rejoicing within the community as a whole (11:1ff.)"; "Romans and the Theology of Paul," 57–58.

daism per se is bad and to be rejected. . . . He was not opposed to the idea of
Judaism per se, nor indeed could he be; he was claiming the high ground that
this, indeed, was what Judaism had always been supposed to be, the historical
people whose identity and destiny were now revealed in the crucified Messiah."[13] In this sense Wright repeatedly insists that Paul's critique of Judaism is
a "critique from within," that is, one Jew (or Jewish group) attempting to define true Judaism (his own brand) over against the false types. Wright assures
us that for this reason Paul can never be labeled "anti-Judaistic."

That Paul did not abandon Judaism means, in the second place, that Paul
brings the "Jewish" *story* and *worldview* to the Gentiles. Indeed, central to
Wright's argument about Judaism in Paul is that while God replaces the *people* of Israel with the church (or the church is the true Israel), nonetheless the
mission of the church is to take Israel's story (a "Jewish" story), whose ending
is in Christ, to the nations. We have already encountered this "Jewish" story.
It is "the true story of Israel's God and his people, the true story (in consequence) of the creator and the cosmos" (*What Saint Paul Really Said*, 40)
which is fulfilled in Christ and thus which Paul announces as the gospel.
"The power of his 'gospel' came precisely from the fact that it addressed the
pagan world with the full weight of Jewish history and tradition behind it"
(48). He brings "a Jewish message of good news for the world" (49). This
Jewish message, story, or worldview may be summed up in "three cardinal
points of Jewish theology in this [Second Temple] period: monotheism, election and eschatology. There is one God, the one true God of all the world; Israel is the people of this one true God; and there is one future for all the
world, a future not very far away now, in which the true God will reveal himself, defeat evil, and rescue his people" (31). While, of course, each of these
points was radically redefined in the crucifixion and resurrection of Jesus,
nonetheless each of them also is a crucial *Jewish* element in the Christian message. Thus, and thus only, is "Judaism" saved from being abandoned in Paul's
theology. The election of Israel and the covenant which God makes with Israel, finally, for Wright's Paul, serve a purpose in a much wider scheme:

> The purpose of the covenant, in the Hebrew Bible and in some subsequent
> writings, was never simply that the creator wanted to have Israel as a special
> people, irrespective of the fate of the rest of the world. The purpose of the cov-
> enant was that, through this means, the creator would address and save his en-
> tire world. The call of Abraham was designed to undo the sin of Adam. (*What
> Saint Paul Really Said*, 33)

Should fleshly Israel, the Jews, fail to fulfill their purpose in this wider creational story, as indeed according to Wright they most thoroughly did, God
would have no problem "redefining" the elect people, such that any promise

---

13. Wright, "Paul's Gospel and Caesar's Empire," 177.

made to Abraham about his descendants "after the flesh" could also be redefined, and "fleshly" nonmessianic Jews simply rendered now as pagans. The Jews are saved not in their flesh as the people of God. Rather, their worldview, appropriately Christianized and universalized, is saved; the story about God the Creator, the world as God's creation, humankind (Adam) as created, fallen, and in need of redemption, a redemption promised *through* (but apparently never *to*) Abraham and his fleshly descendants, but finally enacted only in Jesus Christ. God's election of the Jews thus amounts in fact to the election of a Jewish worldview, borne previously in the Jewish tradition but now fully taken up and corrected by Christians, a worldview which Paul in turn takes to the Gentiles as the gospel they need desperately to hear. "The direction of Paul's message was confrontation with paganism; he had good news for them, but it was good news which undermined their worldview and replaced it with an essentially Jewish one, reworked around Jesus" (*What Saint Paul Really Said*, 79). In his proclamation Paul maintains an "utter and unswerving loyalty to the God of Abraham, Isaac and Jacob, the God who made promises to Abraham, the God who gave the law, the God who spoke through the prophets" (39). Thus does *Paul* remain loyal to "*Judaism.*" But, it seems, *God himself* does not remain loyal to the actual Jewish *people.*[14]

Wright is certainly nervous about the charge of anti-Judaism which might be leveled at such a reading of Paul:

> Believing that God had acted to remodel the covenant people necessarily and Jewishly meant believing that those who refused to join this remodeled people were missing out on God's eschatological purpose. As post-Holocaust thinkers we will be careful how we say all this. As historians of the first century we will recognize that it must be said. As Pauline theologians we will recognize that it contains no shadow, no hint, of anything that can truly be called anti-Judaism, still less anti-Semitism.[15]

Wright himself has not been very careful how he says "all this," certainly not in *What Saint Paul Really Said* or in his essays. It is not at all clear, on the basis of what I showed above, how there is "no shadow, no hint, of anything that can truly be called anti-Judaism" in Wright's Paul. Wright's nervousness is expressed again in another place, where in fact he seems to recognize that his position may be construed as anti-Jewish, but also that there may be no way of avoiding such a charge:

14. See further Wright's "Letter to the Galatians," where he attempts to clarify discussions of Paul's relationship with Judaism. But again, the key question for Wright is not what Paul thinks about *God's* relationship to actual "non-Christian" Jews, but is rather the question of where *Paul* gets his "basic ideas," "thought structure," and "beliefs" (211–12). For Wright, Paul is thoroughly "Jewish" because he gets these in large measure from Judaism: "We should expect Paul therefore to be on the map of first-century Jewish thought about God—and this is indeed the case, though not always in the ways one might imagine" (214). Judaism is saved in the Jewishness of Paul's theology.

15. Wright, "Paul's Gospel and Caesar's Empire," 182.

If he [Paul] had abandoned Judaism and invented a new religion, he would be regarded by many as anti-Jewish. If he had claimed that Judaism's long story had reached its climax, its fulfilment, in Jesus of Nazareth, he would be regarded by many as anti-Jewish. Heads I lose; tails you win. I think he took the second route. Those who object to this on principle need to face the question, whether they would really have preferred him to take the first. (*What Saint Paul Really Said*, 39)

Whether these are the only two alternatives, each anti-Jewish in its own way, for understanding Paul or whether there are others, seems never to enter Wright's mind. But a very large question looms in the background here. If all of Judaism and its Jewish adherents *after* Christ are to be construed theologically on the one hand as mere "compromises" and "parodies" of the Christian message and on the other hand as standing on the same ground with paganism and pagans, can a Christian approach to Judaism and Jews ever be anything other than a full-orbed supersessionism at best and never far from anti-Judaism or anti-Semitism at worst? What, after all, ought Christians to do with paganism?

The Election of Israel Sustained in the Apocalypse of Jesus Christ

The great scholarly authority and self-confidence with which Wright tells us "what Saint Paul really said" certainly presents an intimidating challenge for any who would fundamentally disagree with his basic premises and conclusions. And certainly a full-blown critique of his interpretation of Paul is beyond both the scope of this chapter and the competence of its author. Indeed, a sufficient response would require a major counterreading of Paul supported by extended exegesis of significant passages from the epistles.[16] But this will not prevent me from attempting to place some necessary fundamental question marks against Wright's reading of Paul (in itself a daunting enough task) in an effort to detour and perhaps even in places to derail what seems to be the onward movement of an inexorable "Pauline" supersessionist logic.

I will challenge three of Wright's most important claims. First, do Israel/the Jews exist, in the Old Testament story, to serve a primarily or exclusively *instrumental* role in a much larger story about God's creation of the world, the human fall into sin, God's redemption of humans and the consumma-

16. Such counterreadings are proliferating; see, among many others, the works by Scott Bader-Saye, Neil Elliott, Lloyd Gaston, Richard Hays, Elizabeth Johnson, Mark Nanos, R. Kendall Soulen, and Stanley Stowers listed in note 20 below. So despite Wright's confidence in his own reading, the existence of other readings differing strongly from or opposed to Wright's certainly already places a question mark against it. Wright rarely engages any of these authors, certainly not on the topic under consideration. Indeed, a work like *What Saint Paul Really Said*, with virtually no footnotes, leaves no indication that Wright's interpretation of Paul might be a vigorously contested one. Only Gaston's work is mentioned in the annotated bibliography—and given a bemused dismissal.

tion of creation in the eschaton? Second, is Paul's "story of the Jews," particularly as it is told in Romans 9–11, a story primarily about Israel's "failure" to fulfill its mission, its "rejection" of the gospel, and its "betrayal" of God's purpose, or is it a story about God's actions in fulfilling that purpose? Third, does Paul employ a linear "covenant-historical" narrative in which there is a divinely driven linear movement from Israel, to Christ, to the church, in which historical Israel's role after Christ simply ceases to be of any theological significance, or does Paul display another—I will suggest apocalyptic—way of thinking about Israel in God's purpose? Wright's claims in each of these areas, it seems to me, are the pillars upon which his reading of Paul as a supersessionist is constructed. Each claim, each pillar, is susceptible to some damaging deconstruction in the light of a fundamentally different way of reading Israel's election. Finally, I argue that Wright presents an "evangelical/liberal" reading of Paul that fits nicely into the worldview of late modernity, but fits ill with the apocalyptic/theocentric vision that moved the apostle.

The Purpose of Israel's Election in Moses and Isaiah

As I noted, one of the critical assertions which supports Wright's reading has to do with the purpose of Israel's election:

> Belief in the one true god remained basic (the creator god, hence the god of the whole world), as did belief in Israel's election by this one god. . . . The *purpose* of this election is not so often noticed, but is, I suggest, vital. . . . Israel's vocation had to do . . . with the creator's plan for the whole creation. God called Abraham to deal with the problem of Adam. This theme . . . is central to (e.g.) Isaiah 40–55, and is visible also in the final redaction of the Pentateuch. Both, clearly, are passages on which Paul drew heavily.[17]

Did God really call Abraham "to deal with the problem of Adam"? That is certainly how the early chapters of Genesis are construed in many Christian readings and much Christian theology. The arch of "the biblical narrative" is seen to span the themes of creation, fall, redemption, and eschaton/renewal. Abraham and Israel, and indeed Christ and the church, play their "roles" within this drama, but the plot of the drama is the redemption of humanity and creation after the disaster of the fall from creation's original goodness. Seen from the perspective of this typical Christian understanding of the biblical message, Abraham and Israel mark stages in the "history of redemption," but their purpose as the chosen people finds its end in the coming of Christ and the universalizing of the redemptive message to include everyone and everything. Once Christ comes their purpose is served. Wright reflects this reading with characteristic bluntness: "Israel's fate . . . had not been swept aside. It was not irrelevant. It had reached its climax in the death of Jesus, the representative

17. "Romans and the Theology of Paul," 33.

Messiah of Israel" (*What Saint Paul Really Said*, 48–49). But "Israel's fate" is
that, from that moment on, fleshly Israel and actual historical Jews cease to be
any more theologically relevant for Christian theology than the Norsemen,
Navajo, or Nuer. Israel joins the many peoples of pagan origins and "other religions" as the object of Christian missions.

But, to put the question again, is that really the meaning of Abraham and
Israel in the biblical narrative? Do they serve a merely temporary function,
that is, finally, to serve the purpose of the salvation of the nations or, rather,
of "humanity" as a whole? How does the scriptural testimony portray their
purpose? Wright points with special emphasis to two major biblical texts, Isaiah 40–55 and "the final redaction of the Pentateuch," as texts on which Paul
relied heavily and as places where the "central theme" is clear that "God called
Abraham to deal with the problem of Adam." But it is not so clear. In fact, by
contrast, in each of those stretches of biblical text it seems to be reading more
with the grain to suggest, in the first place, that Adam exists primarily to provide a world-historical *background* to the main story, which is about Abraham
and his descendants (after all, in the final redaction of the Pentateuch only a
very few chapters of the whole are given to Adam and his story—and within
the entire Deuteronomic history it is an even smaller portion); and, in the
second place (in Isaiah 40–55), that the Creator God, beside whom the other
gods are mere nothings, continues to declare his universal rule over the nations *in order that* his declaration to bring "comfort" to his people, whom he
has chosen, will be taken seriously. No other god and no other place will keep
them from God's redeeming power and purpose to restore them to their own
land, since God is the God of all creation. Indeed, as I now demonstrate in
some detail, in each of these sections of biblical text the emphasis on God's
election of Israel for God's sake and for *Israel's* own sake is overwhelming.

Consider first the Pentateuch and the many passages that speak of the election of the patriarchs and of Israel as a people. When Abram is chosen in Genesis 12:1–3, there is no indication that his election simply serves another end,
the redemption of Adam. Earlier chapters account for the "state of the world"
in both its God-created goodness and its human-created misery. Immediately
preceding Abraham's call, in a manner typical of these early chapters of Genesis, we are given two accounts of the worldwide spread of the nations. In Genesis 10 (a genealogy usually passed over in our casual Scripture reading) we discover—before the account of the tower of Babel—that the spread of the
nations, each (already) with its language, is in fact a result of God's blessing
upon the sons of Noah as they respond to the command to "be fruitful and
multiply, and fill the earth" (9:1). Each grouping of descendants is said to live
"in their lands, with their own language, by their families, in their nations"
(10:5, with slight variations in 10:20, 31, 32). In other words, we have here a
surprisingly benign, or rather affirmative, report of the existence of the many
peoples, languages, and cultures, with little indication that they suffer from
Adam's "problem" and stand in need of a "salvation" that will begin with the

call of Abraham. The story of the tower of Babel (11:1–9) interrupts the genealogy of Shem (10:21–31; 11:10–26) to give us another angle on the spread of
the nations. In this story it appears that God judges the temptation to empire
and to cultural-linguistic hegemony so ever-present in human history, even at
the time of the writing of the story (Babel = Babylon). God's answer to that
temptation is, again, to pluralize the peoples and languages.

Then, back to the genealogy of Shem, which proceeds in regular and due
order to its goal, Abram and his wife Sarai. But, we are told, "Now Sarai was
barren; she had no child" (11:30). *That*, and not God's dealing with evil in
the world, becomes the central theme of the chapters to follow (and also for
Paul in Rom. 4:16–25), for God makes the absurd promise to Abram that
he will have countless descendants. But for the story in Genesis these cannot
be Abram's "spiritual" children (such as Eliezer of Damascus, Abram's chief
servant; Gen. 15:2) nor even the children of the handmaiden Hagar; they
must be children of the barren woman. It will require a whole new creative
act of God, a veritable watering of the desert place (cf. Gen. 2). This is not a
story of *redemption* for the nations, but of the *election and creation* of a people. The story of Abram and Sarai is another stage in God's work of *creation*.

When we arrive at the point at which God makes the promise to Abram
about his descendants (12:1–3), we hear this: "I will make of you a great nation, and I will bless *you* and make your name great, so that you will be a
blessing. I will bless those who bless *you*, and the one who curses *you* I will
curse; and in you all the families of the earth [cf. Gen. 10] will be blessed."
While Abram does indeed serve as the mediator of God's blessing to the nations, he does so only *in and as* he himself is the primary object of God's
choosing, creating, and blessing. Indeed, it is in the nations' response of
blessing or curse to Abram as God's proxy (God's image?) that the nations
will receive either blessing or curse from God. And the following story of
Abraham shows this point in several ways—indeed right through to the stories of Joseph and the children of Israel in Egypt, Egypt's receiving either
blessing or curse, depending on how it treats the body of Abraham (Abraham's descendants) in its midst.[18] Wright never seems to consider that Abraham and his descendants after the flesh were chosen both for their own

18. The great climax of the blessing of Israel *among* the nations, *by* the nations, and *to* the nations
comes with the visit by the queen of Sheba to King Solomon in 1 Kings 10. The queen first of all sees the
overwhelming and visible evidence of God's blessing upon Israel (10:1–5; it is worth noting that 4:20–34
echoes the promises to Abram, making it clear that these promises find a decisive—if not final—fulfilment in Solomon's reign); then the queen blesses not only Solomon and his entire court, but also YHWH
who has blessed Solomon, and she gives gifts to Solomon (10:6–10); finally Solomon himself gives gifts
to, that is, blesses, the queen. Of course, the biblical writer never forgets that there is a dark underside to
all of this too (1 Kings 11), but this does not detract from the fact that in Solomon's reign the blessing of
God upon Israel and the mutuality of blessing between Israel and the nations achieves its high point in
Israel's history.

blessing and that, because of this, through them the families of the earth might be blessed.

We could attend to another classic text of Israel's election, Exodus 19:1–6. Israel has reached the mountain of God, after having been "created" by God (15:16) through the separating of the waters at the Sea of Reeds (15:4–8; cf. Gen. 1:6–10). God tells Moses to say to the people: "You have seen what I did to the Egyptians, and how I bore you on eagles' wings and brought you to myself. Now therefore, if you obey my voice and keep my covenant, you shall be my treasured possession out of all the peoples. Indeed, the whole earth is mine, but you shall be for me a priestly kingdom and a holy nation" (Exod. 19:4–6). Certainly the idea of a priestly kingdom suggests that Israel serves a representative, mediating role within a wider world ("the whole earth"), but this is all predicated on Israel's being chosen, created, carried, and treasured by God "out of all the peoples." Israel is more than a functionary within a wider scheme; Israel is the very particular object of God's selective love.

Consider two other classic texts declaring Israel's election:

> It was not because you were more numerous than any other people that the LORD set his heart on you and chose you—for you were the fewest of all peoples. It was because the LORD loved you and kept the oath that he swore to your ancestors, that the LORD has brought you out with a mighty hand, and redeemed you from the house of slavery, from the hand of Pharaoh king of Egypt. Know therefore that the LORD your God is God, the faithful God who maintains covenant loyalty with those who love him and keep his commandments, to a thousand generations, and who repays in their own person those who reject him. (Deut. 7:7–10)

> Although heaven and the heaven of heavens belong to the LORD your God, the earth with all that is in it, yet the LORD set his heart in love on your ancestors alone and chose you, their descendants after them, out of all the peoples, as it is today. (Deut. 10:14–15)

There is no hint in either of these texts of any *instrumental* reason for God's choice of Israel. Israel is God's people because of God's everlasting love. Nor, even in the context of the rigorous call for obedience to the commandments which fills the pages of Deuteronomy, is there any notion that, should Israel "fail" in a supposed instrumental role, God would "redefine" this covenant in such a way that Abraham's descendants after the flesh would simply fall out of God's covenant love for them. Even after the great disobedience which leads to God's curse upon Israel and to Israel's exile, God's abiding love remains:

> When all these things have happened to you, the blessings and the curses that I have set before you [Deut. 28], if you call them to mind among the nations where the LORD your God has driven you, and return to the LORD your God,

and you and your children obey him with all your heart and with all your soul, just as I am commanding you today, then the LORD your God will restore your fortunes and have compassion on you, gathering you again from the peoples among whom the LORD your God has scattered you. Even if you are exiled to the ends of the world, from there the LORD your God will gather you, and from there he will bring you back. The LORD your God will bring you into the land that your ancestors possessed, and you will possess it; he will make you more prosperous and numerous than your ancestors. (Deut. 30:1–5)

Wright's suggestion that in Jesus Christ Israel's exile has ended, that its hopes for a new exodus and return to the land (rooted in this text) are fully summed up and achieved in Jesus alone, appears to render this text a cruel joke. That the people of Israel, Jews, Abraham's descendants after the flesh, should take this text seriously as a promise of their own destiny simply confirms for Wright that they have a sense of "effortless racial superiority" and an "identity marked out by blood and soil, by ancestry and territory." The God of whom the text speaks would appear, in Wright's reading, as a capricious character who can, with a turn of the face, simply abandon the people to whom this promise of fidelity and restoration is made and in their place put a predominantly Gentile church, accompanied by those few Jews who "choose" to put their faith in Jesus. The tables of the Pentateuch have been profoundly turned. God has not remained faithful, in any sense which this text makes, to his people whom he has chosen out of his great love for them.

The same judgment must be made of Wright's reading of Isaiah 40–55. Here the matter is as straightforward and indeed in fundamental continuity with the affirmations of Deuteronomy. In text after text the exilic prophet affirms the great love and fidelity to his covenant which God sustains toward Israel (cf. 43; 44:1–5, 21–22; 45:1–4; 49; 52:1–10; 55:3):

> But you, Israel, my servant,
>   Jacob, whom I have chosen,
>   the offspring of Abraham, my friend;
> you whom I took from the ends of the earth,
>   and called from its farthest corners,
> saying to you, "You are my servant,
>   I have chosen you and not cast you off";
> do not fear, for I am with you,
>   do not be afraid, for I am your God;
> I will strengthen you, I will help you,
>   I will uphold you with my victorious right hand.
>
>   Isaiah 41:8–10

> All of them [idolaters] are put to shame and confounded,
>   the makers of idols go in confusion together.

But Israel is saved by the LORD
   with everlasting salvation;
you shall not be put to shame or confounded
   to all eternity.

Isaiah 45:16–17

   Listen to me, O house of Jacob,
      all the remnant of the house of Israel,
   who have been borne by me from your birth,
      carried from the womb;
   even to your old age I am he,
      even when you turn gray I will carry you.
   I have made, and I will bear;
      I will carry and will save.

Isaiah 46:3–4

For your Maker is your husband,
   the LORD of hosts is his name;
the Holy One of Israel is your Redeemer,
   the God of the whole earth he is called.
For the LORD has called you
   like a wife forsaken and grieved in spirit,
like the wife of a man's youth when she is cast off,
   says your God.
For a brief moment I abandoned you,
   but with great compassion I will gather you.
In overflowing wrath for a moment
   I hid my face from you,
but with everlasting love I will have compassion on you,
   says the LORD, your Redeemer.

Isaiah 54:5–8

Again, the most striking thing about these passages is the profound lack of instrumentality in depicting the relationship between God and Israel. YHWH is bound to his people with a powerful bond of love. It is this love that drives him to seek out and redeem his people from bondage; it is this love that gives the prophet the confidence to declare comfort to God's people (40:1–2).

It is true that the great drama of these chapters is enacted against the backdrop of the nations and indeed of creation as a whole. But it is remarkable that the declarations about God as Creator of all things and all nations serve primarily to warrant the claim that God's power and glory are greater than that of all the gods and idols of the nations (which are mere nothings; 44:9–20) and that YHWH is therefore able to act on Israel's behalf, wherever Israel may be found or bound (cf., e.g., 51:12–16). Even the great pagan emperor Cyrus is only God's anointed servant for this purpose:

> Thus says the LORD to his anointed, to Cyrus,
>> whose right hand I have grasped
> to subdue nations before him
>> and strip kings of their robes,
> to open doors before him—
>> and the gates shall not be closed:
> I will go before you
>> and level the mountains,
>
> . . . .
>
> so that you may know that it is I, the LORD,
>> the God of Israel, who call you by your name.
> For the sake of my servant Jacob,
>> and Israel my chosen,
> I call you by your name.
>> I surname you, though you do not know me.
> I am the LORD, and there is no other;
>> besides me there is no god.
>> I arm you, though you do not know me,
> so that they may know, from the rising of the sun
>> and from the west, that there is no one besides me;
>> I am the LORD, and there is no other.
> I form light and create darkness,
>> I make weal and create woe;
>> I the LORD do all these things.
>
> Isaiah 45:1–7 (cf. 44:28)

Israel's redemption in the midst of the nations, through the instrumentality of the nations, is the decisive vindication of YHWH's faithfulness to Israel and of his power as Creator:

> For I am the LORD your God,
>> the Holy One of Israel, your Savior.
> I give Egypt as your ransom,
>> Ethiopia and Seba in exchange for you.
> Because you are precious in my sight,
>> and honored, and I love you,
> I give peoples in return for you,
>> nations in exchange for your life.
>
> Isaiah 43:3–4

Only as the servant of YHWH "raise[s] up the tribes of Jacob" and "restore[s] the survivors of Israel" does he become "light to the nations"; but precisely as he does so God's salvation reaches "to the end of the earth" (49:6). If YHWH cannot save his people, whom he loves, then the nations and their gods have no reason to bow before his glory. But if YHWH does deliver Israel, then he "will be glorified in Israel" (44:23), Israel itself will become God's glory (46:13;

49:3); only then shall all the nations receive YHWH's teachings and justice (51:1–6), only then shall the nations look to Israel:

> See, you shall call nations that you do not know,
>   and nations that do not know you shall run to you,
> because of the LORD your God, the Holy one of Israel,
>   for he has glorified you.
>
> Isaiah 55:5

It is difficult to see in the entire text of Isaiah 40–55 where Wright could derive the notion that Israel exists only to serve a role, purpose, function, or mission, which if it failed in it, would result in God simply abandoning his people for another, otherwise constituted. Rather, much more to the point, and to the very point at the center of Paul's claim in Romans 9–11, if *God* fails finally to redeem his people, Israel in the flesh, then there is no reason at all to find comfort in the prophet's words. Then this "God" might as well be abandoned.[19] If Jews even today await a final deliverance, one which (from a Christian theological perspective) has already been inaugurated in Jesus Christ, then they stand firmly on the sure words of the Law (Genesis, Exodus, Deuteronomy) and the Prophets (Isaiah). And there is no reason to believe that Paul thought differently.

The Origin and Purpose of Israel's Hardening in Romans 9–11

Does Paul read these Old Testament texts in the way that Wright suggests? Wright's proposal is twofold: (1) Israel failed to live up to its sole purpose, which was to serve the salvation of humanity, that is, as a "light to the nations," and therefore God turns away from and casts off the largest part of Israel according to the flesh; (2) nonetheless, all of Israel's hopes for a "new exodus," deliverance from captivity, and return from exile to the land are fully fulfilled in the death and resurrection of Jesus Christ and the sending of the Holy Spirit. I believe that Wright is correct in holding that the Pentateuch and Isaiah 40–55 are of great importance in Paul's theology. But I showed that Wright's understanding of the thrust of those texts, at least as regards Israel's election and purpose, is dubious, to say the very least. Perhaps that in itself should make us suspicious of his reading of Paul's reading of

19. See the comments on the Old Testament theology of Israel and the nations in God's purpose by Horst Dietrich Preuss in *Old Testament Theology* (trans. Leo G. Perdue; Louisville: Westminster John Knox, 1996), 2:303, 305: "YHWH's salvation was and is first of all earmarked for Israel. And when there was talk also of salvation for the nations and of their praising of YHWH . . . then Israel and its Zion can serve as the mediator of this salvation. . . . One cannot imagine Israel not in this picture, for yhwh himself has placed it there for the realization of his plan for salvation." And further: "God for the sake of his love (cf. only Hos. 11:8f.; Isa. 54:7f., 10) does not fail because of the sin of Israel, and he does not allow Israel to fail during its Old Testament journey. Also, the eschatologization of much theological language is not identical to Israel's failures in this world."

those texts. But does Paul, as he often does, put his own twist on those texts, one that may lie behind Wright's twisted reading?

The most appropriate place to turn for an answer to that question is Romans 9–11.[20] And it is just there that Wright's reading of Paul comes to grief.[21] Wright moves into this passage with most of the assumptions I detailed above about Israel in Paul's theology. Wright acknowledges that "the question throughout [Rom. 9–11] has to do with the character and purposes of God, and particularly his faithfulness to his promises, and hence the justice of his dealings with Israel and the world" (*Climax of the Covenant*, 235), that is, with the righteousness of God. God's righteousness in Paul is, according to Wright, "the covenant faithfulness, the covenant justice, of the God who made promises to Abraham, promises of a worldwide family characterized by faith, in and through whom the evil of the world would be undone" (234). This is a promising beginning. We would expect on this understanding that Romans 9–11 is about God and God's decisions and actions as demonstrations of his righteousness. And so it is: Paul's announced and defended conviction is that the word of God has not failed (9:6). In a remarkable rhetorical tour de force Paul writes the entire passage from 9:6 to 9:27 using nearly twenty active verbs depicting God's action, but using only a few verbs, all passive, with respect to humanity. He thus makes his point absolutely clear, namely that the current "plight" of Israel after the flesh is entirely the result of *God's* decisions and actions. Thus Lloyd Gaston rightly asks: "How is it that people can say that chapter 9 deals with the unbelief of Israel when it is never mentioned, and all human activity, whether doing or believing, whether Jewish or Gentile, is expressly excluded from consideration?"[22]

Despite that, and despite the original promising thesis from Wright that Romans 9–11 is about God's faithfulness, Wright soon turns his attention

20. For the understanding of the theme, shape, and argument of Rom. 9–11 in what follows I am especially reliant, in various ways, on Scott Bader-Saye, *Church and Israel after Christendom: The Politics of Election* (Boulder, Colo.: Westview, 1999), 100–102; Neil Elliott, "Figure and Ground in the Interpretation of Romans 9–11," in *The Theological Interpretation of Scripture: Classic and Contemporary Readings* (ed. Stephen E. Fowl; Oxford: Blackwell, 1997), 371–89; Lloyd Gaston, *Paul and the Torah* (Vancouver: University of British Columbia Press, 1987), 116–50; Richard B. Hays, *Echoes of Scripture in the Letters of Paul* (New Haven: Yale University Press, 1989), 63–83; E. Elizabeth Johnson, "Romans 9–11: The Faithfulness and Impartiality of God," in *Pauline Theology*, vol. 3: *Romans* (ed. David M. Hay and E. Elizabeth Johnson; Minneapolis: Fortress, 1995), 211–39; idem, "Divine Initiative and Human Response," in *The Theological Interpretation of Scripture: Classic and Contemporary Readings* (ed. Stephen E. Fowl; Oxford: Blackwell, 1997), 356–70; Mark D. Nanos, *The Mystery of Romans: The Jewish Context of Paul's Letter* (Minneapolis: Fortress, 1996); R. Kendall Soulen, *The God of Israel and Christian Theology* (Minneapolis: Fortress, 1996), 109–77; Stanley K. Stowers, *A Rereading of Romans: Justice, Jews, and Gentiles* (New Haven: Yale University Press, 1994). Many supersessionist readings of Rom. 9–11 may be found in the classic commentaries on this text, from Origen and Augustine to Käsemann and Cranfield. Wright's interpretation is one in this long line of readings.

21. The key essays are Wright's "Romans and the Theology of Paul" (esp. 56–62) and "Christ, the Law and the People of God: The Problem of Romans 9–11," both in *Climax of the Covenant*, 231–57.

22. Gaston, *Paul and the Torah*, 92.

from God's action to Israel's "failure." "It is not God who has failed, but Israel. That is the emphasis of 9:6–29" (*Climax of the Covenant*, 239). So also, despite the fact that 9:6–29 nowhere attributes any failure to Israel at all, Wright attributes to Israel a whole series of deliberate actions of culpable failure (237): Israel "rejects" the gospel (236); Israel "rebels" against the gospel (237); Israel "clings to the fact of ancestral privilege" (237). To guard against any thought that Israel is a "*tabula rasa* upon which God writes an abstract decree," Paul apparently (where?) draws on the golden calf incident in Israel's history to show that Israel is rather "a rebellious and sinful nation, the people of God maybe but a people, in the bad sense, *according to the flesh*" (238–39, emphasis original). Thus God's justice on Israel "is that of the judge who must judge *sin* properly, . . . who must act to glorify his great name despite the failure of his people" (239, emphasis added). For Wright the point of Romans 9:19–24, regarding the "vessels of wrath," is this:

> [God] sees that the only way of rescuing his world at all is to call a people, and to enter into covenant with them, so that through them he will deal with evil. But the means of dealing with evil is to concentrate it in one place and condemn—execute—it there. The full force of this condemnation is not intended to fall on this people in general, but on their representative, the Messiah. But insofar as they become the place where sin is thus initially focussed (5:20), Israel necessarily becomes the "vessel of wrath." And insofar as Israel clings to her privileged status, and to the Torah as reinforcing it, refusing to recognize the crucified Messiah as the revelation of God's covenant faithfulness, she is bound to remain in that condition. (*Climax of the Covenant*, 239)

We must pose a few hard questions about these claims. Where in Romans 9 does Paul indicate that his theme is how God "will deal with evil"? Is it not rather about God's dealings with Israel, namely that God will remain faithful to Israel, despite the fact that the Gentiles now seem to be receiving God's mercy while Israel does not? Further, Paul insists that the current condition of Israel's "hardening" is entirely God's doing. Israel's actions and moral condition ("clinging" to privilege, "refusing" to recognize Jesus) do not enter the picture at all. If Israel "remains bound" in a condition, it is because God has bound it there (11:32). Indeed, that is precisely the point of Paul noting, with reference to Jacob and Esau, that God's purpose was declared to Rebecca "before they had been born or had done anything good or bad (*agathon ē phaulon*)" (9:11). God's choosing "the younger," Jacob, is not injustice on God's part precisely because the issue is not about moral success or failure but about God's mercy and hardening, enacted not with respect to a moral condition, but strictly with respect to a divine purpose that must be accomplished. So also, Paul's introduction of Exodus 9:16 Septuagint in Romans 9:17 makes precisely that point and only that point:

like Pharaoh, Israel suffers God's hardening "for the very purpose of showing [God's] power in [it], so that [his] name may be proclaimed in all the
earth." Paul is completely silent about Pharaoh as an agent, whether moral
or immoral. The thought that God is dealing with "evil," either in Pharaoh
or Israel or the world, does not enter Paul's argument at all; indeed, he
guards carefully against his readers drawing such a conclusion. For if it were
a matter of moral fault, Paul's fictional interlocutor would not have raised
the question, "Why then does he still find fault?" (9:19). The answer would
be obvious. And if it were a matter of fault and God's righteous condemnation, and the interlocutor was simply confused about that, Paul could settle
the matter easily by saying, "Wait a minute, God really is just in condemn-
ing Israel, because Israel as a people truly is a sinful, rebellious failure in
whom the world's evil is concentrated." But he says no such thing. Rather,
he speaks of the potter's authority over the clay, of the potter's making now
one "vessel" for this end and now another "vessel" for that end. "And what
if he has done so in order to make known the riches of his glory for the objects of mercy [the Gentiles, at this time], which he has prepared beforehand for glory?" (9:23). Paul's point is precisely this: *God* has hardened—
not "condemned"—a portion of Israel in order that the Gentiles might receive God's mercy. Israel's current state (i.e., a portion having been hardened) is the result of *God's* action, not their own. Further, that God has already saved (shown mercy to) a remnant of Israel along with the believing
Gentiles is a sign that God has not simply set aside Israel as a whole. As
Paul will go on to argue (11:1–6, 16), the remnant itself is God's guarantee
that he in fact saves the whole through the part.

In 9:30–33 it might appear that Paul lays some fault at Israel's feet:
"The Gentiles, not pursuing righteousness, attained righteousness, a righteousness which is from faith. But Israel, pursuing a law of righteousness,
did not arrive at that law. Why? Because [they pursued it] not from faith
but as if it were from works" (my translation). There appears to be some
ambiguity about Israel's culpability in this argument. Clearly Israel was
pursuing its aim (which was righteousness nonetheless) by a means that
would not attain the goal. But lest the reader be inclined to attribute the
cause of Israel's misdirected pursuit and present nonarrival at righteousness (except for a remnant, the point of 9:27–29) to Israel's moral failure,
Paul immediately clarifies himself. He again attributes their condition to
God's action. It is the result of God's "laying in Zion a stone that will
make people stumble, a rock that will make them fall" (9:33). Israel
stumbles because God himself trips it up. On the other hand, Paul attributes to Israel ignorance (*agnoeō*) of God's righteousness, despite its obvious zeal for God. Precisely in this ignorance, rather than in culpable
moral failure, Israel pursued a righteousness of its own rather than God's
righteousness, and thus Israel did not submit to God's righteousness. Despite the interpretations of Wright and other commentators, there is no

hint in 9:30–10:3 of "Israel's failure,"[23] but only of God's purpose of bringing righteousness to the Gentiles being worked out through God's own mysterious hardening and tripping-up of Israel, who remains ignorant of that purpose.

Paul sums up God's purpose for the Gentiles in one word: Christ (10:4). He is the righteousness of God which Israel missed because, in its ignorance of God's purpose, it continued to seek the righteousness of Torah. Nonetheless, Paul goes on to say that the Torah (Moses) and the Prophets attest to Christ as God's righteousness for the nations (10:4–13) and to the necessity of Paul's mission as the proclaimer of that righteousness to the nations (10:14–18). Because God has hardened Israel (9:6–10:3), the word about Christ has gone out through Paul to the nations (indeed "to all the earth," "to the ends of the world"; 10:18), who may now believe and confess that word that has come near to them and thereby "call upon the name of the Lord" and be saved.

At this point (10:19) Paul returns to the question of Israel's ignorance: "Again I ask, did Israel not understand?" Not understand what? As the following Scripture citations (10:19–20) make clear, both Moses and the Prophets testify that God at some point would turn to the nations so that he might be found by those who were not seeking him and thereby stir up Israel's jealousy. It is this that Israel might have known, had it read its Scriptures carefully. Perhaps then God's strange ways of hardening and showing mercy might not have been such a hidden mystery to Israel. At the same time, Paul lays no moral fault at Israel's feet, only a certain blindness (a point he will make again in 11:7–10). Further, in 10:21 Paul stresses that God also graciously continues to reach out his hands toward Israel, even as "a disobedient and contrary people."[24] Precisely thus is Paul warranted in denying vigorously that God's turn to the Gentiles means the rejection of his own people (11:1).

23. See, e.g., the chapter title of Joseph Fitzmyer's commentary on Rom. 9:30–10:21: "*Israel's failure*: It is derived from its own refusal"; *Romans* (Anchor Bible 33; New York: Doubleday, 1993), 576. The title for Fitzmyer's comments on 9:30–33 is "Israel has stumbled in its pursuit of uprightness." Such a title emphasizes Israel's "responsibility," whereas Paul puts the emphasis on God's action of causing Israel to stumble.

24. Israel's being a "disobedient and contrary people" (10:21) is stated as neither cause nor effect of God's hardening. It may be another way of describing Israel's hardened state, as, e.g., in 11:30–32, where God's hardening is rendered as God's action of "confining" or "imprisoning" (*sunkleiō*) in disobedience. In any case Paul's quotation of Isa. 65:2 Septuagint in Rom. 10:21 serves as much or more to emphasize God's ongoing "reach" toward Israel—a reach which Paul goes on to explicate in the following verses—as it does to depict Israel's state of being hardened. C. E. B. Cranfield suggests that "in this sentence the statement of Israel's disobedience is strictly incidental . . . , but the statement of what God has done with regard to this people is central and decisive"; *A Critical and Exegetical Commentary on the Epistle to the Romans* (International Critical Commentary; Edinburgh: T & T Clark, 1979), 2:541. I believe it is the assumption that Paul is emphasizing Israel's disobedience rather than God's continuing reach that leads translators to render *de* in 10:21 as a strong contrastive, "but," rather than as "and" or "also"; most trans-

God's ongoing reaching out toward and claim upon his people is attested first by the fact that Paul is himself an Israelite and thus a representative of his own people. On this basis alone Paul is assured that "God has not rejected his people whom he foreknew" (11:2). But there is more: there is also a "remnant" chosen (*eklogē*) by grace (11:5). These chosen obtained (as did the Gentiles) the righteousness from faith; and the rest of Israel was hardened, again because of God's decision and action and not because of any culpable moral failure. "God gave them a sluggish spirit" and eyes and ears that would not function properly (11:8). He allowed "their table [to] become a snare and a trap, a stumbling block (*skandalon*) and a retribution for them," and their eyes to be darkened and their backs bent (11:9–10). In other words, the hardening of the larger portion of Israel is the result both of God's direct action upon Israel and of God's leaving Israel alone in its own pursuit of Torah righteousness. Israel thus stumbles along, as if in a half-sleep, toward a goal which it cannot see clearly, tripping over obstacles which God himself has laid on its path.

But in no sense whatsoever ("by no means!"), according to Paul, are Israel's faltering steps (*paraptōma*) the prelude to its downfall and defeat.[25] They are only the prelude and condition for the salvation of the nations. And if Israel's faltering steps provide the condition for God's pouring out his riches upon the Gentiles, then how much more will Israel's "completion" (*plērōma*) of the race or journey mean? It can only mean, as Paul concludes in 11:15, "life from the dead," the eschatological time of resurrection. For the time being, then, in this time of mercy toward the Gentiles, the chosen

lators render *de* in 10:20 as "and." I should make clear at this point that I am not arguing that Paul is naively assuming or arguing that Israel is sinless or faultless. We may note a few other characterizations of Israel present in Rom. 9–11. In 11:3 Paul quotes 1 Kings 19:10, 14, where Elijah complains that "they [Israel] have killed your prophets, they have demolished your altars . . . and they are seeking my life." But the purpose of this quotation is not to describe Israel's present culpability or to name the cause of God's hardening, but only to set up the argument that a remnant of Israel has been chosen by grace. In Rom. 11:20 Paul writes that a portion of Israel is as branches broken off the tree because of "unbelief." But, as I show, that unbelief is the result of ignorance and God's hardening. That God will remove his hardening and thus the ignorance and unbelief of this portion of Israel and regraft it into the tree, is the hope of 11:23–24. In 11:26–27 Paul, quoting Isa. 59:20–21 Septuagint, affirms that God, "the Deliverer," will banish "ungodliness" and take away the "sins" of Israel. For Paul this is simply to say that God will remove Israel's state of being hardened, as the following verses make clear. None of these verses warrant Wright's interpretation that God has especially "concentrated" sin in Israel. The unbelief of Israel and the disobedience in which Israel is imprisoned under God's hardening are no greater than those of the Gentiles before God showed them mercy.

25. In the context of the Scripture citations in Rom. 11:8–10, with their metaphors of sluggishness, being ensnared, and stumbling in a race or on a journey, it is very unlikely that *paraptōma* in 11:11–12 means "trespass" or "transgression" (so New International Version). There is no indication that Paul shifts from description of God's hardening to judgment of Israel's moral condition. He remains consistent in describing what is happening in the race or journey of the not-chosen portion of Israel; hence *paraptōma* must be translated as "stumbling" (so New Revised Standard Version). On this reading see Gaston, *Paul and the Torah*, 135–50; and Stowers, *Rereading Romans*, 303–16.

remnant part of Israel (those who have attained the righteousness from faith) suffices to stand in for the whole elect people. The chosen remnant is not to be understood as the "saved" minority portion of Israel over against the "lost" majority. The remnant is rather the representative part of the whole, the very means by which the whole of Israel (including the hardened portion) is already made holy. "If the . . . first fruits [are] holy, then the whole batch is holy; and if the root is holy, then the branches also are holy" (11:16).

Indeed, the nations themselves have not come to share in God's kindness and mercy apart from the "tree" of Israel which is made holy through the chosen remnant. Into this tree the nations have been grafted (this also not through their own choosing or action, but through the decision and action of the gardener), in order that they might share in Israel's blessings (11:17–20). On what basis then can the Gentiles boast? None whatsoever. What they have received, they have received because God has shown them kindness. The "severity" of God which now rests upon Israel only serves God's purpose of showing kindness to the nations.

Paul finally summarizes his argument. In the mystery of God's purpose, God has seen fit to put a hardening upon Israel in order that the Gentiles might enter the race and complete it. But Israel itself will be restored and enabled to complete the race, by God's action. "The Deliverer" will come "out of Zion." He will "banish ungodliness" from Israel, "take away their sins," and thus renew the covenant with them (11:26–27). That is, God will as surely lift his hardening as he once imposed it for a season and a purpose. For the sake of the gospel to the Gentiles, Israel is an "enemy." But God will not forsake his promises to Israel's ancestors; nor will he ever abandon his beloved chosen people. These Pauline claims are wholly consistent with the theme at the heart of the texts from Genesis, Exodus, Deuteronomy, and Isaiah examined above. As surely as God's mercy has come upon the once hardened nations (Rom. 1:18–32), so God's mercy will return upon now hardened Israel, for the point of the entire story is that God might "be merciful to all" (11:32).

Throughout the sustained argument of Romans 9–11 Paul has kept a single thesis in view. God may harden and show mercy, now toward the nations, now toward a portion of Israel, as he wills, each in its season and for a purpose (the revelation of God's glory), but God will never reject his chosen fleshly people or allow them to fail in the race of salvation. If Israel of the flesh "fails" as a whole people, God fails. But fleshly Israel as a people neither has failed in its purpose (despite its unbelief and disobedience, i.e., the state of God's hardening) nor can it fail, since its election, purpose, and destiny reside not in itself (as if they were gifts to be given to God in return for God's ongoing faithfulness or mercy; 11:35), but are hidden and preserved in the unsearchable decisions and inscrutable ways of God (11:33–35). If that is Paul's claim, then Wright has given a misleading and quite possibly dangerous reading of Romans 9–11. How do we account for his reading?

Climax of Covenant History versus God's Election and Apocalypse

Wright takes it as one of his chief tasks in reading Romans to make explicit Paul's worldview, which lies for the most part below the surface of the specific arguments of the letter, but which is by and large its driving force:

> The present exercise must involve the tricky attempt to make inferences about Paul's worldview and about the large-scale belief system he held; in other words not simply to study Romans as a rag-bag of loci or topoi within Paul's hypothetical *Compendia* or *Summa*, but to show how the letter belongs within, and indeed acts as a window upon, Paul's symbolic world, his nonreflective praxis, his assumed narrative framework, and his fundamental answers to the key [worldview] questions.[26]

Wright spends a good deal of time, as he sees it, uncovering, teasing out, and putting together that worldview through his particular reading of Romans and the other Pauline letters.[27] In Paul's worldview, according to Wright, Israel is everywhere the subtext, the story beneath the story: as being chosen, covenanted, and given a vocation as God's "means of rescuing the whole world"; as distorting and failing that election, covenant, and vocation; as thus becoming the place where God "concentrates" the sin of the world; as being once and still (in Paul's time) exiled; as awaiting return from exile and restoration; as being led in a new exodus, having its exile ended, and being fully restored, summed up and completed in Christ himself; as thus having its particular "fleshly" election, covenant, and vocation come to an end in the coming of Christ and the calling of the church; as failing to recognize this, its own termination as the people of God, as the "climax" of its story; as needing now, as *individual* Jews, to convert to Jesus Christ. That story of Israel is the effective background narrative in Wright's interpretation of all of Paul's letters. "The critique of Israel . . . emerges constantly in Paul, both in sustained arguments and in frequent 'asides' or allusions, since they frequently give insights into *a whole suppressed train of thought*."[28] Thus, for example, in Galatians 3–4 Paul "tells the story of Israel, the people of God, as the story of Abraham and exodus," despite the facts that Israel and the exodus never seem to come into view in that text and that Israel is mentioned only once and the exodus not at all in the entire letter.[29] While the story of Israel seems (to most readers except Wright) not often to come into view, either explicitly or implicitly, in Paul's

---

26. Wright, "Romans and the Theology of Paul," 32.

27. I say "as he sees it," because I am not convinced that Wright actually "finds" such a worldview "behind" the text, but in fact *puts* it there. It is constructed elsewhere, out of the texts of Judaism of Paul's time; see Wright's *New Testament and the People of God*.

28. Wright, "Christ, the Law, and 'Pauline Theology,'" 14 (emphasis added).

29. Wright, "Letter to the Galatians," 231. See also many of the individual chapters in *Climax of the Covenant*.

letters, for Wright it is in fact always the real and determinative story behind many or most of the particular discussions in Paul's letters.

Further, as I showed above, behind the story of Israel lies another, the story of creation, the fall, and the need of redemption. According to Wright that is the still more foundational and more comprehensive worldview in Paul's theology, a worldview in which Israel itself serves an important—and through its "failure" to fulfill its covenant vocation, a primarily negative—but only temporary function. God's electing, covenanting, and calling of Israel is strictly functional, serving the sole purpose of "dealing with evil" in the created order. Thus, in Romans 9–11, Paul "has told the story of the creator and the world as the story of the covenant god and his people, now understood in a new way on the basis of the death and resurrection of Jesus of Nazareth."[30] Those creational and covenantal narratives are then, for Paul, the stories into which Christ himself enters as a figure. Where Israel fails in its election, covenant, and vocation as God's means of "dealing with evil" in creation, Christ, as himself fully Israel, succeeds. And thus God's purpose for Israel within creation is accomplished in Christ—and comes to an end.

I have already rendered questionable Wright's reading of Israel's story with respect to his interpretations of Genesis, Exodus, Deuteronomy, and Isaiah and with respect to his interpretation of Romans 9–11. His covenant-historical rather than apocalyptic reading of Paul can be rendered equally questionable by proposing the following thesis: Wright contextualizes the coming of Jesus Christ within an account of creation and Israel characterized by historical continuity: Jesus Christ is "the climax of the covenant" with Israel and creation; by contrast, Paul contextualizes creation and Israel within an account of the coming of Jesus Christ characterized as apocalyptic invasion and incorporation: Israel and the creation are judged and incorporated into the apocalypse of Jesus Christ.

Consider the following claim:

If we came "cold" to Romans 9–11, one of the first things that might strike us would be its story line. Paul begins with Abraham, continues with Isaac and Jacob, moves on to Moses and the exodus, and by the end of chap. 9 has reached the prophets and their predictions of exile and restoration. Then, in 10:6f., he expounds the passage in Deuteronomy (chap. 30) which predicts the return from exile, and in 11:1ff. develops this in terms of the "remnant" idea, before reaching, toward the end of chap. 11, the great predictions of covenant renewal from Isaiah and Jeremiah. He narrates, in other words, the covenant history of Israel.[31]

---

30. Wright, "Romans and the Theology of Paul," 58.
31. Ibid., 56. I shall leave aside the fact that such a "story line" has rarely, if ever, been "one of the first things that might strike" "cold" (and even many very "warm") readers of Rom. 9–11. In my judgment, Wright simply drags that story line to the text and superimposes Paul's argument upon it.

After laying out the details of that supposed covenant history at some length, Wright suggests that Paul had laid the groundwork for its story line earlier in Romans: "Paul has told the covenant history of Israel in such a way as to bring out the strange truth of Israel's being cast away so that the world might be redeemed." Thus, the covenant history of Israel provides the context for the coming of Christ: Paul "is simply in fact . . . writing into larger history . . . the truth of the cross. Israel is the Messiah's people according to the flesh (9:5); it has acted out on a grand scale what that [i.e., the cross] means, namely, that it has become the place where sin has been drawn together in order to be dealt with." The "positive result" of Israel's being "cast away" is the inclusion of the Gentiles into God's covenant-history: "*The Gentile mission grows precisely out of this strange covenant purpose.*" "The inclusion of Gentiles is one of the features of the 'return from exile' that takes place after Israel, the servant of the Lord, has borne the sins of many."[32] Hence, what once were Israel's privileges were "transferred" from "Israel according to the flesh, to the Messiah, to the Jew-plus Gentile church."[33] That church is itself now "the fulfilment of the community of Israel" (*What Saint Paul Really Said*, 87). Jews may, if they choose, once again share the blessings of the covenant: "Paul holds firmly to the hope that the renewal of the covenant which has taken place in Jesus the Messiah will be effective not only for Gentiles but also for Jews who will come, as he himself has done, to faith in Jesus as the Jewish Messiah" (109).

Wright thus presents creation and covenant history as a linear historical progression: creation—fall—functional covenant with Israel—Jesus Christ (at which time Israel's "special privilege" is canceled)—the church (which replaces Israel as the people of God)—consummation. "Paul offers his hearers a story in which the whole cosmos was *going somewhere*. Against the essentially ahistorical worldview of paganism, and over against the 'golden age' dreams of some philosophers of history, Paul articulated a linear view of history from creation to new creation" (*What Saint Paul Really Said*, 89–90, emphasis original).

Several objections may be made to that claim. First, in not a single text in the entire Pauline corpus does Paul himself lay out, draw attention to, make use of, or otherwise hint at an extended, continuous, linear historical narrative of creation, Israel, exile, Christ, the church, and the consummation. For example, the claim which Wright makes about the story line behind Romans 9–11 is groundless. Isaac and Ishmael and Jacob and Esau appear in 9:7–13 not as characters in a history of the "covenant people" but as paradigmatic examples or *types* of God's sovereign, selective, and often surprising act of showing mercy toward the one and not the other. Isaac and Jacob as characters of the past are figured into Paul's present to explicate the *current* condition of the Gentiles. Nor does Paul "move on" (in 9:14–18), as if narrating a

32. The quotations are all from "Romans and the Theology of Paul," 58 (emphasis original).
33. Ibid., 59.

continuing story line, to "Moses and the exodus." No story of Moses and the exodus is either told or insinuated in these verses. Rather, "Moses" is simply quoted as declaring that God does indeed show mercy on whomever he chooses. Likewise, Pharaoh appears not as an agent in a narrative of the exodus, but as a *type* of one who is hardened in order that God's name might be proclaimed "in all the earth." Pharaoh is thus also figured into Paul's present in order to explicate Israel's *current* condition. Paul makes no claims about Israel's past or Israel's actions in these texts, only claims about the *present* state of Israel under God's sovereign action of mercy-showing and hardening. There is no "critique" of Israel's history. Nor does Paul, as Wright suggests, continue the narration of a story line on through to "the prophets and their predictions of exile and restoration." In 9:27–29 Paul introduces the notion of the remnant, but again that notion, announced previously by the prophets, becomes for Paul an announcement of the *current* condition of a portion of Israel. Israel's exile is nowhere within the horizon of the text as past event or present reality, nor is return from exile as future event. Israel's restoration appears within the text's horizon only insofar as the remnant chosen by God is a present guarantee that God has not abandoned Israel as a whole and that by means of this remnant God secures the coming restoration of the whole, a point not made fully explicit until 11:1–16. In other words, Paul traces no story line from Israel in the past, through Israel in the present, to Israel (or Israel's replacement, the church) in the future. Paul speaks only of the *present* time, the time of the gospel, the time in which the stories of Israel and the nations have been overtaken by, caught up into, but in no sense dissolved into the momentous event of the apocalypse of Jesus Christ.

That is precisely what is revealed in the relationship between Romans 8:31–39 and Romans 9–11. In 8:31–39, Paul utters his great confession of the conquering and binding love of God demonstrated in the death and resurrection of Jesus Christ, a love from which nothing in all creation can separate those whom God has predestined, called (*kaleō*), justified, and glorified (8:30). "Who will bring any charge against God's elect (*eklektōn*)? It is God who justifies. Who is to condemn?" (8:33–34). It is this binding love of God, enacted in the death and resurrection of Jesus Christ, that gives Paul the confidence ("it is not as though the word of God had failed"; 9:6) to embark on his reading of Israel's current hardening as being both occasioned by and enclosed within God's election of Israel and the apocalypse of Jesus Christ. God will not let his elect people be separated from his love in Jesus Christ ("as regards election [*eklogēn*] they are the beloved, for the sake of their ancestors; for the gifts and the calling [*klēsis*] of God are irrevocable"; 11:28–29). God's abiding and effective love toward Israel, that is, Israel's calling/election, is incorporated into and guaranteed by the history of the gospel (the death and resurrection of Jesus Christ), since in that history alone God has defeated all the powers which might threaten to create a final separation. Israel's story line appears on Paul's apocalyptic horizon in only

one way: as the story not of its own action (whether good or bad) but of
God's action, as the story of its *election* as a corporeal body, which Paul now
understands to be preceded by, drawn up into, and finally sustained in God's
apocalyptic action in Jesus Christ.

Such a fact cannot be accounted for in terms of a historical narrative of Israel that arrives at Jesus Christ and there comes to its end (Paul's supposed
"linear view of history"). For Paul, Jesus Christ does not recapitulate Israel's
history in himself—a view which leads Wright into a plethora of overread-
ings of Pauline texts in search of the supposed story line or worldview hidden behind them ("the tricky attempt to make inferences about Paul's worldview and about the large-scale belief system he held"). Rather, the apocalypse
of Jesus Christ is the recapitulation and sustaining of God's election of historical Israel. It must be so for Paul since, as he is at pains to establish, Israel's
election and the coming of Jesus Christ are *God's* action, and God cannot
contradict or be unfaithful to himself. Israel's history remains for Paul a series of fragments and figures which testify to God's election, but in no sense
does that history, as a history of Israel's obedience or disobedience, constitute the grounds of Israel's election. Only God's action does.[34]

When Paul speaks of Israel, he is interested exclusively in God's action. At
those very few points in his letters where Paul does offer an account of the
action of particular Jews who oppose the gospel (versus an account of God's
action with respect to the people of Israel as a corporate whole), he pronounces no different judgment upon them than he does upon Gentiles who
oppose the gospel. For example, in 1 Thessalonians 2:14–16 (assuming it is
authentically Pauline) Paul locates current opposition from Jews to his prophetic Gentile mission within a history of Jewish persecution of their own
prophets and announces that "God's wrath has overtaken them [not Israel,
but particular Jews] at last" (2:16). He makes this point only for the purpose
of showing that the persecution that the Thessalonian faithful are currently
experiencing from their own fellow citizens is not an isolated incident in
the history of God's people. There has always been disobedience and opposition to God's purposes among Jews as well as Gentiles. So God's wrath
comes not only upon Jews, but also upon the unbelieving and persecuting

34. This understanding differs in some respects from that of J. Louis Martyn, who reads Paul, at
least in Galatians, as rejecting the notion of a binding election of Israel as a people. I think Martyn, who
is rightly critical of the kind of salvation-historical reading of Paul offered by Wright, nonetheless ties
God's election of Israel too closely with the reading of Israel's "covenant-history" as salvation-historical
continuity. Martyn is right to emphasize that for Paul the apocalypse of Jesus Christ interrupts all historical continuities that might serve to establish a "world" for a people apart from Jesus Christ—including Israel's own historical continuity insofar as that is rooted in a narrative about the giving of Torah and Israel's obedience to it. But Martyn does not show, as I think Paul does, particularly in Romans, that God's
action in the apocalypse of Jesus Christ does not contradict, but rather gathers into itself and sustains,
God's action in electing Israel. The continuity rests in God's action, not in the continuous forward
"movement" of history. God's apocalyptic action cannot contradict God's electing action; that, I believe,
is a short summary of Rom. 9–11 in relation to Rom. 8.

Gentile Thessalonians (1 Thess. 1:10). In Romans 1–3 Paul makes clear that
God's wrath is being revealed against all, both Gentiles and Jews, in the
apocalypse of Jesus Christ, a wrath from which neither Gentile nor Jew can
escape except through the righteousness of God, also disclosed in the apocalypse of Jesus Christ. Paul announces God's judgment upon all human action as falling short of the glory of God. But God cannot judge his own action in electing corporeal Israel as his own people, loved forever.

Finally, Wright's fully realized eschatology of the history of fleshly Israel
fails to take into account that Jesus Christ is not the progressive conclusion
of an historical narrative about creation and Israel. Rather, the apocalypse of
Jesus Christ encloses the whole cosmos, and therefore also the church and
fleshly Israel, within itself. The cross of Christ reveals that the present time
of this enclosing is a time of suffering, waiting, and groaning—and for Israel
a time of hardening. While the *ekklēsia* already receives a foretaste of the final victory of God in its present experience of the Spirit (Rom. 8:12–16),
the *ekklēsia*, together with the creation, still awaits the full apocalypse of
God's glory as corporeal and cosmic participation in Christ's resurrection
(the redemption of the body); the church therefore receives its apocalyptic
inheritance in the present primarily as a participation in Christ's crucifixion
(8:17). And if the church, and all creation with it, so also Israel along with
the church and creation. Is it not possible to see Israel's present hardening as
its unique (but unknowing) participation in the crucifixion of Jesus Christ,
not as culpable "failure," but as its own share in suffering, waiting, and
groaning with the church and the whole creation, as it too awaits the final
redemption of all things? Why should we think that fleshly Israel has already
arrived fully at its *telos* (condemnation and cancellation, according to
Wright) in Jesus Christ when neither the church nor the creation has? *All*
things presently suffer, wait, groan together with Christ and the Spirit, even
as all things "will obtain the freedom of the glory of the children of God"
(8:21). But then also, why should we think that while the church and the
creation wait in hope and eager expectation, fleshly Israel's hope has come to
a bitter end in its supposed failure? Does its stumbling attempt to arrive at
the *telos* of God's righteousness through Torah (9:31) finally separate it as a
corporate body from the love of God in Christ Jesus? May it never be! It is
precisely that thought which Paul vigorously opposes in Romans 9–11. The
church and Israel and all things are enclosed in the crucifixion and resurrection of Jesus Christ, the apocalypse of God's love which conquers all the
powers of separation.

Wright's Paul as "Evangelical" and "Liberal"

I conclude this examination and critique of Wright by reflecting briefly
on his reading of Paul as an "evangelical" on the one hand and as a "liberal"
on the other. How is Wright's Paul an "evangelical" in his understanding of
Israel and the Jews? Wright consistently argues that the destiny of the Jews

after the coming of Christ depends upon their conversion to Jesus Christ. Theologically considered, apart from such conversion the Jews as individuals and as a people simply stand in need of salvation along with and under the same condition as the many pagans and pagan peoples of the world. "God has redefined Israel . . . and all forms of Judaism that do not recognize this and conform are at best out of date and at worst dangerous compromises and parodies."[35] Reflecting on Galatians 4:1–11, Wright concludes that for Paul "unbelieving Judaism itself stands revealed as *a compromise with paganism*" (*What Saint Paul Really Said*, 137).[36] There is "no covenant future for those Israelites who refuse to abandon their 'own,' that is, their ethnic status of covenant membership."[37]

In order to share in God's eschatological purpose now fully given over to the church (the "remodeled people of God"), Jews must individually "embrace Jesus as their Messiah"[38] or "come to faith," as Paul himself did, "in Jesus as the Jewish Messiah" (*What Saint Paul Really Said*, 109).[39] Individual Jews, like Gentiles, must come to "see, in Christ, the clue to what the creator/covenant god has righteously been doing in Israel's history, and [to] grasp this in faith—these Israelites can always regain their full covenant status."[40] "The *possibility* that is always held out [in Rom. 11] . . . is not a large-scale last-minute restoration of 'all Jews,' irrespective of Christian faith, but the *chance* that Jews, during the course of the present age, will come to

35. Wright, "Paul's Gospel and Caesar's Empire," 178.

36. Wright continues: "Adherence to Torah, in the way that Paul's opponents [in Galatia] are advocating it, is no better than pagan idolatry. To undergo circumcision is, in effect, to give in to the principalities and powers. It is to step back into a scheme of blood, soil, race and tribe. It is like going back to the paganism renounced at conversion." This is one of many places where Wright confuses the issue of *Gentiles* being persuaded to take up Torah obedience (which Paul vigorously opposes) with the issue of *Jews*, whether messianic or not, continuing to be Torah observant (which Paul assumes they will and nowhere opposes). Paul is troubled by the way that Torah observance becomes or threatens to become a barrier to communion between Jews and Gentiles in the messianic community or to full acceptance of Gentiles into that community on the basis of the faithfulness of Jesus Christ. Wright seems to assume that Paul's criticism of Torah as a problem in the Gentile churches which he is establishing is at the same time Paul's criticism of "Judaism." That assumption is susceptible to serious challenge on many fronts. Most obviously, one wonders why Paul would spend so much effort (below or behind the surface of the text, according to Wright) wrestling with "*Israel's* failure" and *Judaism's* "compromises" when he is writing to *Gentile* churches about the issues they face in their religious, social, and political contexts.

37. Wright, "Romans and the Theology of Paul," 57.

38. Wright, "Paul's Gospel and Caesar's Empire," 176.

39. The mind boggles at the notion that Paul "came to faith." Whether it is according to the accounts in Acts or his own accounts in Gal. 2, Phil. 3, or 1 Cor. 15, Paul is never depicted as "coming to faith" but only as being radically interrupted, accosted, captured, and commissioned in an apocalypse of the risen Lord. Wright's misstep in this characterization of Paul's "conversion," that is, his failure to view it as an apocalyptic seizure of Paul's life, is repeated in his failure to read God's relationship to Israel apocalyptically, that is, as a relationship in which God is the sovereign actor who interrupts and lays hold of Israel for his own purposes.

40. Wright, "Romans and the Theology of Paul," 57.

Christian faith and so be grafted back in" (*Climax of the Covenant*, 248, emphasis added).

Paul thus becomes in Wright's hands an evangelical theologian of individual sin, repentance, conversion, and acceptance of Jesus Christ as personal Lord and Savior through faith, upon receiving an offer of salvation. We might also note how voluntary and self-moved all of this appears in Wright's construal. It is individual Jews, now as generic human beings no different from Gentiles, who, in response to the new possibility of salvation in Christ, "see" what God is doing to Israel, "abandon" their ethnic covenant status, "come to faith in," "grasp in faith," or "embrace" Jesus Christ, and, finally, in so doing, "regain" their covenant status—individual Jews on the proverbial sawdust trail. Perhaps Wright hardly intends it, but in his hands the biblical understanding of the chosen people of Israel is reduced to Jews (with Gentiles) as individual seekers and choosers of Christianity, who participate in the new movement primarily through self-moved individual faith rather than through election into a specific corporate body. While this fits nicely the idea of becoming Christian in the tradition of evangelicalism and revivalism, it is, as we have seen, a long distance from the way in which Paul renders the logic of the gospel—God setting his heart upon and sovereignly electing (and hardening and showing mercy to) and destining for salvation one particular fleshly people out of all the nations of the earth and saving the nations by grafting them into this people.

But, as we have also seen, Wright objects most strenuously to that logic. According to Wright, for Jews to go on, after Christ, affirming and living out of God's election of fleshly Israel is their most culpable and dangerous error. Here we have Wright's "liberal" Paul, who is appalled at the thought that God would bind himself uniquely and forever to one people defined primarily by biological descent, ethnicity (as defined by a particular set of binding practices), and place (as the land of Israel, whether actually possessed or promised). We have already encountered Wright's characterizations of such a thought many times. It betrays the conviction that "Jews . . . enjoy a private covenantal blessing which still depends on a special, privileged, ethnic state."[41] In continuing in this conviction, Israel persists in "her all-consuming interest: her relentless pursuit of national, ethnic and territorial identity" (*What Saint Paul Really Said*, 84). Israel thus "clings to her own special status," showing that it believes that covenant membership is "for Jews and Jews only" (108). It regards the nations with "a sense of effortless racial superiority" (75). "Israel is . . . shown to be guilty of a kind of metasin, the attempt to confine grace to one race" (*Climax of the Covenant*, 240). "From Paul's Christian point of view, those Jews who do not embrace Jesus as their Messiah are thereby embracing instead an identity marked out by blood and soil, by ancestry and territory, in other words, by the 'flesh.' They

41. Ibid., 61.

are, therefore, subject to the same critique as paganism."[42] Such comments, as we have seen, sprinkle page after page of Wright's discussions of Paul on the Jews. Clearly Wright's Paul is revolted by the very idea of God any longer maintaining a special relationship with carnal Israel. So too the "Gentile rejection of an ethnic-based people of god" is, according to Wright's Paul, "quite proper."[43] God in Jesus Christ eradicates any theologically relevant difference between Israel and the nations and establishes a *universal* relationship with the individual members of Israel and the nations in terms of their common humanity as creatures of God who have fallen into sin and stand in need of the redemption offered in Christ.[44]

But while this fits nicely with the idea of how God supposedly ought to relate to humankind according to the liberal indifference to particular bodily, ethnic, and corporate difference, it is a long distance from God's *differential* election, hardening, and mercy-showing, as Paul depicts it in Romans 9–11, in which the difference between Israel and the nations is always strictly maintained. The very basis of Paul's key affirmation that God has not rejected Paul's "kindred according to the flesh" (9:3) is that God has already saved Paul himself, "an Israelite, a descendant of Abraham, a member of the tribe of Benjamin" (11:1); that is, a fleshly Jew who, together with a larger remnant of fleshly Jews, stands in for the whole of fleshly Israel, already rendering the whole body of Israel holy and pointing toward its final salvation (11:16). It is this God who demonstrates faithfulness to fleshly Israel who can also finally be trusted faithfully to show mercy to all, both Israel and the nations; indeed, to the nations only in and through fleshly Israel, from whom, "according to the flesh, comes the Messiah, who is over all" (9:5).

Nor does Paul anywhere argue that, in Christ, Israel and the nations are now "the same" at some higher or deeper level of human existence transcending ordinary carnal, cultural difference. Rather, Paul seeks the harmonious communion (table fellowship) of Jew and Gentile in their corporeal and corporate difference as the great sign of God's reconciliation in Jesus Christ. Christ became a servant not of generic humanity, but of the circumcised, for the sake of the Gentiles, in order that there might be a mutual welcome between Gentiles and Jews and that the nations might rejoice "with God's people" (15:7–12). Such is the illiberal Paul.[45]

---

42. Wright, "Paul's Gospel and Caesar's Empire," 176.

43. Wright, "Romans and the Theology of Paul," 61.

44. See the important critique of Wright's notion of "undifferentiated humanity" (in contrast to Paul's persistent understanding of humanity as always Jew and Gentile) in Terence L. Donaldson, *Paul and the Gentiles: Remapping the Apostle's Convictional World* (Minneapolis: Fortress, 1997), 151–61; the whole chapter entitled "Generic Humanity" (107–64) is pertinent to the issues treated here.

45. Jewish scholar Daniel Boyarin shares Wright's conviction that Paul is a liberal, but unlike Wright sees much more clearly the negative political fallout of such a conviction: "Pauline universalism even at its most liberal and benevolent has become a powerful force for coercive discourses of sameness, denying . . . the rights of Jews, women, and others to retain their difference. . . . This discourse was characteristic of liberal Germany . . . and still persists in the United States of today in such 'liberal' expressions as 'too

I hope that I have by now presented a sufficient challenge to Wright's supersessionist reading of Paul which at the very least renders his reading questionable. In addition, I tried to present an alternative reading of Paul on the Jews and Israel aimed at showing that such a reading is not only possible but also more appropriate with respect to key Pauline texts, particularly Romans 9–11. I also attempted to expose and criticize some of Wright's key enabling assumptions: about the meaning of God's election of Israel as purely instrumental; about the foundational character of worldview and covenant history in Paul's theology; and more generally about the individualistic and universalistic (evangelical and liberal) rendering of the meaning of salvation in Paul. On this last point I hinted at some of the political consequences of Wright's construal. Can his voluntarist, individualist, universalist understanding of the human being in relation to God finally sustain any notion of a people of God, which I argued in the previous chapters is central in Paul's theology? In the end, I believe not. Wright's "Christian" in a strong sense stands alone, an "individual" in relation to a wider unbelieving social order, but unconstituted by participation in the specific people of God. The cancellation of corporeal Israel has become at the same time the cancellation of the corporeal body of Christ.

I hope I showed that the supersessionist interpretation of Paul, of which Wright is one of the most able, unapologetic, and forceful contemporary proponents, is not only less than persuasive, but also seriously damaging to a proper and critically important Christian theology of Israel and the Jews. I turn now to another Christian interpreter of Israel and Judaism who presents a very different, more promising understanding of the place of the Jews in God's purpose.

Israel's Call into Diaspora: Yoder on Paul and the Jews

Diaspora as Normative Judaism

In his later years John Howard Yoder devoted increasing attention to the question of the theological significance of the Jews and Judaism for Christian theology. Central to Yoder's theological engagement with Judaism is his

---

Jewish.' . . . The paradox in such discourse is that nearly always . . . the justification for coercing Jews to become Christian . . . citizens of the world is paradoxically the alleged *intolerance* of—the Jews. The parallels between this modern liberal discourse and that of Paul . . . seem obvious to me"; *A Radical Jew: Paul and the Politics of Identity* (Berkeley: University of California Press, 1994), 233–34. Boyarin captures nicely the strange paradox that lies precisely at the heart of Wright's interpretation of Paul; an interpretation in which *Jews* are persistently blamed for racial domination, nationalism, intolerance, and attachment to "blood and soil," despite the fact that the Diaspora Jews with whom Paul has any dealings at all in his mission are a small, relatively powerless, minority group, often beleaguered by harassment and persecution, seeking only to survive as a distinct people in an intolerant empire in which *Roman* birth, land-ownership, conquest, and political domination were the keys to sociopolitical well-being. Can Boyarin be totally wrong in identifying this "Paul's" supposed liberal universalism as—racism (233)? But, as I tried to show, such a liberal universalist Paul did not exist.

thesis that the history of Diaspora Judaism, from the time of the Babylonian exile to the present day, might be read from a Christian perspective as a history of God's call of his people into a world mission that was not possible when Israel was settled in Judea.

Yoder's thesis is set forth most clearly in his essay "See How They Go with Their Face to the Sun,"[46] a reflection on the significance of the Jewish Diaspora for understanding the role of the people of God among the nations. According to Yoder, the impact of the Babylonian conquest on Israel was historically inestimable and theologically fruitful. The Jews, under God's judgment enacted through the Babylonians, are led into exile. While this event is certainly in one sense a disaster for the nation of Israel, in another sense the exile under Jeremiah's prophetic instruction becomes a calling and a task. Without king, temple, and land the Jews are called into an alternative way of living as a specific people among the nations:

> Thus says the LORD of hosts, the God of Israel, to all the exiles whom I have sent into exile from Jerusalem to Babylon: Build houses and live in them; plant gardens and eat what they produce. Take wives and have sons and daughters; take wives for your sons, and give your daughters in marriage, that they may bear sons and daughters; multiply there, and do not decrease. But seek the welfare of the city where I have sent you into exile, and pray to the LORD on its behalf, for in its welfare you will find your welfare. (Jer. 29:4–7)

Yoder argues that this "Jeremianic dispersion existence," this Diaspora mode of being Jewish among the nations, became a *normative* pattern for Judaism— its divinely appointed mission: "To be scattered is not an hiatus, after which normalcy will resume. From Jeremiah's time on, rather, . . . dispersion shall be the calling of the Jewish faith community" (*For the Nations*, 52).[47] The theology of return, resettlement, and reconquest, played out by Ezra and Nehemiah, the Maccabees, the Zealots and Sadducees, and the messianic revolts up

46. This essay appears in Yoder's *For the Nations: Essays Public and Evangelical* (Grand Rapids: Eerdmans, 1997), 51–78. Many of Yoder's essays on Jews and Judaism were in quasi-unpublished form at the time of his death, available as a manuscript packet directly from Yoder under the title *The Jewish-Christian Schism Revisited: A Bundle of Old Essays* (Notre Dame: Shalom Desktop, 1996). (In order that the reader not be detracted by obvious typographical errors in Yoder's largely unedited text, I silently corrected errors in quotations.) Michael Cartwright and Peter Ochs are currently editing and introducing these and other essays by Yoder on Jews and Judaism for publication by Eerdmans. Other published essays in which Yoder addresses the theme of Jewish Diaspora include "On Not Being in Charge," in *War and Its Discontents: Pacifism and Quietism in the Abrahamic Traditions* (ed. J. Patout Burns; Washington, D.C.: Georgetown University Press, 1996), 74–90; and "War as a Moral Problem in the Early Church: The Historian's Hermeneutical Assumptions," in *The Pacifist Impulse in Historical Perspective* (ed. Harvey L. Dyck; Toronto: University of Toronto Press, 1996), 90–110.

47. Yoder at this point is summing up the message of the play *Jeremiah* by Jewish poet Stephan Zwieg. That message becomes the thesis of Yoder's essay. A similar proposal about Diaspora as the calling of the Jewish community is made by Boyarin, *Radical Jew*, 242–60.

to Bar Kochba in 135 did not become normative. Rather, the stories of Joseph, Daniel, and Esther, being at once faithful to YHWH and publicly useful in the context of their pagan environments, became the normative, canonical stories for a people no longer at home in its own land and no longer in charge of its political destiny.

Indeed, Yoder argues that Jesus' own reform movement may be viewed as a proposal that even in their own land, occupied by the Romans, Jews should take up the Jeremianic Diaspora pattern and learn to live without king and temple and without being in control of the land. Thus, rather than the ethos of the early Christian community being formed "from scratch with only a few words of Jesus [e.g., the Sermon on the Mount] to guide it," Yoder argues that

> Jesus' impact on the first century added more and deeper authentically Jewish reasons, and reinforced and further validated the already expressed Jewish reasons, for the already well established ethos of not being in charge and not considering any local state structure to be the primary bearer of the movement of history. (*For the Nations*, 69)[48]

Not only Diaspora Jews but also the Jews in the land were being called by Jesus to enact their witness to God's will among and for the nations on the model of Jeremiah's instructions to the first Jewish exiles.[49] Dispersion was to be taken up not as a fate or punishment, but as a way of life, as a *mission* and a *service* to the wider world. For Yoder, the history of Diaspora Judaism is testimony that in fact the Jews often understood themselves in precisely this way:

> The life of diaspora Jewry from Jeremiah to the time of Jesus (and since) was characterized more than we usually remember by its public visibility; synagogue life was observable. . . . Jewish life had no secrets. God-fearing Gentiles could observe and understand what was going on when Jews gathered around

---

48. "Thus the move of Judaism, whereby it became able to survive the loss of the Temple, and of such approximation to a Jewish 'state' structure, was a move toward, not away from, accepting Diaspora as the setting for identity and mission. That is parallel to the Jesus move"; *Jewish-Christian Schism Revisited*, 120.

49. Compare the comments of Boyarin (*Radical Jew*, 256): "The Rabbis produced their cultural formation within conditions of Diaspora—that is, in a situation within which Jews did not hold power over others—, and I would argue that their particular discourse of ethnocentricity is ethically appropriate only when the cultural identity is that of a minority, embattled or, at any rate, non-hegemonic. . . . It was a political possession of the Land which most threatened the possibility of continued Jewish cultural practice and difference. Given the choice between an ethnocentricity which would not seek domination over others or a seeking of political domination that would necessarily have led either to a dilution of distinctiveness, tribal warfare, or fascism, the Rabbis de facto chose the former." Boyarin's comments (drawing heavily on the work of W. D. Davies) lend great credence to Yoder's claim that Jesus himself—anticipating in large measure the de facto choice of the rabbis—was calling the Jews in the land, under Roman rule, to live as if they were already then and there a Diaspora people. Boyarin later writes: "The Pharisaic Rabbis 'invented' Diaspora, *even in the Land*, as the solution to [their] cultural dilemma" (256). Perhaps they were not the first Jews to make this proposal!

their Torah, and many Gentiles were in fact attracted by it. Jews earned their livings providing services to the Gentile economies, sometimes to landlords and rulers. Their cosmopolitan connections made them the best cross-cultural translators, scribes, accountants, educators, and compilers of proverbs. Far from being self-contained, they were at home in a world wider than the provincial cultures of Egypt, Mesopotamia, Greece or Rome. (*For the Nations*, 41–42)

Such a mode of existence was possible only on the basis of a uniquely Jewish claim: "Only the Jewish claim that the one true God, known to Abraham's children through their history, was also the Creator and sustainer of the other peoples as well, could enable mission without provincialism, cosmopolitan vision without empire" (*Jewish-Christian Schism Revisited*, 53). The *universal* claim which Israel made about its God was thus validated among the nations not through the Jews being in charge of the nations ("they will make a virtue and a cultural advantage of their being resident aliens, not spending their substance in fighting over civil sovereignty"; *For the Nations*, 71), but through their being present in many places throughout the world, testifying to the one God of Israel through Torah faithfulness and public service. In this way, Yoder claims, Diaspora Judaism after the time of Jesus lived as a "peace church" (*Jewish-Christian Schism Revisited*, 53).

Occasionally privileged after the model of Joseph, more often emigrating, frequently suffering martyrdom nonviolently, they were able to maintain identity without turf or sword, community without sovereignty. They thereby demonstrated pragmatically the viability of the ethic of Jeremiah and Jesus. In sum: *the Jews of the Diaspora were for over a millennium the closest thing to the ethic of Jesus* existing on any significant scale anywhere in Christendom. (*Jewish-Christian Schism Revisited*, 60, emphasis original)

According to Yoder, speaking sociologically, several features of the Diaspora way of life constitute and sustain the identity of Diaspora Jews as a specific people among the nations. First, they gather around and identify themselves by means of a *text* which may be copied and read anywhere. Priesthood and temple are unnecessary; conversely, "decentralization and fidelity are therefore not alternatives" (*For the Nations*, 58). Identity and worship are constituted by reading and singing the scriptural texts. Second, Jewish peoplehood is constituted wherever ten households gather into a "valid local cell of the world Jewish community, qualified to be *in that place* the concretion of the people of God" (58). Here again Yoder emphasizes that no priesthood or hierarchy is necessary. Third, the unity of the scattered people "is sustained by intervisitation, by intermarriage, by commerce, and by rabbinic consultation, needing no high priest or pope to hang together" (59). Fourth, identity is not established by agreement on a doctrinal or philosophical system, but by "the common life itself, the walk, halakah, and the shared remembering of the story behind it" (59). Finally, nothing of Jewish identity depends upon "cultural homogeneity, political control, or autarchy" (59); the narratives about Israel's existence as a nation with a monarch are relativized within the context of other stories about Jews (Abraham, Joseph, Shiphrah and Puah, Moses, Daniel, etc.) living faithfully in contexts where none of these things are in place.[50]

On the other hand, according to Yoder, the Diaspora Jews themselves would have explained their own existence and way of life among the nations theologically rather than sociologically.[51] Diaspora Jews affirm the sovereignty of God over all nations and over their own existence among the nations. Because God is sovereignly bringing about his righteous ends in history in his own way, the Jews do not have to be in charge of history's outcome through acquiring social and political dominance. Rather, God would establish his righteousness finally, for both Jews and the nations, only through the mission of the *meshiach*: "To do his [Messiah's] work for him would be presumptuous if not blasphemous" (*For the Nations*, 67). Thus "the efforts of the Maccabees, the Zealots and Bar Kochba to restore a national kingship had not been blessed by God": it is the Book of Daniel that is included in the Hebrew canon, not the books of the Maccabees (67, 68 n. 40). Indeed, to be placed in a subordinate role among the nations and even to suffer at their hands may sometimes be the chastisement of an "all-righteous God" for the sins of the people: self-defense vis-à-vis the nations "would interfere with that purpose" and perhaps even be "impious" (68). Finally, if righteous Jews do suffer and die at the hands of oppressive Gentiles and nations, God's name would thereby be "sanctified": that is, such suffering and death "makes a doxological contribution on the moral scales of history, which . . . avoidance of suffering (even if unjust) would obviate" (68).[52]

50. For another account of the "sociological innovations" of Diaspora Judaism, see Yoder, "On Not Being in Charge," 78, where he identifies three "culturally unique traits which define 'Judaism' and thereby Christianity in turn": the synagogue as "a decentralized, self-sustaining, nonsacerdotal" community; reading Torah as a community defining practice; and the rabbinate as "a nonsacerdotal, nonhierarchical, nonviolent leadership elite whose power is not civil but intellectual."

51. In addition to "See How They Go with Their Face to the Sun," which I quote here, see "On Not Being in Charge," 78–79.

52. Perhaps in some contrast to Yoder's emphasis on the theological reasons for Diaspora, Boyarin (*Radical Jew*, 258–59) seems to want to emphasize the sociological reasons as the Jews primary contribution to world politics: "I want to propose a privileging of Diaspora, a dissociation of ethnicities and political hegemonies, as the only social structure which even begins to make possible a maintenance of cultural identity in a world grown thoroughly and inextricably interdependent. Indeed, I would suggest that Diaspora, and not monotheism, may be the important contribution that Judaism has to make to the world, although I would not deny the positive role that monotheism has played in making Diaspora possible. . . . Diaspora can teach us that it is possible for a people to maintain its distinctive culture, its difference, without controlling land, a fortiori without controlling other people or developing a need to dispossess them of their lands." Yoder himself asks the question of Diaspora, "Is there something about this Jewish vision of the dignity and ministry of the scattered people of God which might be echoed or repli-

For Yoder the history of the Jews in dispersion, as he sociologically and theologically describes it, is an important and instructive model of the mode of the church's political presence among the nations, that is, a model of "the paradigmatic public role of God's people."[53] Indeed, that agenda dominates not only this essay by Yoder, but also most of his other writings on Jews and Judaism. Those writings are devoted primarily to exploring issues around the "Jewish-Christian schism" as a way of treating in turn crucial questions of Christian discipleship and ecclesial faithfulness (*Jewish-Christian Schism Revisited*, 74–87). Whether and how Yoder's specifically Christian ecclesial, missional, and political concerns may tend to skew his reading of Judaism since Jeremiah to serve his own purposes is a question which cannot be explored in this chapter.[54] The important point for the present purpose is to see how this reading of Judaism both affects and is affected by Yoder's reading of Paul and Judaism.

"Paul the Judaizer"

We appropriately turn now [after a discussion of Jesus and Judaism] to the other most familiar point at which Christians are accustomed to defining Judaism in a particular way and then to negating it. This is the ministry of the apostle Saul/Paul. (*Jewish-Christian Schism Revisited*, 67)

One of the key burdens of the essays in *The Jewish-Christian Schism Revisited* is to argue that Paul remained Jewish through and through, that he never left "Judaism," that he was not rejected in any wholesale way by Judaism, and that blame (or praise) for the Jewish-Christian schism should not be laid at Paul's feet. On the contrary, Paul's mission was in some sense that of "Judaizing" the Gentiles who believed his message. Given Yoder's understanding of the history of Diaspora Judaism and its relevance for a theology of the church and its mission which I outlined above, these claims about Paul may easily be seen as but one aspect of that larger understanding. In-

---

cated by other migrant peoples. . . ?" (*For the Nations*, 78). Clearly he thinks there is. For more on these themes in Yoder, see *Jewish-Christian Schism Revisited*, esp. 53–60. In a review of Boyarin's *Radical Jew*, Stephen Fowl raises the important question—relevant also to Yoder's proposals—"whether or not Jews will ultimately find this [Diaspora focused, rather than State-of-Israel focused mode of political existence] a plausible way to construct their identity" (*Modern Theology* 12 [1996]: 133). Of course this is not the place to answer that question—but see the forthcoming assessments by Cartwright and Ochs in their edition of Yoder's essays on the Jews.

53. The title of chap. 1 in Yoder's *For the Nations*.

54. Some important critical questions about Yoder's claim that "Jeremianic dispersion" is normative Jewish existence are raised by A. James Reimer in "Theological Orthodoxy and Jewish Christianity: A Personal Tribute to John Howard Yoder," in *The Wisdom of the Cross: Essays in Honor of John Howard Yoder* (ed. Stanley Hauerwas et al.; Grand Rapids: Eerdmans, 1999), 444–48. See also the important commentary on and critique of this point in Yoder's essays on Judaism by Jewish theologian Peter Ochs, "Yoder's Witness to the People Israel," part 1 of the editors' introduction to the published edition of *Jewish-Christian Schism Revisited* (forthcoming from Eerdmans), as well as Ochs's commentaries on Yoder's essays throughout the work.

deed, central to his reading of Paul is Yoder's claim that, were the church faithful to Paul, it would readily discover its true character as the Gentile Diaspora people of God whose life would mirror that of Diaspora Judaism.

Paul, Yoder argues, remained consistently Jewish, even at the very heart of his theology. He was not, as is often assumed or argued, "the great hellenizer" who took an originally Jewish message and shaped it into something essentially Greek and Gentile. On the contrary, "what Saul or 'Paul' did was not to found another religion but to define one more stream within Jewry. More narrowly; he created one more stream within *pharisaic* Jewry" (*Jewish-Christian Schism Revisited*, 6, emphasis original). For this reason we find Paul engaged in an intra-Jewish, intra-Pharisaic debate about the looseness or rigorousness with which *halakah* ought to apply to Gentiles who wished to be integrated into the Diaspora Jewish community, which was "already bicultural, bilingual, long before 'Paul' came on the scene" (7). The synagogues were already making proselytes of varying degrees of integration. They were already working out "wise, modest compromises about table fellowship, like those spelled out in Acts (15 and 21) and 1 Cor 8–10" (7). There were already, before Paul appeared on the scene, extensive discussions and disagreements about these issues, particularly in the synagogues of the Diaspora.[55] "The policy of 'Paul' was marginally more open on these matters than the other contemporaries we know of, but still it was only a little more of the same thing" (7). Paul himself never quit attending Diaspora synagogues (and the temple when he was in Jerusalem) because of his position on these matters. Further, that he was occasionally (or frequently) disciplined by leaders of Diaspora synagogues indicates that he "insisted on claiming Jewish identity and demanding a hearing in the synagogues he visited" (8). But Paul was *not* disciplined for holding a relatively loose application of *halakah* for Gentiles. Rather, table fellowship was the issue: Paul was disciplined for "teaching that messianic Jews could and in fact should eat with Gentiles who (for their part) would not have to keep the rules" because the messianic age had now dawned. "Precisely because the messianic age has dawned, Gentiles do not need to become Jews in order to come under the Torah of the Messiah. Yet because Jesus is the Messiah of the Jews, there is no reason either for Jews to renounce their observant custom" (69). Paul himself did not simply cease his own Jewish observance.[56]

What then was Paul's "conversion" about, according to Yoder? Again, it is not a matter of Paul's being changed from a Jew into something non-Jewish. Rather, Paul

55. For a helpful discussion of the various positions and debates among Jews of Paul's time which confirms Yoder's point, see Donaldson, *Paul and the Gentiles*, 51–78.

56. As I show in the following chapter, the view that Paul did not expect Christ-believing Jews to forsake Torah observance is widely shared among Paul scholars.

was changed from a Pharisee who (because *meshiach* had not come) defended the halachic boundaries of the community, to a Pharisee who (because the age to come had begun) celebrated the ingathering. That is to say . . . that what has changed is not the man but the world. The messianic "Paul" is no less a Jew, no less a Pharisee, than Saul. What has changed is that a new age has begun. It has begun with the Resurrection, which only a Pharisee could believe in. (*Jewish-Christian Schism Revisited,* 9)[57]

Paul, as one who now lives in the new world, the new age, thus goes out to the nations with none other than a thoroughly Jewish message that he hopes will take root also among the Gentiles, who are now called to live in this "whole new world":

Far from being the great hellenizer of an originally Jewish message, Paul is rather the great Judaizer of hellenistic culture. He comes with his monotheism into a polytheistic world, with his ethical rigor into a hedonistic world. He teaches Aramaic prayers to gentile believers and expands the Pharisaic *chabourah* or love feast into a celebration of inter-ethnic unity. (*Jewish-Christian Schism Revisited,* 70)

In just this way Paul represents one strand of Judaism in the first century, a century during which there "was no such thing as normative Judaism" (*Jewish-Christian Schism Revisited,* 24), but only a quite wide variety of types of Judaism both within Palestine and in the Diaspora. Hence, not only does Paul not reject normative Judaism, since such did not exist; he also presents his own messianic form of Judaism as *normative,* implying thereby the non-normative character of any of the other strands:

Paul never surrendered his claim that a true child of Abraham must share the faith in the son of the promise made to Abraham. Those Israelites who had not yet seen in Jesus the Promised One were not thereby for Paul mainline Jews, or authentic Jews, but rather Jews not yet accepting the fulfilment of the promises made to their father. In all of his polemic against people who were making what he considered to be a wrong use of the values of the Hebrew heritage (the law, the ritual, circumcision, *kaschrut*), Paul never suggested that his adversaries were typical Jews, or that the values they were using wrongly were unimportant, or that he wanted his own disciples to be anything other than good Jews. (*Jewish-Christian Schism Revisited,* 26–27)[58]

57. Yoder's argument that the age to come means, apocalyptically, the arrival of a new world, is made most fully in an essay on 2 Cor. 5:17 first published in 1980: "'There Is a Whole New World': The Apostle's Apology Revisited," in his *To Hear the Word* (Eugene, Oreg.: Wipf & Stock, 2001), 9–27. Referring to this essay, Yoder writes: "II Cor 5:17 describes a 'new creation' or 'whole new world' which is not a born-again individual but a transformed cosmos"; *Jewish-Christian Schism Revisited,* 9 n. 18.

58. Yoder writes in a footnote that when he first presented the essay (1977) this claim was "a debatable thesis. Since then it has come to seem much less daring, thanks to the work of Stendahl, Gaston, [Alan] Segal, and Nanos."

Yoder's point in stressing the Jewishness of Paul, his message, and his claims is not to address the question of whether Paul's type of Judaism supersedes other types, but the question of whether what Paul establishes as churches through the preaching of the gospel are intended by Paul to be anything other than a thoroughly Jewish phenomenon, religiously, ethically, intellectually, sociopolitically, and theologically. Yoder's answer is, No, not at all. Paul intended no "schism" with Judaism, no departure from already existing ways of being Jewish. Rather, "what Paul added [to an already existing pattern of Diaspora Jewishness] . . . was the pastoral and political power of a strong mind and will, with which he founded and led *messianic synagogues in this already available style*" (*Jewish-Christian Schism Revisited*, 8, emphasis added):

> This meant structuring a confessing community on non-geographical grounds, an identity that could be voluntarily sustained by a minority of people scattered in lands under other sovereignties. There were two groups of Jews who did this successfully. . . . There were the messianists, later called Christians, and there were the rabbis.
>
> Both of these movements were Jewish. Neither was more Jewish than the other, although the "Christian" side of the tension had been crystallized earlier. They had almost the same moral traditions, almost the same social structures. They differed from one another only about one very Jewish but also very theological question, namely on whether the presence of the Messianic Age should be conceived of as future or also already as present. (*Jewish-Christian Schism Revisited*, 25)

In other words, Paul was simply taking the Jeremianic dispersion mode of being God's people among the nations and applying it to the new messianic, predominantly Gentile communities which were being formed through his preaching about Jesus the Messiah. He established these communities in a thoroughly Jewish way of life marked by an identity focused on the worship of the one God of Israel and his Messiah Jesus, the study of the Jewish Scriptures, local communal gathering, peaceable relations with the wider world, and a system of networks with messianic communities in other cities.

Empire, Schism, and the Church's Fall into Paganism

Clearly, according to Yoder, Paul certainly never intended, promoted, or practiced a schism with "Judaism." Indeed, there is no schism during the New Testament period or during most of the century immediately following it. Yoder draws this conclusion after a study of the period from 70 C.E. to the Bar Kochba revolt of 135 C.E.:

> Nobody withdrew from anybody; neither "religion" ejected the other or left the other; but later Judaism is more marked by its rejection of the Messianic Jews' claims than the New Testament is marked by any rejection of what the

other Jews stood for. The Christian "New Testament" includes significant sections—most of James and the Apocalypse, sections of the letters of Peter (as, at the other end, most of the teachings of Jesus) which are not uniquely messianic and could have been written by non-Christians.

Nothing in the Christianity of the apostolic canon is anti-Jewish, or even un-Jewish or non-Jewish, unless it be read in the light of later Christian prejudice. Christian anti-Judaism arose well *after* the apostolic/canonical period, from causes running counter to the apostolic experience and witness. Thus "normative Christianity," when defined by the Christian canon rather than by the fourth century and its anti-Jewish precursors, was documented, as a Jewish movement, before the Jewish-Christian split. (*Jewish-Christian Schism Revisited*, 39)

Had the church thus remained true to its canonical, normative sources of self-description there might have been a continuing, relatively open relationship between messianic and nonmessianic Jews, lasting indefinitely.[59] In fact, there are theological reasons why such a relationship might have been expected. In the first place, for Paul what happens with the coming of Christ "is the fulfillment and not the abolition of the meaning of Torah as covenant of grace. 'Fulfillment' is a permanently open border between what went before and what comes next" (*Jewish-Christian Schism Revisited*, 72). A Jew who is still waiting for the messianic age is nonetheless waiting for something that *might* come. For such a Jew, another Jew's claim that the messianic age has *already* come cannot be ruled out in principle; it has simply not yet been sufficiently demonstrated for the Jew who denies it. In the second place, from the Christian side, Christians must follow Paul in continuing to make the claim to Jews that Jesus is indeed the one for whom they are waiting. There should always have been an open border from Christians toward Jews, rather than an increasingly principled exclusion of the Jews from the messianic story:

Christians gave up their messianic claim in its most authentic and original form . . . when they renounced their claims regarding the first coming [of the Messiah] and the Jews: i.e., when they granted to the non-Messianic synagogue that it had the right to exclude them [a right which Paul did not grant it], and then went on to give further occasion for the rebuilding of other barriers by forsaking the dietary compromises that had originally been accepted [Acts 15], and by sliding culturally into an increasing Romanization and Hellenization. (*Jewish-Christian Schism Revisited*, 72–73)

In Yoder's account, it is the cultural slide into romanization and hellenization that finally seals the fate of the Jewish-Christian schism for many centu-

---

59. "Not only was [the] affirmation of Jewish identity the center of the mission of Jesus in the first generation and of Paul in the second. The social fences remained down between church and synagogue for two or three more generations at least. The first Christian (i.e., messianic Jewish) communities remained basically Jewish in style and language even in the hellenistic cities" (*Jewish-Christian Schism Revisited*, 118).

ries to come and cuts Christianity off both from its Jewish roots and ways and from the Jews themselves. This is the fall of the church into paganism. The first stage of this fall is hellenization, primarily the result of the efforts of the early Christian apologists to make the Christian message "credible or palatable to the authorities of gentile culture, be they philosophers, priests, or princes, by sloughing off the dimensions of Jewish particularity. Thereby the faith became an ahistorical moral monotheism, with no particular peoplehood and no defenses against acculturation, no ability to discern the line between mission and syncretism" (*Jewish-Christian Schism Revisited*, 76).[60] The second stage is romanization. Christians over time came to discern God's historical purpose not primarily through what God is doing in history through his vulnerable but identifiable chosen people, specifically distinguishable from the nations, but what God is doing through the empire, since now the emperor is seen to be the chosen instrument of God's historical purposes. The church's otherness from the dominant social and political order now becomes "spiritual" and invisible in a manner in which the Jews refuse to allow their otherness to become invisible:

> With the age of Constantine, Providence no longer needed to be an object of faith, for God's governance of history had become empirically evident in the person of the Christian ruler of the world. . . . Before Constantine, one knew as a fact of everyday experience that there was a believing Christian community [the visible church] but one had to "take it on faith" that God was governing history. After Constantine, one had to believe without seeing that there was a community of believers [the invisible church], within the larger nominally Christian mass, but one knew for a fact that God was in control of history.[61]

The visible Christian body is now simply identical with the empire. Whereas Jews go on circumcising only those who are born or become Jewish, the church simply baptizes everyone in the empire. This situation persisted without contradiction until the time of the Radical Reformation. It was only then that the Radical Reformation churches reclaimed something of the Jewishness of their identity (though probably without identifying it as Jewishness).

Yoder draws out the correspondences between the Radical Reformation churches and the Jewishness of the Jews and the early church. First is a recovery of "decentralized vitality." "The anticlericalism, the anticentralism, the warning against antinomianism, the rejection of national-governmental control of the churches, which had marked early Christianity, were rooted jewishly just as truly as was the nonviolence of the free churches" (*Jewish-Christian Schism Revisited*, 77). Second is a recovery of an eschatological vi-

60. Yoder neglects to take account of the many ways in which Jews, whether in Palestine or in the Diaspora, were also "hellenized" to greater or lesser extents already by the time of Jesus and Paul.

61. Yoder, "The Constantinian Sources of Western Social Ethics," in *The Priestly Kingdom: Social Ethics as Gospel* (Notre Dame: University of Notre Dame Press, 1984), 136–37.

sion of history. Rather than blessing the existing social and political order, as established religion tends to do, Judaism and the Radical Reformation understand that God stands and acts in a critical relationship to that order, a stance also to be taken up by the people of God. Third, Jews and the radical churches are "unembarrassed about particularity" (78). They are not surprised that "their view is not generally acceptable. They expect to be outvoted" (78). Fourth, both groups derive their "ongoing social identity, including [their] capacity to change, from the presence in [their] midst of a *book*" (78, emphasis original). The first leaders of the Anabaptist movement were called "readers" or "teachers" rather than priests. The reading of the Bible itself, unmediated by ecclesiastical authority or a scholastic class of interpreters, became a focal identifying practice of the Radical Reformation movement. "In creating a new critical sub-culture around the text of their Scriptures, the Anabaptists were doing something more like the synagogue than like anything else going on in Europe at the time" (78). Sixth, the Jews and the radical churches are similar in "their seriousness about a distinctive moral commitment," which led the mainline reformers to accuse the radicals of "representing a new monasticism or new Judaism" (78). Finally, the Anabaptists and Mennonites, like the Jews, are willing to accept imposed migration and exile as a way of life for a people whose true home is not in any one land or nation. To be sure, historically where Jews and Mennonites were received and given protection they were sometimes appreciated and granted some privileges as "useful subjects"; indeed, they in turn sometimes became uncritical of their host rulers when those rulers treated other minorities with injustice. Nonetheless, "even when tolerated, they never fit in completely": they maintain their distinctive identifying practices, "thus reminding themselves that they are not fully at home anywhere" (79).

In these ways what was lost with the rise of Constantinianism, namely an understanding and practice of the church as a people of God modeled after Diaspora Judaism, is in some measure recovered by the Radical Reformation churches. A great deal of the impetus for Yoder's own study and recovery of Diaspora Judaism as a way of life relevant to Christian theology may be found here, in his conviction that Diaspora Judaism has much to teach the church about how to be the church according to its normative delineation in the thoroughly Jewish Pauline teaching and practice.[62]

The Jews: Exemplary or Elect People?

Clearly Yoder's primary interest in the Jews and Diaspora Judaism is to pay attention to their history and way of life as an instructive example for

62. Much more could and needs to be said about Yoder's essays on Judaism than I have said here. My main point, as the following discussion shows, is to present the central ideas of Yoder's writings on Judaism and to test them in light of Paul's theology of Israel. The kind of detailed, critical examination which Yoder's work calls for has been started in a marvelous way by Ochs and Cartwright in their introductions to *Jewish-Christian Schism Revisited*. Ochs provides a valuable Jewish perspective on Yoder.

the Christian church. Of course this is not merely an accidental choice of an example. The historic roots of the church are in the "Judaism" of the time of Jesus and Paul and before. Indeed, Yoder is at pains to stress the historical continuity and ongoing relationship between that Judaism and the early church, arguing that there are finally no definitive reasons, only historically contingent ones, why the church and nonmessianic Judaism should have finally split and entered into an antagonistic relationship. Both sociologically and theologically they shared a virtually identical call to be God's people in the midst of the nations in a particular way, bearing witness nonviolently to God's sovereignty over the nations and God's faithfulness and grace to his people.

On these terms it seems clear that Yoder maintains a strong conviction that non-Christian Jews continue to be God's people despite their refusal to believe that Jesus is their long-awaited Messiah. But we must probe that conviction a little deeper. What is its theological basis? Or, more pointedly, does Yoder hold to a doctrine of Israel's election, and what is the shape of that doctrine?

Yoder acknowledges that since World War II theologians have been debating the question of "whether Christians should give a special place to Israel" within their theological visions or systems (*Jewish-Christian Schism Revisited*, 16). There has been a variety of proposed answers to this question across the theological spectrum. This is not, however, the question Yoder sets himself to address in any focused manner:

> I note for now only that for it to be a question at all one must assume the profound uniqueness which sets Jews apart from everyone else as a theological challenge to Christian thought. [The current] alternatives [regarding Israel's place in Christian theology] are ways out of the question raised for us by the assumption that Jews, like all non-Christians, are outside the salvation story, in such a way that we must adjudicate among the several different available views of how or whether to bring them the Gospel of Jesus Christ. But if as the woman at the well said, "salvation is of the Jews," that might be the wrong question. (*Jewish-Christian Schism Revisited*, 16–17)

The right question then is whether the Jews are simply "like all non-Christians" and therefore "outside the salvation story." Yoder responds at greatest length to this question in an essay in *The Jewish-Christian Schism Revisited* entitled "Judaism as a Non-non-Christian religion" (113–24). As the title of that essay indicates, Yoder makes it quite clear that Judaism beyond the New Testament cannot simply be regarded as one religion among many, as simply equivalent theologically to Hinduism or Buddhism. Yoder rejects the "supersession thesis, according to which Christians have replaced the Jews as the people holding the right understanding of the abrahamic and mosaic heritage and as the bearers of the salvation history" (113). That kind of supersessionism, whether in earlier or more modern versions, resulted in a variety of types of anti-Judaism in Western Christianity, as well as a variety of attitudes toward Christian mission to the Jews.

On the other hand, there are various types of "philo-Judaism" as well, some of them supersessionist, others not. The Enlightenment and liberal Christianity have their own version of seemingly respectful supersessionism. Judaism is rendered as one of the religions of "moral monotheism," which is the higher and more universal truth beyond the particularities of the religions of Christianity, Judaism, and perhaps Islam. On this understanding Judaism can be treated by liberal Christians "as one more Christian denomination," and Jews are therefore in no need of evangelizing (*Jewish-Christian Schism Revisited*, 115). At the opposite extreme the dispensationalists, following the tradition of John Nelson Darby and the Scofield Bible, are in some sense nonsupersessionist. They understand the Jews to "have a permanent priority as the people possessing inalienably the promises of God, in no way superseded by Christianity" (115). For the dispensationalists, however, evangelization of the Jews is nevertheless crucial, "since their conversion has a key place in the divine timetable, quite distinct from mission to Gentiles" (115). In the end-time there will be a massive conversion of Jews to Jesus as Messiah, the one who will then restore the throne of David and establish the sovereignty of Israel over all the nations of the earth.

Finally, according to Yoder, there is "the most profound" type of respect for Judaism, which "arises from biblical and theological renewal, rather than the mere dilution of Christian specificity or from an esoteric eschatology" (*Jewish-Christian Schism Revisited*, 116). This type, proposed most directly and thoroughly by Karl Barth, asserts the irrevocable character of Israel's election, an election which is not only not thwarted by Jewish rejection of Jesus the Messiah, but in fact proved by it. God's grace toward Israel persists despite the fact that, as the elect people, Israel nonetheless rejects that grace. This view assumes and depends on the ongoing survival of Judaism in Christendom:

> There is surely some mystery in the survival of Jewry, as no other people has done, without common territory, common political authorities, common language. . . . There is also an evil mystery in the sense of scandal, in the way in which the various host cultures, amidst whom the Jews have lived, have sought their destruction. The facticity of survival and of scandal reinforces the theological confession of election. (*Jewish-Christian Schism Revisited*, 117, ellipsis original)

In the end, however, Yoder does not take up and develop any one of these three available models for honoring Judaism. Certainly he would reject the first two. But even the third model depends, he suggests, on a hardening of the categories Christianity and Judaism that is the result of a history of mutually adversarial and exclusionary self-definition that began after an initial period of mutual openness. Judaism, at least in the Western world, was shaped in significant measure by its response to an increasingly dominant and often oppositional Christianity; thus rabbinic Judaism as we know it today is a "post-Christian phenomenon" (*Jewish-Christian Schism Revisited*, 119), owing something of its particular shape and existence to Christianity, just as much as Christianity historically owes its existence to Judaism. For Yoder the hope of a fruitful dialogue between Jews and Christians depends on taking account of that historical fact and remembering a day when it was not so and need not have become so. There is more to learn from the days when nonmessianic Jews and early Gentile churches shared a common sociopolitical stance with respect to the wider world than there is from the subsequent history. In any case, Yoder does not call further attention to the doctrine of election as a serious point of departure from which Christians might rethink their relation to Jews: he never engages in any extended reading of Romans 9–11. The promise of Jewish-Christian relations is to be found more in the exemplary character of Diaspora Judaism than in the Pauline doctrine of Israel's election.

Comparing Yoder and Wright

A comparative reading of Yoder and Wright sheds further light on Yoder's contribution. Yoder's focus of attention opens up a perspective on the Jews in God's purpose which Wright has not and, on his terms, cannot imagine. And yet, Yoder also makes many moves in his theology of the Jews that are remarkably similar to those of Wright and, like Wright's, theologically questionable from a Pauline perspective.

On Reading Jewish History

It would be difficult to find a stronger point of contrast between Yoder and Wright than in how they read the history of Judaism since the exile. For Wright the exile and subsequent Diaspora are read exclusively under the sign of God's punishment of an unfaithful people which is destined thus to suffer in the condition of exile until the day when God regathers his people from the ends of the earth and restores their fortunes and power in the land under a new king. While Wright can write extensively about Israel's calling to mission as a people in *the land*—a mission which he believes they ultimately fail to fulfill—he nowhere considers that Israel's mission might be being fulfilled, indeed fulfilled according to God's will, by a people in *Diaspora*. Hence, when Jesus comes announcing the arrival of God's reign, and yet fleshly Israel is evidently not gathered from exile and restored to and in the land, God's reign must mean for Wright that God finally and fully ends Israel's exile—executes its final punishment and restoration—in this one Jew alone who wholly submits to God's reign. On the other hand, virtually the whole of Israel, except for those few who believe in and follow Jesus, are cast off for their failure to submit to that reign. After Christ the history of Judaism must be read at best as an inexplicable anachronism, at worst as a history of blatant disobedience by those Jews who live in a Christian context, yet refuse to believe in Jesus. It means nothing for Wright, from the point of view of a Christian interpretation of Judaism, that communities of Jews both before and after Christ lived faithful lives among the nations—often under severe pressure of opposition, often from Christians—testifying by their faithfulness that the one God of Israel sustains both them and the nations in his electing and providential care.

Wright nowhere accounts for the canonical prominence of stories of paradigmatic Jews as resident aliens, the stories of Abraham, Joseph, Daniel, and Esther. Reading Israel's story as a fairly straightforward linear historical movement from patriarchs, to exodus, to entry into the land, to kingship and decline, to exile, to return and hope for full restoration, Wright misses the fact that these paradigmatic canonical characters all exhibit ways of being faithful among the nations as a concrete possibility for a people in exile.[63] Wright is thus equipped to read Jesus only in terms of Israel's story of kingship, exile, and restoration, that is, in terms of the story of Israel as nation in its land with its king. Wright limits Israel's divine calling and destiny to one and only one option—ethnic and national self-determination vis-à-vis the other nations and empires of the world—and then condemns them as ethnocentric nationalists for actually pursuing that option. If the actual Gospel narratives of Jesus depict him "fulfilling" that story in some way, if Israel's calling and destiny so construed is in some manner completed in Jesus, as Wright argues it is, it can be in only some highly "interpreted" sense: Jesus sums up, indeed *is himself* Israel, land, king, and temple. There is nothing left of a calling and destiny for Israel as an historical people. The meaning of "Israel" as a people is now thoroughly absorbed into the doctrine of Christ and the church.

Yoder raises the possibility of reading both Jewish history and Jesus' relation to it differently. By reading the Jewish exile in the light of Jeremiah 29:4–7 and the patterns of faithfulness-in-exile exhibited in the stories of Joseph, Daniel, and others, Yoder opens up the history of Judaism as a positive model of the church's own way of faithfulness. Further, he opens up a new way of understanding Jesus' mission and his message of the reign of God. God reigns and is sovereign over the nations, bringing about his purposes, even when his people is in charge of neither the nations nor its own nation. Jesus issues a call to Israel to submit to God's reign precisely in these terms. When the God of Israel reigns over his people, his people need not reign, or rather, may in fact reign with Christ as they take up the way of the cross as a concrete political alternative to the way the rulers of this world exercise their

---

63. See the section entitled "The Basic Story" in Wright's *New Testament and the People of God*, 216–17.

dominion. In doing so they participate in God's reign. Yoder's point is this: Jesus was neither the first nor the last Jew to believe and live in this way. The pattern was there among Jews and in the Jewish Scriptures before Jesus came, and it was lived faithfully by many Jews throughout the Diaspora after Jesus came. Jesus' resurrection and exaltation are God's vindication of the finality and ultimacy of this pattern, as the way in which God works in this world through his people. Thus, if nonmessianic Jews after Christ go on being faithful to this pattern as a Diaspora people, they must be regarded as God's people who live the way of Jesus, even though they do not confess Jesus as the Christ. That is, they also must be acknowledged (by Christians) as faithful participants in God's reign announced by Jesus and inaugurated in his life, death, and resurrection.

Indeed, Yoder's reading of the history of the Diaspora precisely reverses the relationship between the church and synagogue that Wright sets up. For Wright the nonmessianic synagogue can represent only Israel's refusal, rebellion, and rejection of God's purpose in Jesus Christ, its fall into paganism, from which it can recover only by listening to the church, which has now taken the place of Israel and has the message and way of life that the Jews must believe and learn. Yoder, on the other hand, presents the relationship between church and synagogue as characterized by potentially open borders and mutual learning. Under the conviction that the Jews remain God's people, Yoder calls the church to recover from *its* fall into paganism (hellenization and Constantinianism) by paying careful attention to the theological convictions and sociopolitical stance which characterize the life of the nonmessianic synagogues of the dispersion.

Wright's and Yoder's opposing judgments on Jewish history, interestingly, depend in large measure on where they look, which Jewish history they tend to focus on. Wright's focus is "Palestinocentric," leading him to emphasize the various ways in which movements in Palestine at the time of Jesus and Paul believed they could contribute by their beliefs and practices to the restoration of the national fortunes of Israel. Wright thus tends to see only ethnocentric nationalism and sees this as the primary form of Israel's unfaithfulness. He in turn projects this onto all Jews everywhere—it is the "Jewish sin"—unqualified by whether actual Jewish belief and practice in the Diaspora is the same as beliefs and practices within Palestine. Even the Diaspora Jews who oppose Paul's mission (if in fact they are Jews, as Wright assumes) are, according to Wright, motivated by ethnocentric, nationalistic zeal. While Yoder agrees with Wright that a kind of restoration nationalism motivated Jewish movements in first-century Palestine (this is Yoder's premise in his reading of Luke in *The Politics of Jesus*), he nonetheless turns his attention also toward Diaspora Judaism, rejecting the idea that the Palestinocentric vision is the only important background to understanding the missions of Jesus and Paul. Rather, the clue to understanding both of those missions is for Yoder precisely "Jeremianic dispersion existence," the dynamic form of Jewish faithfulness beyond Palestine to which Jesus called the Jews living in Palestine and to which Paul looked for a model for the messianic Jew-and-Gentile synagogues—*ekklēsiai*—that sprang up with his proclamation of the gospel of Jesus Christ.

Wright's reading of Jewish history in the end perpetuates a common Christian myth about Judaism, namely that it can finally be summed up under a single category which happens to be opposed to Christianity—now not legalism and works-righteousness, as in Christian theology before the new perspective on Paul, but "ethnocentric nationalism." Yoder, by paying careful attention to Diaspora Judaism and other important strands of the Old Testament story, provides a powerful and persuasive alternative to Wright's reading of and judgment upon the history of Judaism. It remains a task of more detailed scholarship to determine how fruitful Yoder's approach may be for understanding Jesus' and Paul's missions historically from the perspective of Diaspora Judaism. In the meantime, however, Yoder's perspective at the very least holds promise as a significant resource to enable the church to move beyond its entrenched supersessionism, rooted in a negative image of Judaism and a misreading of Paul, and to begin learning from faithful Judaism a great deal about the church's own calling and mission in a world wracked by violent nationalisms and tribalisms.

Moral History or God's Election

Despite the obvious differences, Wright and Yoder also share a common focus in their attempts to develop a theology of Israel, Jews, and Judaism, a focus which sets both of them at odds with Paul. Like Wright, Yoder gives far more attention to the question of *Jewish* faithfulness than to that of *God's* faithfulness. I explored in some detail above how Paul, in contrast to Wright, is not concerned to address the question of Israel in God's purpose in terms of a moral history of the Jews and Judaism, that is, to tell a lengthy story of the sin of the Jews. Rather, Paul concerns himself with what *God* is doing with Israel, given that the larger part of Israel is not believing Paul's gospel and accepting his mission. Paul's answer in Romans 8–11 is that God will not, cannot, contradict his election of carnal Israel, but rather sustains that election in and through the apocalypse of Jesus Christ. Nothing in all creation can separate the elect people from God's love in Christ Jesus. For that reason the Gentiles who are grafted into Israel can be assured of their own participation in God's salvation. Jews, even nonmessianic Jews, continue to be sharers in and recipients of the strange differential movement of God's mercy-showing.

Paul does not in Romans or his other letters engage in a moral history of Judaism. Both Wright and Yoder do, and a great deal of their judgments about the irrelevance or continuing relevance of Judaism for Christian theology is based on that moral history. Indeed, we have seen that Yoder in fact shows almost no interest in the doctrine of Israel's nonsuperseded election, even as he at the same time also seems to assume it. Yoder, like Wright, is in-

terested in a form of "Jewishness." Wright holds that Israel's election bears
fruit and is sustained, finally, in the Jewishness of the story and worldview
that Paul brings to the Gentile world. Yoder emphasizes the Jewishness of
the Diaspora form of life as the peculiar gift of the Jews to the world. In
both cases the biblical and Pauline doctrine of God's election of a specific,
nonsubstitutable, fleshly historical people tends to disappear behind a set of
"Jewish" ideas or practices.

Finally, it seems, for Yoder as for Wright that the emphasis upon the election of carnal Israel carries with it the danger of the self-assertion of an ethnocentric nationalism. Israel as a nation in charge of its own land is also for
Yoder the one thing to be avoided in a Christian theology of Israel. Zionism
lurks as a problem in the background of Yoder's entire *The Jewish-Christian
Schism Revisited* (as perhaps it does also in Wright, though that is not so evident).[64] But the avoidance of Zionism can be accomplished, it seems, in another way than by occluding God's irrevocable election of Israel. Consider
Jesus. Jesus is sent by God on a mission to Israel, and he sends his own disciples out in the first place on a mission to Israel. Jesus issues a call to the Palestinian Jews of his time to be a faithful people in a land and a kingdom that
they are not to seize as a possession by their own violent force but to receive
only as a gift from God. This is nonetheless a call that he makes explicitly—

64. This is especially evident in the final essay in Yoder's *Jewish-Christian Schism Revisited*: "Earthly
Jerusalem and Heavenly Jerusalem," 125–32. Yoder's theme is Jerusalem as the "holy city." He asks "*why*
Jerusalem matters as *more than* a place or a population. The answer to that question must be a statement
not about the city itself but about the God who some three millennia ago chose it for a special function"
(127, emphasis original). In choosing Jerusalem, God reveals something of his own character. First, it reveals his "extraterritoriality," since the chosen city did not belong originally to any one of the tribes of Israel. "The transcendence of the Most High is acted out in the fact that *the place of his manifestation is not
our own turf. . . .* God chooses neutral ground—or even foreign ground—as the way to be graciously in
our midst" (127). This fact, according to Yoder, reveals that God cannot be possessed by anyone and
shows his compassion for "the others, the outsiders, the nations, the sojourners" (128). "We" are saved
from "provincial self-definitions that reduce the Most High God to a graven image by reducing his causes
to ours" (128). Christians have been guilty of such provincialism by reducing God's cause to that of imperial Rome; other religions do the same with other cities; Jerusalem has suffered the same fate from Jews,
Christians, and Muslims. Further, God reveals his transcendence by not binding his reign to this particular city. God is sovereign over all the nations, and therefore the Jews may go out among the nations confident of his presence and power in those places. Yoder concludes: "We can state the common witness of all
authentic monotheism to the transcendence of God's claims upon us in favor of the others, the outsiders.
The *Most High God* . . . accentuate[s] transcendence . . . in the interest of relativizing our claims to locate
Him on our own turf and make Him the enemy of our enemies" (130). This authentic "Hebraic" understanding of Jerusalem is expressed in the idea that in addition to the empirical, earthly Jerusalem is a
promised Jerusalem which is "above" or "heavenly" or "to come." That dualism of cities is another way of
saying that Jerusalem belongs to God, not to any particular earthly people; the dualism of earthly and
heavenly points toward a prophetic judgment on all current earthy claims to Jerusalem as "our city." "The
dualism points toward new possibilities for this world, toward promises which both condemn and redeem" in relation to the earthly city (131). Yoder's implied point throughout this essay, commissioned for
a conference convened by the Anti-Defamation League of B'nai B'rith, is to "relativize mainline Zionism"
(132). The theme of earthly and heavenly Jerusalem was set for him by the conference organizers.

and even in some sense exclusively—to "the lost sheep of Israel," the chosen people of God. As I am sure Yoder would agree, there is no necessary link between Jews affirming their corporeal election and their taking forceful possession of the land of Palestine. Abraham is chosen as God's friend and Israel created as God's people while the land is still only *promised*, and as the exile shows, the land may be temporarily taken away (or the people sent out of the land) and again set before the people as a promise, without the chosen people thereby ceasing to be chosen.

Because Yoder does not make the election of Israel the point of departure in his theology of the Jews, his attention is drawn toward the moral and even voluntary character of Judaism. He chooses to concentrate on Jewishness as a *way of life*, to be freely reaffirmed by Jews and taken up by Gentiles, as the place to focus the discussion of the relation between Jews and Christians.[65] As I showed above, a great deal can be learned from that focus about how to be God's people in the world; from a Pauline perspective, however, it is not the primary or most promising theme for beginning a theological discussion of the relation between messianic Jews and Gentiles on the one hand and nonmessianic Jews on the other.[66] The question that begs to be asked at this point, but that I cannot pursue further, is whether any adequate ecclesiology must give priority to election over ethics, the faithfulness of God over the faithfulness of Jews and Gentiles. Paul would say yes! So too, I think, would Yoder. But he does not develop a response to that question in his essays on Judaism.

Recovering Israel's Election in Theology

The recovery of the doctrine of the irrevocable election of Israel is increasingly becoming an important feature of Christian theology, though still only

65. Consider the following comments in response to the dictum "a person is born a Jew but must become a Christian." The dictum, Yoder argues, is "insufficient on both sides." "Since Constantine, most Christianity is not voluntary. The sacramental practice of baptism, which originally meant voluntarily entering a new community, was retained, but its meaning was reversed. It came to be done to an infant who had no choice, and soon it was done at the behest of a government that gave the parents no choice. When it was challenged by reformation radicals, infant baptism was defended by the reformers on the grounds that it was the modern equivalent of Jewish circumcision; that is, a ritual of birth, not choice. On the other hand, to be Jewish after Jeremiah often included *some element* of freedom. Not only were Gentiles able to join the synagogue community; children of Jewish parents could also lose themselves in the crowd. Sometimes in fact the surrounding [culture] exerted on Jews a positive pressure to abjure; thus Jewish identity persisted because it was voluntary. . . . Thus the Judaism with which we are able to converse has faced the freedom to apostatize no less directly than has Catholicism"; *Jewish-Christian Schism Revisited*, 123, emphasis original.

66. This judgment is not intended to undervalue in any way the importance of Yoder's attention to "Jewishness" for understanding the nature and mission of the church, only to set it in its proper theological order. For further detailed exploration of some of the themes that Yoder opens up, and a confirmation of the fruitfulness of those themes, see the important work by Markus Bockmuehl, *Jewish Law in Gentile Churches: Halakhah and the Beginning of Christian Public Ethics* (Edinburgh: T & T Clark, 2000).

a few theologians have made it a central theme in their systematic presentation of Christian doctrine.[67] The first and most notable exception is, of course, Karl Barth's treatment of election in the second volume of his *Church Dogmatics*.[68] Examination of Barth's treatment lies beyond the scope of this study.[69] Here, in conclusion, I simply draw attention to two works in which consideration of the biblical and Pauline doctrine of Israel's election promises to reshape and renew central topics in Christian theology.

R. Kendall Soulen's *God of Israel and Christian Theology* provides an important resource for challenging the kind of supersessionist reading of the biblical story which undergirds Wright's reading of Paul. Soulen draws attention to the way in which "the church's standard canonical narrative" moves from God's creation of the cosmos and humankind, to the "fall" of humankind from its original purpose, to God's work of restoring humankind to that purpose in the redeeming work of Jesus Christ, and finally to God's consummation of creation in the eschaton. "This account of the Bible's narrative unity has exercised unparalleled influence on the church's theological imagination from the second century to the present day."[70] What Soulen rightly discerns, however, is the way in which that account

> makes God's identity as the God of Israel largely indecisive for shaping theological conclusions about God's enduring purposes for creation. The model renders the center of the Hebrew Scriptures—the eternal covenant between the God of Israel and the Israel of God—ultimately indecisive for understanding how God's works as Consummator and as Redeemer engage creation in lasting and universal ways.[71]

In other words, the church's standard canonical narrative—what Wright calls a worldview—can be told either without reference to Israel or with reference to Israel only as Israel serves the purely preparatory function of leading up to (whether negatively or positively) the coming of the Redeemer of "human-

67. For an excellent survey of important works of Christian theology on this theme by Karl Barth, Rosemary Radford Ruether, Paul van Buren, Clark Williamson, R. Kendall Soulen, and Oliver O'Donovan, see Bader-Saye, *Church and Israel after Christendom*, 73–94. There has also been a renewal of interest in the doctrine of election among Jewish theologians. Two of the most important works are Michael Wyschogrod, *The Body of Faith: Judaism as Corporeal Election* (Minneapolis: Seabury, 1983); and David Novak, *The Election of Israel: The Idea of the Chosen People* (Cambridge: Cambridge University Press, 1995).

68. Another example, usually overlooked, of making discussion of Israel a significant topic in systematic theology, is the treatment by Hendrik Berkhof in *Christian Faith: An Introduction to the Study of the Faith* (trans. Sierd Woudstra; orig. 1973; repr. Grand Rapids: Eerdmans, 1979), 221–65. Berkhof does not, however, say much about Israel's election; his interest is primarily religious-historical.

69. For a study of Barth's doctrine, see Bader-Saye, *Church and Israel after Christendom*, 73–77; Soulen, *God of Israel and Christian Theology*, 81–106. A longer, detailed study is Katherine Sonderegger, *That Jesus Christ Was Born a Jew: Karl Barth's "Doctrine of Israel"* (University Park: Pennsylvania State University Press, 1992).

70. Soulen, *God of Israel and Christian Theology*, 15.

71. Ibid., 16.

kind," who in turn ends Israel's purely functional purpose. "The standard model drives an *historical* wedge between the gospel and the God of Israel *by collapsing God's covenant with Israel into the economy of redemption in its prefigurative form.*"[72] We have seen how that standard narrative has a powerful and destructive effect on Wright's reading of Israel's election in Paul. The first part of Soulen's work shows how that supersessionist narrative is at work in Christian theologians from Irenaeus to Barth.

In the second part of his book Soulen attempts a thorough retelling of the canonical narrative in such a way that, according to the biblical story of Israel in God's purposes, God's election of Israel is *decisive* for the Christian doctrines of creation, humanity, redemption, and consummation. In other words, no central Christian doctrine can be rightly delineated without reference to the election/creation of Israel and the constitutive difference thus created between Jew and Gentile:

> Since God promises to bless Abraham and "in him" all the families of the earth, the human family participates in covenant history in a particular way, namely, as Israel and the nations, as Jews and Gentiles. Covenant history encompasses but does not derive from God's work of creation. Rather, God's election of Israel, and therefore Jewish and gentile identity, is a "new creation" above and beyond creaturehood in the image of God. . . .
>
> Ultimately, both dimensions of human religious identity—creaturehood in God's image and partnership in the economy of Israel and the nations—are necessary to account for the human condition in the context of God's work as the Consummator of creation.[73]

Soulen's groundbreaking work marks a crucial correction for all future Christian theology by pointing to the fact that such theology simply cannot be properly done, in any of its aspects, without reference to God's irrevocable election of corporeal Israel.[74]

A more thorough and comprehensive study of the Christian theology of Israel may be found in Scott Bader-Saye's *Church and Israel after Christendom: The Politics of Election*. As the subtitle reflects, Bader-Saye's work is a rich study of the social and political significance of the doctrine of election for the life and mission of the church. As I have already noted with respect

72. Ibid., 110 (emphasis original).

73. Ibid., 136–37. A comparable though somewhat different thesis is argued by Gerhard Lohfink in *Does God Need the Church: Toward a Theology of the People of God* (trans. Linda M. Maloney; Collegeville, Minn.: Liturgical, 1999).

74. See further Soulen, "YHWH the Triune God," *Modern Theology* 15 (1999): 25–54. Soulen's proposals for a nonsupersessionist theology of Israel raise important issues for the Christian doctrine of God, which he explores in this essay. Those issues are taken up as well by Bruce Marshall, "Israel," in *Knowing the Triune God: The Work of the Spirit in the Practices of the Church* (ed. James J. Buckley and David S. Yeago; Grand Rapids: Eerdmans, 2001), 231–64; and idem, *Trinity and Truth* (Cambridge: Cambridge University Press, 2000), 169–79.

to Wright, it is precisely a supersessionist account of Israel and the church that leaves the church with a truncated version of its political witness, whether under the conditions of the earlier forms of Christendom (the church's incorporation into the Holy Roman Empire) or the later (the church's incorporation into the modern liberal nation-state). A recovery of the doctrine of Israel's corporeal election is crucial, Bader-Saye argues, not only for the well-being of Jews and Judaism, but also for the present and future faithful witness of the church in and for the world:

> If the church is understood as that body of people grafted into and thus carrying forward Israel's covenantal politics (alongside the Jews), then this means we can no longer read the New Testament as superseding the social concerns of the Old Testament. We cannot divide the Christian community from the explicitly political identity of Israel. The church, as much as the Jews, exists within the one covenant of God, which leaves no arena of life unaccounted for, including politics. This means that attending to Israel as a way to rethink ecclesiology will mean resisting the depoliticizing of the church. Such depoliticizing of ecclesiology has both internal and external roots. Internally, the church has lost its political witness because of its inadequate understanding of election, which sought to leave the Jews and their materiality behind. Externally, the churches in the West have been depoliticized by their accepting their place in a modern liberal polity that renders them largely irrelevant to the public square.[75]

As Bader-Saye fills out this argument, we find a vision of the church and Israel that provides the larger context within which the concerns and insights of Yoder might find their proper place. As we have seen, Yoder finds in Diaspora Judaism a pattern of fundamental importance for the church's political existence and witness in the world, but he does so largely without reference to the doctrine of Israel's election. Indeed, in some respects Yoder's insights might be developed solely on the basis of the *exemplary* character of Diaspora Judaism's model. Yoder loses sight of the church as a people constituted by God's apocalyptic action, and he tends to emphasize human action (as he does also in his accounts of the "sacraments" or characteristic practices of the church). Bader-Saye provides the crucial theological setting for Yoder's retrieval of the Diaspora model, a model which Bader-Saye himself exploits for the development of ecclesiology.[76] Yoder's work is best read, I suggest, as a complement to Bader-Saye's work, but it must be corrected by Bader-Saye's maintaining the priority of God's action in electing Israel.

Finally, in a surprising way, Bader-Saye also provides not only an alternative to the supersessionist reading of Wright (of whom Bader-Saye is also critical),[77] but also a way to retrieve and correct Wright's attempts, which I

75. Bader-Saye, *Church and Israel after Christendom*, 2–3.
76. Ibid., 135–48.
77. Ibid., 95–97.

noted above, to read Paul politically and for the political witness of the church. There is a tendency for Wright's Pauline politics to look suspiciously liberal-democratic and voluntarist. But such a reading runs against the grain of Paul's theology and sets Paul up for Boyarin's criticism of Paul as the fount of the liberal vision of human nature. One might hope that an influential theologian and New Testament scholar such as Wright might take another look at the theology of Paul and at the election of Israel as presented by non-supersessionist readers such as Soulen and Bader-Saye and provide a corrected, more adequate version of "what Saint Paul really said."

What Paul does say is that God irrevocably elects a specific people—Israel and through Jesus Christ the *ekklēsia* as Israel's extension into the nations—in order that God might bring glory to his name among the nations through this people. In the following chapter I explore in greater detail what God's election of a people might mean for that people as it seeks to live faithfully in a world in which it is constantly encountering and engaging other peoples of other gods and lords.

5

Culture

Religion and Pluralism in Pauline Perspective

Christians in late-modern, post-Christian Western societies are not the first to engage the challenges raised by religious and cultural plurality. Paul's world, as he encountered it in his ever-expanding movement among the Gentile peoples, was as pluralist as our own, in many respects more so. There was indeed what we might call a world religion of the time, the religion of imperial Rome, the *Pax Romana* established under the rules of Julius Caesar and Augustus. Augustus especially was hailed as the lord and savior of the whole world: he established his own cult and the cult of the goddess Pax in Rome and throughout the Roman Empire.[1] The universal rule of the *Pax*

---

1. See the helpful description of the *Pax Romana* in Ulrich Mauser, *The Gospel of Peace: A Scriptural Message for Today's World* (Louisville: Westminster John Knox, 1992), 84–89. See also the introduction (by Richard Horsley) and the first seven chapters (by a variety of authors) in Richard A. Horsley (ed.), *Paul and Empire: Religion and Power in Roman Imperial Society* (Harrisburg, Pa.: Trinity, 1997), 1–137. These essays provide a wide range of general and detailed accounts of the way in which imperial power was established and exerted through the imperial cult in the Roman Empire. Accounts of the divinizations of Julius Caesar and Augustus are given in Hans-Josef Klauck, *The Religious Context of Early Christianity: A Guide to Graeco-Roman Religions* (trans. Brian McNeil; Edinburgh: T & T Clark, 2000), 288–301. Klauck's volume is an expansive, detailed, and beautifully presented account of the subject matter which illumines much of what I write in this chapter.

209

Romana was itself the universal reign of the gods of Rome. "What was most novel in the Roman attitude to their empire was the belief that it was universal and willed by the gods."[2]

Unthreatened for centuries by any other such world-dominating religions, the Roman imperial order could thus afford to tolerate many other gods and lords throughout the empire, so long as they remained merely local, personal or private, and made no counterclaims about universal truth and world dominion. Ultimately all gods and lords would have to serve and sustain the cause of the Roman Empire. So there was indeed a world religion, but there were also many other public and private cults, places of worship, images and statues of the gods, ritual practices and sacrifices, and recurrent festivals in honor of the numerous greater and lesser deities. There were mystery cults and religious associations, seers and oracles, magicians and astrologers, miracle workers and philosophers. The cosmos was believed by most people of the time to be populated with many good and evil spirits, and numerous folk religious practices were designed to manipulate these spirits. All of these "varieties of religious experience" pervaded the Gentile worlds and the daily life of the peoples to which Paul took his gospel of the one God of Israel and the one Lord Jesus Christ.[3]

Western societies at the beginning of the third millennium are growing increasingly pluralist or, as some argue, fragmented, as Christianity's wanes in significance as the religious glue binding those societies into unified wholes.[4] All of the countries of Western Europe and North America are now host to numerous world religions, sects, cults, ancient and new age spiritualities, occult practices, beliefs, and philosophies, not to mention the virtually countless Christian denominations. Franz Cumont, a Belgian historian of Hellenistic and Roman religion appears to have had, according to Hans-Josef

2. P. A. Brunt, "*Laus Imperii*," in *Paul and Empire: Religion and Power in Roman Imperial Society* (ed. Richard A. Horsley; Harrisburg, Pa.: Trinity, 1997), 25.

3. All of this in its huge and fascinating array is described in Klauck, *Religious Context of Early Christianity*. See also the shorter accounts by David Aune, "Religions, Graeco-Roman," in *Dictionary of Paul and His Letters* (ed. Gerald F. Hawthorne, Ralph P. Martin, and Daniel G. Reid; Downers Grove, Ill.: InterVarsity Press, 1993), 786–96; Clinton E. Arnold, *Powers of Darkness: Principalities and Powers in Paul's Letters* (Downers Grove, Ill.: InterVarsity Press, 1992), 19–54.

4. There are many helpful analyses of the contemporary pluralist context. See especially Lesslie Newbigin, *The Gospel in a Pluralist Society* (Grand Rapids: Eerdmans, 1989); William Placher, *Unapologetic Theology: A Christian Voice in a Pluralist Conversation* (Louisville: Westminster John Knox, 1989); Richard J. Mouw and Sander Griffioen, *Pluralisms and Horizons: An Essay in Christian Public Philosophy* (Grand Rapids: Eerdmans, 1993); Philip D. Kenneson, *Beyond Sectarianism: Re-imagining Church and World* (Harrisburg, Pa.: Trinity, 1999). Jonathan Wilson, following Alasdair MacIntyre, makes a helpful distinction between pluralism and fragmentation, arguing that late-modern Western societies are better thought of as fragmented than pluralist. There are not enough deep connections to traditions, however different, to sustain an authentic pluralist conversation between those traditions. Instead, late-modern people in the West retain only bits and pieces—unconnected fragments—of their traditions; see Jonathan Wilson, *Living Faithfully in a Fragmented World: Lessons for the Church from MacIntyre's "After Virtue"* (Harrisburg, Pa.: Trinity, 1997), 24–38.

Klauck something of a "prophetic gift" when he wrote the following at the beginning of the twentieth century:

> Let us for a moment suppose that modern Europe [or North America] were to witness the believers abandoning the Christian churches in order to venerate Allah or Brahma, to observe the commandments of Confucius or Buddha, to accept the fundamental principles of Shintoism; let us imagine a great congeries of all the races of the world, with Arabic mullahs, Chinese literary scholars, Japanese bonzes, Tibetan lamas, Hindu pandits preaching at one and the same time fatalism and predestination, the cult of ancestors and the adoration of the divinised ruler, pessimism and redemption through self-annihilation, while all these priests built temples in foreign styles in our cities and celebrated their various rites in them—this dream (which the future may perhaps one day see realised) would give us a rather accurate picture of the religious confusion which characterised the ancient world of Constantine.[5]

Today Cumont's prophecy has been fulfilled in our midst! As Klauck notes, "now that we have reached the end of the [twentieth] century, we find ourselves confronted by the slogan of the 'multicultural' society, which will always be a multireligious society too."[6] We seem to be in a world which in some significant respects resembles closely the worlds of Constantine and, before him, the apostle Paul. As Paul and the early Christian churches encountered, witnessed to, and lived in a pluralist context as a minority religion, so too, it seems, do the churches in today's Western societies.

The situations are not, however, so nearly similar as we may think. Jonathan Wilson provides an important analysis of some of the significant differences:

> The early church did not have to live with the history of its having shaped the Mediterranean culture. So, for example, where the early church knew that it was encountering an alien, resistant, even hostile culture, the contemporary church in the West tends to think of the culture as benign, if not friendly, toward the gospel. Where the early church knew that its message was new and strange, the contemporary church presents its message as familiar and comfortable. Where the early church sought to make its message understood, the contemporary church assumes that it is understood and seeks to persuade its hearers to accept what they understand.[7]

These differences noted, there is nonetheless a good deal that we can learn from the early churches' response to their pluralist contexts. But, as Wilson goes on to note, there are also other differences of a less benign nature:

5. F. Cumont, *Die orientalischen Religionen im römischen Heidentum* (repr. Darmstadt, 1975), 178–79; quoted in Klauck, *Religious Context of Early Christianity*, xiii.
6. Klauck, *Religious Context of Early Christianity*, xiii.
7. Wilson, *Living Faithfully in a Fragmented World*, 20.

For example, the early church did not have to answer for the way that its life had been intertwined with injustice, such as the church's support for slavery and segregation in the American South and apartheid in South Africa. Nor did the early church have the legacy of anti-Semitism to confess. Nor did the early church have a history of visible support for unjust and immoral rulers. All of this history has an effect on how we are to live faithfully today, and the practices of the early church give us limited guidance here.[8]

As I show below, I do not fully share Wilson's opinion that Paul and the early church can provide only limited guidance in light of these negative and oppressive aspects of the church's history. But Wilson notes some important factors in the contemporary context that play a decisive role in current attitudes toward cultural and religious pluralism. The most significant of these, to my mind, is the close alliances which the churches, Roman Catholic, Orthodox, and Protestant alike, have persistently established with worldly political powers from the fourth to the twentieth centuries. Because of such alliances the churches have been able, often coercively and violently, to subdue, exclude, and sometimes destroy religious and cultural others and enforce their own (but not often authentically Christian) forms of life on all the peoples in a given region, nation, or even empire. With the decline of Christendom in the West and increasing awareness of and sensitivity to those who are culturally/religiously other, there is now a widespread rejection of the proposal that the Christian message is one of nontranscendable and universally binding validity. A universal truth claim (of any kind), when tied to worldly power, whether political, economic, industrial, or technological, is now seen to be a very dangerous thing indeed.

Consider some of the assessments of the claim of Christian uniqueness made in a widely read volume of essays on the theology of religious pluralism. Gordon Kaufman asks:

How, in all our diversity, can we humans learn to live together fruitfully, productively and in peace in today's complexly interconnected world, instead of regularly moving into the sort of conflict and struggle that may erupt into a nuclear holocaust that will destroy us all? These are questions that raise special issues for Christians because of the absolutistic claims about divine revelation and ultimate truth that have often been regarded as central to faith; these claims require careful theological scrutiny.[9]

Along with Kaufman, John Hick in an essay in the same volume notes that many "thinking Christians" are now abandoning "Christian absolutism" be-

8. Ibid., 21.
9. Gordon Kaufman, "Religious Diversity, Historical Consciousness, and Christian Theology," in *The Myth of Christian Uniqueness: Toward a Pluralistic Theology of Religions* (ed. John Hick and Paul F. Knitter; Maryknoll, N.Y.: Orbis, 1987), 3.

cause of its "collaboration with acquisitive and violent human nature, [which] has done much to poison the relationships between the [powerful] Christian minority and the non-Christian majority of the world's population by sanctifying exploitation and oppression on a gigantic scale."[10] Kaufman, Hick, and many other contributors to *The Myth of Christian Uniqueness* go on to engage in "careful theological scrutiny" in an effort to significantly reduce or disqualify any "absolutistic claims about divine revelation and ultimate truth" which have traditionally been made about the Christian message. By rejecting the universal validity of Christianity among the religions and embracing religious pluralism, the authors hope in some way to contribute to ending the dominating, coercive, and violent history of Christianity as a cultural and political force in the world.

It is certainly correct to say, following Wilson, that Paul did not have the coercive and often violent history of Christendom to live with, or live down, when he went out among the nations with their religions and forms of life. The contemporary Christian encounter with and mission to the religions bears the burden of that history, and still so often repeats it in new ways. In this respect Paul's encounter with the Gentile peoples differs markedly from the Christian encounter with the plurality of religions and forms of life in our time. Nonetheless, one of the central aims of this chapter is to argue that precisely in light of the history of Christendom we need to listen to Paul anew about the normative form of Christian witness in a pluralist context.

To achieve that aim I will first set forth what can only inaccurately be called a "theory of religion." I make use of the works of a few postliberal and postmodern theologians who are able to take us beyond the usual modernist notions of religion as a "universal dimension" of human existence. In place of religion they propose the notions "form of life" and "culture," and I will indicate why I think these notions are more helpful, especially when we ask what Paul was doing in his pluralist context when he took the gospel of Jesus Christ to the Gentile peoples. In the next two sections, I pay close attention to two of Paul's letters (Romans and 1 Corinthians) where he addresses questions about the form of life or culture which the gospel calls forth from the people of God. I propose that Paul in fact never works with a notion of religion, but rather with the idea of "a people" which by the shape of its life bears testimony to the world-transforming power of the good news of Jesus Christ. In Rome Paul calls for the formation of one people out of two cultures (Jew and Gentile), while in Corinth he calls for the formation of an "other" people in the midst of a common culture. In each case, however, as I argue, the gospel not only calls forth a people, but also shapes a new specifically Christoform culture among that people. Finally, I draw on the forego-

10. John Hick, "The Non-Absoluteness of Christianity," in *The Myth of Christian Uniqueness* (ed. John Hick and Paul F. Knitter; Maryknoll, N.Y.: Orbis, 1987), 17. While I disagree with Kaufman and Hick in their reductions of the universal validity of the Christian message, I do not find the language of "absoluteness" very helpful.

ing studies in Romans and Corinthians to develop a set of "Pauline notes to-ward a theology of culture and religions."

From Religion to Culture

Typically in the modern era, questions about Christianity and the religions have been treated under the assumption that religion is a *genus* of which there is a variety of species. Often the hope is to overcome the differences among religions by identifying that genus. But when it is asked, Species of what? the answers have been many: worship of "God"; the way of salvation; enlightenment; apprehension of "the Real"; the spiritual dimension of human existence; the aspect of faith; etc. The assumption that religion is a genus is now under intense scrutiny and criticism. Every attempt to define the genus or "essence" of religion seems to have failed, for at least two reasons. First, there is virtually no agreement among students of the religions about how to define the commonness that would yield up the characteristics of a genus. Second, every proposal seems from the beginning to inscribe another particular *theological* description of what is common. That is, the hope that one might define a "neutral," nonspecific transcendent reality or universal dimension of human experience in which all religions in some sense participate, or at which they might arrive, comes to grief over the fact that such transcendences and universal dimensions are themselves the products of local and particular convictions—usually those of Western, or Western-educated, academic elites of generally Kantian persuasion—and therefore amount to no more than competing religious proposals on the same plane as those made by already available particular religions.[11]

It is perhaps obvious that the inability to define its subject matter might cause a crisis in the discipline of religious studies and make it difficult to know what we are talking about when we use the word *religion*. And so it has.[12] As one possible solution to the crisis, it is now often proposed that less specific, less religious, more general and encompassing definitions of religion might help. Paul

11. This problem in modern discussions of the religions is detected and analyzed by many writers. Virtually every author in *Christian Uniqueness Reconsidered: The Myth of a Pluralistic Theology of Religions* (ed. Gavin D'Costa; Maryknoll, N.Y.: Orbis, 1990) makes the point in one way or another. Subsequent books by the same authors (Gavin D'Costa, Francis X. Clooney, J. A. DiNoia, Paul J. Griffiths) and many others develop this postliberal critique of liberal versions of religion and the religions. I find especially illuminating Paul J. Griffiths's *Problems of Religious Diversity* (Malden, Mass.: Blackwell, 2001). Also notable in this regard is S. Mark Heim, who challenges the widely held conviction that all religions "finally" aim for and arrive at the same end; see his *Salvations: Truth and Difference in Religion* (Maryknoll, N.Y.: Orbis, 1995) and *The Depth of the Riches: A Trinitarian Theology of Religious Ends* (Grand Rapids: Eerdmans, 2001).

12. See the discussion of this crisis in Paul J. Griffiths, "The Very Idea of Religion," *First Things* 103 (May 2000): 30–35. This essay is a helpful introduction to the issues as well as to Griffiths's fuller treatment in *Problems of Religious Diversity*. Reviews and discussions of the issues surrounding the "crisis of religious studies" are a regular feature in the journal *Religious Studies Review*.

Griffiths is one who wishes to continue to use the word *religion* and, in order to do so, provides one example of a more generalized nonreligious definition: "A religion . . . [is] a form of life that seems to those who inhabit it to be comprehensive, incapable of abandonment, and of central importance."[13] In speaking (in Wittgensteinian terms) of a form of life, Griffiths helpfully takes us beyond the type of definitions that in some sense already presuppose an idea of the religious subject matter, then conform the definitions to it. Griffiths gives us a definition that can account for whole ranges of human social and cultural activity as the site of the religious. Yet it is not clear that his definition, as he states it, is helpful in every respect. It may indeed account for those forms of life that seem to their inhabitants to be "comprehensive, incapable of abandonment, and of central importance" (e.g., some versions of Christianity, Buddhism, Islam), but it does not account for those forms of life, which we might normally think of as religious, that are practiced but do not seem to their participants to be "comprehensive, incapable of abandonment, and of central importance." Do magical practices or fetishes fit this definition of religion? Do cultic attempts to manipulate multiple good or evil spirits? In the ancient Roman Empire, would the imperial cult count as a religion, while the cult of a civic deity or a household god would not (even though in most modern definitions of religion it would be the reverse)? Do the thoroughly polytheistic forms of life practiced in India constitute a religion called "Hinduism"?[14] What about the many ways of being Christian in America which often seem to exist and be practiced for the sake of the higher thing, Americanism, which is in fact the form of life that seems to its participants to be more comprehensive, less capable of abandonment, and of greater importance than Christianity? In this case, Americanism is the religion by Griffiths's definition, but many forms of Christianity in America are not. Griffiths does not take account of the fact that many if not most human beings often engage in multiple forms of life that we might designate religious according to the usual understandings (e.g., participating in practices having to do with deities or spirits), as well as and alongside of others that would be religious by Griffiths's understanding but that we would not normally think of as such (e.g., participating in practices having to do with national or political or economic values and ideals). Griffiths's definition does not seem to account for polytheism, which itself is

13. Griffiths, *Problems of Religious Diversity,* 7. The more expansive definition is also more informative: "A religion . . . [is] a form of life that seems to those who belong to it to be comprehensive, incapable of abandonment, and of central importance to the ordering of their lives. It is the great circle that seems to religious people to contain all the smaller circles representing their non-comprehensive forms of life; it is a form of life the abandonment of which seems to those who inhabit it to be tantamount to the abandonment of their identity; and it is a form of life that permits address to the questions that seem to those who belong to it to matter more than any others" (12).

14. I place "Hinduism" in quotes here in part because it is not at all clear that Hinduism is one thing identifiable as *a* religion. Is Hinduism better understood as the totality of life (linguistic, cultural, social, political) on the Indian subcontinent? If so, it seems to meet Griffiths's definition, but if it is the multiplicity of relatively unconnected cultic practices called forth by the multitudinous deities, then it seems not to.

never *a* religion, but typically an eclectic combination of relatively nonintegrated sets of convictions and practices produced by or with reference to the powers at work in the cosmos. Comprehensiveness, unsubstitutability, and ultimacy do not apply to polytheism, and yet specific social and cultural forms of life do take shape among peoples with reference to those powers.

To further clarify this matter, I turn to John Milbank, who notes that the more generalized, nonreligious definitions of religion (e.g., religion as a "form of life" or "what binds a society together") "turn out to be so all-encompassing as to coincide with the definition of culture as such":

> What we are often talking about when we speak of the religious, are the basic organizing categories for an entire culture: the images, word-forms, and prac-tices which specify "what there is" for a particular society. The commonness that pertains between different religions, is therefore not the commonness of a genus, or of a particular specified *mode* of human existence; instead it is the commonness of Being, or the fact of cultural—as opposed to natural—exist-ence itself. And there is nothing *necessarily* analogical within this community of cultural Being; instead, Being—both cultural and natural—or "what there is," can get construed in sheerly different and incommensurable ways by the many religions.[15]

Milbank's concept of culture is similar to Griffiths's "form of life," but the ad-vantage in Milbank's construal is that it allows for a multiplicity of religious visions, practices, and forms of life to make up the total fabric of the cultural: a polytheistic culture (e.g., "Christian America") is imaginable in Milbank's terms, while a polytheistic religion seems unimaginable in Griffiths's terms (the religion would have to be either Christianity or Americanism). The spec-ification of "what there is" for a particular society is the specification of the religious subject matter (whether that is singular or plural). Milbank thus goes on to state: "It follows that comparative religion should give way to the con-trasting of cultures (although the implied ahistoricity and ignoring of shared roots, infractions, and overlaps in this program must be in turn superseded)." If we further account (as perhaps Milbank does not) for the fact that *a* culture (singular) exists hardly anywhere on earth, but rather that nearly everywhere there are always multiple smaller and larger cultures in play, overlapping, in-teracting, mutually influencing, and modifying one another, then we have a concept that, I believe, gets us closer to understanding Paul's engagement with the Gentile world/worlds of his mission.[16]

15. John Milbank, "The End of Dialogue," in *Christian Uniqueness Reconsidered: The Myth of a Plu-ralistic Theology of Religions* (ed. Gavin D'Costa; Maryknoll, N.Y.: Orbis, 1990), 177 (emphasis original).

16. For a helpful critique of Milbank's notion of culture, see Kathryn Tanner, *Theories of Culture: A New Agenda for Theology* (Minneapolis: Fortress, 1997), 96–102. I am also indebted to Tanner's criticism of modern understandings of culture (38–56) and her postmodern reconstruction of the idea of culture (56–58).

Kathryn Tanner's attempt to define a theologically useful postmodern account of culture in *Theories of Culture* gives additional help toward understanding what Paul was about in his mission. Here I simply list the important features of her account:[17]

1. Cultures may be characterized by "taken-for-granted meanings" and "stable configurations of cultural elements" that may be shared by most or all participants in a society. Such meanings, configurations, and agreements are, however, "won" through historical processes in which many agents, personal and corporate, are continuously at work attempting to define those meanings and configurations. Thus "homogeneity, consistency, order, are no longer unempirical, a priori presumptions; sometimes they occur, sometimes they do not" (*Theories of Culture*, 56). Cultures are always in some state of flux.

2. While the concept of "culture as a whole" is not impossible, cultures must be thought of as "contradictory and internally fissured wholes" that generate their own "characteristic sites of resistance and contradiction." Around any cultural consolidation "swirl opposed meanings and ways of articulating cultural elements that have not been forced finally from the field," since the power of culture is never "concentrated solely in one party's hands" (*Theories of Culture*, 57).

3. Culture may still be considered "an essentially consensus-building feature of group living. That consensus becomes, however, extremely minimalistic: it forms the basis for conflict as much as it forms the basis for shared beliefs and sentiments. Whether or not culture is a common focus of *agreement*, culture binds people together as a common focus for *engagement*" (*Theories of Culture*, 57, emphasis original).

4. Cultural difference is not primarily a matter of "boundaries separating self-contained cultures. . . . Cultural elements may cross such boundaries without jeopardizing the distinctiveness of different cultures." The distinct identities of cultures are established not through isolation, but through the way common cultural elements are "handled and transformed" by segments of a society. "Cultural identity becomes . . . a hybrid, relational affair, something that lives between as much as within cultures. What is important for cultural identity is the novel way cultural elements from elsewhere are now put to work, by means of such complex and ad hoc relational processes as resistance, appropriation, subversion, and compromise" (*Theories of Culture*, 57–58).

5. Cultural self-criticism is not the product only of the encounter with the "external cultural 'others,'" but may also be the result of "the complexity and diversity that exist within any one culture. . . . A culture includes its own alternatives" (*Theories of Culture*, 58).

17. Ibid., 56–58.

Tanner's explication enables us to gain some sense of the complex dynamism, plurality, relationality, and changeability of culture(s), depending on the wide variety of agents and forces at work in a society. While a finite number of cultural goods or elements may be available at any given time in a society's history, the ways of handling, rearranging, and transforming these is potentially nearly infinite. I am convinced, as the rest of this chapter shows, that Paul's mission to and engagement with the Gentile peoples may be understood more clearly through these clarifications of the religious subject matter made by Griffiths, Milbank, and Tanner.

Two Cultures, One People:
Gentile Believers and the Synagogues in Rome

If, following Griffiths, Milbank, and Tanner, we substitute the idea of a form of life or culture for that of religion, I think we have a tool that enables us to understand something of Paul's own mission to the Gentile peoples, and of his aim as God's chosen messenger to them. *For Paul's aim was not to propose another religion to the nations, but to call out and build up a people in their midst, a people formed by allegiance to the one God of Israel and his Son, Jesus the Messiah.*

It seems likely that the way Paul originally hoped to establish a people for God's name, called out from the nations, was by incorporating his Gentile converts into the existing Jewish communities and synagogues of the Diaspora; that is, not to establish "free-standing" Gentile churches, but to persuade Jewish synagogues to welcome the new thing that God was doing among the Gentiles through the gospel and Paul's mission.[18] For Paul's convictions about the apocalyptic theological significance of Jesus included the conviction that those Gentiles who believed his message about Jesus and through him came to worship the one God of Israel were now fully members of Abraham's family. They should therefore be welcomed as members of the Diaspora Jewish communities, with full participation in the life of the synagogues, without having to take up observance of Torah. The Torah was no longer to be used as a barrier to such life together among Jews and messianic Gentiles. Indeed, believing Gentiles need not even be circumcised. Rather, Jews and messianic Gentiles together would now constitute the one people of God. The synagogues, however, were not very receptive of these terms of Paul's message and mission to the Gentile peoples. For a variety of reasons, often theological, but also often having to do with the political, social, and economic situations of the Diaspora communities vis-à-vis their host societies, Paul's difficult challenge to the Diaspora communities was by and large rejected (cf. Acts 18:1–17). The re-

___

18. See Mark Nanos, *The Mystery of Romans: The Jewish Context of Paul's Letter* (Minneapolis: Fortress, 1996), 109–10.

sult was that, contrary to Paul's original intentions, the synagogues or "citizens' assemblies" (*ekklēsiai*) that Paul formed were largely, though not exclusively, Gentile.

What might have happened, culturally, if the Diaspora communities had fully welcomed Paul's Gentile converts and granted them full rights of participation in synagogue life? While the answer to that question is largely speculative, it is easy to imagine that the blending of the two peoples would have led over time to transformations of both cultures, with the synagogue functioning as the primary site of engagement and argument over the "final" shape of an agreed-upon cultural configuration. Doubtless, the presence on site of nonobservant Gentiles would not have been a complete cultural shock to the Jewish community in a given locale, since such a community would already have been in some measure a product both of its own Torah observance and of Gentile cultural elements which would have "crossed the boundaries" into the Jewish community. To look for synagogues of "pure Judaism" in Paul's time would be anachronistic. Further, questions surrounding Gentile relationship to the God of Israel and to the Torah, as well as questions about how Jews and Gentiles were to dwell together, were far from settled within the Jewish communities of the Diaspora in Paul's time. As Terence Donaldson and others show, there was a good deal of debate over such questions, as well as considerable variation in practice with respect to Jewish association with Gentiles.[19] Diaspora Hellenistic Jewish communities were themselves already, before the arrival of Paul and his message, relatively various and fluid "cultural consolidations" characterized by the kinds of contradictions and "internal fissures," "opposed meanings and ways of articulating cultural elements," hybridizations, and relationships of "resistance, appropriation, subversion and compromise" with the surrounding cultures, which Tanner explicates. So it is safe to assume that at least some measure of change to existing Diaspora Jewish cultures may have been a by-product of Jewish acceptance of Gentiles on Paul's terms. And perhaps the threat of that worried the leaders of many synagogues.

But there is no reason to think that some Judaizing of the Gentile culture of the converts would not also have taken place and would likely have been the primary direction in which the cultural shift would have flowed. Paul nowhere suggests that *Jews* should reject their Torah observance, and in fact seems to assume that they would and should remain committed to it (1 Cor. 7:17–20; cf. Gal. 5:3; Acts 21:17–24).[20] Indeed, in the Galatian churches, according to Mark Nanos, the Gentile believers may have been quite eager to Judaize, in accordance with the wishes (and pressure) of the local syna-

19. See Terence Donaldson, *Paul and the Gentiles: Remapping the Apostle's Convictional World* (Minneapolis: Fortress, 1997), 51–74, and the texts and literature cited in the notes.
20. See Markus Bockmuehl, *Jewish Law in Gentile Churches: Halakhah and the Beginning of Christian Public Ethics* (Edinburgh: T & T Clark, 2000), 170–71.

gogues, in part to escape the social and political liminality and perhaps even danger to which their rejection of Gentile gods, including the emperor, had consigned them; but also in part because the Jewish way of life itself may have been perceived to sustain more directly an appropriate faithfulness to the God of Israel even for these Gentiles.[21]

In order for such a merging of cultures to have taken place in the Diaspora synagogues, however, there would have to have been agreement with Paul by the synagogues that Jesus was in fact the Messiah of Israel and, moreover, that this same Jesus had such powerful, apocalyptic significance that because of him neither Jewish birth nor full proselytism to Torah observance were any longer the sole conditions for full participation in the elect community. Those Gentiles called by God through their participation in Jesus Christ would also be full members of the family of Abraham. On this, historically, few if any Diaspora synagogues agreed with Paul. And for Paul's part, he would not compromise on insisting that Gentile converts be accepted by the synagogues *solely* on the basis of the believing Gentiles' incorporation into Israel through the death and resurrection of Jesus Christ.

It was that full primary acceptance that Paul was after. That a certain amount of subsequent, voluntary Judaizing of Gentile believers would have occurred, once they were fully incorporated into the synagogues on the basis of their being "in Christ," seems not only inevitable but desirable.[22] Paul is intent on Gentiles becoming obedient to the God of Israel and dwelling together in peace with their Jewish fellow believers. As we discovered in chapter 2 with respect to Galatians, Paul's primary question was about which *power* (or which god and lord) would be at work in shaping the life of this new Jew-and-Gentile Diaspora community. If the Torah, which itself was good, was nevertheless allowed to be determinative of the messianic Gen-

---

21. For an account of this argument, see Mark Nanos, "The Inter- and Intra-Jewish Political Context of Paul's Letter to the Galatians," in *Paul and Politics: Ekklesia, Israel, Imperium, Interpretation: Essays in Honor of Krister Stendahl* (ed. Richard A. Horsley; Harrisburg, Pa.: Trinity, 2000), 146–59; for a full account see idem, *The Irony of Galatians: Paul's Letter in First-Century Context* (Minneapolis: Fortress, 2002).

22. The very fact that the early Gentile churches had only the Jewish scriptures would have virtually guaranteed a measure of Judaizing of Gentile culture in these churches, insofar as the churches read their own way of life as in some sense an extension of the way of life of Israel. The impact of Jewish moral discourse (*halakhah*), via Paul, on the form of life of the early Gentile churches is explored in Bockmuehl, *Jewish Law in Gentile Churches*, 167–73; and more extensively in Peter J. Tomson, *Paul and the Jewish Law: Halakha in the Letters of the Apostle to the Gentiles* (Minneapolis: Fortress, 1990). On this point Michael Wyschogrod, in his otherwise helpful essay, "Christianity and Mosaic Law," *Pro Ecclesia* 2 (1990): 451–59, misses the point when he writes: "Paul assumes that circumcision and the law remain obligatory for Jews. The question is, is it obligatory for Gentiles? Paul's position is not only is it not obligatory for Gentiles, it is forbidden for Gentiles." There is, however, no suggestion in Paul's writings that Torah observance is "forbidden" for Gentiles, only that they should not submit to efforts to make it a *requirement* for their life together with Jews.

tiles' full inclusion into the Jewish community (i.e., as authentically "Abraham's offspring" through Christ; Gal. 3:29), then the Torah itself would be the effective power in the community, a power equivalent to those that formerly enslaved the Gentiles (4:1–11). But the Gentiles were not delivered from those enslaving powers by the Torah, but by the power of the gospel and the Spirit: "You foolish Galatians! Who has bewitched you? It was before your eyes that Jesus Christ was publicly displayed as crucified! . . . Does God supply you with the Spirit and work miracles among you by your doing the works of the law, or by your believing what you heard" (3:1, 5). It was to the God of Israel, his Messiah, and the life-giving Holy Spirit that the community of both Jews and Gentiles in Christ owed its existence and allegiance. Given that, the Torah was primarily available to both Jews and Gentiles as the scripture which bore faithful testimony to God's deed in Christ and the Holy Spirit and only secondarily available as a set of practices identifying one particular group within that community, the Jews.

Paul does not reject either the Torah or Jewishness as the form of life (culture) for Jews, whether messianic or not, as their appropriate manner of faithful response to God's gracious faithfulness to them (also in Jesus Christ). He rejects only the belief that Torah observance rather than God's apocalyptic deed in Christ and the Spirit finally determines the destiny of Gentiles as full sharers in Abraham's family. Potentially, every one of Paul's *ekklēsiai* might have been the site of engagement between Jewish and Gentile cultures (in those places where there were Jewish populations), two peoples coming together to become one assembly of God's people, to shape a new form of life from these two cultures under the lordship of Jesus Christ and in the power of the Holy Spirit. That vision seems rarely if ever to have materialized as a result of his own mission efforts, but it seems that Paul held out a strong hope that precisely this might happen in the city of Rome, and to that end he wrote his letter to the Romans.

In a remarkable departure from his usual practice, Paul does not address his letter to the "church" or "churches" in Rome (the word *ekklēsia* appears only in chapter 16, and not with reference to the addressees of the letter). Rather, he addresses his letter to "all God's beloved (*agapētois theou*)," those "called (*klētois*) to be saints" in Rome (1:7). The called and elect of God are those who can never be separated from the love of God in Jesus Christ (8:30, 33, 38–39); and this, as I showed in the previous chapter, certainly includes all of those nonmessianic Jews who, by virtue of their election and calling, are also "beloved" by God (11:28–29) and therefore inseparable from God's love in Jesus Christ. In this noteworthy greeting, therefore, Paul appears to make no distinction between messianic Jews and Gentiles on the one hand and nonmessianic Jews on the other. He includes them *all* in his address, and his letter will be of interest and concern to all of them, even though the "implied readers" throughout the letter—the ones in need of and receiving Paul's explicit instruction (1:6, 13; 11:13–14 [and Rom. 9–11 as a whole];

15:15–16)—are Gentiles.[23] The assumption in Paul's greeting is that the Gentile believers in Jesus are in close relationship with Jews and the synagogues, messianic and possibly also nonmessianic, in Rome; indeed, in the kind of relationship where Paul feels warranted to greet them all together as God's beloved. The messianic Gentiles are not addressed as their own distinct assemblies; Paul's address does not separate them from the Jewish assemblies, the synagogues. This consideration among others lead some commentators on Romans to propose that the entire thrust of the letter concerns the ongoing participation of the Gentiles in the Jewish synagogues in Rome and the behaviors which Paul exhorts the Gentile believers to practice in order to maintain their fellowship with the synagogues as full sharers in God's Abrahamic family.[24] For while Paul argues vigorously that Gentiles must be fully received as Gentiles by the Jews, a serious issue remains. Markus Bockmuehl identifies it succinctly: "It is one thing to say that Jews and Gentiles together constitute the people of God; quite another, to define the common life of that new covenant people."[25]

For Paul to call for a particular set of behaviors from Gentile believers in order for them to share a common life with the Jewish community in Rome may sound like a contradiction of Paul's message to the Galatians. But an important contextual difference between Galatia and Rome suggests otherwise. The Jewish communities in the Galatian cities seem to have been insisting on the full proselytism of Gentiles, that is, on their circumcision and obedience to "the entire [Sinaitic] law" which is implicit in circumcision (Gal. 5:3), in order for the Gentiles to share fully in the life of the Jewish communities and synagogues (and thus perhaps also to come under the same political considerations and protections as were granted the Jews).[26] In Rome, however, it appears that the synagogues were requiring only (or Paul is assuming they were requiring only) that the messianic Gentiles fulfill the obligations of the so-called Noachide commandments in order for there to

---

23. For arguments for Gentiles as the "implied readers" or "encoded audience" of Romans, see Stanley Stowers, *A Rereading of Romans: Justice, Jews, and Gentiles* (New Haven: Yale University Press, 1994), 21–33; Nanos, *Mystery of Romans*, 75–84. The implied readers or audience are not the same as the "empirical audience," which may in fact have been both Gentiles and Jews. Nanos writes: "Thus, we must be careful to distinguish between what we can know about the makeup of the congregation(s) in Rome [the empirical audience] and what we can conclude about Paul's intentions toward the implied readers/hearers of the message. In other words, our concern is not so much with who was present, but rather, with whom he was really instructing" (76). I am suggesting that while Paul in Rom. 1:7 (as also in Rom. 16) *greets* both Gentiles and Jews (the empirical audience), he nonetheless sets it as his task in the letter to *instruct* Gentiles only. For a critique of Stowers's argument for Gentiles exclusively as the implied audience, see Richard B. Hays, "'The Gospel Is the Power of God for Salvation to Gentiles Only'? A Critique of Stanley Stowers' *A Rereading of Romans*," *Critical Review of Books in Religion* 1996: 35–37.

24. This proposal is made most persuasively by Nanos in *Mystery of Romans*; see also the extensive literature which he draws upon to support his thesis.

25. Bockmuehl, *Jewish Law in Gentile Churches*, 145.

26. As argued by Nanos in *Irony of Galatians*.

be full fellowship between Gentiles and Jews. These commandments were a relatively small—and during Paul's time, still fluid—set of rules gleaned primarily from Genesis 1–11 and the laws in Leviticus, rules that pertained to resident aliens in the land of Israel and that marked out "righteous Gentiles" outside the land, that is, those Gentiles with whom, according to some traditions, Jews could have fellowship. Such rules included prohibitions against idolatry, blasphemy, fornication, bloodshed, and eating meat with blood in it.[27] In other words, "even if Gentiles are saved as Gentiles, they must be exhorted to abide by those commandments that already apply to them [precisely as Gentiles] in Scripture and its interpretative tradition."[28]

Such commandments were in fact set forth for Gentile converts in the Apostolic Council described in Acts 15. There a distinction is made precisely *Acts* between the requirement that Gentile believers "be circumcised and ordered to keep the law of Moses" (15:5—i.e., what seemed to be required of them in Galatia), which is rejected, and the Noachide requirement that they "abstain only from things polluted by idols and from fornication and from whatever has been strangled and from blood" (15:20, 29). As Bockmuehl notes, these rules would provide sufficient conditions for the common life of Jews and Gentiles, the possibility of their dwelling together as one community rather than two: "If it is indeed the case that in Christ these Gentiles have a portion in the world to come . . . then it suffices to apply to them the same ethical principles that would in any case apply to righteous Gentiles living with the people of Israel, i.e., resident aliens."[29] According to the arguments of Nanos, Bockmuehl, and Peter Tomson, it is these scriptural requirements which Paul asks the Gentile believers in Rome to fulfill (in Rom. 12–15) as their "obedience of faith" in order to continue to be well received by the Jews and synagogues (messianic or nonmessianic) in Rome.[30] Such requirements would not make Jews of the Gentiles who were obedient to them; rather, in Paul's understanding they would share full communion with Jews, through Jesus Christ, precisely as Gentiles who are nonetheless called to live by God's revealed law for Gentiles.

The result would not have been one religion (Christianity) replacing another (Judaism), but one new people of Jews and Gentiles being formed to bear witness to the one God of Israel who had reconciled them to one an-

27. See the important discussion of the Noachide commandments in Bockmuehl, *Jewish Law in Gentile Churches*, 145–73. Bockmuehl writes: "Briefly put, the *topos* of Noachide Law in rabbinic thought governs relations between Jews and non-Jews, and is thus a kind of functional equivalent to the *ius gentium*. Its basis lies in the conviction that God gave certain pre-Sinaitic laws equally to all humankind, laws that may therefore form the ethical foundations of Jewish dealing with Gentiles" (150). As Bockmuehl makes clear, the rabbinic teaching on the Noachide laws is not yet fully worked out during Paul's time.

28. Ibid., 167.

29. Ibid., 165.

30. Nanos, *Mystery of Romans*, 166–238.

other through Jesus Christ and the gift of the Spirit. The two radically different cultures involved in this reconciliation and new social project would be
challenged to adapt to each other through mutual accommodation. In Rome
it seems that the Gentiles to whom Paul sends his instructions have not
adopted an accommodating spirit vis-à-vis the Jews. Rather, they are proud
and boastful of their being called to be God's people and have come to suppose that nonmessianic Jews have been rejected as God's people. In response,
while Paul reaffirms (as he did with the Galatians) the gospel of God's apocalyptic reconciliation of the Gentiles through Jesus Christ and the Holy Spirit
(Rom. 1–8) and thus their full incorporation into God's people apart from
Torah observance, he nonetheless even more forcefully reminds them of
their indebtedness to Israel as the olive tree into which they have been
grafted. If the Gentile believers are the people of God, they are so insofar as
they have now also been made members of the people Israel (Rom. 9–11),
who is God's original beloved, whom God will never cast away. In other
words, the nonmessianic Jews continue to have a priority in God's electing
purposes with respect to the Gentile believers, a priority that Paul calls the
Gentile believers to acknowledge and even to submit to.[31]

For the sake of the formation of God's people in Rome, therefore, Paul requires the submission of the "strong" (i.e., Gentile believers who are tempted
to "boast" over the Jews) to the "weak" (i.e., messianic or nonmessianic Jews)
whose faith is nonetheless faith, who nonetheless eat and drink and give
thanks and observe days "in honor of the Lord" (14:6), whose Lord is none
other than the one Lord of Israel and the nations, whose same Lord "is able
to make them stand" (14:4), and whom the strong are therefore not to
judge. For these reasons Paul exhorts the strong to take up the scripturally
warranted Gentile dietary restrictions set forth by the Apostolic Council

---

31. This last point, namely that Paul calls the Gentile believers in Rome to submit even to the nonmessianic synagogues in Rome, is argued by Nanos with respect to Rom. 13 in *Mystery of Romans*, 289–
336. The "governing authorities" (13:1) are, according to Nanos, the rulers of the synagogues, who have
their authority from God to maintain the political well-being and good order of the synagogues. In many
cities in the Roman Empire they performed not only or even primarily religious functions for the synagogue, but also political, social, and economic functions—they were often benefactors and philanthro-
pists. Nanos's proposal is a radical departure from the usual interpretations of Rom. 13, which almost
universally assume that the governing authorities are Roman civil and/or imperial officials. His proposal
has not been widely accepted, even though there are arguments to commend it—not least because it enables a *seamless* reading of Romans, including a reading of Rom. 9–15 in which the relation of Jews and
Gentiles is consistently the focus of Paul's argument. Nanos's proposal solves the persistent problem of
the apparent "intrusiveness" of Rom. 13 into the argument as a whole. While at this stage Nanos's proposal about this text remains a minority opinion, his discussion merits further serious attention. I suspect
that agreement with Nanos would be less a matter of further exegetical focus on Rom. 13 by itself and
more a matter of agreement with his wider proposal that the point of Romans as a whole, and therefore
in its parts, is to encourage, or rather strongly insist, that the Gentile believers in Rome remain in close
fellowship with the Jewish community there, living with the Jews the common life of the people of God.
I find that thesis of Nanos quite persuasive, and therefore I also find his argument about Rom. 13 to have
merit.

(14:13–23). It is that kind of cultural "service" on the part of the Gentile believers that will lead to the creation of one people of God in full mutual
communion, while at the same time honoring the theologically warranted
and sustained cultural difference (Torah observance or nonobservance) between the two: "Each of us must please our neighbor for the good purpose
of building up the neighbor. For Christ did not please himself" (15:2–3);
rather, "Christ has become a servant of the circumcised on behalf of the
truth of God . . . and in order that the Gentiles might glorify God for his
mercy" (15:8–9). Through the Gentiles' imitation of Christ's servanthood—
that is, Gentiles becoming in this regard servants of the Jews (messianic or
not) for their "mutual upbuilding" (14:19)—Paul hoped that the social
space of the Jewish communities and synagogues in Rome would become a
space of cultural harmony, "so that together you [Gentiles and Jews] may
with one voice glorify the God and Father of our Lord Jesus Christ" (15:6).
That would have amounted to a clear and profound testimony, in the very
heart of the imperial capital, that the one God of Israel and the one Lord
Jesus Christ was the ruler and reconciler not only of the Jews but also of the
nations and of the Jews *in communion with* the nations. This same God was
creating, through the reconciling apocalypse of Jesus Christ, a startlingly
new cultural-social-political order—a counterempire—through which his
glory would be revealed among the nations.

One Culture, Two Peoples:
Forming the Gentile Assembly in Corinth

We do not know whether Paul's hope became a reality in Rome. We do
know that he had to adopt another approach to the formation of the people of
God in the churches that he established in his mission. What would he do in
those contexts where the Gentile believers had to shape their lives as a people in
relative independence from the synagogues? To that question we now turn.

In the previous chapter I proposed, following John Howard Yoder, that for
Paul the communities of the Jewish Diaspora were at the very least the *model*
for Paul's *ekklēsiai*. Those communities, by remaining faithful to Torah and
meeting regularly as the synagogue, were able both to dwell among the nations, "seeking the welfare of the cities" in which they were located, and at the
same time to maintain a specific identity as the people of the God of Israel.
While faithful Torah observance in these communities ensured a good measure of nonassimilated cultural identity across space and time, it did not pre-
clude participation in and use of a great deal of the available elements and
goods of the host culture(s). Testimony to that is given in that there was a
good deal of visible difference among the various Diaspora communities, not
least in the languages that were spoken (cf. Acts 2:5–11). Those scattered communities thus displayed (in Tanner's terms) aspects both of shared "taken-for-
granted-meanings" and "stable configurations of cultural elements," provided

would H.
agree (see
earlier
chapter)

primarily by Torah observance, as well as significant differences among them as
a result of "boundary crossings." Common cultural elements of the wider culture (e.g., language, goods, customs) were incorporated, handled, and transformed by the Jewish communities to create "hybrid" Jewish communities in
one place that were not exactly like those in other places of the Diaspora.

Because the synagogues by and large rejected Paul's message and mission, the
Gentile believers in Jesus were largely left to work out the question of their form
of life without the help of the Jewish people. Further, by acknowledging that
through Christ the Gentiles were acceptable to God as Gentiles, Paul was in
principle also bound in some sense to embrace existing Gentile forms of life, albeit forms that were subject to the transforming power of the gospel and the
Holy Spirit. The task for Paul, therefore, was to shape synagoguelike assemblies
of Gentile believers more or less "from scratch." That is, rather than shaping one
people from two cultures, as he hoped would happen in Rome, he was bound to
call out and shape from one culture (Gentile) another people, a people of the
one God of Israel, created by the preaching of the gospel and the power of the
Holy Spirit. As I argued in chapter 1, Protestant readers of Paul have often been
preoccupied with relatively abstract theological themes such as grace, faith, and
works, separated from their concrete contexts in Paul's letters. What often goes
missing in these readings is an awareness of the all-encompassing paganism of
the Greco-Roman world of Paul's time, whether in its imperial or more local and
personal forms, and the radical strangeness and otherness of Paul's message
within that paganism. Paul's profoundly Jewish missionary aim was to convince
Gentiles that in the life, death, and resurrection of a crucified Jew the God of the
Jews (who is the one and only God of all peoples) had acted decisively to save
Gentiles, not from "good works," but from the imperial and local paganisms,
polytheisms, and idolatries in which they were held captive and from the personal, social, and political disorder and injustice which resulted from their honoring of false gods and false lords (Rom. 1:18–32).

The gods and lords of the Gentiles, whether the divinized emperor or the
deities of city, social club, and household, exercised real and effective power
over those who honored them. The Gentiles by their habitual honoring of
these gods were in fact, according to Paul, enslaved by them. The forms of life
(personal, social, political) of the Gentiles reflected their bondage, a bondage
from which it was difficult to be delivered even for those who had in some
sense renounced the gods and lords by believing the gospel and joining the
community of the true God.[32] "Since some have become so accustomed to
idols until now, they still think of the food they eat as food offered to an idol;

32. That the Gentile peoples are in fact enslaved (rather than, say, liberated, saved, and helped, as
they might think) by their gods is for Paul not a conclusion which he draws from a "neutral" analysis of
"the human situation" and therefore not one to which the Gentile peoples might be led through a similar
analysis. It is, rather, something Paul knows because the one true God has made it known to his own people, Israel, and now in Jesus Christ has revealed to the Gentile peoples (through Paul's preaching of the
gospel of liberation from idolatrous bondage).

and their conscience, being weak, is defiled" (1 Cor. 8:7). Apart from the powerful intervention of the God of Israel among the Gentile peoples they would remain in their bondage, believing that life, hope, well-being, and peace were graciously granted to them by the achievements and powers of the Roman emperor and the pantheon of Greek and Roman deities.

Salvation arrived for the Gentile peoples as an act of God's invasive power through Paul's preaching of the gospel (Rom. 1:16). I have delineated the apocalyptic character of Paul's message in the previous chapters. I simply re-iterate that for Paul the purpose of God's apocalyptic action in the crucifix-ion and resurrection of Jesus Christ is in the first place to mount an attack on the powers that enslave the Gentile peoples. As Richard Horsley states, "Paul's gospel of Christ announced doom and destruction not on Judaism or the Law, but on the 'rulers of this age.'"[33] Horsley goes on to draw out one of the implications of this fact, given that the widest context of Paul's mis-sion was the Roman Empire: "Ironic as it may seem, precisely where he is borrowing from or alluding to 'imperial' language, we can discern that Paul's gospel stands counter primarily to the Roman imperial order, 'this world, which is passing away.'"[34] In other words, when Paul in his mission engages the religions of his day, he has to do not only with the many smaller cults to be found in each town and city, but also with the world religion which dom-inated life in the Roman Empire from top to bottom of the social order. The power of the Roman imperial-religious order also had to be countered by an-other power, the Wholly Other power of God's imperial rule.

It is thus quite clear that for Paul the religions of the Gentiles must in some sense be engaged as the workings and manifestation of *powers*, whether personal, sociopolitical, or "divine." The rituals, habits, customs, and social and political practices in which the Gentile peoples participated were the ef-fective instruments of the powers, the means by which the powers laid hold of persons and peoples for their causes and sustained them in those causes. Different powers of different orders each produced and required their own sets of rituals, customs, and practices in order to be available and effective for the participants in those practices. Paul thus does not have an "essential-ist" notion of religion (indeed, the concept of religion or religions does not appear in his letters), that is, of religion as an abiding and distinct sphere or dimension of human existence with its own raison d'être and focal point, which can be either discerned or discussed without reference to the everyday practices of personal, social, and political life in relation to the various pow-ers at work in and through them.[35] Rather, we may say that Paul engaged the

33. Richard Horsley, "General Introduction," in *Paul and Empire: Religion and Power in Roman Im-perial Society* (ed. Richard A. Horsley; Harrisburg, Pa.: Trinity, 1997), 6.

34. Ibid., 7.

35. For illuminating accounts of the origins of the idea of religion and the politics from which the idea originates and is sustained, see William T. Cavanaugh, "'A Fire Strong Enough to Consume the House': The Wars of Religion and the Rise of the State," *Modern Theology* 11 (1995): 397–420; Griffiths,

whole of Gentile social and cultural existence as the manifestation of the powers at work among the nations. It is also clear, then, as we have already seen, that Paul was not proposing in his mission that the Gentile peoples accept another religion. The "competition" into which Paul entered with his mission to proclaim the gospel was a power struggle in which nothing less was at stake than the formation of a new people with its own distinctive habits, customs, practices, and social and political order, all oriented by, to, and in the service of its own distinctive Power. Paul sought not to establish a religion, but a people among other peoples, distinct from those other peoples by virtue of the specific power at work in it, the power of the God of the gospel. The engagement with the "other," whether as person or society, was for Paul always immediately and intrinsically a theological engagement and always immediately and intrinsically an argument about the shape of political, social, cultural, and personal existence. As Horsley states:

> It is . . . simply anachronistic to think that Paul was founding a religion called Christianity that broke away from a religion called Judaism. Paul's mission and communities would not have appeared as distinctively religious to his contemporaries in the Roman empire. The term he uses for the movement as a whole as well as for particular communities, *ekklēsia*, was primarily political, the term for the citizens' "assembly" of the Greek *polis* (city-state).[36]

Paul consistently addresses his letters to these citizens' assemblies, not to Christians as members of another religion. The question of which power is at work and given allegiance in the Pauline assemblies is crucial to every letter that Paul writes. Is it the apocalyptic power of the one God of Israel, unleashed in the crucifixion and resurrection of Jesus and now working among the Gentile peoples through the Holy Spirit, or is it another power? By what power shall this new people be formed? "For I will not venture to speak of anything except what Christ has accomplished through me to win obedience from the Gentiles, by word and deed, by the power of signs and wonders, by the power of the Spirit of God" (Rom. 15:18–19).

We may make the claim, then, that for Paul powers, peoples, and cultures are inextricably bound up with one another. There is not only one power at work in the world, but a plurality of powers, earthly and "heavenly," each having its own sphere of influence. Paul engages the Gentile world/worlds as the space of the work and manifestation of complex and interrelated systems

---

"Very Idea of Religion," 30–35; and Milbank, "End of Dialogue," 174–91. Griffiths writes of the continuing attempts of scholars in religious studies to "preserve the idea that religion is a sui generis dimension of human experience, recognizable cross-culturally and not to be analytically reduced to other categories such as culture, economics and power. And yet at the same time they want to deny the ontological commitments that would make sense of such an idea" (33).

36. Horsley, "General Introduction," 8.

of powers holding sway among the Gentile peoples. These powers create the kinds of cultic, social, political, and cultural arrangements and practices that constitute the Gentiles as a people (at the level of empire) or as numerous relatively distinct local peoples. It is these powers that, according to Paul's gospel, God engages in war in the apocalyptic event of the crucifixion and resurrection of Jesus Christ.

Yet Paul is no smasher of idols or destroyer of pagan temples, nor does he encourage his converts to become so. Nor, of course, does he require his Gentile converts to become Jews or to leave their pagan environs or to cease to be in some measure the Gentiles they had been before hearing and believing Paul's message. Paul's aversion to all things idolatrous seems to coexist alongside patience with actual Gentile idolaters and acceptance of many Gentile cultural forms of life within the life of the people of God. In other words, Paul made some crucial discriminations between the powers at work among the Gentiles and the forms of Gentile enslavement to them on the one hand and the actual Gentile forms of life produced by those relationships between powers and peoples. How does Paul make such discriminations? What are his criteria of judgment? What is the character of the radically new and other power unleashed among the Gentile peoples through the preaching of the gospel, and what is the shape of the people called into existence by that power?

The most promising place to seek answers to those questions is 1 Corinthians. For despite the fact that there was a Jewish community in Corinth in Paul's time (cf. Acts 18:1–17), the messianic community there seems to have been predominantly Gentile in make-up and thoroughly Gentile in sensibility and to have had little by way of a positive relationship with the synagogue. As Richard Hays notes, "This meant that Paul was faced with a massive task of *resocialization*, seeking to reshape [without the aid of the synagogue] the moral imagination of these Gentile converts into patterns of life consonant with the ways of the God of Israel."[37] Apparently the "resocialization" was only partially complete, even though Paul, according to Acts 18:11, spent eighteen months in Corinth establishing the *ekklēsia* there before he moved on to other regions. Between the time he left and the correspondence we have in 1 Corinthians a great deal happened in the new community to prompt an extensive set of responses from Paul to a variety of issues raised by the attempts of the community to live as God's people in Corinth. This raises the important question that has engaged Pauline historians for a century or more: What happened after Paul left Corinth?[38]

That question has often been answered by attempting to find a single interpretative key to the problems in the Corinthian church, such as the influ-

37. Richard B. Hays, *First Corinthians* (Louisville: John Knox, 1997), 4 (emphasis original).
38. This question forms the title of Bruce W. Winter's *After Paul Left Corinth: The Influence of Secular Ethics and Social Change* (Grand Rapids: Eerdmans, 2001).

ence of "gnostic" ideas or an "overrealized eschatology" in the Corinthians'
understanding of Christian faith. Such suggestions, however, have a tendency to assume that the issues are primarily religious, or about theological
ideas, that is, that heresies are either already present or in the making in
Corinth.[39] That assumption has been questioned by Hays: "In many cases,
the practices of the Corinthians were motivated by social and cultural factors—such as popular philosophy and rhetoric—that were not consciously
theological at all."[40] Some fascinating and valuable studies on the sociocultural history of Corinth by Bruce Winter explore and substantiate Hays's
point. Winter argues "that the problems which arose subsequent to Paul's
departure [from Corinth] did so partly because the Christians were 'cosmo-
politans,' i.e., citizens of this world and, in particular, citizens or residents of
Roman Corinth. They had grown up in, and imbibed that culture before
they became Christians. They reacted to some issues that arose after Paul left
on the basis of the learnt conventions and cultural mores of Corinthian *Ro-
manitas*."[41] Those problematic "conventions and cultural mores" are by no
means all in the realm of what we might designate as religious. Many social,
political, and cultural (as well as cultic) habits and practices threatened to
impede the formation of the new citizens' assembly, the body politic of
Christ in Corinth. Winter identifies these:[42]

- "professional competitiveness" among rhetors and teachers, which spills
  over into competition among the students loyal to their teachers—reflected in 1 Corinthians 1–4
- lenience in legal punishment toward those of higher social standing
  who contravene moral order—reflected in 1 Corinthians 5
- the use of often unjust "secular" law courts (subject to the influences of
  power, status, and bribery) to bring "vexatious litigation" against competitors and/or enemies—reflected in 1 Corinthians 6:1–8
- "elitist ethics" among the socially and economically privileged, used to
  justify "gluttony, drunkenness, and sexual indulgence" under the slogan "all things are permitted for me"—reflected in 1 Corinthians 6:12;
  10:23; 15:29–34

39. Such assumptions and theories about "the Corinthian heresy" seem almost to presuppose a
"Christianized" Corinthian community—that is, a community that has had a significant history of
"thinking about" Christianity in theological terms. But that is hardly the case. The Corinthians are only
in the early stages of making appropriate distinctions (or not) between the ritual, cultural, social, and political habits and practices formed through lifelong participation in the body politic of Corinth (including its gods and lords) on the one hand and the habits and practices consistent with their participation in
the new corporate body called forth by the God of Israel and Jesus Christ on the other.

40. Hays, *First Corinthians*, 8.

41. Winter, *After Paul Left Corinth*, 27.

42. Ibid., "Part I: The Influence of Secular Ethics," 31–211.

- social elitism displayed (e.g., in men covering their heads) in liturgical activities and cultic rites—reflected in 1 Corinthians 11:2–16
- the hosting of "private dinners" to which each participant brought and ate their own meal, rather than sharing food with all who gathered (thus displaying and perpetuating socioeconomic disparities)—reflected in 1 Corinthians 11:17–34
- the use of religious curses, that is, calling upon the gods and spirits to bring calamity upon one's competitors and/or enemies—reflected in 1 Corinthians 12:1–3
- the practice of patronage to establish dominance and wield influence in social, political, and cultic contexts—reflected by its transformation into service in 1 Corinthians 16:15–18

In addition to this list (not necessarily exhaustive) of Corinthian social, cultural, and political habits and practices that affected ecclesial life in Corinth, Winter also shows how other external social changes posed challenges for the Corinthian churches.[43] Such events include a grain shortage, the establishment of the imperial cult in Corinth, the resituating of the Isthmian Games from Corinth to nearby Isthmia, and the removal of provisions of kosher meat in the Corinthian meat market. Each of these raised new questions for the Corinthian believers after Paul left Corinth—questions having to do with marriage in a time of crisis, attendance at the temple of the imperial cult and public festivals celebrating the Isthmian games, and eating meat offered to idols. At the heart of many, if not all, of the issues which these challenges, internal and external, raised for the Corinthian assembly was the threat that this fledgling community of God's people would be torn asunder into several competing groups. Each group seemed to be seeking some kind of ascendancy with respect to the other groups of believers and perhaps some kind of advantage in the wider Corinthian social and political order as well. Paul's task in the letter is to prevent this community from falling apart by slipping back into the forms of life they were used to before they were rescued by the gospel.

That task begins for Paul, crucially, by reminding the Corinthians *who* they are (1 Cor. 1:1–9). He asserts their being as God's people, the *ekklēsia* or citizens' assembly "of God," a people "sanctified" or set apart from the wider Corinthian society by virtue of God's "call" upon them to be "holy ones" in that place. They in turn, together with others "in every place," have come to "call on the name of our Lord Jesus Christ" and have become recipients of God's grace and made rich in spiritual gifts. They have been placed into a story which culminates with the final apocalypse of Jesus on "the day of our Lord Jesus Christ" and may be confident until that day that "God is faithful; by him [they] were called into the fellowship of his Son, Jesus Christ our Lord." In this way Paul lets the church of God in Corinth know that, like Is-

---

43. Ibid., "Part II: The Influence of Social Changes," 213–301.

rael, it has been incorporated into a name, a story, a communion, a purpose, and a goal that is not of its own making. Their existence as a people is from beginning to end God's work, a work that, despite the many apparent failures of the Corinthians to live up to their calling, God will complete among them. "God is faithful." Everything that Paul says subsequently is said in the light of God's calling of the Corinthian community and of God's faithfulness to that calling. As we have already seen in an earlier examination of 1 Thessalonians, Paul's theology of election is as foundational for his understanding of the Gentile people of God as it is for his conviction that nothing can separate corporeal Israel from the love of God in Jesus Christ.

Only after he has reminded the Corinthian assembly of their election and calling does Paul go on to offer his apostolic discernment and instruction with respect to the issues and questions raised for the church by the Corinthian context. Further reading of 1 Corinthians reveals the criteria at work as Paul sorts his way carefully through the issues. Most important, in 1 Corinthians 1–4 Paul reasserts the message which he originally announced to the Corinthians, the apocalyptic gospel of the crucified Christ in which the present world order ("the rulers of this age") is fundamentally challenged by the power of God. The cross of Christ is the central criterion of Paul's discernment of the present situation. What counts as wise, powerful, and rich (the sources of Corinthian "boasting") in the present order is revealed as precisely its opposite in the searching light of the gospel:

> For the message about the cross is foolishness to those who are perishing, but to us who are being saved it is the power of God. . . . Has not God made foolish the wisdom of the world? . . . We proclaim Christ crucified, a stumbling block to Jews and foolishness to Gentiles, but to those who are the called, both Jews and Greeks, Christ the power of God and the wisdom of God. For God's foolishness is wiser than human wisdom, and God's weakness is stronger than human strength. (1 Cor. 1:18-25)

Thus, right from the beginning of Paul's instruction he calls attention to this *other* power besides human wisdom, wealth, and strength, which ought to establish another social order than that created by the competitive pursuit of ascendancy in the community. In order for the Corinthian assembly to live its life as the people of God, its members must live by the power of this God, a power revealed in the cross of Christ. While the Corinthian believers continue to be enticed by the elitism and patronage so prevalent in Corinthian society, questing after social status and dominance and the advantages that come with them, Paul insists that the social shape of God's people must be "cruciform" through and through.[44] As Winter notes, even in their gatherings as an assem-

44. An extensive and illuminating account of cruciformity as the characteristic mark of Paul's theology is provided by Michael Gorman, *Cruciformity: Paul's Narrative Spirituality of the Cross* (Grand Rapids: Eerdmans, 2001).

bly, ostensibly to worship the God and Lord who had called them to be a people, the Corinthian believers offered "yet another example of the replication in the Christian community of the contentious conduct of those involved in the power politics in the body politic in Roman Corinth in the first century."[45] The changing of the gods had done little to change the form of life of this assembly. Indeed, in that respect the Corinthians had rendered the change wrought by the gospel as merely religious. Paul's goal for the Corinthians, on the other hand, is vastly more far-reaching: he looks for nothing less than the full transformation of the Corinthian form of life by the power of the gospel, a power revealed with utmost clarity in the cross of Christ.

That transformation begins with the Corinthians giving up their quests for ascendancy (quests fulfilled in part by being disciples of the "best" teacher, whether Apollos or Paul) and instead becoming disciples of only one teacher and model, Jesus Christ himself. "Let no one boast about human leaders. For all things are yours, whether Paul or Apollos or Cephas or the world or life or death or the present or the future—all belong to you, and you belong to Christ, and Christ belongs to God" (3:21–23). The imitation of Christ, who did not seek his own advantage but that of the other (cf. 10:24), is the touchstone for all of Paul's transformative instruction in 1 Corinthians.[46] Only through imitation of Christ's power-in-weakness revealed in the crucifixion will the body politic of Jesus Christ in Corinth be built into a social order that is fundamentally different from that of the wider competitive Corinthian society and thus be an authentic witness to the power of the crucified Christ and the one God of Israel in their midst.

But the transformation of Corinthian life is also specifically shaped by some other factors. First, Paul expects the messianic assembly to render just judgments, uninfluenced by the prestige of the guilty parties (1 Cor. 5), and he considers the assembly fully competent to judge grievances among its members (6:1–8). More positively, Paul believes that the *ekklēsia* has been supplied by the Holy Spirit with all the authority, gifts, and competencies necessary to function as its own specific social body (1 Cor. 12). These are the practices and characteristics of the Diaspora synagogue, which is clearly Paul's model also for the Gentile assemblies. They, like the synagogues, are to work together and be built up together as a distinct people, and not to have the authorities and courts of the "secular" *polis* ruling and judging their affairs. Second, Paul expects the members of the community to live lives of purity, to abstain from sexual immorality, greed, gluttony, and drunkenness (6:9–10), and he dismisses the self-justifying rationalizations of the elite in this regard who have adopted the aphorism, "all things are permitted for me." Rather, "you were washed, you were sanctified, you were justified in the name of the Lord Jesus Christ and in the Spirit of our God" (6:11). Finally,

45. Winter, *After Paul Left Corinth*, 141.
46. See Gorman, *Cruciformity*, 222–38; and Hays's entire commentary, *First Corinthians*.

Paul requires that the Corinthian believers not eat meat offered to idols, and that they separate themselves from banquets and celebrations associated in any way with idolatry, in order that they might avoid becoming "partners with demons" (10:21). In brief, it seems clear that Paul expects that the Corinthian assembly no less than the Gentiles in Rome ought to give glory to the God of Israel, who calls the Gentiles also to be his people, by honoring the stipulations for Gentile fellowship with Jews as taught in Scripture and affirmed in the Apostolic Council of Acts 15.[47] Even in Corinth, then, where the Gentile believers have had to form their own assembly separate from the synagogue, they are nonetheless to "give no offense to Jews or to Greeks or to the church of God"; rather, like Paul, they are to "try to please everyone in everything [they] do, not seeking [their] own advantage, but that of many, so that they might be saved" (1 Cor. 10:32–33). "Gentiles turning to faith in the Christ of Israel need not (must not!) become Jews; however, *equally important*, they must not remain pagans, nor offend their Jewish brothers and sisters by disregarding purity behavior operative for guiding the lifestyles of 'righteous gentiles' in their midst. . . . They must live in purity if they want respect for their claims of having turned from idolatry to the worship of the One God."[48]

In summary, then, Paul's task in Corinth amounted to this. After having been rejected by the synagogue, he formed another assembly that included some Jews but was predominantly Gentile. Corinthian society was thoroughly pagan and idolatrous at every level, from the imperial and civic governments to the households of the slaves. The gods were numerous. The social order was characterized by fierce competition, elitism, and patronage. Immoral sexual practices were commonly embraced, particularly by the privileged. From this, Paul had to shape a people who would bring glory to the God of Israel. He did so by announcing the good news of how this God had invaded the world of Corinth and its culture through Paul's message about the crucifixion and resurrection of Jesus Christ. A new power was unleashed in the city, a power able to deliver the Corinthians from their enslavements to the many lords, powers, and practices that had laid claim to their lives. God was creating a new people in the midst of Corinthian culture, by choosing, calling, and setting apart those who believed the message that Paul proclaimed. Four things would characterize this people. First, they would know themselves to have been incorporated by the power of the Holy Spirit into the story about the one God of Israel who in these last days had acted in mercy toward the nations (because he is also the God of the nations) in Jesus Christ. Second, they would receive Jesus Christ as the one who had freely

47. See Nanos, *Mystery of Romans*, 201–7, for a discussion of the oft-repeated claim by scholars that Paul ignored the Apostolic Decree in his mission. See especially the criticisms of that claim by various authors reported by Nanos on 202 n. 95 and 205–6 n. 112.
48. Ibid., 199.

given up power, status, and privilege and handed himself over to be crucified, thereby delivering the Corinthian Gentiles from their bondage to the
many gods and many lords of Corinth and the empire. They would also receive this same Jesus as their "Lord," who himself had demonstrated the fundamental cruciform pattern of life (not seeking his own advantage, but that
of the other) that was to take shape among the Corinthian believers. Third,
the assembly of Corinthian believers was to function in the city of Corinth
in the manner of a Diaspora synagogue, ruling their own affairs and settling
their own disputes, in justice, in self-sacrifice, and for the sake of building
up the corporate body. Fourth, the practices of members of the Corinthian
assembly were to conform to the pattern of Noachide laws, thereby demon-
strating on the one hand their turn from idolatry and its associated habits,
practices, and forms of life and on the other their allegiance and obedience
to the one God of Israel and the one Lord Jesus Christ.

Combined, these four elements would distinguish the Gentile people of
Israel's God in Corinth from the people of Corinth as a whole, even as at the
same time a great deal of Corinthian culture would be held in common between these two peoples. Thus the Corinthian assembly would, in Tanner's
terms, itself constitute a "contradiction" and "fissure" in Corinthian culture,
an alternative way of "articulating cultural elements" available in the Corinthian context. Under the transforming power of the gospel, commonly held
cultural elements in Corinth would be "handled and transformed" into
something new, "by means of such complex and ad hoc relational processes
as resistance, appropriation, subversion, and compromise."[49] The synagoguelike messianic Corinthian citizens' assembly, the body politic of Jesus Christ,
would thus form a concrete sign of the redemption of Gentile Corinthian
culture, in the very heart of cosmopolitan Corinth.

The Gospel as Culture

With reference to Romans and 1 Corinthians we have seen how in each
letter Paul aims to shape a people: in Romans he works toward the creation
of one people from two cultures, Gentile and Jewish; in 1 Corinthians he
works toward the creation of a distinct people drawn out of the larger culture of pagan Gentile Corinth. But the relationship of people to culture in
each case requires further clarification. There is a sense in which in both
Rome and Corinth the new people created by the gospel is itself also a *new
cultural reality*. For it is not the case that the goods and elements of the preexisting cultures (Jewish and Gentile in Rome; Gentile in Corinth) are simply there, available, and ready to hand for new "uses." Rather, as previous
chapters showed, the goal of the apocalypse of Jesus Christ is to bring about
a new creation. In the cosmic war for this new creation, the world created

49. Tanner, *Theories of Culture*, 57–58.

and ordered by the rebellious powers and principalities of "the present age" had to be invaded by the one Creator God of Israel and reordered to his purposes. That invasion occurred in the crucifixion and resurrection of Jesus Christ. It is constitutive of the new creation; the people called to be and live this new creation through their worship of the God of Israel and his Messiah in the power of the Holy Spirit must therefore imagine the world, society, and culture otherwise. The world must *become* otherwise for them as it has been *made* otherwise through the death and resurrection of Christ. That requires an alternative account of, in Milbank's words, "Being itself" or "what there is." As Yoder writes, it is the task of worship to bring about that alternative account:

> Worship is the communal cultivation [no doubt, a deliberately chosen word] of an alternative construction of society and history. That alternative construction of history is celebrated by telling the stories of Abraham (and Sarah and Isaac and Ishmael), of Mary and Joseph and Jesus and Mary, of Cross and Resurrection and Peter and Paul, of Peter of Cheltchitz and his Brothers, of George Fox and his Friends. How pointedly, and at what points, this celebrated construction will set us at odds with our neighbors, will of course depend on the neighbors.[50]

When Paul writes gospel truth to Rome or Corinth he has no other aim than to offer a different account of Being itself from what is currently available in those cities, an "alternative construction of society and history" rooted in the worship and stories of an Other God, the one God of Israel and Jesus Christ. The political order (e.g., dominance and subservience), social relations (e.g., eating and drinking), goods and elements (e.g., food and drink) of the culture in Rome or Corinth before the gospel arrives are in some sense *different things* from what they become after the gospel arrives and recreates them otherwise. The Romans and Corinthians are called by Paul to participate in the task of the creation of a new culture shaped by the gospel, in which social order and material goods are redescribed by being reinscribed within another, scriptural narrative and another, cruciform, social practice.

For the Gentile believers in Rome, Paul argues, the world can no longer be constituted by their separation from and condescending attitude toward the Jews in Rome and their refusal to honor the claims of the Jewish Scriptures on their Gentile lives. According to Paul's letter, the world of Jesus Christ in Rome is the world in which Gentiles are reconciled with Jews, one in which they offer mutual welcome and praise of the one God of Jews and Gentiles (Rom. 15:1–13). The struggle to realize this new world among the Gentile believers in Rome is the struggle against their own imaginations in bondage, through deeply ingrained beliefs, habits, and practices, to a well-

50. John Howard Yoder, "The Hermeneutics of Peoplehood," in *The Priestly Kingdom: Social Ethics as Gospel* (Notre Dame: University of Notre Dame Press, 1984), 43.

established sense of what it is to be "Roman." It appears that to be Roman for the Roman believers in the Messiah, Jesus had come to be defined in some sense as to be "not Jewish" and "not Israel," indeed, to suppose that the God of Jesus Christ had himself turned finally away from Israel and toward Rome (God himself, perhaps, being enamored of Roman "power"). Paul argued otherwise, by reading Israel's hardening in the light of the larger biblical narrative of Israel's irrevocable election (Rom. 9–11). So he exhorts the Gentile believers: "Do not be conformed to this world [in which Romans think themselves superior], but be transformed by the renewing of your minds, so that you may discern what is the will of God—what is good and acceptable and perfect" (12:2). The world and culture which Paul insists must come into being in Rome among the Gentile believers and Jews is the world and culture of God's reconciliation, in which Gentile believers not only honor Israel as the still-living tree into which they have been grafted (11:17–24), but also obey Israel's scriptural requirements specified for life in peaceable and worshipful fellowship with the Jews (Rom. 13–15).

Thus, whereas Paul in one sense urges the reconciliation of Gentile and Jewish cultures in the one people of God in Rome, in another sense he also recognizes conflict between the new culture coming into being in Jesus Christ and the old culture of traditional Rome. The Gentile believers in Rome are engaged in a conflict of cultures as a consequence of the incommensurable accounts of "what there is" given by their Roman traditions on the one hand and by the gospel of Christ and Israel's Scriptures on the other. They must therefore constantly guard against the ancient and powerful beliefs, habits, and practices that continue to bind them to the patterns and forms of life of the old creation and that still have a grip on some members of the community:

> I urge you, brothers and sisters, to keep an eye on those who cause dissensions and offenses, in opposition to the teaching that you have learned; avoid them. For such people do not serve our Lord Christ, but their own appetites, and by smooth talk and flattery they deceive the hearts of the simple minded. For while your obedience is known to all, so that I rejoice over you, I want you to be wise in what is good and guileless in what is evil. (Rom. 16:17–19)

Surely those on whom Paul urges his "brothers and sisters" to "keep an eye" are also among the recipients/hearers of his letter, indeed are also his "brothers and sisters." They are us! The struggle to realize the new world and culture of God's apocalypse in Jesus Christ is as much an intracommunal, indeed innerpersonal, struggle as it is a struggle with those outside (cf. also 1 Cor. 5). More important, however, the Roman believers may be confident that it is the world that God himself will most surely bring into being through his own final apocalyptic act: "The God of peace will shortly crush Satan under your feet. The grace of our Lord Jesus Christ be with you" (Rom. 16:20; cf. 8:18–39).

One of the many struggles to live the new creation in Corinth centered around the issue of food offered to idols. If in Rome the primary cultural question might have been framed as "Who are we (Romans), and who are they (Jews)?" in Corinth the cultural question with respect to food is "What is this?" In 1 Corinthians 8–10 Paul attempts to help the Corinthians discern an answer to that question, for it is not at all obvious what the food is. Certainly it is not merely food, existing neutrally, which can be picked up and used one way or another. That is what some of the arrogant Corinthians "in the know" seemed to believe (8:1–4). Paul, however, regards the food as something thoroughly constituted by idolatrous custom and conscience (8:7) and contextualized within a social order at odds with the gospel (8:12). It is therefore a cultural "good" in the service of the powers of defilement and destruction (8:7, 9, 11). Paul's lengthy discussion in these chapters is an effort to instruct the Corinthians in the fact that cultural goods are always *what they are* by virtue of the powers, orders, and ends they serve. Food first offered to idols and then taken and eaten without regard for the conscience of the other is one thing—participation in the life of an idol or "demon," slavery, and destruction for both oneself and another (10:1–22). Food received thankfully as a gift on the grounds that "the earth and its fullness are the Lord's" and in full respect of the conscience of another, "not seek[ing one's] own advantage, but that of the other . . . so that they might be saved" (10:24, 33) is another thing—participation in Christ, true liberty, and the glorification of God.

Paul's efforts to provide another account of "what there is," his attempts to provide an "alternative construction" of eating and drinking (some of the core aspects of culture) within a social order limned by the gospel, thus rely upon three moves: (1) affirming the gospel confession, which the Corinthians already believe in some sense, of "one God, the Father, from whom are all things and for whom we exist, and one Lord, Jesus Christ, through whom are all things and through whom we exist" (8:6); (2) drawing the Corinthians into his own story of the imitation of Christ, that is, of self-denial and self-discipline for the sake of others (9:1–27); and (3) renarrating the Corinthians' identity through a scriptural story of Israel's eating and drinking, which was supposed to be their life-giving participation in Christ, but became instead their death-dealing participation in idolatry (10:1–13). In each of these moves Paul engages the Corinthians in the struggle to distinguish the culture being called into being through God's power revealed in Jesus Christ and the Holy Spirit from that culture and realm of powers in which they formerly participated and that defined for them both who they were and what the world and its goods were.

In summary, for Paul there is an intrinsic and coinherent relation between powers, peoples, and cultures. For him it is not enough to name a god (or power). It is also necessary to specify who this God is—the God of Israel and Jesus Christ—and what people is called into being by this God—Israel and the church. Further, there is a specific form of life or culture to which this people is called. Religion (either as religious experience or beliefs) cannot simply be laid softly upon a preexisting people or a preexisting culture. Rather, the imperial power of God apocalypsed in Jesus Christ calls out from among the Gentile peoples nothing less than a new people, in fundamental continuity with the people Israel, whose form of life is conformed to Jesus Christ and the Scriptures through the power of the Holy Spirit. This God, this people, this culture, cannot, in the first instance, be anything other than different in a fundamental sense from any other culture of another people and another god. And that difference precedes and sets the norm of discernment for any engagement with other religions or cultures.

Pauline Notes toward a Theology of Culture and Religions

Drawing on the foregoing discussions of powers, peoples, and cultures in Romans and 1 Corinthians, I now turn attention to some of the issues surrounding religious and cultural pluralism identified at the beginning of this chapter. The shaping of a Christian theology of culture, religions, and Christian witness in a pluralist context remains one of the most important tasks for our time, particularly under the conditions of multiculturalism and globalization.[51] As I indicated earlier, I am convinced that Paul's efforts to shape the beliefs and practices of the earliest messianic communities have much to teach us, even if, as Wilson notes, the context in which contemporary Western Christians must make their witness differs in significant ways from that of Paul. Paul's work makes a contribution in at least four areas: (1) the nature of the difference between Christianity and the other religions, (2) the nature of the universality of Christian claims, (3) the problem of power in Christian witness, and (4) a Christian understanding of the other.

The Difference of Election

A great deal of effort is expended in interfaith discussions over questions of the similarities and differences between religions. Topics for examination and comparison cover the range from conceptions of God (or, more generically, the ultimate reality), the self, the world, salvation, and the afterlife, to sacred texts, rituals, traditions, social practices, and moral and ethical patterns. No one can deny the many benefits such careful, detailed study and comparison has yielded for mutual understanding among the various traditions, whether those happen to be across the world or across the street from each other. The work of Christian mission has not only been one of the chief beneficiaries of comparative religion and interfaith dialogue, but also one of the primary motivations for pursuing those disciplines.

51. Each of these terms is likely susceptible to some serious deconstruction, which is beyond the scope of this work.

And yet, from a Pauline perspective, comparison and evaluation of religious similarities and differences does not come close to naming the one thing that finally makes the difference between Christians and others. As I showed in this chapter with reference to Paul's letters to the Romans and Corinthians (and earlier with reference to 1 Thessalonians), the first and constitutive distinguishing feature of the *ekklēsiai* to which he writes is that they are called and chosen by God. It is *God* who has specified and distinguished these assemblies in the midst of the nations; it is in the first place God's *election* of these communities which makes the difference, rather than a religious experience or a set of human behaviors, whether cultic, moral, or social.

In most interfaith discussions the claim of God's specific election of a particular people is not likely to be seen as a helpful starting point for dialogue and understanding. For example, Martin S. Jaffee makes a useful distinction between what he names "metaphysical monotheism" and "elective monotheism."[52] While the two are often linked, they are not the same. The former is a monotheism developed out of reflection "on the nature of the one Being who sustains all beings . . . [a] philosophical speculation about first principles" ("One God, One Revelation, One People," 759). Elective monotheism is something quite different. "The essential marker of elective monotheism is not the uniqueness of God alone. *Rather, it lies in the desire of the unique God to summon from out of the human mass a unique community established in his name and the desire of that community to serve God in love and obedience by responding to his call"* (760, emphasis original). Jaffee identifies Judaism, Christianity, and Islam as just such elective monotheisms. These communities are characterized, he goes on to argue, not only by a particularly intense relationship with their God, but also by profoundly exclusionary relationships with religious others, "obsessively defining themselves not only over against some hypostasized 'polytheism' but, more importantly, over against each other" (757):

> The possession of divine love, at least at the level of the historical testimony to its presence within the community, is itself the warrant for ontological hatred of the very existence of the Other. It is perhaps some comfort that such hatred can be overcome eschatologically. But the eschatological ethic of inclusiveness in redemption makes only rare appearances on the historical stage on which the various elected communities struggle for domination. On the plane of history, the capacity of God to love intensely and exclusively is translated, as often as not, into the human capacity to hate intensely. ("One God, One Revelation, One People," 774)

52. Martin S. Jaffee, "One God, One Revelation, One People: On the Symbolic Structure of Elective Monotheism," *Journal of the American Academy of Religion* 69 (2001): 753–75.

While there may be reasons to dispute Jaffee's global characterization of the historical testimonies of one or more of the communities of elective monotheism, I believe he is right in at least one thing and shares a widespread conviction in another. First, his definition of elective monotheism is an accurate description of the biblical understanding of God's election of Israel and the church. Jews and Christians have little or nothing at stake in defending the bland moral or metaphysical monotheisms of the various philosophical traditions, including those of modernity, but everything at stake in affirming elective monotheism. Paul, as we have seen, is an "elective monotheist" precisely in keeping with Jaffee's definition.

Second, Jaffee voices a common conviction that elective monotheism is "the warrant for ontological hatred of the very existence of the Other." That conviction is now increasingly shared even by many Jews and Christians, who wish to relinquish this embarrassing and often dangerous biblical doctrine in favor of one brand or another of relatively benign metaphysical monotheism. For what are the possibilities of dialogue and understanding among religions—among these monotheisms in particular—if Jaffee is right in his assessment of the implications of the very structure of elective monotheism? What is the hope for peaceable relations among them? And how do Jews and Christians avoid the charge that opposition, conflict, hatred, and violence are intrinsic to their most basic theological convictions about who they are?

I am convinced, however, that God's election of a people is at the very heart of Pauline theology and therefore that that doctrine must be central to the church's witness also in our time. The rejection of biblical elective monotheism is perhaps the first and most critical move toward conceiving of Christianity as a religion, a kind of value-added spiritual "dimension" that can be laid over the "self-evident" validity of forms of life (e.g., Greco-Roman, Western European, North American) already in play before this religion arrives and continuing in play even as this religion thrives, often as the "chaplain" of those forms of life.[53] By contrast, Paul's entire engagement with Gentile culture, the "religious other," arises out of a message about the God who once chose Israel as his people and is now also calling a people for his name from among these Gentile nations, a people whose existence is itself to become a form of life that witnesses to this God's will for all humanity and all creation. The citizens' assemblies called out to be God's people are commissioned to be timely, local signs of God's judgment upon and healing of a society and culture, a visible sociocultural witness of God's apocalyptic triumph over the rebellious and destructive rulers of this age at work in a given locale. In Pauline theology, God's missionary aim from the foundation of the

---

53. See Rodney Clapp, *A Peculiar People: The Church as Culture in a Post-Christian World* (Downers Grove, Ill.: InterVarsity Press, 1996), esp. chap. 1; and Barry A. Harvey, *Another City: An Ecclesiological Primer for a Post-Christian World* (Harrisburg, Pa.: Trinity, 1999).

world (at work in Paul's own mission) is "to bring about the obedience of faith among all the nations" (Rom. 1:5; cf. 15:16–19; 16:25–26), "to make everyone see what is the plan of the mystery hidden for ages in God who created all things; so that through the church the wisdom of God in its rich variety might now be made known to the rulers and authorities in the heavenly places" (Eph. 3:9–10). The church itself is that body which God "chose . . . in Christ before the foundation of the world to be holy and blameless before [God] in love" (1:4). The church's mission to the world is thus fundamentally compromised where it does not acknowledge, affirm, and live by the fact that, joined to Israel through Jesus Christ, it is God's elect people, assigned a unique and unsubstitutable place in God's purpose for creation. The difference of election is a nonsoluble difference.

The conviction about "the uniqueness of the elect community" suggests therefore, as George Lindbeck shows, a certain "untranslatability" at the very core of the gospel message and mission; for by very definition the idea of an elect people does not translate into a generally accessible set of experiences, concepts, or principles which might form the "common ground" of conversation between religions: it "makes interreligious dialogue more difficult." Indeed, Lindbeck acknowledges that while the reaffirmation of election and untranslatability may increase the chance of "intrareligious authenticity, faithfulness and honesty," it may also increase "potential for interreligious combativeness and violence."[54] The difference of election is a difficult difference indeed. Nonetheless, precisely because election is *particular*, that is, of a particular people by a particular God for a particular way of life, there is a limit to the generalizations that can be made. As we will see shortly, Jaffee's claim that elective monotheism is justification for "ontological hatred of the very existence of the Other" cannot be sustained as an adequate reading of the Pauline theology of election.

The Scandal of Universality

In view of the frequent relativizing moves thought necessary to sustain interreligious dialogue, the difficulty of election is further exacerbated by the fact that the church as the elect people believes it has a message and way of life which is "good news" for *all* peoples. Crucial to Pauline theology is the claim that the electing God of Israel and the church is the one God of Jews and Gentiles, the one God of creation and all nations, the one God whose singular and unsubstitutable cosmic-apocalyptic deed in Jesus Christ is finally the reconciliation and redemption not only of Israel and the church, but of all creation (Rom. 8:18–39; cf. Col. 1:15–20). In other words, added to the scandal of particular election and apocalypse is the scandal of the *universal* purpose of God revealed and enacted in election and apocalypse. The

---

54. George Lindbeck, "The Gospel's Uniqueness: Election and Untranslatability," *Modern Theology* 13 (1997): 424–27.

universality of God's purpose in Jesus Christ is as intrinsic to the Christian claim as the particularity of God's election of a people in Jesus Christ. Christians affirm the truth of Jesus Christ as the good news for all nations because he is himself the God of Israel acting decisively on behalf of the nations.

That said, there is often a temptation to misplace the universality claim, to shift it from a claim about God's act in Jesus Christ for Israel and the nations to a claim about the universality of Christianity as a religion and its supposed mission to establish itself (by various means of persuasion) as the one, true religion in or over all the nations. Many problems attend this misplaced universality, not the least of which is a tendency of Christians to seek, as part of their missionary mandate, to be "in charge" not only of the church itself but also of the nations or, alternatively, to bind up the cause of the Christian religion very closely with the cause of those rulers or nations that would promote, defend, or spread it. That tendency leads in turn to the histories of warring, coercion, and domination noted above by Jaffee, Kaufman, Hick, and others, who in turn are prepared to trim back all so-called absolutist or universalist claims about Israel, Jesus Christ, and the church in order to avoid such Christian "imperialisms."

But it is precisely here that a Pauline perspective on the church's mission is able to save the church from itself. First, to reiterate, the gospel which Paul preaches does not establish one other religion among others, but calls forth a specific people (the *ekklēsia* of God as an extension of historical Israel) that as such does not relate to its worldly context as soul to body but, more accurately, as "nation" to "nation." While the God of Israel is intent on saving the peoples of the earth through the power of the gospel, he does so by calling forth a people from among the peoples. The mission is universal, the means is always particular, timely, and local. There is no indication in Paul that he expects the people of God to become simply coextensive with the peoples of the earth. Even in this or that region or city, Paul expects that God will not coercively lay hold of the majority population, but rather, by the cruciform power of the gospel, will call out and create a people who will be faithful to the form of life which being "in Christ" or having "the mind of Christ" will shape among them.

Second, the task of this people-among-peoples is not to acquire control of the helm of worldly history, but to enact an alternative history as a witness to the lordship of the crucified Christ among them and to bring praise to the God of Israel among the nations. For this very reason Paul instructs believing Gentiles and Jews in Rome how to dwell together in peace as one people, in which at the same time the (judged and transformed) traditions of both are honored and sustained. In the same way he instructs the Corinthians how to be a people which, by their mutual self-giving, service, and upbuilding, might become an alternative body politic, the body of Christ, in that most destructively politicized city. In either case the cosmic-apocalyptic triumph of God in Jesus Christ comes to concrete (and indeed partial) frui-

tion in the particular, local battles won by this people, in the power of the
Holy Spirit, against false gods and lords and rulers, against the principalities
and powers of this age, against the stories, imaginings, habits of mind, and
practices that form the (often invisible) barriers to obedience to the God of
Israel.[55] For Paul, the primary task and indeed mission of the church is its
own ongoing conversion to the lordship of Jesus Christ. Virtually all of his
letters are written to that end. As such, however, the church as a converted
and converting people is also itself a constant invitation and call to the citizens of the wider world to enter the life of the people of God and therein
also to participate in the life and purpose of the triune God.[56]

An understanding of the task and mission of the church conceived along
these Pauline lines should allay the fears of those who cannot see how the
joint convictions of election and universality are not intrinsically dangerous
and thus an insuperable barrier to interreligious dialogue. But the history of
the church, in stark contradiction of Paul's approach, has given good—very
good—reasons for those concerns. As Wilson notes, that history of unholy
alliances with worldly power, coercion, and domination is a history of which
Paul did not have to take account. But *we* must. How?

Yoder addresses this issue in an essay entitled "The Disavowal of Constantine: An Alternative Perspective on Interfaith Dialogue."[57] "Constantine" of course is not simply the name of the fourth-century emperor who
"began to tolerate, then supported, then administered, then finally joined
the church," but also "the symbol of a sweeping shift in the nature of the
empirical church and its relation to the world" (*Royal Priesthood*, 245). As a
symbol, Constantine represents "the alliance between Rome-as-Empire and
Church-as-Hierarchy, which the fourth and fifth centuries gradually con-
solidated." But since the God of Scripture "calls his people to a propheti-
cally critical relationship to structures of power and oppression," that alliance must be seen as "not merely a possible tactical error but a structured
denial of the gospel" (245). It is Constantine the symbol of this alliance
which must be "disavowed." Such a disavowal requires an open confession
and repentance:

55. Compare this comment by Stanley Hauerwas: "The great task before Christians today is to un-
mask the invisibility of those stories that constitute our lives which we assume, wrongly, are commensu-
rate with our being Christian"; "In Defense of Cultural Christianity: Reflections on Going to Church,"
in Hauerwas's *Sanctify Them in the Truth: Holiness Exemplified* (Nashville: Abingdon, 1998), 164.

56. For an excellent, lengthier discussion of the themes of this paragraph, see David J. Bosch, *Transforming Mission: Paradigm Shifts in Theology of Mission* (Maryknoll, N.Y.: Orbis, 1991), 149–54. The
whole of chap. 4, "Mission in Paul: Invitation to Join the Eschatological Community," 123–78, is valuable reading.

57. John Howard Yoder, "The Disavowal of Constantine: An Alternative Perspective on Interfaith
Dialogue," in *The Royal Priesthood: Essays Ecclesiological and Ecumenical* (Grand Rapids: Eerdmans,
1994), 242–61.

It might change the whole tone of interfaith encounter if . . . Christians were to receive the grace to say, "We were wrong. The picture you have been given of Jesus by the Empire, by the Crusades, by struggles over the holy sites, and by wars in the name of the 'Christian West' is not only something to forget but something to forgive. We are not merely outgrowing it, as if it had been acceptable at the time: we disavow it and repent of it. It was wrong even when it seemed to us to be going well. We want our repentance to be not mere remorse but a new mind issuing in a new way—*metanoia*." (*Royal Priesthood*, 251)

That kind of confession and repentance may be brought out into the open by the church because confession and repentance are themselves ingredient in the gospel message by which the church itself lives and which it brings as good news for the world. Confessing and repenting of the false universality of Christianity established in the Constantinian mode opens the way for a new hearing and reception of an authentic gospel universality established in the Pauline mode—the continual calling out of a people who will enact a history that is precisely a cruciform alternative to Constantine. That people's engagement with and witness to the religious and cultural other therefore requires an appropriate politics.

The Politics of Witness

The calling out and creation of a people, as Paul well knew, is an intrinsically political act. A people is shaped by power, purpose, and polity. There cannot be a people without a politics. This too is disturbing in the context of interreligious conversation, where it is often believed that the best chance for dialogue and understanding is to have "free and frank" discussions about the religions, as far removed from their political contexts as possible. But the hope for a worthwhile depoliticized dialogue among religions is a vain one, for at least two reasons. First, as Kenneth Surin devastatingly demonstrates with reference to several theologies of religion, the idea of religious dialogue is itself a product and practice of Western intellectual elites and their Western-trained counterparts from other religions and regions—all of whom share in some way in the politics of the privileged.[58] They dialogue about the world religions as single, global realities—and, in the pluralist mode, also about the "common human experience" shared by them all—and yet such global religions and common human experience seem to exist nowhere in particular. Surin is worth quoting at length here:

Only someone who is not aware of the always particular "location" from which he or she theorizes can celebrate the new "global city" and propound a world or global theology in this apparently unreflective way: impoverished

---

58. Kenneth Surin, "A 'Politics of Speech': Religious Pluralism in the Age of the McDonald's Hamburger," in *Christian Uniqueness Reconsidered: The Myth of a Pluralistic Theology of Religions* (ed. Gavin D'Costa; Maryknoll, N.Y.: Orbis, 1990), 203–4.

peasants from Kedah in Malaysia find it well-nigh impossible to accept that they and a wealthy landowner *from their own village* are situated in the same moral or social location, and yet we are urged by [Wilfred] Cantwell Smith and Co. to believe that such Malay peasants, their landlord and even the Duke of Westminster or the Hunt brothers inhabit the same global city or share a common human history.

The global space of the discourses of "religious pluralism" . . . , "inclusivism" . . . , and "liberal exclusivism" . . . , effectively incorporates, and thereby dissolves, the localized and oppositional "spaces" of people like peasants in Malaysia. Local attachments, with their always specific histories and politics, are displaced and dispersed by a global and "globalizing" topography as the local is subsumed under the regime of the universal.[59]

Those who thus seek to rescue the religions from ethnocentrism, parochialism, and exclusivism, themselves simply instantiate just one more such vision (that of liberal intellectual elites who have achieved the "global gaze") and propose it as the universal truth. From a Pauline perspective it can only be one of the principalities and powers, one more false universal that enslaves not only its true believers, but also all those who have been included in its global gaze and therefore also occluded by it.

Second, as I have argued, Christianity as a religion apart from a people and a politics is an abstraction from a Pauline perspective. A Pauline response to the charges Surin brings against interreligious dialogue should by now be quite evident. Paul describes his own politics of witness in his letters (Rom. 15:14–33; 1 Cor. 1–4; 9; much of 2 Corinthians). In 1 Corinthians 9 in particular he writes of how he constantly works to become a participant in the concrete, local life of the people to whom he brings the gospel. The primary point here is not that Paul adapts himself to the *cultural* forms of life of the people to whom he comes (he seems to suggest that there are limits to that for him; 9:21), but that he adopts a particular *political* stance in their midst. He does not make use of any of his freedom and rights (9:12, 15, 18), choosing rather to make himself "a slave to all, so that I might win more of them" (9:19). This is the kind of "power" which Paul exercises when he proclaims the gospel and calls out a people for God's name, for it is the kind of power that is intrinsic to the message he preaches: "For the message of the cross . . . is the power of God" (1:18). For Paul to come to the Corinthians asserting his own human wisdom and power would be to empty the cross of its power (1:17):

When I came to you, brothers and sisters, I did not come proclaiming the mystery of God to you in lofty words or wisdom. For I decided to know nothing among you except Jesus Christ, and him crucified. And I came to you in weakness and in fear and in much trembling. My speech and my proclama-

59. Ibid., 195–96 (emphasis original).

tion were not with plausible words of wisdom, but with a demonstration of
the Spirit and of power, so that your faith might rest not on human wisdom
but on the power of God. (1 Cor. 2:1–5; cf. Gal. 3:1–5)

Paul's politics of witness requires that he assume no higher ground than that
which his hearers occupy, no global gaze which "dissolves the oppositional
'spaces'" of those to whom he comes with the gospel. Precisely so, his coming
to the Corinthians is a coming in weakness and fear and much trembling. He
comes in vulnerability and in no position to guarantee the responses of those
to whom he witnesses (opposition is always possible and many times actual
for Paul; 2 Cor. 11:21–33); he refuses any form of persuasion other than the
message of Christ crucified and the working of the Holy Spirit. His weakness
is his "glory" precisely because it is his sharing in the power of Jesus Christ:
"So, I will boast all the more gladly of my weaknesses, so that the power of
Christ may dwell in me. Therefore I am content with my weaknesses, insults,
hardships, persecutions, and calamities for the sake of Christ; for whenever I
am weak, then I am strong" (12:9–10). Or, in Yoder's words: "The herald believes in accepting weakness, because the message is about a Suffering Servant
whose meekness it is that brings justice to the nations."[60]

As we have seen, Paul calls for that same kind of politics to shape the life
of the people of God, whether in Rome or Corinth; the politics in which the
members do not seek their own advantage, but that of the other; the politics
in which they become servants of one another; the politics of mutual upbuilding. But Paul also calls for this cruciform politics to shape the ongoing
relationships between the people of God and the surrounding peoples:

Give no offense to Jews or to Greeks or to the church of God, just as I try to
please everyone in everything I do, not seeking my own advantage, but that of
many, so that they may be saved. (1 Cor. 10:32–33)

Bless those who persecute you; bless and do not curse them. . . . Do not repay
anyone evil for evil, but take thought for what is noble in the sight of all. If it
is possible, so far as it depends on you, live peaceably with all. . . . Do not be
overcome by evil, but overcome evil with good. (Rom. 12:14, 17–18, 21)

So then, whenever we have an opportunity, let us work for the good of all, and
especially for those of the family of faith. (Gal. 6:10)

See that none of you repays evil for evil, but always seek to do good to one another and to all. (1 Thess. 5:15)

The alternative to "the politics of speech" which characterizes the kinds of interreligious dialogue which Surin criticizes is, therefore, the politics of the

---

60. Yoder, "Disavowal of Constantine," 256.

cross of Christ, exemplified in Paul's own missionary stance and in the stance of the missionary people of God in relation to the other peoples in a specific, local social and political space. Yoder speaks of this as "the congregational structure of the mission":

> The alternative to a book about dialogue is not a better book but a way of conversing. The alternative to an elite dialogue carried on by gurus and professors is not to change elites but to discover the theologianhood of all believers. The alternative to speculation about "anonymous Christians" is becoming locally explicit about Jesus. The alternative to abstract treatment of the tension between the particular and the universal is not a steadily deepening redefinition of terms, or a retraction into the indefinable, but the particular experience of confessing Jesus as Christ here and now. . . . This is enough: . . . we need no apologetic prestructure, no metaphysical infrastructure, no social victory, no conciliar definitions to be able to move along.[61]

"Becoming locally explicit about Jesus" is the calling, task, and mission of the people of God in their particular contexts. The church's claim about the universal validity of the gospel is not warranted from on high by the powerful elites, whether politicians, religious leaders, or academics. It is warranted when the reign of Christ among his people becomes concretely and locally visible in many places around the world. "This is enough." Indeed, to wish and work for more is to reject the Pauline politics of witness and once again to take up the way of Constantine.

The Face of the Other

Because Paul's witness and mission is carried out according to the politics of the cross, in the concreteness of actual, patient encounter with the other, he is able to take the true measure of the other as other. That means he takes a *complex* measure of the other, in contrast to any simple homogenization under one category. For example, the other as "sinner" is certainly one of the ways in which Paul characterizes the other—although not only the other: "While *we* still were sinners Christ died for *us*" (Rom. 5:8); "should *we* continue in sin in order that grace may abound?" (6:1). But "sinner" is neither the sole nor the determinative category under which Paul thinks of the recipient of the gospel.[62] While I cannot explore this question in detail, a short list with commentary will illustrate Paul's complex engagement with the other as both nonbeliever and believer.

Jew or Gentile. The categorization of the whole of humanity into two "halves," into Jew or Gentile, is as near to the center of Paul's anthropology as we are likely to get. There is no ultimate dissolution of this basic categorical

---

61. Ibid., 253–54.

62. This is in stark contrast to a great deal of Protestant theology and preaching about the non-Christian other.

difference between the two groups of humanity either in sin or in grace. Even as Paul understands "all," both Jews and Gentiles, as having sinned or come "under the power of sin" (Rom. 3:9), each group does so in its own way and under its own conditions (Rom. 2). Hence, there is not for Paul a "universal human condition" or "humanity as such."[63] Even in Christ, while Jew and Gentile are indeed made one, the point is that in Christ and through baptism into his death and resurrection Gentiles and Jews are reconciled in their difference, joined together, Gentile *with* Jew, into the one family of Abraham. The entire point of Paul's letter to the Romans, as we have seen above, is that these two are *not* called to eradicate the difference, but to "welcome one another" and join in the common praise of the God of Israel.[64] The church is that place where Jews welcome Gentiles as friends and vice versa. A Gentile church which views the Jew (messianic or otherwise) either as the enemy or as another human being "just like us" has not taken the proper measure of this other. *This* other stands before the Gentile church as *the* other with whom the Gentile has to do, as the chosen image of God's own particular Otherness with respect to, in the midst of, and for the sake of the Gentile peoples (cf. Gen. 12:1–3). Jesus is this Jew, supremely and representatively, but he is never without his people, of whom he became a servant "on behalf of the truth of God in order that he might confirm the promises given to the patriarchs, and in order that the Gentiles might glorify God for his mercy" (Rom. 15:8–9). Gentile enmity vis-à-vis (i.e., "face to face" with) the Jew is Gentile enmity with God. The salvation of the Gentiles as such thus depends on the friendship established between Jews and Gentiles, the welcome of Gentiles into the family of Abraham through the death of Christ.

Subject to Powers. Both Jews and Gentiles (in their own ways) are subject to a complex system of powers. Paul himself does not systematize these powers; indeed he shows no interest in how the Gentiles might do so (as, e.g., the Colossian believers might have done). But he regards these powers as having persons and peoples in their grasp, and therefore the persons and peoples to whom he brings the gospel of Christ crucified are not simply free individual "choosers" of their own destinies. They require deliverance from bondage to, among other things, empire, ethnic apartheid, social hierarchy, dominance through patronage, pagan cult practices, and magic. There are also the powers of sin and death and even the Torah when it is functioning (having been captured by sin; Rom. 7; Gal. 4) as a condition of Gentile participation in Abraham's family or as barrier to fellowship between Jews and Gentiles.

Freedom from these powers is not the result of self-help. It comes only when a superior power invades the realms of the other powers to deliver peo-

---

63. See the extended argument to this effect in Donaldson, *Paul and the Gentiles*, 107–64.

64. Paul's statement in Rom. 10:12 that "there is no distinction (*ou . . . diastolē*) between Jew and Greek" is not a statement about Jews and Greeks in themselves, but about the lordship under which they both stand as Jews and Greeks: "The same Lord is Lord of all and is generous to all who call on him."

ples from them. For Paul the gospel in the first place is that superior power, because it is the power of the one God of Israel, the creator of all things. At the same time, the power of the gospel is so radically other, as this God is Other, that it looks like the very opposite of the powers the Gentiles know. Gospel power is the crucifixion, a crucifixion brought on by the rulers of this age who know nothing of God's wisdom, secret and hidden. But to those who in the power of the Holy Spirit hear and believe the gospel, the crucifixion is revealed as the true wisdom and power by which the cosmos and humans are saved and rightly ordered. Having this revelation shape the people of God requires the kind of instruction in the "mind of Christ" that Paul gives and the kinds of shifts in concrete social and political practice that he calls for in his letters.

Paul thus knows the other (person or people) as deeply enmeshed in a multifarious, multilayered, overlapping, interrelated, mutually conditioning set of participations—social, political, cultic, suprahuman—that have a great deal to do with defining who he is addressing as a recipient of the gospel. The only way to know this other is to enter the world in which the other participates and engage the powers in the concrete specificity with which they shape the lives of a person and people. That kind of entry, always under the sign of the cross, characterizes Paul's missionary "method" from beginning to end. He shares *life* with the Gentiles. He knows their world. Even so, Paul's letters to the Romans and Corinthians are not abstract, homogenized, globalized treatments of Christian doctrine applied to specific situations; they are displays of Paul's direct and specific engagement with the ways in which the multifarious worldly powers continue to maintain some grip on the lives of the believers; powers that need to be challenged and overcome by the power of the gospel—"the particular experience of confessing Jesus as the Christ here and now" (Yoder). Paul's letters are decisive interventions in a battle in which the rulers of this age are once again attempting to reclaim this people whom the God of Israel has called out from the world.

Agents of Self-Destruction. At the same time, Paul does not engage the other merely as a victim of forces beyond human control. Quite the contrary, the other is a participant and agent in his or her own destruction. In Romans 1:18–32 Paul presents a complex relationship in which God acts as the revealer of his "eternal power and divine nature" and as the judge who "hands over" the idolatrous Gentiles to the gods of *their own* making as their sentence for "suppress[ing] the truth" revealed by the one Creator God. That entire text is a complex mix of passive and active verbs depicting the Gentile peoples under the wrath of God revealed in the gospel. God's judgment comes upon them not as victims, but as those who have done what they ought not to have done and not done what they ought to have done. Indeed, in 1 Corinthians 6:9–11 Paul identifies (some of) the Gentiles by their unrighteous deeds: "Do you not know that wrongdoers (*adikoi*) will not inherit the kingdom of God? Do not be deceived! Fornicators, idolators, adulterers, male prostitutes, sodomites, thieves, the greedy, drunkards, revilers, robbers—none of these will inherit the kingdom of God. And this is what some of you used to be." There is no neat distinction between the sin and the sinner here. Paul does not see the other in terms of an "inner person," untouched by bodily actions and willing participations in wrongful practices and habits. He sees the other in need of a "bath" and a wholly other set of bodily participations and actions: "But you were washed, you were sanctified, you were justified in the name of the Lord Jesus Christ and in the Spirit of our God. . . . Do you not know that your bodies are members of Christ? Should I therefore take the members of Christ and make them members of a prostitute? Never! . . . Shun fornication! . . . For you were bought with a price; therefore glorify God in your body" (6:11, 15, 18, 20). Nothing prevents Paul from holding the other responsible for their own deeds, whether those are done in bondage to the powers or in the power of the gospel and the Holy Spirit.

Doers of Good. Nor, then, are unbelieving others to be seen simply, unqualifiedly as doers of evil and unrighteousness, incapable of doing good, destined only for eternal destruction. Paul seems to share something of the Jewish tradition of recognizing the "righteous Gentile." Even (a few) unbelieving Gentiles, whose very reason for existing is to do the good for which they were created, can do that good and please God. While many or perhaps most "store up wrath" for themselves by their self-seeking, rejection of the truth, and wickedness (cf. Rom. 1:18–32), there are others who swim against the stream of Gentile wickedness, who "by patiently doing good seek for glory and honor and immortality." To these, God will "give eternal life" (2:6–7). The usual Protestant readings of Paul cannot countenance that conclusion. There have been many attempts to explain it away under the conviction that Paul's understanding of "the human condition" is univocal, that is, that the "sinful human condition" is present identically everywhere and in every individual.[65] Paul's conclusion in 2:6–7 that there may be a few righteous Gentiles does not detract for a moment from his conviction that the non-Jewish nations as a whole are under the reign of malignant powers, including the powers of sin and death, and stand in need of God's decisive act of cosmic deliverance in the apocalypse of Jesus Christ. In fact, it is the very purpose of that apocalypse to break open the prison-world of the Gentiles in order that they might all live the obedience of faith and share in the blessings of Abraham. Further, God's judgment of human deeds is made "through Jesus Christ" (2:16), and therefore no Gentile or

65. See Donaldson, *Paul and the Gentiles*, 89, for some of the attempts to reconcile this passage with Rom. 3. See also the thorough and helpful discussion of 2:6–11, against many typical Protestant interpretations, in Kent L. Yinger, *Paul, Judaism, and Judgment according to Deeds* (Cambridge: Cambridge University Press, 1999), 146–82. In the end, however, Yinger attempts a more systematic correlation of the themes of judgment according to deeds and "justification by faith" than is warranted from Paul, not least, I think, because he does not entertain the possibility of rendering *pistis Christou* as the "faith of Christ."

Jew is simply "free standing" in this regard. But the point I emphasize here is that Paul's assessment of the relationships between the powers, peoples, and persons and the doing of good and evil seems again to be complex, variegated, and multivocal. The other whom Paul encounters in his mission to the Gentiles is constituted in a complex way, a complexity of which Paul was fully able to take account.

Bearers of Distinct and Transformable Cultures/Forms of Life. The same must be said for the products of the influences of the powers on the cultures and forms of life of the Gentiles. While the rulers of this age are ultimately bent on the destruction of God's purposes, the results of their workings among peoples are not univocally negative, without reserve. Were that the case, Paul could not have come to the Gentiles with the gospel he did, since at the very heart of that gospel is the claim that they are received as Gentiles; and that means in some sense as they are—"by their families, their languages, their lands, and their nations" (Gen. 10:20; cf. 10:5, 31–32). The cultural other whom Paul meets in his mission is neither an embodiment of evil nor an empty cipher, but the other as a participant in and bearer of a distinct and transformable form of life—a form of life in need of the radical judgment of the gospel, but nonetheless a form of life which, so judged, is itself worthy of honor and acceptance—even by a Pharisaic Jew like Paul. Indeed, that is precisely the point of Paul's gospel to the Gentile peoples. The gospel does not transport the socially/culturally constituted Gentile into the Jewish culture (which is what Paul means by being saved by works); rather the gospel calls the Gentile to a Gentile form of life consistent with the confession that Jesus is Lord.

Dead in Christ. "For the love of Christ urges us on, because we are convinced that one has died for all; therefore all have died" (2 Cor. 5:14). The radicality of this claim is often short-circuited. It is often claimed that this requires that we view the other as one "for whom Christ has died"; but that is only half the truth of what Paul declares here. Not only has Christ died for all; all (and therefore this other who stands before me, and all particular others) are also already dead in Christ, all are caught up already into the crucifixion, all stand reconciled to God through the death of Christ, all are in this sense already in Christ. This is not the same as declaring that all are Christians or that some are "anonymous Christians" (Karl Rahner). It is, rather, declaring that in the apocalypse of Jesus Christ the world has changed. "From now on, therefore, we regard no one from a human point of view. . . . So if anyone is in Christ, there is a new creation: everything old has passed away; see, everything has become new!" (5:16–17). The new creation being asserted here is not a claim about the state of the Christian; it is a claim about how the world, and in particular the other human being, must be acknowledged as new creation by the Christian, who knows that the old creation has been invaded, challenged and judged, in the death of Christ. "See, everything has become new!" The other who stands before me is already a cosharer in that new creation; the task of the Christian in the face of this other is to call attention to that fact. "All this is from God, who reconciled us to himself through Christ, and has given us the ministry of reconciliation; that is, in Christ God was reconciling the world to himself, not counting their trespasses against them, and entrusting the message of reconciliation to us" (5:18–19). It can hardly be the first task of the proclaimer of the gospel or the Christian in interreligious dialogue to "count trespasses" against the other. Being there as a messenger of reconciliation is the first task.

Called to Live for God. The ministry of reconciliation begins by seeing the other as a sharer in God's new creation through Christ's reconciling death and by calling this other to "live no longer for themselves, but for him who died and was raised for them" and to "be reconciled to God" (2 Cor. 5:15, 20). That call must come, of course, from one who is already living a cruciform life, a life of reconciling ministry. And the call may be refused. It is intrinsic to the vulnerability of the gospel and commission of its messenger that this be the case. In fact, this too is the ministry of reconciliation, which is prepared to suffer such a refusal for the sake of honoring this other. Nonetheless, the love of God (for the messenger, for this other) urges us on to make this plea that the other become a cosharer with us in the life of the triune God.

Friends. To read the opening and closing greetings in Paul's letters and to sense the passion that pulses in them is to become aware that Paul knew his Gentile and Jewish others as friends, brothers and sisters, those whom he loved. It seems unlikely that Paul's friendships began only after someone became a believer. His mission was conducted in and from the homes of friends and through his own "tent-making" business. Far from being a street-corner preacher or a "mass" evangelist, Paul took his gospel into the lives and homes of the Gentiles who would welcome him. He met and talked with them face-to-face. He knew their names. He urged them to live in the freedom and holiness of the gospel. He invited them to become partners in his work and to share life with the people of God.

The other for Paul can never fully be accounted for under a single category or even a multiplicity of categories. He regards the other in their full humanity, that is, in the full complexity and particularity of multiple passive and active participations in personal, social, cultural, and political realities, in relation also to the gods and lords (or the one God and one Lord) with whom they have to do. The other, then, including of course the religious other encountered in the work of mission, in interreligious dialogue, or in the course of everyday life, must, in Pauline terms, be known as more than "a Hindu" or "a Muslim" or a "non-Christian." To know the other in their full humanity depends on the one hand on knowing this other in the truth of God's election of Israel and the apocalypse of Jesus Christ and on the other hand on knowing this other in the concreteness of everyday life. Each of these kinds of knowing appears all too rarely on the horizon for Christians engaged in interreligious dialogue.

Such are some of the directions and contours for a Christian theology of religion, culture, and pluralism which a study of Paul's mission to the nations engenders. At the heart of such a theology is Paul's focus not on a "dimension" of human experience, but on the people whom God calls out from among other peoples. A full development of that central point in the production of a Christian theology of religions is an agenda for another day.

Conclusion

Preaching Paul
beyond Christendom
and Modernity

What difference might the reading together of Paul and the postliberals that I offer here make for preaching or teaching Paul in the churches today? In this brief conclusion I provide a few hints of where I think what I proposed in the preceding chapters would lead in preaching and teaching Paul—orientations for a rediscovery of Pauline theology. Before addressing the specifically Pauline themes, however, a few comments about Christendom and modernity are in order.

Christendom identifies that arrangement, pertinent mostly in the Christian West, in which the church or churches find themselves in some sense established, accepted, and perhaps even in possession of some recognized power, within the dominant social and political order. That arrangement characterizes the condition of the church less frequently now than it did for about fifteen centuries, but it persists in some form in many places, most obviously in America (much less obviously in Canada). Many Christians and churches believe it is, or ought to be, the normative condition of the church. The reader of this book will by now be aware that I do not share that conviction. Neither do Paul and the postliberals. That is not because I think that the church must, de facto, accept a condition of marginality when that is all that is being offered in a given time and place. It is, rather, because the church lives by the wisdom, power, and riches of God revealed in the cross of Christ, which are irreconcilable with the wisdom, power, and riches by which principalities and powers, societies, and empires rule the world. Christendom forgets that. I hope my work on Paul and the postliberals is a helpful reminder

255

of it. The following orientations for preaching Paul focus therefore on God's action in calling out a *people* from among the nations, a people whose very being is made possible and sustained by the "foolishness of the cross."

Modernity names the negative reaction, primarily in the post-Enlightenment West, to particularity, limit, finitude; and it names the attempts intellectually, culturally, and politically to transcend those conditions. Modernity, and often the church with it, dissociates itself from the specificity of YHWH, Israel, Jesus Christ, the one, holy, catholic, and apostolic church, Scripture. It prefers to speak of the divine, faith communities, mediators of religious experience, and sacred texts. Churches and theologians have had a three-hundred-year love affair with modernity. The evidence of that affair comes in many forms: the love of universal reason and the rational arguments for Christian beliefs based on it; the search for universal human experience or a common religious subject and the appeal to that in the defense and promotion of the Christian religion; the love of general theological or religious themes like God (of no particular people) as naming the transcendent, or faith, love, grace, freedom, justice, and peace as naming the shape of the general, universal relationship of transcendence and immanence. By embracing modernity, the churches hoped to do better for themselves among the powers (intellectual, social, political) by not being pinned down by the locality and vulnerability of their specific provenance. I hope that my work on Paul and the postliberals is a reminder that the cosmos and humanity are lost apart from the act of YHWH in choosing Israel to be his beloved people, choosing one vulnerable, killable Jew to be crucified in Jerusalem and through whom to deliver the creation from its bondage to decay, and choosing a people for his name from among the nations and empowering them in the Holy Spirit to bear faithful witness to YHWH of Israel and his Messiah. The following orientations for preaching Paul therefore focus on God's action in calling out a *specific* people through whom God makes known his purpose for all the peoples of the earth and for the whole creation.

Pauline theology as I understand it takes the church on a road beyond Christendom and modernity, one on which a new form of the church's faithfulness awaits. How shall this understanding take shape in the teaching and preaching of the church? I offer the following suggestions.

Preaching Justification

- Justification is God's action.
- Justification is God's invasion and rectification of the enslaved cosmos through the death and resurrection of Jesus Christ, the gift of the Holy Spirit, and the creation of the *ekklēsia*.
- Justification is God's mercy to the Gentile peoples, God's deliverance of them from their bondage to idols, principalities, powers, and cosmic principles.

- Justification is God's rectifying action whereby he reconciles the Jewish and Gentile peoples to one another and creates one people from the two.
- Justification, as God's rectifying justice for all things, is accomplished through the faithfulness of the Just One, Jesus Christ. Justification by faith is justification by Jesus Christ's loyalty and faithfulness toward the God of Israel, which culminates in his death by crucifixion, at the hands of the powers.
- Justification, as God's rectifying justice for all things, is accomplished through God's own faithfulness, demonstrated in the vindication of Jesus' faithfulness by raising him from the dead.
- Justification, as God's rectifying justice, is accomplished in the creation of the church, the worldly space in which God's rectifying justice is done in the world by and among God's people. Justification bears world-transforming fruit in the body politic of Jesus Christ.
- Justification is the powerful action of the Holy Spirit, by which God convinces persons of the truth of the gospel and calls them and sustains them in communion with himself through participation in his people, the *ekklēsia*, and its constitutive practices—preaching, baptism, Eucharist, reconciliation. Justification and ecclesial participation are inseparable.
- Preaching justification has little or nothing to do with preaching (human) faith; it has much to do with preaching faithful, active, bodily participation in God's work in Jesus Christ, through a way of life that corresponds to the pattern of Jesus Christ's own faithfulness, by taking up the way of the cross and eagerly waiting for God's vindication of the people of God and the whole creation in the coming resurrection. Preaching justification proposes no hiatus between trust in God and faithful human action—they are coinherent, coconstitutive, and inseparable.
- Preaching Pauline justification is helped by reading Karl Barth.

Preaching Apocalypse

- Apocalypse is God's action.
- Apocalypse is God's power enacted in the crucifixion and resurrection of Jesus Christ, of which the apostles are witnesses. It is the good news which God apocalypsed to Paul.
- Apocalypse is and defines God's power in relation to the powers of this world. God's power as the cross and resurrection of Jesus Christ exposes what the world names as power, wisdom, and riches as their opposite. Conversely, the truth about God's power and wisdom is revealed in the gospel story of the self-giving vulnerability of Jesus' crucifixion at the hands of the rulers of this age.
- Preaching the Pauline apocalypse enables the people of God rightly to identify and expose the powers of the present age for what they are, the

enemies of God's reign established in the crucifixion and resurrection
of Jesus Christ. It enables the people of God to see how these powers
persistently and often subtly maintain a measure of influence and even
dominance among the people of God.

- Preaching the Pauline apocalypse is to call the people of God to reject
the prior claims which the gods, lords, rulers, powers, ideologies, and
ways of life in our time make upon the church and its members. To
preach apocalyptically is to say that the absolute priority of Jesus Christ
in the church is a matter of life and death for it; that the church's witness and therefore its very reason for being dies when it becomes the
servant of another master (the North American way, freedom and justice, democracy) than Jesus Christ.
- Preaching the Pauline apocalypse is to call the people of God to trust in
its own peculiar raison d'être and form of life as the work of God, with
its intrinsic and compelling rationality, sociality, and polity.
- Preaching the Pauline apocalypse is helped by reading Stanley Hauerwas.

Preaching Politics

- Politics is the reign of God.
- Jesus Christ is the substance and the form of God's reign among God's
people—whether Israel or the church.
- The politics of the reign of God in Jesus Christ calls the people of God
to recognize this Other ruler, this Other empire, this Other citizenship,
as having the prior and primary claim upon its existence as a people,
indeed, as identifying the very existence of that people as such, in distinction from all other "peoplehoods."
- The politics of the reign of God is a fundamental criticism of the politics of the rulers of this world and of the claims of "divine right" they
wish to make upon God's people. Preaching politics is to expose those
claims as false and a contradiction of the gospel.
- Preaching Pauline politics is intrinsic and critical to instructing the people of God. It is instruction in the normative form of the social and political existence of the people of God. It is an aspect of preaching Christology, ecclesiology, the sacraments, and eschatology.
- Preaching Pauline politics is in the first place to call the people of God
to shape its own sociopolitical life together in accordance with the
shape of God's reign apocalypsed in the life, death, and resurrection of
Jesus Christ. It is not in the first place (or second) to preach about how
God's people should "get involved" in the political processes of the
wider world.
- Preaching Pauline politics is preaching about the transformation of the
structures of daily life according to the gospel, in which the politics of

the humility, servanthood, and self-giving of the Son of God become normative for all spheres and relationships.
- Preaching Pauline politics is preaching what makes for peace: the people-building gifts of the Holy Spirit among the people of God, the reconciliation of enemies, peaceable relations with strangers and outsiders, submission to the powers that be, rejection of violence and "the sword," resistance to the pressure of ideologies and -isms that call the people of God to war for their sake.
- Preaching Pauline politics as ecclesial life is preaching the transformation of life in the world by the gospel, whereby the church itself becomes a sign to the watching world of its proper destiny under the reign of Jesus Christ.
- Preaching Pauline politics is helped by reading John Howard Yoder.

Preaching Election

- Election is God's choice of a specific people for his name and glory.
- Preaching election is preaching God's mercy toward Israel, God's choice of Israel to be his "treasured possession," a "priestly kingdom and a holy nation."
- Preaching election is preaching God's faithfulness to his irrevocable covenant with historic, corporeal Israel, a faithfulness revealed in the fact that God incorporates and sustains his election of fleshly Israel in the apocalypse of Jesus Christ.
- Preaching election is preaching the specific, strange work of God through the people Israel as the way in which God brings the Gentile peoples to share in God's blessings to Israel.
- Preaching election is preaching the engrafting of the Gentiles into the tree of Israel. The church appropriates, but does not expropriate, the name *Israel* to itself, because God through Jesus Christ incorporates the Gentiles into Israel.
- Preaching election is to preach the indissoluble otherness of Jews and Gentiles and to speak of the reconciliation and friendship of these others made possible in the cross of Jesus Christ. Preaching election is preaching the gospel of reconciliation.
- Preaching election is to maintain focus on the *specificity* of the biblical witness—the election of Abraham, Isaac, and Jacob; the election of the people Israel; the election of the *ekklēsia* from among the nations; the election of Jesus Christ, in whose apocalypse God's election of his people (Israel and the church) is incorporated and sustained. Preaching election is preaching Jesus Christ.
- Preaching election is not preaching about the destinies of individual persons for salvation or damnation.

- Preaching election is helped by reading R. Kendall Soulen, Scott Bader-Saye, the history of the Jews, and Jewish theologians.

Preaching Culture

- Preaching religion should not be done.
- Preaching culture is preaching the lordship of Jesus Christ over all creation and all peoples, including their cultural activity and products.
- Preaching culture is preaching God's calling out of and laying claim to a specific *people* in the entirety of its life as a people.
- Preaching culture is preaching critical discernment of the ways in which the practices and goods of the wider cultural world are often captive to the purposes of false gods and lords.
- Preaching culture is preaching the transformative power of the gospel on the "givens" and goods of the cultural wider world which enter and pervade the *ekklēsia* in the minds and bodies of the church's members.
- Preaching culture is preaching the transformation of a people and persons through constant enactment of and participation in the constitutive ecclesial practices of preaching, baptism, and Eucharist.
- Preaching culture is preaching the missionary action of the people of God as the timely, local action of discernment and transformation of the specific cultures in which the church is being created and built up.
- Preaching culture is helped by reading the works of John Howard Yoder, Stanley Hauerwas, Rodney Clapp, John Milbank, and a whole host of their postliberal and "radically orthodox" friends and coworkers.

The above are only a few ways to orient preaching Paul beyond Christendom and modernity. These orientations are not meant to "sum up" the apostle or substitute for the careful reading of his letters. They are meant, rather, to give direction, to lead the preacher or teacher back to Paul's letters with new eyes and ears, there to see and hear again the life-giving good news that God once apocalypsed to the apostle to the nations. By availing ourselves of the help of some of the Pauline scholars and contemporary theologians whom I identify in this book, I believe this gospel might also be received again as God's apocalypse for the people of God in our own time.

Bibliography

Achtemeier, Paul J. "Apropos the Faith of/in Christ: A Response to Hays and Dunn." Pp. 82–92 in *Pauline Theology*, vol. 4: *Looking Back, Pressing On*. Edited by Elizabeth Johnson and David M. Hay. Atlanta: Scholars Press, 1997.

Albrecht, Gloria. "Article Review: *In Good Company: The Church as Polis*." *Scottish Journal of Theology* 50 (1997): 219–27.

Arnold, Clinton. *Powers of Darkness: Principalities and Powers in Paul's Letters*. Downers Grove, Ill.: InterVarsity Press, 1992.

Aukerman, Dale. *Reckoning with Apocalypse: Terminal Politics and Christian Hope*. New York: Crossroad, 1993.

Aune, David. "Religions, Graeco-Roman." Pp. 786–96 in *Dictionary of Paul and His Letters*. Edited by Gerald F. Hawthorne, Ralph P. Martin, and Daniel G. Reid. Downers Grove, Ill.: InterVarsity Press, 1993.

Bader-Saye, Scott. *Church and Israel after Christendom: The Politics of Election*. Boulder, Colo.: Westview, 1999.

Balch, David L. "Household Codes." Pp. 318–20 in vol. 3 of *Anchor Bible Dictionary*. Edited by D. N. Freedman et al. New York: Doubleday, 1992.

Bammel, E., and C. F. D. Moule (eds.). *Jesus and the Politics of His Day*. Cambridge: Cambridge University Press, 1984.

Barth, Karl. *Church Dogmatics*, vol. 4.1: *The Doctrine of Reconciliation*. Translated by Geoffrey W. Bromiley. Edinburgh: T & T Clark, 1956.

———. *The Epistle to the Romans*. Translated by Edwyn C. Hoskyns. Oxford: Oxford University Press, 1933. Reprinted 1968.

———. *Der Römerbrief.* Zurich: EVZ, 1940.

Barth, Markus. *Ephesians*. 2 vols. Anchor Bible 34–34A. Garden City: Doubleday, 1974.

———. "Jews and Gentiles: The Social Character of Justification in Paul." *Journal of Ecumenical Studies* 5 (1968): 241–67.

———. *Rediscovering the Lord's Supper: Communion with Israel, with Christ, and among the Guests*. Atlanta: John Knox, 1988.

Bauckham, Richard. *God Crucified: Monotheism and Christology in the New Testament*. Grand Rapids: Eerdmans, 1998.

261

Beker, J. Christiaan. *Paul the Apostle: The Triumph of God in Life and Thought.* Philadelphia: Fortress, 1980.

———. *Paul's Apocalyptic Gospel: The Coming Triumph of God.* Philadelphia: Fortress, 1982.

———. *The Triumph of God: The Essence of Paul's Thought.* Minneapolis: Fortress, 1990.

Berkhof, Hendrik. *Christ and the Powers.* Translated by John Howard Yoder. 2d edition. Scottdale, Pa.: Herald, 1977.

———. *Christian Faith: An Introduction to the Study of the Faith.* Translated by Sierd Woudstra. Reprinted Grand Rapids: Eerdmans, 1979.

Biggar, Nigel. "Is Stanley Hauerwas Sectarian?" Pp. 141–60 in *Faithfulness and Fortitude: In Conversation with the Theological Ethics of Stanley Hauerwas.* Edited by Mark Thiessen Nation and Samuel Wells. Edinburgh: T & T Clark, 2000.

Bockmuehl, Markus. *The Epistle to the Philippians.* Peabody, Mass.: Hendrikson, 1998.

———. *Jewish Law in Gentile Churches: Halakhah and the Beginning of Christian Public Ethics.* Edinburgh: T & T Clark, 2000.

Bosch, David J. *Transforming Mission: Paradigm Shifts in Theology of Mission.* Maryknoll, N.Y.: Orbis, 1991.

Boyarin, Daniel. *A Radical Jew: Paul and the Politics of Identity.* Berkeley: University of California Press, 1994.

Brunt, P. A. "*Laus Imperii.*" Pp. 25–35 in *Paul and Empire: Religion and Power in Roman Imperial Society.* Edited by Richard A. Horsley. Harrisburg, Pa.: Trinity, 1997.

Carter, Craig A. *The Politics of the Cross: The Theology and Social Ethics of John Howard Yoder.* Grand Rapids: Brazos, 2001.

Cassidy, Richard. *Paul in Chains: Roman Imprisonment and the Letters of St. Paul.* New York: Herder & Herder/Crossroad, 2001.

Cavanaugh, William. "The City: Beyond Secular Parodies." Pp. 182–200 in *Radical Orthodoxy: A New Theology.* Edited by John Milbank, Catherine Pickstock, and Graham Ward. London: Routledge, 1999.

———. "A Fire Strong Enough to Consume the House: The Wars of Religion and the Rise of the State." *Modern Theology* 11 (1995): 397–420.

Clapp, Rodney. *A Peculiar People: The Church as Culture in a Post-Christian Society.* Downers Grove, Ill.: InterVarsity Press, 1996.

Coakley, Sarah. *Powers and Submissions: Spirituality, Philosophy, and Gender.* Oxford: Blackwell, 2002.

Coenen, Lothar. "Church, Synagogue." Pp. 291–307 in vol. 1 of *The New International Dictionary of New Testament Theology.* Edited by Colin Brown. Grand Rapids: Zondervan, 1975.

Cranfield, C. E. B. *A Critical and Exegetical Commentary on the Epistle to the Romans.* 2 vols. International Critical Commentary. Edinburgh: T & T Clark, 1975–79.

Dawn, Marva J. *Powers, Weakness, and the Tabernacling of God.* Grand Rapids: Eerdmans, 2001.

D'Costa, Gavin (ed.). *Christian Uniqueness Reconsidered: The Myth of a Pluralistic Theology of Religions.* Maryknoll, N.Y.: Orbis, 1990.

de Boer, Martinus C. "Paul and Jewish Apocalyptic Eschatology." Pp. 169–90 in *Apocalyptic and the New Testament: Essays in Honor of J. Louis Martyn.* Edited by Joel Marcus and Marion Soards. Sheffield: JSOT Press, 1989.

———. "Paul, Theologian of God's Apocalypse." *Interpretation* 56 (2002): 21–33.

Donaldson, Terence L. *Paul and the Gentiles: Remapping the Apostle's Convictional World.* Minneapolis: Fortress, 1997.

Donfried, Karl P. "The Imperial Cults of Thessalonica and Political Conflict in 1 Thessalonians." Pp. 215–23 in *Paul and Empire: Religion and Power in Roman Imperial Society.* Edited by Richard A. Horsley. Harrisburg, Pa.: Trinity, 1997.

Donfried, Karl P., and I. Howard Marshall. *The Theology of the Shorter Pauline Epistles.* Cambridge: Cambridge University Press, 1993.

Dunn, James D. G. *The Epistle to the Galatians.* Peabody, Mass.: Hendrickson, 1993.

———. "The New Perspective on Paul." Pp. 183–214 in Dunn's *Jesus, Paul, and the Law: Studies in Mark and Galatians.* Louisville: Westminster/John Knox, 1990.

———. "Once More, Πίστις Χριστοῦ." Pp. 61–81 in *Pauline Theology,* vol. 4: *Looking Back, Pressing On.* Edited by Elizabeth Johnson and David M. Hay. Atlanta: Scholars Press, 1997.

———. *Romans.* Word Biblical Commentary 38A–38B. Dallas: Word, 1988.

———. "The Theology of Galatians: The Issue of Covenantal Nomism." Pp. 125–46 in *Pauline Theology,* vol. 1: *Thessalonians, Philippians, Galatians, Philemon.* Edited by Jouette M. Bassler. Minneapolis: Fortress, 1991.

———. *The Theology of Paul the Apostle.* Grand Rapids: Eerdmans, 1998.

———. *The Theology of Paul's Letter to the Galatians.* Cambridge: Cambridge University Press, 1993.

Dunn, James D. G., and Alan M. Suggate. *The Justice of God: A Fresh Look at the Doctrine of Justification by Faith.* Grand Rapids: Eerdmans, 1993.

Elliott, Neil. "The Anti-Imperial Message of the Cross." Pp. 167–83 in *Paul and Empire: Religion and Power in Roman Imperial Society.* Edited by Richard A. Horsley. Harrisburg, Pa.: Trinity, 1997.

———. "Figure and Ground in the Interpretation of Romans 9–11." Pp. 371–89 in *The Theological Interpretation of Scripture: Classic and Contemporary Readings.* Edited by Stephen E. Fowl. Oxford: Blackwell, 1997.

———. *Liberating Paul: The Justice of God and the Politics of the Apostle.* Maryknoll, N.Y.: Orbis, 1994.

———. "Romans 13:1–7 in the Context of Imperial Propaganda." Pp. 184–204 in *Paul and Politics: Ekklesia, Israel, Imperium, Interpretation: Essays in Honor of Krister Stendahl.* Edited by Richard A. Horsley. Harrisburg, Pa.: Trinity, 2000.

Everts, J. M. "Conversion and Call of Paul." Pp. 156–63 in *Dictionary of Paul and His Letters.* Edited by Gerald F. Hawthorne, Ralph P. Martin, and Daniel G. Reid. Downers Grove, Ill.: InterVarsity Press, 1993.

Fitzgerald, John T. "Haustafeln." Pp. 80–81 in vol. 3 of *Anchor Bible Dictionary.* Edited by D. N. Freedman et al. New York: Doubleday, 1992.

Fitzmyer, Joseph A. *Romans: A New Translation with Introduction and Commentary.* Anchor Bible 33. New York: Doubleday, 1993.

Fowl, Stephen E. *Engaging Scripture: A Model for Theological Interpretation.* Oxford: Blackwell, 1998.

————. "Learning to Narrate Our Lives in Christ." Pp. 339–54 in *Theological Exegesis: Essays in Honor of Brevard S. Childs.* Edited by Christopher Seitz and Kathryn Greene-McCreight. Grand Rapids: Eerdmans, 1999.

————. Review of *A Radical Jew: Paul and the Politics of Identity* by Daniel Boyarin. *Modern Theology* 12 (1996): 131–33.

Fowl, Stephen E., and L. Gregory Jones. *Reading in Communion: Scripture and Ethics in Christian Life.* Grand Rapids: Eerdmans, 1991.

Fredriksen, Paula. "Paul and Augustine: Conversion Narratives, Orthodox Traditions, and the Retrospective Self." *Journal of Theological Studies,* n.s. 37 (1986): 3–34.

————. "What You See Is What You Get: Context and Content in Current Research on the Historical Jesus." *Theology Today* 52 (1995): 75–97.

Frei, Hans W. *The Eclipse of Biblical Narrative: A Study of Eighteenth and Nineteenth Century Hermeneutics.* New Haven: Yale University Press, 1974.

————. *Theology and Narrative: Selected Essays.* Edited by George Hunsinger and William C. Placher. Oxford: Oxford University Press, 1993.

————. *Types of Christian Theology.* Edited by George Hunsinger and William C. Placher. New Haven: Yale University Press, 1992.

Friesen, Duane K. *Artists, Citizens, Philosophers: Seeking the Peace of the City: An Anabaptist Theology of Culture.* Scottdale, Pa.: Herald, 2000.

Gager, John G. *Reinventing Paul.* New York: Oxford University Press, 2000.

Gaston, Lloyd. *Paul and the Torah.* Vancouver: University of British Columbia Press, 1987.

Gaventa, Beverly Roberts. *First and Second Thessalonians.* Louisville: John Knox, 1998.

————. "The Singularity of the Gospel: A Reading of Galatians." Pp. 147–59 in *Pauline Theology,* vol. 1: *Thessalonians, Philippians, Galatians, Philemon.* Edited by Jouette M. Bassler. Minneapolis: Fortress, 1991.

Georgi, Dieter. *Theocracy in Paul's Praxis and Theology.* Translated by David E. Green. Minneapolis: Fortress, 1991.

Gorman, Michael J. *Cruciformity: Paul's Narrative Spirituality of the Cross.* Grand Rapids: Eerdmans, 2001.

Griffiths, Paul J. *Problems of Religious Diversity.* Malden, Mass.: Blackwell, 2001.

————. "The Very Idea of Religion." *First Things* 103 (May 2000): 30–35.

Gustafson, James. "The Sectarian Temptation: Reflections on Theology, the Church and the University." *Proceedings of the Catholic Theological Society* 40 (1985): 83–94.

Harink, Douglas. "For or against the Nations: Yoder and Hauerwas, What's the Difference?" *Toronto Journal of Theology* 17 (2001): 167–85.

Harvey, Barry. *Another City: An Ecclesiological Primer for a Post-Christian World.* Harrisburg, Pa.: Trinity, 1999.

Hauerwas, Stanley. *After Christendom? How the Church Is to Behave If Freedom, Justice, and a Christian Nation Are Bad Ideas.* Nashville: Abingdon, 1991.

————. *Against the Nations: War and Survival in a Liberal Society.* Notre Dame: University of Notre Dame Press, 1992.

————. *A Better Hope: Resources for a Church Confronting Capitalism, Democracy, and Postmodernism.* Grand Rapids: Brazos, 2000.

———. *Christian Existence Today: Essays on Church, World, and Living in Between.* Grand Rapids: Brazos, 2001.

———. *Dispatches from the Front: Theological Engagements with the Secular.* Durham: Duke University Press, 1994.

———. "Failure of Communication *or* A Case of Uncomprehending Feminism." *Scottish Journal of Theology* 50 (1997): 228–39.

———. *The Hauerwas Reader.* Edited by John Berkman and Michael Cartwright. Durham: Duke University Press, 2001.

———. *Sanctify Them in the Truth: Holiness Exemplified.* Nashville: Abingdon, 1998.

———. *Wilderness Wanderings: Probing Twentieth-Century Theology and Philosophy.* Boulder, Colo.: Westview, 1997.

———. *With the Grain of the Universe: The Church's Witness and Natural Theology.* Grand Rapids: Brazos, 2001.

Hauerwas, Stanley, and Jeff Powell. "Creation as Apocalyptic: A Tribute to William Stringfellow." Pp. 107–15 in *Dispatches from the Front: Theological Engagements with the Secular.* Durham: Duke University Press, 1994.

Hauerwas, Stanley, and William Willimon. *The Truth about God: The Ten Commandments in Christian Life.* Nashville: Abingdon, 1999.

Hauerwas, Stanley, et al. (eds.). *The Wisdom of the Cross: Essays in Honor of John Howard Yoder.* Grand Rapids: Eerdmans, 1999.

Hawthorne, G. F. "Philippians, Letter to the." Pp. 709–11 in *Dictionary of Paul and His Letters.* Edited by Gerald F. Hawthorne, Ralph P. Martin, and Daniel G. Reid. Downers Grove, Ill.: InterVarsity Press, 1993.

Hays, Richard B. "Christology and Ethics in Galatians: The Law of Christ." *Catholic Biblical Quarterly* 49 (1987): 268–90.

———. *Echoes of Scripture in the Letters of Paul.* New Haven: Yale University Press, 1989.

———. *The Faith of Jesus Christ: An Investigation of the Narrative Substructure of Galatians 3:1–4:11.* Chico, Calif.: Scholars Press, 1983.

———. *First Corinthians.* Louisville: John Knox, 1997.

———. "'The Gospel Is the Power of God for Salvation to Gentiles Only'? A Critique of Stanley Stowers' *A Rereading of Romans.*" *Critical Review of Books in Religion* 1996: 35–37.

———. "Jesus' Faith and Ours: A Rereading of Galatians 3." Pp. 257–68 in *Conflict and Context: Hermeneutics in the Americas.* Edited by Mark Lau Branson and C. René Padilla. Grand Rapids: Eerdmans, 1986.

———. "Justification." Pp. 1129–33 in vol. 3 of *Anchor Bible Dictionary.* Edited by D. N. Freedman et al. New York: Doubleday, 1992.

———. "The Letter to the Galatians." Pp. 181–348 in vol. 11 *The New Interpreter's Bible.* Nashville: Abingdon, 2000.

———. *The Moral Vision of the New Testament: Community, Cross, New Creation.* San Francisco: Harper San Francisco, 1996.

———. "Πίστις and Pauline Christology: What Is at Stake?" Pp. 35–60 in *Pauline Theology,* vol. 4: *Looking Back, Pressing On.* Edited by Elizabeth Johnson and David M. Hay. Atlanta: Scholars Press, 1997.

———. Review of *Galatians* by J. Louis Martyn. *Journal of Biblical Literature* 119 (2000): 373–79.

Heim, S. Mark. *The Depth of the Riches: A Trinitarian Theology of Religious Ends.* Grand Rapids: Eerdmans, 2001.

———. *Salvations: Truth and Difference in Religion.* Maryknoll, N.Y.: Orbis, 1995.

Herzog, W. R., II. "Sociological Approaches to the Gospels." Pp. 760–66 in *Dictionary of Jesus and the Gospels.* Edited by Joel B. Green et al. Downers Grove, Ill.: InterVarsity Press, 1992.

Hick, John. "The Non-Absoluteness of Christianity." Pp. 16–36 in *The Myth of Christian Uniqueness.* Edited by John Hick and Paul F. Knitter. Maryknoll, N.Y.: Orbis, 1987.

Holland, Scott. "The Problems and Prospects of a 'Sectarian Ethic': A Critique of the Hauerwas Reading of the Jesus Story." *The Conrad Grebel Review* 10 (1992): 157–68.

Horsley, Richard A. "1 Corinthians: A Case Study of Paul's Assembly as an Alternative Society." Pp. 242–52 in *Paul and Empire: Religion and Power in Roman Imperial Society.* Edited by Richard A. Horsley. Harrisburg, Pa.: Trinity, 1997.

——— (ed.). *Paul and Empire: Religion and Power in Roman Imperial Society.* Harrisburg, Pa.: Trinity, 1997.

——— (ed.). *Paul and Politics: Ekklesia, Israel, Imperium, Interpretation: Essays in Honor of Krister Stendahl.* Harrisburg, Pa.: Trinity, 2000.

Howard, George. "Faith of Christ." Pp. 758–60 in vol. 2 of *Anchor Bible Dictionary.* Edited by D. N. Freedman et al. New York: Doubleday, 1992.

Hurtado, Larry W. "Convert, Apostate, or Apostle to the Nations: The 'Conversion' of Paul in Recent Scholarship." *Studies in Religion/ Sciences Religieuses* 22 (1993): 273–84.

Jaffee, Martin S. "One God, One Revelation, One People: On the Symbolic Structure of Elective Monotheism." *Journal of the American Academy of Religion* 69 (2001): 753–75.

Johnson, E. Elizabeth. "Divine Initiative and Human Response." Pp. 356–70 in *The Theological Interpretation of Scripture: Classic and Contemporary Readings.* Edited by Stephen E. Fowl. Oxford: Blackwell, 1997.

———. "Romans 9–11: The Faithfulness and Impartiality of God." Pp. 211–39 in *Pauline Theology,* vol. 3: *Romans.* Edited by David M. Hay and E. Elizabeth Johnson. Minneapolis: Fortress, 1995.

Johnson, Luke Timothy. *Reading Romans: A Literary and Theological Commentary.* New York: Crossroad, 1997.

Joint Declaration on the Doctrine of Justification of the Lutheran World Federation and the Roman Catholic Church. Grand Rapids: Eerdmans, 2000.

Kallenberg, Brad. *Ethics as Grammar: Changing the Postmodern Subject.* Notre Dame: University of Notre Dame Press, 2001.

Käsemann, Ernst. *Commentary on Romans.* Translated and edited by Geoffrey W. Bromiley. Grand Rapids: Eerdmans, 1980.

———. *Perspectives on Paul.* Translated by Margaret Kohl. Philadelphia: Fortress, 1971.

Kaufman, Gordon. "Religious Diversity, Historical Consciousness, and Christian Theology." Pp. 3–15 in *The Myth of Christian Uniqueness: Toward a Pluralistic Theology of Religions.* Edited by John Hick and Paul F. Knitter. Maryknoll, N.Y.: Orbis, 1987.

Kenneson, Philip D. *Beyond Sectarianism: Re-imagining Church and World*. Harrisburg, Pa.: Trinity, 1999.

———. *Life on the Vine: Cultivating the Fruit of the Spirit in Christian Community*. Downers Grove, Ill.: InterVarsity, 1999.

Klauck, Hans-Josef. *The Religious Context of Early Christianity: A Guide to Graeco-Roman Religions*. Translated by Brian McNeil. Edinburgh: T & T Clark, 2000.

Lindbeck, George. "The Gospel's Uniqueness: Election and Untranslatability." *Modern Theology* 13 (1997): 424–27.

———. *The Nature of Doctrine: Religion and Theology in a Postliberal Age*. Philadelphia: Westminster, 1984.

———. "What of the Future? A Christian Response." Pp. 357–66 in *Christianity in Jewish Terms*. Edited by Tikva Frymer-Kensky et al. Boulder, Colo.: Westview, 2000.

Lohfink, Gerhard. *Does God Need the Church? Toward a Theology of the People of God*. Translated by Linda M. Maloney. Collegeville, Minn.: Liturgical, 1999.

Lowe, Walter. "Barth as Critic of Dualism: Re-reading the *Römerbrief*." *Scottish Journal of Theology* 41 (1988): 377–95.

———. "Prospects for a Postmodern Christian Thought: Apocalyptic without Reserve." *Modern Theology* 15 (1999): 23.

Marshall, Bruce. "Israel." Pp. 231–64 in *Knowing the Triune God: The Work of the Spirit in the Practices of the Church*. Edited by James J. Buckley and David Yeago. Grand Rapids: Eerdmans, 2001.

———. *Trinity and Truth*. Cambridge: Cambridge University Press, 2000.

Martin, Dale B. *The Corinthian Body*. New Haven: Yale University Press, 1995.

Martin, Ralph P. *2 Corinthians*. Word Biblical Commentary 40. Waco: Word, 1986.

Martyn, J. Louis. "The Apocalyptic Gospel in Galatians." *Interpretation* 54 (2000): 246–66.

———. "Events in Galatia: Modified Covenantal Nomism versus God's Invasion of the Cosmos in the Singular Gospel: A Response to J. D. G. Dunn and B. R. Gaventa." Pp. 160–79 in *Pauline Theology*, vol. 1: *Thessalonians, Philippians, Galatians, Philemon*. Edited by Jouette M. Bassler. Minneapolis: Fortress, 1991.

———. *Galatians: A New Translation with Introduction and Commentary*. Anchor Bible 33A. New York: Doubleday, 1997.

———. *Theological Issues in the Letters of Paul*. Nashville: Abingdon, 1997.

Mauser, Ulrich. *The Gospel of Peace: A Scriptural Message for Today's World*. Louisville: Westminster John Knox, 1992.

McCormack, Bruce L. *Karl Barth's Critically Realistic Dialectical Theology: Its Genesis and Development, 1909–1936*. Oxford: Oxford University Press, 1995.

McGrath, A. E. "Justification." Pp. 517–23 in *Dictionary of Paul and His Letters*. Edited by Gerald F. Hawthorne, Ralph P. Martin, and Daniel G. Reid. Downers Grove, Ill.: InterVarsity Press, 1993.

Milbank, John. "The End of Dialogue." Pp. 174–91 in *Christian Uniqueness Reconsidered: The Myth of a Pluralistic Theology of Religions*. Edited by Gavin D'Costa. Maryknoll, N.Y.: Orbis, 1990.

———. *Theology and Social Theory: Beyond Secular Reason*. Oxford: Blackwell, 1990.

Milbank, John, Catherine Pickstock, and Graham Ward (eds.). *Radical Orthodoxy: A New Theology*. London: Routledge, 1999.

Morrison, Clinton D. *The Powers That Be: Earthly Rulers and Demonic Powers in Romans 13:1–7.* London: SCM, 1960.

Mouw, Richard J., and Sander Griffioen. *Pluralisms and Horizons: An Essay in Christian Public Philosophy.* Grand Rapids: Eerdmans, 1993.

Munck, Johannes. *Paul and the Salvation of Mankind.* Translated by Frank Clarke. London: SCM, 1959.

Nanos, Mark. "The Inter- and Intra-Jewish Political Context of Paul's Letter to the Galatians." Pp. 146–59 in *Paul and Politics: Ekklesia, Israel, Imperium, Interpretation: Essays in Honor of Krister Stendahl.* Edited by Richard A. Horsley. Harrisburg, Pa.: Trinity, 2000.

———. *The Irony of Galatians: Paul's Letter in First-Century Context.* Minneapolis: Fortress, 2002.

———. *The Mystery of Romans: The Jewish Context of Paul's Letter.* Minneapolis: Fortress, 1996.

Newbigin, Lesslie. *The Gospel in a Pluralist Society.* Grand Rapids: Eerdmans, 1989.

Newman, C. C. "God." Pp. 412–30 in *Dictionary of the Later New Testament and Its Developments.* Edited by Ralph P. Martin and Peter H. Davids. Downers Grove, Ill.: InterVarsity Press, 1997.

Niebuhr, H. Richard. "The Doctrine of the Trinity and the Unity of the Church." *Theology Today* 3 (1946): 371–78. Reprinted *Theology Today* 60 (1983): 150–57.

Novak, David. *The Election of Israel: The Idea of the Chosen People.* Cambridge: Cambridge University Press, 1995.

O'Brien, Peter T. *Colossians, Philemon.* Word Biblical Commentary 44. Waco: Word, 1982.

Placher, William C. "Postliberal Theology." Pp. 115–28 in vol. 2 of *The Modern Theologians: An Introduction to Christian Theology in the Twentieth Century.* Edited by David F. Ford. Oxford: Blackwell, 1989.

———. *Unapologetic Theology: A Christian Voice in a Pluralist Conversation.* Louisville: Westminster John Knox, 1989.

Preuss, Horst Dietrich. *Old Testament Theology.* 2 vols. Translated by Leo G. Perdue. Louisville: Westminster John Knox, 1995–96.

Rasmusson, Arne. *The Church as Polis: From Political Theology to Theological Politics as Exemplified by Jürgen Moltmann and Stanley Hauerwas.* Notre Dame: University of Notre Dame Press, 1995.

Reid, Daniel G. "Principalities and Powers." Pp. 747–49 in *Dictionary of Paul and His Letters.* Edited by Gerald F. Hawthorne, Ralph P. Martin, and Daniel G. Reid. Downers Grove, Ill.: InterVarsity Press, 1993.

Reimer, A. James. "Theological Orthodoxy and Jewish Christianity: A Personal Tribute to John Howard Yoder." Pp. 430–48 in *The Wisdom of the Cross: Essays in Honor of John Howard Yoder.* Edited by Stanley Hauerwas et al. Grand Rapids: Eerdmans, 1999.

Richard, Earl. "Early Pauline Thought: An Analysis of 1 Thessalonians." Pp. 39–51 in *Pauline Theology,* vol. 1: *Thessalonians, Philippians, Galatians, Philemon.* Edited by Jouette M. Bassler. Minneapolis: Fortress, 1991.

Rutgers, Leonard Victor. "Roman Policy toward the Jews: Expulsions from the City of Rome during the First Century C.E." Pp. 93–116 in *Judaism and Christianity in First-Century Rome.* Edited by Karl P. Donfried and Peter Richardson. Grand Rapids: Eerdmans, 1998.

Sanders, E. P. *Paul.* Past Masters. Oxford: Oxford University Press, 1991.
————. *Paul and Palestinian Judaism: A Comparison of Patterns of Religion.* Philadelphia: Fortress, 1977.
————. *Paul, the Law, and the Jewish People.* Philadelphia: Fortress, 1983.
Schreiner, Thomas R. "Works of the Law." Pp. 975–79 in *Dictionary of Paul and His Letters.* Edited by Gerald F. Hawthorne, Ralph P. Martin, and Daniel G. Reid. Downers Grove, Ill.: InterVarsity Press, 1993.
Schroeder, David. "Lists, Ethical." Pp. 546–47 in *The Interpreter's Dictionary of the Bible: Supplementary Volume.* Edited by Keith Crim. Nashville: Abingdon, 1976.
Schweitzer, Albert. *The Mysticism of Paul the Apostle.* Translated by William Montgomery. London: Black, 1931.
Simpson, J. W., Jr. "Thessalonians, Letters to the." Pp. 932–39 in *Dictionary of Paul and His Letters.* Edited by Gerald F. Hawthorne, Ralph P. Martin, and Daniel G. Reid. Downers Grove, Ill.: InterVarsity Press, 1993.
Smith, Abraham. "The First Letter to the Thessalonians: Introduction, Commentary, and Reflections." Pp. 671–737 in vol. 11 of *The New Interpreter's Bible.* Nashville: Abingdon, 2000.
Sonderegger, Katherine. *That Jesus Christ Was Born a Jew: Karl Barth's "Doctrine of Israel."* University Park: Pennsylvania State University Press, 1992.
Soulen, R. Kendall. *The God of Israel and Christian Theology.* Minneapolis: Fortress, 1996.
————. "YHWH the Triune God." *Modern Theology* 15 (1999): 25–54.
Stackhouse, Max L. "Liberalism Dispatched vs. Liberalism Engaged." *Christian Century* (Oct. 18, 1995): 962–67.
Stendahl, Krister. "The Apostle Paul and the Introspective Conscience of the West." *Harvard Theological Review* 56 (1963): 199–215. Reprinted on pp. 78–96 in Stendahl's *Paul among Jews and Gentiles.* Philadelphia: Fortress, 1976.
————. *Final Account: Paul's Letter to the Romans.* Minneapolis: Fortress, 1995.
————. *Paul among Jews and Gentiles.* Philadelphia: Fortress, 1976.
Stout, Jeffrey. *Ethics after Babel: The Languages of Morals and Their Discontents.* Boston: Beacon, 1988.
Stowers, Stanley. *A Rereading of Romans: Justice, Jews, and Gentiles.* New Haven: Yale University Press, 1994.
Surin, Kenneth. "A 'Politics of Speech': Religious Pluralism in the Age of the McDonald's Hamburger." Pp. 192–212 in *Christian Uniqueness Reconsidered: The Myth of a Pluralistic Theology of Religions.* Edited by Gavin D'Costa. Maryknoll, N.Y.: Orbis, 1990.
Tanner, Kathryn. "Creation and Providence." Pp. 111–26 in *The Cambridge Companion to Karl Barth.* Edited by John Webster. Cambridge: Cambridge University Press, 2000.
————. *Theories of Culture: A New Agenda for Theology.* Minneapolis: Fortress, 1997.
Tillich, Paul. *Dynamics of Faith.* New York: Harper & Row, 1957.
Tomson, Peter J. *Paul and the Jewish Law: Halakha in the Letters of the Apostle to the Gentiles.* Minneapolis: Fortress, 1990.
Toole, David. *Waiting for Godot in Sarajevo: Theological Reflections on Nihilism, Tragedy, and Apocalypse.* Boulder, Colo.: Westview, 1998.

Volf, Miroslav. "Soft Difference: Theological Reflections on the Relation between Church and Culture in 1 Peter." *Ex Auditu* 10 (1994). An on-line article accessed Oct. 26, 2000, at http://www.northpark.edu/sem/exauditu/papers/volf.html.

Wanamaker, Charles A. *The Epistles to the Thessalonians: A Commentary on the Greek Text.* Grand Rapids: Eerdmans, 1990.

Wannenwetsch, Bernd. "The Political Worship of the Church: A Critical and Empowering Practice." *Modern Theology* 12 (1996): 269–99.

Webster, John. *Barth's Moral Theology: Human Action in Barth's Thought.* Grand Rapids: Eerdmans, 1998.

Webster, John, and George Schner (eds.). *Theology after Liberalism: A Reader.* Oxford: Blackwell, 2000.

Wells, Samuel. *Transforming Fate into Destiny: The Theological Ethics of Stanley Hauerwas.* Carlisle, Cumbria: Paternoster, 1998.

Wilson, Jonathan. *Living Faithfully in a Fragmented World: Lessons for the Church from MacIntyre's "After Virtue."* Harrisburg, Pa.: Trinity, 1997.

Wink, Walter. *Engaging the Powers: Discernment and Resistance in a World of Domination.* Minneapolis: Fortress, 1992.

———. *Naming the Powers: The Language of Power in the New Testament.* Philadelphia: Fortress, 1984.

———. *Unmasking the Powers: The Invisible Forces That Determine Human Existence.* Philadelphia: Fortress, 1986.

Winter, Bruce W. *After Paul Left Corinth: The Influence of Secular Ethics and Social Change.* Grand Rapids: Eerdmans, 2001.

Work, Telford. *Living and Active: Scripture in the Economy of Salvation.* Grand Rapids: Eerdmans, 2002.

Wright, N. Thomas. *The Climax of the Covenant: Christ and the Law in Pauline Theology.* Minneapolis: Fortress, 1991.

———. *Jesus and the Victory of God.* Vol. 2 of *Christian Origins and the Question of God.* Minneapolis: Fortress, 1997.

———. "The Letter to the Galatians: Exegesis and Theology." Pp. 205–36 in *Between Two Horizons: Spanning New Testament Studies and Systematic Theology.* Edited by Joel B. Green and Max Turner. Grand Rapids: Eerdmans, 2000.

———. *The New Testament and the People of God.* Vol. 1 of *Christian Origins and the Question of God.* Minneapolis: Fortress, 1992.

———. "Paul's Gospel and Caesar's Empire." Pp. 160–83 in *Paul and Politics: Ekklesia, Israel, Imperium, Interpretation: Essays in Honor of Krister Stendahl.* Edited by Richard A. Horsley. Harrisburg, Pa.: Trinity, 2000.

———. "Romans and the Theology of Paul." Pp. 30–67 in *Pauline Theology,* vol. 3: *Romans.* Edited by David M. Hay and E. Elizabeth Johnson. Minneapolis: Fortress, 1995.

———. *What Saint Paul Really Said: Was Paul of Tarsus the Real Founder of Christianity?* Grand Rapids: Eerdmans, 1997.

Wyschogrod, Michael. *The Body of Faith: Judaism as Corporeal Election.* Minneapolis: Seabury, 1983.

———. "Christianity and Mosaic Law." *Pro Ecclesia* 2 (1990): 451–59.

Yeago, David S. "'A Christian Holy People': Martin Luther on Salvation and the Church." *Modern Theology* 13 (1997): 101–20.

Yinger, Kent L. *Paul, Judaism, and Judgment according to Deeds.* Cambridge: Cambridge University Press, 1999.

Yoder, John Howard. "The Apostle's Apology Revisited." Pp. 115–34 in *The New Way of Jesus: Essays Presented to Howard Charles.* Edited by William Klassen. Newton, Kans.: Faith & Life, 1980.

———. "Armaments and Eschatology." *Studies in Christian Ethics* 1 (1998): 43–61.

———. *Body Politics: Five Practices of the Christian Community before the Watching World.* Nashville: Discipleship Resources, 1992.

———. *For the Nations: Essays Evangelical and Public.* Grand Rapids: Eerdmans, 1997.

———. *The Fullness of Christ: Paul's Revolutionary Vision of Universal Ministry.* Elgin, Ill.: Brethren, 1987.

———. "How H. Richard Niebuhr Reasoned: A Critique of *Christ and Culture.*" Pp. 31–89 in Glen H. Stassen, D. M. Yeager, and John Howard Yoder's *Authentic Transformation: A New Vision of Christ and Culture.* Nashville: Abingdon, 1996.

———. *The Jewish-Christian Schism Revisited: A Bundle of Old Essays.* Notre Dame: Shalom Desktop, 1996.

———. "On Not Being Ashamed of the Gospel: Particularity, Pluralism, and Validation." *Faith and Philosophy* 9 (1992): 285–300.

———. "On Not Being in Charge." Pp. 74–90 in *War and Its Discontents: Pacifism and Quietism in the Abrahamic Traditions.* Edited by J. Patout Burns. Washington, D.C.: Georgetown University Press, 1996.

———. *The Politics of Jesus: Vicit Agnus Noster.* 1st edition. Grand Rapids: Eerdmans, 1972.

———. *The Politics of Jesus: Vicit Agnus Noster.* 2d edition. Grand Rapids: Eerdmans, 1994.

———. *The Priestly Kingdom: Social Ethics as Gospel.* Notre Dame: University of Notre Dame Press, 1984.

———. *The Royal Priesthood: Essays Ecclesiological and Ecumenical.* Edited by Michael G. Cartwright. Grand Rapids: Eerdmans, 1994.

———. *To Hear the Word.* Eugene, Oreg.: Wipf & Stock, 2001.

———. "War as a Moral Problem in the Early Church: The Historian's Hermeneutical Assumptions." Pp. 89–110 in *The Pacifist Impulse in Historical Perspective.* Edited by Harvey L. Dyck. Toronto: University of Toronto Press, 1996.

Detailed Table
of Contents

Index of
Scripture References

Index of Authors
and Names